Diverse Performances

*To Richard
with best
wishes from
Ross Brown*

Also by David Haldane Lawrence:

'Such a Humble Branch of Our Art: The Victorian Theatre Orchestra', *Theatre Notebook* 61, 1 (February 2007)

'Sowing Wild Oats: The Fallen Man in Late-Victorian Society Melodrama', *Literature Compass* 4, 3, 888–898 (March 2007)

'Performing Working Boys: the Representation of Child Labour on the Pre- and Early Victorian Stage', *New Theatre Quarterly* 24, 2 (May 2008)

'Masculine Appearances: Male Physicality on the Late-Victorian Stage', *Critical Survey*, 20, 3 (September 2008)

'Chorus boys: words, music and queerness (c.1900–c.1936)' *Studies in Musical Theatre* Volume 3 Issue 2 (2009)

'Charles Dickens and the World of Opera', *The Dickensian*, 483, 107, 1 (Spring 2011)

Also by Ross Burgess:

The Automated Office, with Joseph St John Bate (Collins, 1985).

Editor, *IBM: Small and medium systems* (Pergamon Infotech State of the Art Report 14:1, 1986).

UNIX Systems for Microcomputers (Blackwell Scientific Publications, 1988; 1990).

'The Croydon Group, 1971–' in *Out of the Shadows: a History of the pioneering London Gay Groups and Organisations 1967–2000*, ed. Tony Walton (Bona Street Press, 2010).

Many articles for the *UK LGBT History Project*: www.lgbthistoryuk.org.

David Haldane Lawrence

Diverse Performances

Masculinities and the Victorian Stage

Edited by Ross Burgess
With a Foreword by Jeremy Kingston

Paradise Press

Diverse Performances: Masculinities and the Victorian Stage
by David Haldane Lawrence, edited by Ross Burgess

First published in Great Britain in 2014 by
Paradise Press, BM Box 5700, London WC1N 3XX.
www.paradisepress.org.uk
www.foxearth.net/diverseperformances

Copyright © the estate of the late David Haldane Lawrence and Ross Burgess 2014

The moral right of David Haldane Lawrence and Ross Burgess
to be identified as the authors of this work has been asserted in accordance
with the Copyright, Designs and Patents act 1988.

All rights reserved. No part of this publication may be reproduced, stored in a retrieval system, or
transmitted in any form or by any means, electronic, mechanical, photocopying, recording or
otherwise, without the prior permission of the copyright owner.

A CIP catalogue record for this book is available from the British Library.
ISBN 978-1-904585-74-9

10 9 8 7 6 5 4 3 2

Printed and bound in Great Britain by
Berforts Information Press, King's Lynn.

Cover design by David Tilbury; front cover illustration: 'Fanny and Stella'
(Ernest Boulton and Frederick Park), 1869.

Set in Times New Roman, with headings in Clarendon LT
and title page in OrnellaD and K22 Monastic

Contents

List of Illustrations vii
Foreword by Jeremy Kingston ix
Editor's Preface xi
    Acknowledgements xiii
Introduction: Masculine ideology versus the stage 1
Chapter One: Men in the audience 11
    Men in the gallery 12
    The 'Swell' and masculine self-promotion 19
    Men and prostitutes in the audience 22
    Gentlemen voyeurs: admiring the ballet-girls 24
    The male gaze and the female performer 29
    'Margeries', 'Poofs' and 'Mary-Annes' 34
    Oscar Wilde and wearers of the green carnation 43
    Dissent and gentrification 48
Chapter Two: Men before and behind the scenes 53
    Musicians in the theatre orchestra 53
    The backstage labour force 62
    Shifting the scenery 65
    The lighting men 69
    The scene painter's shop 74
    The carpenters' shop 78
    Wilhelm: masculine influence in costume design 80
    The invisible army 85
Chapter Three: Men on the stage 89
    Actor-managers: at the top of the hierarchy 91
    Matinée idols and the cult of manliness 97
    Conviviality and rivalry: Charles Dillon 112
    Bonds of male friendship: Irving, Toole and Stoker 116
    Homosexuality among actors 122
    Male transvestism on the stage 125
    Men versus women on the stage 130
    Husbands and wives in the Victorian theatre 136

Actors and fatherhood 145
Social acceptance: the actor as a 'gentleman' 150
Chapter Four: Plays and playwrights: the struggle for control 157
The homosocial world of the male playwright 160
Demands on the dramatist 162
Originality versus adaptations from the French 169
The financial position of the dramatist 171
Dion Boucicault: raising the status of dramatists 177
The dramatist as director of his own plays 181
Censorship and the call for reform 188
Jacob Grein, an 'unconventional' foreign influence 196
The legacy of the Victorian era 204
Chapter Five: Masculinity in comedy and melodrama 207
Defenders of the Empire: sailors in melodrama 211
H.M.S. Pinafore: parodying naval melodrama 221
Soldiers on the stage 225
Factory Lads: working-class men in melodrama 239
A Lancashire lad led astray 247
Divided self: *The Corsican Brothers* and *The Bells* 255
Challenging male supremacy: *The Magistrate* 266
Philanderers and profligates in the 'New Drama' 274
Wilde, dandyism and Uranian subtexts 282
The changing reflections of masculinity 298
Conclusion: Changing power structures in the Victorian theatre 301
Appendix: The hard life of the Victorian actor 305
Getting on the stage 305
Managers and agents 307
The harshness of conditions for actors 310
The actor on tour 316
The economics of acting 317
Notes and references 323
Select Bibliography 337
Books and articles 337
Plays Cited 351
Sources for illustrations 355
Index 357
Some recent books from Paradise Press 369

List of Illustrations

Figure 1. Leaving the Pavilion Theatre, Whitechapel 1
Figure 2. Coventry Street, 11.15 p.m. 2
Figure 3. Interior of the Gaiety Theatre, 1868 13
Figure 4. The Fairy Queen's rebuke 20
Figure 5. Introducing a well-feathered *protégé* 25
Figure 6. Eight o'clock p.m. 'The Opera'. The audience at Her Majesty's Theatre in the 1850s: note the men in the audience with opera-glasses. 26
Figure 7. George Augustus Sala 27
Figure 8. Seven o'clock p.m. 'Behind the scenes' 28
Figure 9. An admirer of the ballet girls 30
Figure 10. Royal Italian Opera, c. 1847. Possibly depicting what is now Her Majesty's Theatre in the Haymarket, rather than Covent Garden as the caption suggests. 35
Figure 11. A pair of 'swells' going arm-in-arm to the theatre 37
Figure 12. Boulton and Park 39
Figure 13. Oscar Wilde 45
Figure 14. John Gray 46
Figure 15. Mr Irving considering the incidental music: the Lyceum Theatre orchestra 61
Figure 16. Behind the scenes at Drury Lane: in the flies 64
Figure 17. Lifting a fairy: stagehands operating a 'trap' at Drury Lane 67
Figure 18. Limelight equipment 71
Figure 19. Limelight men in the fly-gallery 72
Figure 20. The scene-painter's studio, Drury Lane: painting 'the trans' (i.e. the transformation scene for a pantomime) 75
Figure 21. The carpenters' shop, Drury Lane: 'profiling' a mermaid (i.e. shaping a piece of scenery to fit the painting) 79
Figure 22. C. Wilhelm: 'A Burmese Phantasy': costume designs for Drury Lane 82
Figure 23. Sir Squire Bancroft 90
Figure 24. Sir Henry Irving 92
Figure 25. Sir Herbert Beerbohm Tree 94
Figure 26. 'Hence, horrible shadow! Unreal mockery, hence!' (*Macbeth*) (illustrating early-Victorian 'historical' costume) 98
Figure 27. William Terriss, c.1880 102

Figure 28. F. R. Benson 105
Figure 29. Sir George Alexander as Aubrey Tanqueray in *The Second Mrs Tanqueray* 108
Figure 30. Lewis Waller as Henry V: Lyceum Theatre, 1900 111
Figure 31. Charles Dillon as Othello, 1856 114
Figure 32. John L. Toole 117
Figure 33. Bram Stoker 119
Figure 34. El Niño Farini as 'Lulu' 129
Figure 35. William Charles Macready as Henry IV 133
Figure 36. Dame Ellen Terry in 1886 135
Figure 37. Charles and Ellen Kean in *Macbeth* 138
Figure 38. Marie Effie Bancroft (née Wilton) 142
Figure 39. William and Madge Kendal in W. S. Gilbert's *Pygmalion and Galatea*, 1872 144
Figure 40. Edward Bulwer-Lytton, Lord Lytton 175
Figure 41. Dion Boucicault 178
Figure 42. Thomas William Robertson 183
Figure 43. W. S. Gilbert as 'Ironmaster at the Savoy' 186
Figure 44. Henry Arthur Jones 193
Figure 45. J. T. Grein 197
Figure 46. George Bernard Shaw 202
Figure 47. Mr T. P. Cooke as 'William' in *Black-Ey'd Susan* 214
Figure 48. Poster for *H.M.S. Pinafore.* 223
Figure 49. Interior of Astley's Royal Amphitheatre 228
Figure 50. William Terriss as Lt Dudley Keppell in *One of the Best* 238
Figure 51. Tom Taylor 248
Figure 52. Poster for *The Ticket-of-Leave Man*, Royal Princess Theatre, Edinburgh 251
Figure 53. *The Corsican Brothers*: duel scene from the 1852 production (from the watercolour by Edward Henry Corbould) 259
Figure 54. Henry Irving in *The Bells* 262
Figure 55. Arthur Wing Pinero 267
Figure 56. Poster for *The Magistrate*, Royal Lyceum Theatre, Edinburgh 272
Figure 57. *The Profligate*, Act IV, at the Garrick Theatre: Dunstan Renshaw rejects committing suicide 279
Figure 58. Marc-André Raffalovich, aged about 16 284
Figure 59. *The Importance of Being Earnest*: Allan Aynesworth (Algy) and Sir George Alexander (Jack) in the original production 291

Foreword by Jeremy Kingston

Jeremy Kingston is a celebrated playwright, author of *Oedipus at the Crossroads* and *Making Dickie Happy*. He has also been drama critic for *The Times* and previously for *Punch*.

I DON'T SUPPOSE I am alone in always wanting to find out what goes on behind the scenes, whether faced with a hotel or office door marked Staff Only or a stately home's kitchen garden glimpsed through a keyhole or indeed kitchens anywhere. Wanting at the age of eight to find out how Dick Whittington's ship had been made to sink on the way to Morocco led me eventually into the world of the theatre, and here we have a book that both creates and satisfies the wish to learn what went on behind the scenes in that long-vanished Victorian world where a visit to the theatre was the only indoor public entertainment available.

David Lawrence takes us literally behind the scenes—behind the painted scenery where underpaid stagehands worked in astonishingly awful conditions to create the spectacles that thrilled nineteenth century audiences. He goes on to tell us what went on in front of the scenery as well, not only on the stage but in the audience, with its strictly determined boundaries between the affluent and the poor; in the manager's office; and in the lives theatricals enjoyed or endured outside the theatre. Turning from the performers to what was performed, he provides a marvellous mass of information about the plays, most of them intoxicatingly patriotic, that packed theatres throughout the land, in city and market town alike.

The title of the book could refer to the behaviour of people in almost any walk of life. Diversity rules. The sub-title restricts the territory to the Victorian theatre but masculinities? What are they exactly—or inexactly, perhaps, because, as Lawrence points out, notions of maleness are forever shifting. They must have something to do with manliness but that too is open to question and answered with different definitions at different times. The nineteenth century seems to have been particularly bothered by the need to be precise. An ambitious man might hope his upward mobility would bear him to a point where he could be regarded as having become a gentleman. This was certainly considered a good and proper thing to be, and Lawrence lists the qualities that, in general, defined him.

Interestingly, most of these qualities were exhibited by the working-class heroes of early-nineteenth-century drama—sailors who sprang to the defence of those in need, young farmers irreproachably honest (though accused of crimes by villains), factory workers unshakably devoted to their sweethearts. But no matter how virtuous, steadfast and noble-hearted these heroes were—and such they always were—the low position they occupied in society always worked against their rise. But then rising was not required of them: their role in Victorian drama was to persuade working-class audiences that honourable behaviour—manly behaviour—was entirely within the reach of all. The unspoken implication of such plays was that there was no need to start chucking stones at their betters or start a revolution, which is what so many of their confrères in other European nations were repeatedly bent on doing.

For those who worked in the theatre a more troublesome assumption hindered their rise towards respectable manliness. Theatres were regarded as discreditable places of employment, and almost certainly hives of immorality. While carpenters and other artisans might only be faintly contaminated, it was the actor whose character was always suspect. He openly pretended to be somebody he was not—and not just one somebody but a succession of them—and this worked against everything a properly masculine man held to be most precious: truth, consistency, stability, decorum. The biographical section of Lawrence's book traces the laborious route taken by successful actors and managers (often one and the same) to become accepted as properly admirable men. The knighthood conferred upon Henry Irving in 1895—announced in the same week that Oscar Wilde was sentenced to two years hard labour—showed that the unusually gifted *and decently masculine* man could join these ranks. The difficulties facing those lower down the theatrical hierarchy, and the repeated efforts by determined individuals to alter how masculinity was defined, are a richly absorbing area of theatrical history.

Jeremy Kingston

Editor's Preface

DAVID HALDANE LAWRENCE was born in New Zealand in 1940, and educated at Auckland Grammar School until the age of 17. I first met him in the late 1960s when he was living in London with his then partner Alfred (they had moved together from New Zealand some years before). Our paths crossed from time to time thereafter, for instance when I did a short IT consultancy study for the British Library and discovered that David was working there and living in the heart of the West End's theatre district. We then lost touch, and when I next met him he was living with his long-term partner, Keith, in South London.

David worked for the British Library for about 24 years, while developing his interest in the theatre, opera, and costume. He also studied for a degree in English Literature at Birkbeck, University of London. Having gained first class honours, he went on to do an MA and subsequently a PhD, and became well known as an expert on several aspects of theatre history, before his death in 2009.

This book had its origins in David's PhD 2006 thesis.* In the following years, he did further work on the text, with a view to having it published. After his death, an amended version was offered to Ashgate Publishing. A report commissioned by Ashgate said that it contained 'excellent and painstaking archival research', but 'did not grapple with the fundamental re-thinking of the trajectory of Victorian theatre history which has been undertaken by scholars in the last two decades'. Consequently Ashgate felt unable to publish it. Keith was extremely disappointed at this rejection, and I volunteered to edit the book and get it published.

After starting work on the book I was surprised to discover that the version rejected by Ashgate was by no means the final version: David

---

* The thesis, entitled *Masculinities and nineteenth-century British theatre: 1829 to 1901*) can be consulted online (login needed, no charge) at:
    http://ethos.bl.uk/OrderDetails.do?did=16&uin=uk.bl.ethos.437393

had produced a further version containing a large number of additions, corrections and amendments. Internal evidence suggests that he was still working on it up to his untimely death.

In preparing the work for publication I have mainly used this further version, which clearly represents David's final thoughts on the subject, while checking it against the earlier versions, and reinserting the passage about *H.M.S. Pinafore*. I have also included in an Appendix a substantial passage from the earlier versions as being interesting in itself.

The main structural change from David's versions is that I have removed the many references to source documents from the main text and converted them to end-notes in a 'References' section at the end of the book, where they are available for the specialist to refer to, without disrupting the flow for the general reader. I have also removed or shortened a number of passages where David repeats or summarises points that he had already made—no doubt appropriate in a PhD thesis, but perhaps excessive in a work for general publication.

I have silently corrected a number of minor points of spelling, punctuation, and grammar, and made a few other changes to the wording. In conformity with present-day British usage I have omitted the full stops after 'Mr', 'Mrs', etc., and attempted to standardise the use of hyphenated or non-hyphenated words (the *New Oxford Spelling Dictionary*, alongside *New Hart's Rules*, has been my guide). I've also slightly shortened some of the section headings. I've added footnotes (marked as '—*Ed.*') where I felt that further explanation was necessary for the general reader: in many cases these reflected my own ignorance or confusion, being by no means an expert on the Victorian theatre. All other footnotes are by David (identified where necessary as 'DHL').

Included in the thesis, but not in the later versions, are a number of illustrations. I have inserted most of these in the text in what seemed the most appropriate places; I've also added some further illustrations showing some of the major personalities mentioned in the text and some nineteenth-century theatre interiors and posters.

In the versions that I picked up, a small number of the references were still marked as unknown or to be confirmed. Having spent some time, both online and in the London Library, searching for the missing items, I couldn't fail to be impressed by the vast amount of work that David must have expended in marshalling the various resources that he used. In a few cases I've not been able to resolve the references: I would welcome any information from readers. Also, given the history of this book, it is very possible that some errors may have crept into the text. Readers who come across any are invited to let me know via Paradise Press.

Acknowledgements

Had David lived to see this book published, as he'd dearly wished, he would no doubt have paid thanks to many people who had assisted him with the writing, including colleagues and supervisors at Birkbeck, and his partner Keith Steadman. No doubt many others will have assisted him: it's now not possible to thank them by name, but I hope they will see this book, and recognise that they played some part in its creation.

I would also like to thank Keith, for allowing me access to David's files, for his hospitality (along with Alexandre) and of course for giving me the opportunity to prepare the book for publication.

Thanks are also due to the members of the Gay Authors Workshop for their support, particularly Rod Shelton who has guided me on some of the more obscure aspects of formatting and publishing, Christopher Preston who encouraged me to trim some of the more repetitive passages, and Jeremy Kingston who advised on the overall structuring of the book as well of course as writing the Foreword.

Thanks also to John Stock Clarke for his very valuable comments and corrections from his own extensive knowledge of nineteenth-century literature, to David Tilbury for his striking cover design, and finally to Roger, my civil partner and soon to be husband, for his proofreading skills and for his love, support and forbearance over the course of this project.

Ross Burgess

Introduction:
Masculine ideology versus the stage

IN 1901, AT THE CUSP OF THE VICTORIAN AND EDWARDIAN PERIODS, the journalist Arthur St John Adcock* observed the audience leaving an evening of melodrama at the Pavilion Theatre in Whitechapel and contrasted the scene with those leaving West End theatres.

Figure 1. Leaving the Pavilion Theatre, Whitechapel

---

* 1864–1930; Also a novelist and poet —*Ed.*

In Whitechapel he noted that 'the first hundred or so to burst into the open air from the front entrances' were 'all men'. Men, as well as boys, led the way out of the theatre, streaming into public houses, whelk stalls and fish and chip shops.[1]* Meanwhile, in the West End, 'crush-hatted men† in evening dress' emerged from performances at up-market theatres, singly or in pairs, or escorting elegantly dressed ladies to their carriages or to supper at fashionable and bohemian restaurants in the Strand or by Leicester Square.[2]

Figure 2. Coventry Street, 11.15 p.m.

St John Adcock's article reveals men of both the working and upper classes as leaders—they are the first to emerge from the theatres, they lead the way to public houses, to elegant carriages, or to fashionable

---

* Numbered references are to the notes in the References section at the end of the book.
† A crush hat, or opera hat, was a top hat with springs, designed to be folded up when in the theatre. —*Ed.*

restaurants. This conforms to the nineteenth-century view of men taking precedence; and in the theatre, whether they were in the audience, on the stage, or behind the scenes, men were as dominant a force as they were in just about every other sphere of Victorian life. From the actor-manager down to the stagehand, the Victorian theatrical workforce was almost completely under male control.

The key personalities of this period have been the subject of numerous biographies and articles, but there are aspects of their lives that remain pertinent to a study of masculinity on the Victorian stage. A prime case is Sir Henry Irving, the predominant figure of late-nineteenth-century British theatre. Aspects of his extraordinarily variegated career are highly relevant, notably his role as a father, his marital complications, his professional relationships with men and women, and his elevation to a gentlemanly status. Oscar Wilde is another unavoidable presence, as are figures as varied as William Charles Macready or Boulton and Park. Far less is to be found regarding the careers of more minor figures in the Victorian theatre. While I feel it is essential to include major presences where they have a crucial bearing on the subject discussed, I have also included, wherever possible, personalities less well known in the twenty-first century.

Any discussion of masculinity would be incomplete without the inclusion of women. Despite the predominance of men in the Victorian theatre, women could also exert considerable power, not only as actresses, but also as managers of theatres. The theatre was one of the few spheres in which they could work alongside men. Men and women shared many of the difficulties and advantages of theatrical life. Throughout the century it was common for a married couple to be an acting and management team. Leading men of the theatre tried to emulate bourgeois familial respectability. However, the theatrical world, with its 'bohemian lifestyle', tended to subvert the middle-class notion of established, respectable family life. Men and women in the theatre worked strange hours; on stage, they wore make-up and dressed in exotic costumes; their morality was considered dubious. The theatrical life-style set them apart from ordinary life. Yet, throughout the Victorian period, actors and actresses strove for acceptance and tried to emulate the ideals of middle-class respectability.

A major subject of this book is the struggle of leading actors to achieve gentlemanly status and to be fully received into society. This was mainly due to the 'gentrification' of the theatre that gradually occurred from around the mid-1850s.[3] Victorian theatre history could therefore be roughly divided into two halves: pre- and post-gentrification. This gentrification was largely due to the encouragement of an affluent middle- to upper-class audience. Up till then, the legitimate theatre had been largely deserted by the upper classes; this was partly due to the prevalence of prostitution and an influx of lower-class spectators brought in by the growth of urbanisation. The largely uneducated audiences demanded popular fare. This necessitated an intensely demonstrative and visual presentation, with bills comprising four or more hours of action, emotion, sentiment, comedy, spectacle and novelty. The theatre therefore became part of a popular culture fostered by increasing urbanisation and the growth of industry. The focus was on acting and staging rather than works of great literary merit. The result was vigorous and variegated entertainment—offering a release from the often dreary conditions of industrialisation.

With its themes of morality, patriotism, and close familial ties, the early-nineteenth-century British theatre became part of a popular culture rooted in protestant ethics. An adherence to ideals of right and wrong, of masculinity and femininity, of the importance of success and the prominence of the family, united all classes and created shared tastes. Audiences of all social levels appreciated melodrama, were fascinated by crime and criminality, indulged in profound sentimentality and believed in retribution.

Until the *fin de siècle* there was no artificial distinction between highbrow and lowbrow. Distinctions between cultural forms were merged. Popular novels were adapted for the stage. Socially relevant paintings were reproduced in stage productions. Plays were staged and framed like paintings. Illustrations in serialised novels influenced the staging of their adaptations. Theatre, in turn, influenced the novel with its use of melodramatic situations. The stage also aspired to become educational. History was brought to life through costumes and scenery in the Shakespearean revivals of William Macready and Charles Kean, and later those of Henry Irving and Beerbohm Tree.[4]

While there was a proliferation of provincial theatrical activity, the main focus was on London. Its numerous theatres ranged from the 'serious' and fashionable venues of the West End to the 'transpontine' playhouses south of the river and those in the East End.

Under laws dating back to the 1660s, theatres had been divided between the patent houses and a number of unpatented 'minor' theatres. The patent system was designed to protect the 'legitimate' or spoken drama, which was restricted to the three West End patent theatres: the Theatres Royal at Drury Lane and Covent Garden* and, in the summer, the Theatre Royal in the Haymarket. This meant that the so-called 'minor theatres' were forced to present musical entertainments, or insert songs and music into plays.[5] The Theatre Regulation Act of 1843 did away with this distinction: the minor theatres were now able to perform spoken drama like the patent theatres. Breaking the patent theatre monopoly meant that by the mid nineteenth century London and the provinces had a diverse range of theatres catering to all social levels. However the Act also placed unprecedented power in the hands of the Lord Chamberlain, whose tight censorship continued to stifle British drama until 1968, well into the twentieth century.

The move toward a more literate theatre began in the early years of Queen Victoria's reign. William Macready produced plays by Browning; Charles Kean attempted historical accuracy in the design of Shakespearean revivals at the Princess's Theatre; Samuel Phelps presented Shakespeare and Jacobean drama at Sadler's Wells. Squire and Marie Bancroft's management of the Prince of Wales's Theatre† in the 1870s could be seen as the culmination of the move toward respectability. It also defined a class hierarchy among audiences. As the nineteenth century progressed toward its close, the middle to upper classes began to patronise the theatre again, while the masses turned toward the music hall.[6] Drama became more questioning and serious. The variegated bill was gradually replaced by an evening devoted to a single play. Matinée

---

* The Theatre Royal Covent Garden became the Royal Opera House in 1892 —*Ed.*
† Previously the Queen's Theatre, and later the Scala Theatre, Charlotte Street. Not to be confused with the present Prince of Wales Theatre, Leicester Square, nor with other Queen's Theatres, including the current one on Shaftesbury Avenue —*Ed.*

performances became popular with female spectators coming into the West End from the suburbs. The social acceptance of actors and actresses culminated with the knighthood of Henry Irving in 1895.

In the Victorian era, masculinity was constrained at all levels by an illusory set of ideals. The 'ideal man' should exemplify many qualities including physical courage, chivalry, virtue, patriotism, earnestness, selflessness and integrity. These were values largely influenced by concepts both of ancient Greek platonic friendship and of medieval chivalry. They contributed to a middle-class emphasis on patriotism, morality and the family—ideals that not only permeated literature and art, but were also a major theme of stage melodrama.

To embody these moralistic concepts, it was necessary to be 'a gentleman'. In the bourgeois society of nineteenth-century England, becoming a gentleman was not always a matter of gentle birth:

> The true definition of a gentleman must not be drawn according to circumstances of birth. English gentlemen form an order to which any man may aspire to belong. They do not form a caste. ... There is nothing, therefore, *de jure* to prevent one of inferior birth from becoming a gentleman, or one of the highest birth from ceasing to be.[7]

The true worth of a gentleman was measured in both moral and material terms. An upwardly mobile middle class had been fostered by the industrial revolution, and a 'gentleman' could be created through his own financial endeavours. Acquired wealth made it possible for the lower class man to move up the social scale. It was less easy for an actor to reach this elevated status. Actors were popularly considered to be profligate and 'bohemian'. Only those who had worked their way up the hierarchy to positions of power and authority achieved the rather dubious status of being a 'gentleman'. Yet, by the *fin de siècle*, there was a proliferation of actors from upper-class backgrounds, who would automatically have been classed as 'gentlemen'.

Conforming to qualities advocated by proponents such as Samuel Smiles* meant that a middle-class male had to live up to a high set of

---

* The leading proponent of the ideals of helping oneself up the moral and social scale was Samuel Smiles. In his enormously successful treatise *Self-Help*, he maintained that to be brought up a gentleman was the foundation of a manly character: 'The crown and glory ideals. He was always supposed to be the leader, to be able to set standards of moral behaviour, to exercise authority over the lower, less privileged ranks of society. However, despite Smiles's insistence that gentlemanliness was within easy reach of any virtuous Briton, being 'a gentleman' had much to do with social acceptance. The only sure way of knowing you were accepted as a gentleman was if you were treated as such. A man was more likely to be looked upon as a gentleman in some walks of life than in others—for instance, the professional ranks of the army and navy, the law, civil service, medicine or clergy. With wealth becoming more diffused, many men could rise in the ranks and assume the trappings of gentility. The hierarchy of birth became less certain and the concept of a gentleman became infused with mental and moral qualities of respectability. It was a concept that ultimately enabled men of the theatre to attain a gentlemanly status. Ideally, a 'true gentleman' was not involved with a bohemian sphere such as the theatre. Most gentlemen were employed in the public spheres of government, industry and commerce. For a man involved with industry or commerce, a working life meant the competition of other males. Competition was supposed to strengthen a man's character:

> There can be no question nowadays, that application to work, absorption in affairs, contact with men, and all the stress which business imposes on us, gives a noble training to the intellect, and splendid opportunity for discipline of character. ... A man's business is his part of the world's work, his share of the great activities which render society possible. He may like it or dislike it, but it is work, and as such requires application, self-denial, discipline.[8]

This competitive spirit applied as much to the theatre as to business and commerce. Competition was endemic between rival managers, actors and dramatists.

Outside of employment (whether in the theatre or in commerce), masculine respectability depended on a properly ordered household and a commitment to family life. The home was supposed to provide a release

---

of life is Character. ... Men of character are not only the conscience of society, but in every well-governed State they are its best motive power; for it is moral qualities in the main which rule the world'. See Smiles 1879: 383.

and comfort after the competitiveness of the masculine world of work. The idealised depiction was of the affluent *paterfamilias* ruling over his household with a loving and obedient wife by his side. A wife was meant to be the bearer of his children, organiser of the household and provider of much-needed comfort. Ideally, she fulfilled all these functions, while lacking the same matrimonial rights as her husband. The law gave absolute power to husbands over their wives and families. A married woman's property automatically passed to her husband. It was not until 1893, after several Married Women's Property Acts had been passed, that her property rights began to be fully affirmed.

The ideals of masculinity, home and family were largely aimed at a middle class world. The working-class man and his family posed a different set of concerns. For a working-class family to survive economically, the whole family often had to go out to work. Throughout the nineteenth century there was extreme poverty, and for many working men prospects for employment were eroded by economic depressions. Together with problems such as a decline in apprenticeship and having to spend prolonged periods within the home, those who worked as casual labourers became unreliable breadwinners. In working-class households, paternal authority was often diminished, due to the absences in pubs or the supposed laziness of the so-called head of the family. Idle men could take to drink or beat their wives. Young unemployed men formed groups that attempted to submerge a working-class identity. They indulged in fantasies that emulated the masculine habits of an outmoded aristocracy—with nights on the town, and homosocial group activities such as boxing, gambling and aggressive behaviour in theatre galleries.[9]

Working-class disaffection posed a threat to the stability of the status quo. The middle classes only had to hear or read about political disturbances in France, Italy, and elsewhere in Europe, to be made to feel uneasy about their position in relation to the labouring masses in Britain's industrialised cities.

The stability of middle-class family life could also be threatened from within, by the different codes of conduct for men and women. The nineteenth-century British husband usually had a life beyond the confines of the home and commerce. Men had more freedom than women to move between public and private worlds. They formed close bonds, creating a homosocial sphere that excluded wives and families. Male camaraderie applied to all levels of society. For the working man, solace and companionship could be found in the public house or the all-male conviviality of the 'free-and-easy' sing-song evening. The middle-class or upper-class man inhabited the world of the gentleman's club, all-male dinner parties and societies. He was also inclined to venture into the secretive sexual sphere of the *demi-monde*. Beyond domestic respectability and the surface code of moral purity, there was the 'man's world' of mistresses, visits to casinos, brothels and 'night houses'. The *demi-monde* also embraced the sphere of furtive homosexual* liaisons.

For those who transgressed sexually, the attendant fear of scandal constituted a threat to livelihoods and domestic stability. Many a middle- to upper-class man found the world was a less secure place than the cosy depictions of domestic harmony found in popular paintings and literature. At the same time, art and literature were unafraid to depict familial disintegration through issues such as drink or immorality. Sexual scandal could mean the loss of a career and financial security, imprisonment, or the necessity to go into exile abroad.

Another escape from domestic and feminine ties could be found through emigration to the outposts of the Empire. It was the mission of 'real men' to go out and expand the colonies. Many young unattached men emigrated to find work and adventure—particularly in Africa, India, Canada and Australasia. Here they presided over indigenous populations—employed as civil servants, serving in the Army, enforcing law and order, or administering plantations for commodities such as sugar, tea or rubber. It was also common practice for upper-class young men to be sent abroad to the colonies by their families because of financial or sexual misdemeanours (a theme which occurs in several *fin-de-siècle* problem plays). By the end of the century, the British Empire became a place of the imagination where male comradeship and class hierarchy could find full scope.

The components of an idealised view of manhood were exhibited and reiterated throughout nineteenth-century British art and literature. The

---

* The word 'homosexual' is used here and elsewhere for convenience, although the term itself would have been unknown for most of the period covered by this book. —*Ed.*

stage, with its mass appeal, was also a potent platform for enacting these ideals. Nineteenth-century drama contains many of the stereotypes of masculine ideology—the moralistic hero, the transgressive villain, as well as prodigal sons, stern fathers and moral arbiters. Strong moral and patriotic messages aimed to elicit appropriate responses from masculine spectators: the British 'tar' patriotically defending his country; the labourer fighting to maintain the honour of his family; evangelically inspired heroes fighting evil and defending virtue. With its pictorial representation, popular nineteenth-century drama could reach those who lacked education or were illiterate. It could even provide moral examples for those perceived to have strayed from the confines of masculine respectability. Writers and campaigners, including Charles Dickens, advocated the moral worth of drama. However, theatre was primarily for entertainment. It constituted 'a world apart' from the realities of life. British drama of the nineteenth century may have upheld the ideals of masculinity, but theatres remained places of diversion, offering a few hours' escape from the everyday world, giving groups of men in the audience the opportunity to assert themselves.

Chapter One:
Men in the audience

THROUGHOUT THE NINETEENTH CENTURY, men of all classes gathered for convivial entertainment. With the rise of industry and a subsequent growth in the urban population, cities increased in size and diversity. Experiencing the wide variety of attractions offered by the so-called 'metropolis' became a male pleasure. This extended to the notion of a masculine 'right' to the city—a 'right' that lent itself to attention-seeking behaviour. Parties of middle- to upper-class young men visited places of entertainment such as the theatre or music hall as part of a night on the town. An evening's 'spree' (or excursion) usually included drinking, gambling, visits to supper rooms and the search for sexual pleasure. Meanwhile, working-class men found solace from intolerable living and working conditions by visiting theatres and music halls and drinking together in public houses. For men in both groups, upper class and working class, visiting the theatre offered freedom from social constraints.

Men of all classes therefore formed a considerable majority among theatre audiences. They visited the theatre alone, in pairs or in groups, in the company of mistresses, or with wives and families. Watching four or more hours of variegated entertainment provided a diversion from the burdens and duties of everyday life. This applied as much to the industrialist living in luxury, as to the working class man domiciled in cramped conditions and poverty.

For men of all levels, visiting the theatre could allow for relief from stifling moral codes. The theatre, with its gaudiness, artificiality and larger-than-life emotions, invited a vociferous response. It allowed for the release of non-conformist behaviour among audiences. But it was men, rather than women, who were usually seen as the leaders of disruption. Masculine dissidence among theatre audiences was apparent at all social and economic levels—ranging from the working man in the gallery, to the clerk in the pit* and to the upper class 'swells' found in the stalls and dress circle.

Men in the gallery

Arguably, the gallery, located at the highest level, was the liveliest part of the audience. It was mainly patronised by working-class men, women and children, as well as by low-paid clerks and shop workers, all of whom paid cheaper prices of admission. The galleries of transpontine theatres were also visited by well-to-do young men out on a spree, visiting the East End for fun. Other male visitors included journalists and observers, such as Charles Dickens, who wrote and reported on working-class audiences for a largely middle-class readership.

The gallery (popularly known as 'the gods') often covered a considerable area of the auditorium and could hold a large number of spectators.† For instance, in 1836, the gallery of the Victoria Theatre,‡ which was considered 'the most commodious of any gallery in London', seated '1,200 or 1,400 persons'.[1] For the working man, the theatre building must have offered a glamorous alternative to the outside world. Once inside a theatre such as the Pavilion in Whitechapel, he would have found himself in a glittering, ornately decorated space. From his position in the gallery, he would have gazed down on mock-Renaissance splendour, complete with a 'superb chandelier' modelled on the one at Covent Garden.[2] Surroundings such as those found in the Pavilion provided a contrast to the drab working and living conditions of most working-class men.

Theatres, even those in poorer areas, were structured to provide separate areas for different economic and social groups. A horseshoe or

---

* For instance, disturbances in the pit at the Vaudeville Theatre on 29 May 1880, were claimed to be led by 'a gang of ill-favoured, loud-talking young men.' See An Old First-Nighter, *Theatre* August 1880: 67–68.

† Evidently, it was the great eighteenth-century actor, David Garrick, who coined the term 'gods' for the gallery. In 'one of his celebrated prologues ... when apostrophising that portion of the audience in the immediate neighbourhood of the ceiling, he exclaimed, "And you, ye gods! To merit never blind – | A fellow-feeling makes us wondrous kind." ' See Grant 1836: 83.

‡ Now the Old Vic —*Ed.*

oval shaped auditorium was divided into boxes, dress circle, pit,* and gallery. Each of these areas had a separate entrance, ensuring that wealthier patrons in the better seats were kept separate from the tradesmen in the pit and the rowdier elements of the gallery.

Figure 3. Interior of the Gaiety Theatre, 1868

Theatre buildings often located the gallery entrance at the side of the building, away from the view of smart patrons entering at the front. The structure of theatres thus encapsulated the rigid class hierarchy that permeated society. At the same time, theatre-going brought together all levels of society under one roof, to share in the mutual experience of a performance. It also meant that one level of society was forced to tolerate the behaviour of another.

---

* The pit (not to be confused with the orchestra pit) was the lowest level of the auditorium, often with backless benches. By the end of the century it had largely been replaced by higher-priced, more comfortable stalls seating See Page 143. —*Ed.*

Visiting the theatre could be a communal experience. As Dickens remarked of the gallery audience at the Britannia Theatre in Hoxton: 'We had all come together in a place where our convenience was well consulted and where we were well looked after, to enjoy an evening's entertainment in common.'[3] An evening at the theatre offered warmth and companionship, as well as excitement and entertainment. Fairly substantial food and drink could be purchased. Dickens, in 1850, noted that at the Royal Standard Theatre: 'Huge ham sandwiches, piled on trays like deals in a timber yard, were handed about for sale to the hungry; and there was no stint of oranges, cakes, brandy-balls, or other similar refreshments.'[4] This method of food distribution persisted until late in the century. At the Britannia in 1896, after the first part of the performance 'strong men without coats, and huge baskets on each arm, came among the audience, and dispensed sandwiches, saveloys, bread, pasties, ginger-beer and oranges'.[5] For the working man with his family, an evening at the theatre supplied more than just entertainment and an escape into luxurious surroundings. It could also be a necessary source for nourishment with its provision of cheap and sustaining food and drink.*

The gallery attracted workers from a wide range of trades. The occupations of gallery audiences reflected the location of theatres and the type of employment in the area. For instance, many weavers attended the City of London Theatre in Bishopsgate. The Standard in Shoreditch attracted mechanics and their children as well as silk weavers from Spitalfields. Sailors from the docks could be found among the spectators at the Pavilion in Whitechapel.[6] Charles Dickens, in his well-known description of the gallery of the Britannia Theatre, claimed to have found a wide range of low- and high-paid workers, mostly male, both skilled and unskilled: 'mechanics, dock-labourers, coster-mongers, petty tradesmen, small clerks, milliners, stay-makers, shoe-binders, slop workers, poor workers in a hundred highways and bye-ways'.[7] On another visit he noted 'a few mechanics and artisans in broadcloth and dark tweed'.[8]

---

* The food on sale in East End theatres was not always fresh or wholesome. T. W. Erle, visiting the Royal Effingham Theatre, found that the pies sold in the auditorium were 'of a violently adipose character, and given to glisten in a manner which is apt to overwhelm the consumer with consternation and discomforture'. See Erle 1880: 21.

These depictions of spectators were intended to build up local colour. However, unless Dickens questioned members of a large gallery audience as to their various trades, it is more than likely that his descriptions were based on supposition. Later in the century there was a more reliable description of the trades of men in the gallery of Henry Irving's Lyceum Theatre. The spectator Alfred Wareing recalled how Irving's performances attracted working men of various trades from different London areas. In the gallery at the Lyceum he was likely to meet 'the master boot-maker from Hoxton, the foreman compositor from Marylebone, the Soho dressing-case maker, and such like'.[9]

Obtaining a seat in the gallery often meant a scramble. There were many reports of injuries and even fatalities caused by the crush of would-be spectators. Seats were not reserved and there were fights to obtain the best places. The struggle to get into the gallery gave another opportunity for male aggression. Aggressive behaviour was, to a large extent, fostered by the greed and ignorance of managers whose main concern was for profit. They crammed audiences into as many seats as possible with total disregard for the health and safety of the spectator.

Unhealthy, cramped conditions particularly applied to the gallery. This was an area that could be extremely noisy and smelly. There was often a woeful lack of sanitation. Men, women and children were affected by these unhealthy conditions. In his 1888 manual on *Theatre Hygiene*, Walter Roth commented on how the narrowness of the cheaper seats created a cramped sitting position which could be the cause of 'stiff arms and legs, aching back, sore knees, cramped toes, a worse temper, and a smashed-up hat'.[10] The inadequate provision of latrines created further problems—their construction and ventilation was often so primitive that 'vitiated air from urinals and closets' carried into the auditorium.[11] Few urinals and water-closets meant that in some theatres audiences were forced to relieve themselves on the stairs or in adjacent streets.[12]

These cramped, unventilated gallery areas were permeated with the smell of unwashed bodies, particularly masculine body odours. In summer, young men took off their coats because the 'temperature in their sixpenny heaven is so high'. This added to the stench of the so-called 'great unwashed'. A French visitor to the Britannia in 1870, while seated in the stalls, became aware of a 'strong smell of poverty'. Although men in the gallery sat in their shirtsleeves, sweat still streamed down their faces, making their clothes stick to their skin.[13] *The Sketch*, visiting the Britannia in 1896, noted that among men in the gallery 'coats were scanty, waistcoats few and far between, collars and neckties practically unknown'.[14] Many spectators did not like attending the theatre on the evening after a matinée, or on Saturday night after five days of performances, because of the 'vitiated' atmosphere. The 'imperfect removal of air' from the previous night's performance was claimed by Walter Roth to be the cause of headaches and 'other troubles'.[15] The 1892 Report of the Chairman of the London County Council's Theatres and Music Halls Committee stated that bad ventilation resulted in conditions such as 'theatre headache' and 'theatre diarrhoea'.[16]

Gallery conditions seemed to encourage working-class male aggression. Rowdiness led by men or boys created a problem in many theatres, particularly those in predominantly working-class areas. The working-class man—disenfranchised, often unemployed, his patriarchal status undermined—could find in visiting the theatre gallery an outlet for his insecurity. From his seat in the gallery, he looked down upon those sections of society he was usually forced to look up to. The gallery was a sphere from which he could both verbally and physically give release to pent-up aggression and class enmity.

In *Some Habits and Customs of the Working Classes* (1867), Thomas Wright describes 'the celestials ... discharging nutshells, peas, orange-peel and other annoying though harmless missiles' at the heads of the devoted occupants of the regions below—making theatre-going hazardous for those in the pit. The 'chaff' of the gallery audience 'often assumes an unpleasantly personal tone'.[17]

Wright divides the gallery audience into three masculine-dominated hierarchies: 'the roughs, the hypocrites or snobs, and the orderlies'. 'The roughs' are the most numerous. They come to the theatre with 'unwashed faces and in ragged and dirty attire ... bring bottles of drink with them' and '*will* smoke' in spite of the notice that prohibits smoking and states that 'officers will be in attendance'. The roughs 'favour the band with a stamping accompaniment, and take the noisy part in applauding or giving "the call" to the performers'. Their female companions 'are generally accompanied by infants, who are sure to cry and make a disturbance at some interesting point in the performance'. The snobs are those who claim to prefer the gallery to other parts of the house; 'nevertheless they seem very ill at ease in the place of their choice, and shrink from the glance of the occupants of the pit and boxes'. Snobs also 'stand on the back seats, talking loudly among themselves 'but *at* other occupants of the gallery'. They are 'at great pains to inform you that that they have merely come into the gallery for a 'spree', or 'just to see what kind of a place it is'; although strangely enough they are to be found there 'two or three nights a week'. 'Orderlies' go into the gallery because it is 'the *cheapest* part of the house', although it is the least comfortable and respectable; 'they can go into that part twice for the same amount of money that they would have to pay to go into any other part once'.[18] All three elements exhibit rowdy, inattentive behaviour, with the poverty-stricken 'roughs' being the most aggressive.

Gallery noise often drowned out the words of the actors. This was usually the case on Saturday and public holiday nights when unruly youths thronged the cheaper seats. Saturday, being pay-day in the East End, meant a noisier, rougher audience. Having been paid, young men tended to go the theatre to pass away their evening, while their wives and mothers went to the local markets to buy food for the week.[19] The release from a week of long working hours, not to mention pay spent on drink, gave an excuse for rowdy, infantile behaviour. Even after the theatre had become 'gentrified', with audiences more socially divided, unrest continued in the gallery. By the 1890s 'obstreperous' behaviour had become associated with men of a lower-class social group. Managers were more likely to use socially divisive methods in an attempt to make this section of the audience less audible and visible to upper-class patrons in expensive seats.[20]

In the mid nineteenth century, managers of neighbourhood theatres were eager to assure journalists and other commentators of the respectability and good behaviour of their audiences. However, there were reports of sexually abusive and drunken behaviour by men in the gallery—very often from young toffs visiting lower-class theatres while out on a spree.

A serious incident occurred at the City of London Theatre in 1870 when a drunken spectator molested a girl of sixteen in the gallery. 'Being annoyed by a fellow' the girl paid an extra penny to move into a private box. The 'fellow' followed her there with his companions 'and after sprinkling her with filthy water from ginger beer bottles, indecently assaulted her'. Sentencing the 'fellow' to two months imprisonment the magistrate said that the facts disclosed in the case 'were horrible to contemplate'. An outraged *Hackney and Kingsland Gazette* suggested that the City of London Theatre was far from being respectable. It claimed that the public had 'a right to know farther' about a 'place of entertainment in which doings are carried on that are "horrible to contemplate".' [21] The case brought into question not only the respectability of minor theatres, but also the behaviour of young men in the audience, particularly those visiting from more affluent areas.

Despite the many reports emphasising bad behaviour by men in the gallery, other commentators claim that working-class gallery audiences were better behaved than such articles would suggest, and that even in provincial towns there were men in the gallery audience who were more knowledgeable and literate than was usually supposed. In the 1830s, the actor-manager, Robert Dyer, claimed that: 'The audience of a manufacturing town are strictly critical, and even the poor mechanic in the gallery pretends to judgement. ... He has read your author, and understands his beauties; it is not unusual to see him with a play-book and candle, following the actor in every line, ready to convict him in an error'.[22]

Observing the audience of the Victoria Theatre in the middle of the century, Charles Dickens saw the gallery filled with 'attentive faces, rising one above the other, to the very door in the roof, and squeezed and jammed in regardless of all discomforts'. He was impressed with 'a sense of its being highly desirable to lose no possible chance of effecting any mental improvement in that great audience'. He insisted that the leisure habits of the working class should be viewed with sympathetic understanding and that theatre was central to its amusements.[23]

However the reports of middle-class commentators were often patronising toward the working classes. For instance, Henry Morley, reviewing Shakespearean performances at Sadler's Wells for the *Examiner* in 1857, found the audience

> mainly composed of hard-working men who crowd a sixpenny gallery and shilling pit. ... There sit our working-classes in a happy crowd, as

orderly and reverent as if they were at church, and as yet as unrestrained in their enjoyment as if listening to stories told them by their own firesides.[24]

Journalists such as Henry Morley tend to affect surprise that members of the gallery could behave themselves, be attentive, and appreciate 'higher drama'. Making his rather patronising observations for the benefit of a bourgeois readership, the male middle-class journalist seated in the gallery seemed like an intruder into this predominantly working-class, lower-income area of the theatre.

The 'Swell' and masculine self-promotion

In the mid nineteenth century, the behaviour of some upper-class men in the audience could be just as disorderly as that of working-class youths up in the gallery. These were groups of indolent, fashionable young men out on a 'spree'—popularly known as 'swells'.

The swell assumed a theatricality that rivalled that of the actor on stage; he also offered an alternative to rigidly coded norms of masculine behaviour. Like the actor he was continually on display, constantly provoking attention and offering himself for the gaze of others.

An example of a swell's misbehaviour appeared in the journal *Here and There* on 1 June 1872. The swell came forward in his stage-box and

> in full sight of the audience in the stalls arranged his collar, stroked his hair and whiskers, bowed elaborately to an acquaintance, bent low and whispered loud to one of the ladies, coolly surveyed the audience in the most leisurely manner through his lorgnette and finally smiled saucily in approval of the charms of the actress who was enacting the Fairy Queen.

The swell deliberately made himself conspicuous. He paid no attention to the play and 'would do all he could to prevent others from paying any attention to it'. He stared impudently at every pretty girl in the audience and talked incessantly to the ladies of his party who encouraged his 'senseless chatter'. The players were disturbed by his behaviour. Finally, the actress playing the Fairy Queen, insulted by his 'impertinent attentions', strode up to his stage box and struck the astonished swell over the head with her wand.[25]

Along with the supper-club and the saloon, the theatre auditorium provided a venue for display and showing-off, especially among groups of indolent upper-class young men. They could be particularly obstreperous during forays into theatres of the East End.

Figure 4. The Fairy Queen's rebuke

For instance, a group of 'gentlemen' seated in a private box at the Pavilion Theatre were reported to have been typically boisterous and infantile—talking and laughing aloud, smoking, and knocking each other's hats off. After being reprimanded, they moved to a stage box where they repeated the conduct and created a further nuisance. Although they assaulted the sergeant who arrested them, the magistrate found discrepancies in the evidence; they were only made to pay bail and keep the peace for six months.²⁶ It was their 'gentlemanly' status that allowed them to escape a more severe penalty.

The upper-class swell believed he had a 'right' to the city. This allowed him to behave with extreme arrogance. He was notorious for making noisy, late entrances into West End theatres at half-price admission time.* Action on stage was often interrupted by 'scions ... of hereditary legislators, ... baronets, guardsmen and their hangers-on' as well as 'gentlemen whose days are given to commercial pursuits in the City, and whose evenings are devoted to enjoyment at the West End'. To these were added parties of gentlemen from provincial towns 'bent on a metropolitan holiday'. The manners of these late-comers did not have the reserve of 'the purely society audience'. They made 'critical comments from the stalls ... mostly of a strikingly personal nature ... in a tone so loud that the actors can overhear'.²⁷

The arrogant behaviour of the swell was the subject of much scathing commentary. As Wilkie Collins (writing in *Household Words* under the pseudonym of 'John Bull') remarked in 1859:

> Don't we all know what a blessing it is for the audience who have been fools enough to pay the whole price, to be invaded at nine o'clock by another audience who have been wise enough to pay half price? Don't we all know how it improves the closing scenes of an interesting play, and how it encourages the actors who happen to be on stage at the time, to hear the silence in the theatre suddenly interrupted by a rushing and scraping of feet and a rapid opening and shutting of box-doors? ²⁸

His clattering, late entry into the stalls, dress circle or boxes gave the swell a chance to draw attention to himself as well as disturbing the other spectators.

Thomas Wright claimed that it was the working-class man in the god' who brought to order 'those two stupid-looking and half-drunken swells' who 'have come into the audience at half-price time' and 'annoy the audience by talking and laughing in a very loud tone'. Whereas 'scornful

---

* Half-price admission was aimed mainly at clerks and shop assistants who had long working days. Some theatres also offered more than one piece during the evening, for instance ending with a one-act farce starting at 9pm. By the 1870s working hours were shorter, an evening at the theatre typically comprised a single play starting at 8pm or so rather than 6:30 or 7, and half-price admission was abandoned. —*Ed.*

looks and indignant hushes from the pit and boxes' had no effect on their behaviour, it was only threats from the gallery that could make them 'subside into silence, and suddenly become very much interested in the playbill'.[29]

The swell was popularly represented as brainless, idle, foppish, and effeminate. Music hall songs such as George Leybourne's 'Champagne Charlie' (1866) projected the image of the intoxicated, bankrupt, indolent swell. The innuendo and emphasis of a music hall performance gave a knowing wink to the traditional exploits of the young men about town. It suggestively pointed to homosocial groups thumbing their noses at authority and tasting the forbidden pleasures of low life. In the song, Champagne Charlie says he is 'good for any game at night' and invites like-minded young men to join him on a spree.[30]

For working lads in the audience the elegant, rakish and flamboyant figure of the music hall swell fulfilled a fantasy of a good life in the West End. His boasting of an easy life of drink, money and women represented a life-style that few working-class men could hope to obtain. The music hall performer's emphasis on the 'counterfeit swell' seemingly reassured the masculine working-class spectator that he could overcome social difficulties and take on the persona of a 'Champagne Charlie'.

Men and prostitutes in the audience

For young gentleman out on a 'spree', the theatre could be a venue for sexual encounters. In the early Victorian period, before the theatres became gentrified, 'ladies of the town' with their clients formed a considerable portion of the audience. Prostitutes (along with thieves and pickpockets) cruised around and inside theatres on both sides of the Thames. Men in the audience were often a willing target for loose women.

Even the illustrious patent theatres, Drury Lane and Covent Garden, attracted numbers of prostitutes, openly soliciting men and indulging in sexual acts.[31] Many of these were young girls, shamelessly exploited, not only by their male clients, but also by older women—the madams who exerted power over them. According to *The Swell's Night Guide* (1840) 'old harridans' closely watched the conduct of their *protégées* in the saloons or from boxes in the theatre. They could nightly be seen, ensconced in the corner of a box, scrutinizing both the girls and their lovers and occasionally pointing out to the inexperienced those persons whom they consider to be well stocked with money, and whom they think most likely to be caught by the splendour of false diamonds, satins &c.[32]

For the client and prostitute, the private box provided a space conducive to sexual activity. At Covent Garden private boxes had snug and secret retiring anterooms, with 'voluptuous couches and all things requisite for the comfort and convenience of the debauchee'. Drury Lane had doors to private boxes that fastened on the inside so that 'visitors' were 'not so liable to be intruded upon'.[33]

The private, secretive nature of these areas in early nineteenth-century theatres makes them appear to have been deliberately planned for furtive sexual activity. The occupants, intent on their own performance, are unlikely to have paid much attention to the performance on stage.

Flora Tristan, a visitor from France, described the situation when she attended Drury Lane in 1840. At half price admission times, 'throngs of prostitutes and men of every station crowd into the theatres'. In the foyers, loose women 'receive as if in their own drawing rooms'. A young man was even undressed in the lobby by a group of whores who stole his clothes, leaving him completely naked. Prostitutes and their clients keep going in and out of boxes 'and one is constantly exposed to the draughts sweeping through the doors they leave open behind them'. The corridors are 'full of raucous laughter and ribaldry. ... It is as if one were surrounded by the dregs of so-called civilisation.'[34]

Despite efforts by managers to make their lobbies more elegant, 'many decent men and women' were put off attending theatres because of the presence of prostitutes. Certain theatre managements were reluctant to take active steps against prostitution. The presence of soliciting women was a draw for a number of men in the audience and it increased the sale of half-price tickets.[35] William Acton, in his treatise on prostitution, recalled that: 'It was the fashion formerly for those wishing to see life ... to go to the Theatre Royal, and between the acts to stroll into the saloons, and there look at the stout, over-dressed women who frequented these places and resided in houses of ill-fame in the neighbourhood slums.' After the performance it was 'the correct thing' for young men to be taken to brothels and a 'notorious saloon in Piccadilly'.[36]

Later in the century, prostitutes created problems in music halls, where they began to congregate after the closure of night houses and casinos. They soon became the target of moralistic and reforming groups. In 1886 there was an attempt to prevent fallen women cruising the Alhambra, the Pavilion and the Criterion.

The most famous episode occurred in 1894, when the campaigner Laura Ormiston Chant tried to close down the notorious promenade at the Empire Music Hall in Leicester Square. The Empire promenade (known as the 'American Bar') was an infamous space for solicitation.[37]

Under pressure from Mrs Ormiston Chant, the LCC committee decided that the Empire could only be re-licensed if no drinks were sold in the auditorium. This meant that screens would have to be put up around the lounges, and the promenades filled with fixed seating. The Empire management claimed that this would throw some seven hundred people out of work, but the LCC upheld the ruling.[38] There was a comical aspect to the near-riot that ensued. Male spectators, angered by the removal of one of the Empire's main attractions, attacked the flimsy canvas screens shutting off the promenade. According to the *Pall Mall Gazette*,

> Well-dressed men—some of them almost middle-aged—kicked at it from within, bursting the canvas, but hardly affecting the woodwork. ... The attendants ... watched in helpless and amused inactivity.[39]

Among those who led the attack was a young Winston Churchill with a party comprising his fellow Sandhurst cadets and gentlemen armed with walking sticks. Mrs Ormiston Chant and her campaigners were thwarted. Within two years the LCC allowed the Empire to pull out the seats and re-open the promenades. This was because prostitutes continued to visit the theatre and could not be barred if they were orderly. The promenades were forbidden in theatres built after 1889 (the Empire had opened in 1884). Prostitutes continued to cruise older theatres until 1916 when London vigilantes finally dislodged them.[40]

Gentlemen voyeurs: admiring the ballet-girls

For many men in the audience, the theatre was a venue for voyeuristic indulgence. The horseshoe-shaped auditorium gave an opportunity to admire and ogle the beauties both on stage and in the audience. Auditoriums were not darkened until late in the century, so spectators could view not only the performance on stage, but each other decked out in all their finery. For wealthy gentlemen it gave an opportunity to display their wealth and position through placing an elaborately gowned, bejewelled female companion at the front of their boxes. Usually the man stood or sat behind her, as etiquette demanded.[41]

Figure 5. Introducing a well-feathered *protégé*

Apart from ladies in the audience, there were female performers on stage to be admired and even sought after. Gentlemen made visits backstage and to the Green Room for assignations with actresses or ballet girls, often attempting to lure them to late night suppers in *chambres privées*. It was even claimed that actresses paid commission-money to 'spend-thrift peers' for introductions to young men, their 'well-feathered *protégés*, as pigeons that may be safely plucked'.[42]

Such was the sexual allure of the actress, that wealthy, often dissolute, young men went to exorbitant lengths to acquire introductions. In 1840 the 'Hon. F. L. G.' exclaimed that 'Actresses are in greater demand among men of gallantry, than any other class of women whatsoever.' The actress became a desirable object, a prize to be gained for the pleasure of men.

Figure 6. Eight o'clock p.m. 'The Opera'. The audience at Her Majesty's Theatre in the 1850s: note the men in the audience with opera-glasses.

Young men were advised that 'To gain the favour and companionship of an actress some little tact is required.' The best plan to 'capture' a favoured actress was for 'a party of gentlemen' to get up a private performance of a play and invite her to perform in it. The present of a ring or trinket may assist in 'capitulation'. After all, actresses were considered 'the most mercenary of their sex'.[43] Like the prostitute, the actress was on public display, led an independent life and was financially vulnerable. These were qualities that made her desirable to the drunken swells and Guardsmen who endeavoured to get into green rooms or dressing rooms, or loitered outside the stage door.[44]

Tracy Davis has commented that 'Open prostitution for any type of female performer was out of the question.' Theatres were in the areas frequented by prostitutes, and recognition by a manager could mean 'instant dismissal without a recommendation'.⁴⁵

Figure 7. George Augustus Sala

However, the author of *The Swell's Night Guide* assured his male readers that there was no difficulty in acquiring actresses, as many frequented 'some of the French Introducing Houses'. These appear to have been discreetly concealed brothels—'A showy brass plate would lead the passer-by to imagine that a physician of eminence was the occupant of the house.' Or it would be fronted by premises for a suitably feminine trade, with erotic connotations, such as millinery, corset-making or 'stay-building'.⁴⁶ Such hidden venues were possibly discreet enough for a low-paid supporting actress to supplement her income by indulging in prostitution.

Almost two decades later, the journalist George Augustus Sala* described lecherous aristocrats and dissipated swells visiting the 'forbidden region' of the Green Room. Here they try to fulfil their fantasies through meeting ballet girls dressed in revealing costumes, 'abridged muslin skirts and flesh-coloured continuations of ballet-girlhood'.⁴⁷

Sala's pure, hardworking British ballet-girl is the unwitting prey of degenerate upper-class males. He sees the green room as a place of failed

---

* Probably the most prolific journalist of the Victorian period, and author of a bawdy pantomime called *Harlequin Prince Cherrytop*. See also page 65. —*Ed.*

assignations where virtuous ballerinas hold out against unwanted male attention. However, despite Sala's emphasis on their moral purity, many a poorly paid, overworked ballet girl was tempted away from 'her rude and stern lot' with promises of 'broughams and diamond *aigrettes*, dinners at Richmond and villas in St John's Wood'.[48]

Figure 8. Seven o'clock p.m. 'Behind the scenes'

As one ballet girl explained (in a letter to *The Era*) no other girl was subject to so many temptations. Backstage she was constantly addressed by 'men of fortune and talent'. For an ignorant girl, men held out 'great temptations' as well as many 'bright promises'—which could easily be broken once the seduction had been accomplished.[49]

According to an 1888 tract, *Tempted London*, to get behind the scenes was the aim of all young men considering themselves 'fast'. However it was a privilege reserved for those with plenty of money and position. The 'standing' of champagne and tipping officials was 'beyond the scope of a clerk's modest income'.[50] Some managers positively encouraged upper class swells behind the scenes. 'A nobleman had only to present his card to the stage door keeper to gain access to any part of the theatre'.[51] 'Young lords, or stage door loungers as they were sometimes called' were permitted to hang about the wings where they attempted 'familiarities with female artistes'. In the mid-1880s, there were still one or two theatres dependent on the patronage of 'mashers' and dissipated aristocrats 'who make the theatre a rendezvous and pay their money merely to gaze upon their mistresses in tights'.[52]* Well-to-do swells and dissipated aristocrats were able to go backstage and create a nuisance, while the majority of 'misguided youths' hanging about stage-doors of theatres were clerks whose appearance 'suggests their ambition'.[53]

By the 1890s the green room had apparently become more respectable. It was now the waiting room for 'the leading artistes in the intervals of their parts'. In major theatres this area was 'very comfortably, not to say luxuriously, fitted up' for the benefit of leading performers. It was no longer accessible to 'ladies of the ballet, still less to supers'.†[54] Nor was it supposedly accessible to well-to-do men seeking the favours of actresses and ballet girls.

Unauthorised backstage visits were claimed by most West End theatre managers to be forbidden. Yet at some theatres and music halls, including the Alhambra, male spectators were able to obtain paper and envelopes in the stalls and write notes to fancied actresses or ballet girls, attempting to make appointments with them. The notes were passed to theatre attendants who delivered them backstage. By supplying notepaper and messengers the management was complicit in continuing to allow the solicitation of female performers by dissolute upper-class men.[55] It is an example of the hypocrisy and double standards surrounding male behaviour: while backstage physical harassment appears to be forbidden, solicitation is able to continue by means of pen and paper.

The male gaze and the female performer

The musical entertainments of the Victorian theatre, from burlesque to musical comedy, had an overwhelming emphasis on femininity. An abundance of attractive women on stage was deliberately manipulated for the erotic arousal of the male spectator. This particularly applied to

---

* A 'masher', according to the *Urban Dictionary*, www.urbandictionary.com, is 'a man who attempts to force his unwelcome attentions on a woman'. —*Ed.*

† Supernumerary actors —*Ed,*

dancers. In 1839, Dr Michael Ryan castigated the sensuality of women on the stage:

> Who has not seen actresses appear in ... dresses as white as marble and fitting so tightly that the shape of their bodies could not be more apparent, had they come forward in a state of nature? Again, opera dancers appear nightly before crowded moral audiences, in dresses made for the express purpose of exposing their shape and figure, while the style of dancing is such as to excite the most wanton thoughts and lascivious desires.[56]

Figure 9. An admirer of the ballet girls

The ballet girl held her male admirers in the audience in sexual thrall. Her movements on stage were imbued with sensuality. She wore costumes that revealed, rather than concealed, certain portions of her body. A low cut bodice showed naked arms, bare shoulders and cleavage. Her short skirts displayed her ankles and even her legs. The twirling, layered muslin of a ballerina's *tarlatan* could arouse fetishistic desires in an era when petticoats, corsetry and frilly undergarments were objects of male arousal.

The combination of freely flowing draperies, unrestricted movement and unfettered femininity were sources for voyeuristic indulgence by men in the audience.[57] Not only could actresses and dancers be viewed on the stage: images of them appeared in openly displayed prints in notorious Holywell Street, near the Strand. Female performers appeared on postcards, while provocative drawings, photographs, and articles appeared in erotic journals such as *The Exquisite* and *The Day's Doings*, and toward the end of the century in *The Mascot* and *Photobits*. Men were able to study erotic images of female performers in the privacy of their chambers or studies.

Actresses and dancers in revealing costumes, making seemingly sensual gestures, were blamed by moral campaigners for leading young men astray. The effect of subjection to the male gaze on half-clad ballet girls was not usually considered. In 1888, the tract *Tempted London* warned that a young man attending the theatre with 'two or three companions' could become more or less enamoured of 'a singing chambermaid' or 'leading lady' both of whom 'display their personal attractions with more emphasis than modesty'. He could easily lose his head at the sight of the leading lady 'clad in a white robe, her hair flowing loosely in extravagant luxuriance down her back, her white arms bare to her shoulder, her neck and bosom by no means jealously guarded from the vulgar gaze'. He was in danger of carrying away a mental impression of her 'which can do him no good and may do him much harm'.[58]

Even when coming out from the auditorium, the theatre bar offers further temptation. It is usually presided over by 'young women who have been carefully selected for their good looks'.[59] On leaving the theatre the youth, 'his imagination excited and his senses in a whirl', comes out into the Strand, haunt of prostitutes and leading to Holywell Street. The sight of 'brilliant bars and supper rooms' as well as 'the gaily dressed women who flit around him with laughing eyes' gives him little inclination to return to his 'dismal suburb and his own sparsely furnished bedchamber'.[60] Through the influence of women on the stage, a respectable young man is liable to be harmed by excessive masturbation, consorting with prostitutes, and venereal disease.

By the end of the century moral campaigners were concerned with the effect of female performers on middle-class husbands, brothers and sons.

In 1894, Laura Ormiston Chant cited the impact of female ballet costumes which created an impression of nudity on men in the audience at the Empire.[61] Campaigners tried to prohibit a male-orientated pleasure without success. For many men, the erotic enjoyment of watching ballet girls was a diversion from duties of home, family and the workplace. Venues such as the Alhambra and the Empire provided a form of erotic escapism for middle-class men. That this was an indulgence that could be enjoyed in the company of other men lends to an apparently heterosexual pleasure a decidedly homoerotic undertone.

Defying the campaigns of moralisers, an article by Arthur Symons,* published in the *Savoy* magazine for 1896, describes the erotic interplay between ballet girls on the stage and men in the audience at the Alhambra Music Hall. Whereas in 1859 Sala's dissipated swells actively roamed backstage seeking *coryphées*, Symons in the 1890s sees the men in the audience as passive voyeurs. The front row of the stalls is 'filled entirely by men'. They have not come to the theatre 'from an abstract, aesthetic interest in the ballet'. Those who cannot get seats stand by the bar with 'intent eyes, the gray smoke curling up from their cigarettes' as they gaze at the girls on stage.[62]

The gentlemen at the Alhambra indulge in the passive enjoyment of female sexuality gyrating in front of them on the stage. Their 'friends on the other side of the footlights' are very much aware of their admirers in the audience. The women on stage know the power they can exert over the men seated in the front row.† The moment they come on stage, they 'will look down ... to see who are in the front row, and who are standing by the bar at the side'. When the performance concludes 'The whole front applauds violently; and if one observes closely, it would be seen that every man, as he applauds, is looking in a different direction.' Each man

---

* Arthur Symons poet, writer and critic, was a central figure in the Rhymers Club. He and his friends would meet Alhambra girls after the show and take them to the 'Crown' pub for drinks and serious talk. See Carter 2005: 96.

† John Hollingshead also attested to the sexual power of the Alhambra ballet-girls: 'The few ballet girls who stood out from the mass, principally owing to their great physical beauty, were the prize strawberries on the top of the bottle. They proved the power—the old and everlasting power—which existed long before Helen of Troy, one of God's greatest gifts'. See Hollingshead 1895: I, 230.

applauds his favourite among the dancers, and each of the dancers becomes an object for desire.[63] The ballet at the Alhambra, as described by Symons, reveals a fascination with illusion and artificiality. For most men in the audience the female dancer remained an unattainable object of desire, only to be gazed upon night after night. She became part of the 'man's world' of forbidden pleasure, but divided by the less than respectable world of the music hall stage, notions of wantonness and a lower social class.

A 1913 novella, *The Actor Manager* by Alice and Claude Askew, gives the reverse view—that of men in the audience as seen from the stage by a showgirl. The men who comprise most of the stalls audience at the fictional Comet Theatre were:

> nearly all of them young men, well-dressed, nice-looking boys for the most part, boys who looked as if they had been cut out after some identical pattern. And the faces of these youths lacked character—lacked strength; but, of course, they were all smart boys—that went without saying.[64]

The lack of 'strength' and 'character' in their faces suggests moral weakness and depravity. The heroine of the novel, overwhelmed by the male gaze, rushes off the stage in panic during her musical comedy debut. Her feelings of shame and degradation are possibly similar to the reactions of other young women making their first appearance on stage confronted by the eyes of men:

> It was only when Sheila was facing her audience that the knowledge of the truth came to her, and she knew in a flush of troubled comprehension that she was being set up to be stared at—devoured by men's eyes—that it was her beauty that was on sale—her spotless womanhood. She was only conscious of a feeling of misery and shame, of the devouring gaze of hundreds of eyes. She wanted to throw a cloak over herself, she longed for a veil to hide her face. All they wanted to do was stare at her, taking in the grace of her young body, to gaze with bold eyes at her slim form.[65]

There is an underlying sexual titillation in the situation of a vulnerable young girl alarmed by the voyeuristic penetration of a number of men's eyes. Like Arthur Symons's article, the episode may be seen to work on different levels. Another layer of 'gazing' comes from the readership of the novel—male readers could identify with the fictional audience and find erotic stimulation in the plight of a heroine being metaphorically undressed by the eyes of men.

There were also female performers who enjoyed and encouraged the attention of men in the audience. This could be achieved through teasing confusions of gender, with 'girls travestied as boys, so boyish sometimes, in their slim youth; the feminine contours now escaping, now accentuated'.[66] Since the maligned male dancer had been banished from performing leading roles during the 1870s, female dancers at venues such as the Empire and Alhambra appeared *en travesti*.*[67] Male costume revealed the contours of the female body, freeing it from the constraints of nineteenth-century feminine fashion. Boots, tights, short tunic, doublets and jerkins showed off legs and tightly drawn waists, accentuating hips, breasts and buttocks. A paradox was created by which the travesty performer was even more sexually appealing than those playing feminine roles.[68] However, while Symons' cross-dressed Alhambra ballet girls may have exuded a teasing sexuality for men, male impersonation in drama and in the music hall raised other questions. In pantomime, no effort was made to pretend that the fleshly principal boys were men. It was customary for women to take the roles of boys in drama, making themselves as convincing as possible.

On the music hall stage, female performers dressed in male attire and sang songs about boys, making the same sort of leering invitations to come on a spree as Champagne Charlie. At the same time they introduced a feminine perspective. Male disguise gave the impersonator the opportunity to express the feelings of women in the audience. She was able to mock the pretensions of a 'man's life' through the innuendo of her performances. She exuded an androgynous appeal that deliberately threw masculine instincts into further disarray.

'Margeries', 'Poofs' and 'Mary-Annes'

The nineteenth-century theatre undoubtedly attracted a homosexual coterie among the groups of men who visited it together. The theatre

---

* In the late nineteenth century, male dancers in ballets at the Alhambra and elsewhere mainly appeared in mime or character roles, although foreign dancers were occasionally imported to play heroes and princes.

represented a radical and liberal space, where the sexual hypocrisy of the surrounding world could be challenged. Its bohemianism endorsed an alternative behaviour; a reversal of conventions of masculine identity.[69]

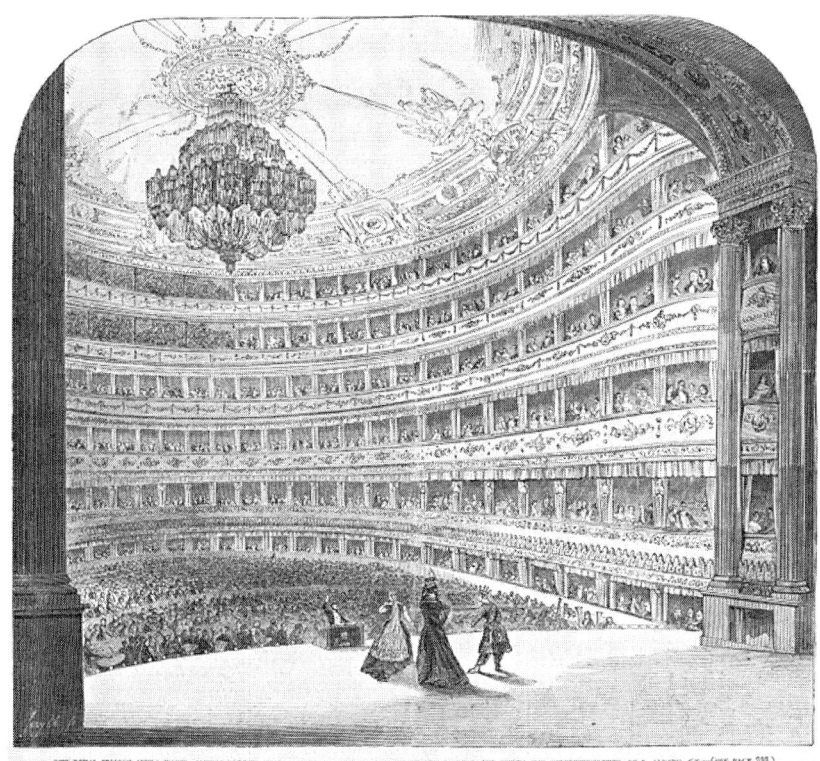

Figure 10. Royal Italian Opera, c. 1847. Possibly depicting what is now Her Majesty's Theatre in the Haymarket, rather than Covent Garden as the caption suggests.

According to the *Yokel's Preceptor* (c.1850), a rather scurrilous guide to the sexual underworld, the West End of London was 'actually thronged with ... Margeries, Pooffs &c' who 'flock the saloons and boxes of theatres, coffee-houses &c' (although particular theatres are not specified).[70] This points to a substantial homosexual presence among mid-Victorian theatre audiences. The guide also refers to the 'notorious Margeries' or male prostitutes who thronged the West End. The areas of the West End frequented by male prostitutes, such as Regent Street Quadrant, the Haymarket, the streets toward Trafalgar Square and the Strand, were conveniently located close to theatres.

Like female prostitutes, 'renters'* were to be found inside the theatres and music halls. The dark recesses of the Olympic, the Adelphi and the Italian Opera† were used for homosexual liaisons.‡

Later in the century, the standing room area behind the circle at the Alhambra was a well-known cruising ground for male prostitutes (at least until the 1930s).[71] Renters and their homosexual hangers-on also frequented part of the Empire Music Hall, the Pavilion, and the bar of the St James's Theatre.[72] The Criterion Bar in Piccadilly was considered 'a great centre for inverts'. It attracted 'men in evening dress, men in mufti, guardsmen and garrulous music hall artists, City men, well-known racing men, and popular jockeys—all sorts and conditions of men'.[73]

The homosexual presence in theatres and music halls could be a target for aggression by the management. In 1894, a member of the audience at the Empire complained about the front-of-house manager, Robert William Ahern, 'dragging, kicking and punching a pacific man from the gallery'. He explained that the man was a '*sodomite*' and that more than half the audience in the 'shilling promenade' was 'of that class'. He turned out 'half a dozen a night & gave them a good kicking'. According to Ahern, the shilling gallery of the Empire 'was the only place in London where this class of people congregated'; he boasted that 'he could lay his hands on 200 sods every night in the week if he liked.'[74]

Ahern may have been exaggerating, but his claim points to a considerable amount of homosexual activity in London theatres and music halls in the years prior to the arrest and trial of Oscar Wilde. It also raises the question as to why the moral campaign against the Empire in 1894 ignored the question of queers§ and renters up in the shilling gallery and

---

* Young male prostitutes. I've substituted this term for DHL's 'rent boys' which seemed to strike an anachronistic note for the period on question. —*Ed.*

† This presumably relates to the post-1847 period when the "Italian Opera" referred to Covent Garden. Prior to that date it would have referred to what is now Her Majesty's Theatre in the Haymarket. —*Ed.*

‡ The 'fields of adventure' of *Case XIX* in Havelock Ellis's *Sexual Inversion* include 'the dark recess in the gallery of the Olympic Theatre' as well as the Adelphi and the Italian Opera. See Ellis and Symonds 2008: 148.

§ As with 'homosexual', the term 'queer' in this sense is strictly speaking anachronistic for this period. Contemporary terms in common use would have included 'sodomites' and 'inverts'. —*Ed.*

concentrated on women parading in the more affluent promenade. As Tracy Davis has pointed out, so far as Laura Ormiston Chant was concerned, indecency meant the covert enjoyment of female sexuality by men away from the moralistic sphere of wife and family.[75] She seemed unaware that there were also a number of middle-class married men not averse to picking up renters in the lower-priced areas of certain theatres or music halls.

Figure 11. A pair of 'swells' going arm-in-arm to the theatre

Because homosexuality was criminalised, many men who indulged in homosexual activities (in theatres or elsewhere) were vulnerable to arrest or blackmail. While practising homosexual men were forced to remain hidden, strong and emotional platonic male friendships were extolled by society. For a man to remain a bachelor was a common condition throughout the Victorian era. Society's acceptance of bachelorhood was useful for those of Uranian* inclinations. This, together with the overt

---

* 'Uranian' was a term used amongst literary circles in the late nineteenth century to mean homosexual. It was sometimes used in the more specific sense of men who had platonic attachments to boys. —*Ed.*

emotionalism of many male friendships, offered protection for same-sex lovers. It also creates conjecture about the sexual orientation of men reported visiting the theatre in pairs and in groups. Some of the elegantly dressed pairs of 'swells' were possibly queer couples. After all, 'swell' was one of the terms used for the clients of male prostitutes.[76]

Same-sex relations between swells were hinted at in an article which appeared in *The Era* in 1877. It compared the 'Swell' and his companion with literary and mythological male friends and lovers: 'the Swell is but a fragment without his brother exquisite. You might as well take Damon from Pythias, or Sandford from Merton, as part this youthful Aeneas from his faithful Achates.'*[77] (The ideal of platonic male-to-male relations, as exemplified by classical heroes such as Aeneas and Achates, is derided when applied to the presence of a pair of ridiculous swells. That the Greek heroes were also lovers seems to hint at a homosexual presence among swells in theatre audiences.

Indolent young men, such as swells, mashers or dandies, were considered effeminate. Their leisured inactivity seemed to defy notions of duty and moral purpose associated with manliness. Indulging in a lifestyle that rejected these tenets was considered to be absolute unmanliness. The frivolity of the swell, with his fashionable clothes, spendthrift habits and effeminate manner of speech, equated him with the cross-dressed 'margery' and homosexual 'poof'. Along with his brother dandies and mashers, he was considered duplicitous, lacking masculine qualities of frankness, openness and candour.[78] As James Eli Adams has observed, these flamboyant male figures intruded on a position in Victorian life reserved for the feminine.[79] However their effeminacy was not necessarily associated with same-sex desire, because there was an 'intractable element of theatricality in all masculine self-fashioning, which inevitably makes its appeal to an audience, real or imagined'.[80] But, as the Boulton and Park case was to prove, the dandy and the swell could easily be involved with sodomitic desire and merge into the *demimonde* of men who 'passed' as women.

---

* Damon and Pythias were devoted friends in ancient Greece; Tommy Merton and Harry Sandford were the heroes of a children's book by the eighteenth-century writer Thomas Day; Achates was the loyal companion of Aeneas in Virgil's *Aeneid*. —Ed.

Figure 12. Boulton and Park

The Boulton and Park case points to the presence among theatre audiences of men who dressed as women. Ernest Boulton and Frederick Park (known as 'Fanny' and 'Stella') are possibly the best-known examples of Victorian transvestites. The events of their arrest and trial have been well documented and are included in nearly every discussion of nineteenth-century male dissidence. Nevertheless their case uniquely combines masculine deviancy with elements of the theatre. My concern, therefore, is with their association with the theatre and its reflection of alternative male behaviour.

Boulton and Park, two young middle-class gay* men who dressed as women, gave performances, both on the stage and off. As members of the

---

* 'Gay', here and elsewhere, is used in its modern sense; in the nineteenth century it would generally have referred to prostitution: its association with homosexuality arose well into the twentieth century. —*Ed.*

audience they were regularly seen in theatres and music halls of the West End during the 1860s and 70s. They also ventured as far afield as the Surrey Theatre in Blackfriars. In the guise of actresses, they gave stage performances in halls and theatres located in London and the provinces. Finally, they were arrested on leaving the Strand Theatre (which attracted prostitutes of both sexes) on 28 April 1870. Both were fashionably gowned and coiffured at the time of their arrest.

From the evidence of the numbers of arrests, men dressed as women formed a considerable subculture. It has been suggested that most of them were middle-class and they belonged to self-identified networks. They constituted a threat to the self-image of the Victorian bourgeoisie.[81] Yet the presence of 'Female Personators' was not apparent to everyone. The journalist Percy Fitzgerald wrote that in the trial of Boulton and Park 'an extraordinary picture of a society, unsuspected by many, was revealed. ... It appeared there were a number of persons who affected this effeminate mode of disguising themselves'. Cross-dressing was considered part of the decadence of the age; according to Fitzgerald it was 'the outer eruption significant of a deeper social disease within'.[82]

Evidence suggests that a cross-dressed element was to be found in theatre audiences, but none attracted the same kind of attention as Fanny and Stella. Part of the outrage they provoked was due to their respectable middle-class backgrounds. In theatres and music halls their behaviour proved too unconventional for the comfort of management and patrons. They carried theatricality to an extreme, deliberately challenging codes of respectability by openly displaying deviant personas.

The pair seemed to delight in creating confusion among 'respectable' theatregoers by appearing dressed as women on one night and as men on another. Or they could take on the appearance of painted Piccadilly renters. John Reeves, Staff Superintendent of the Alhambra Music Hall in Leicester Square, observed their behaviour in the auditorium for two years.[83] He saw them one night dressed as men 'but their faces painted, their necks fully displayed by low collars and powdered. They wore waistcoats fully opened ... they looked more feminine than masculine.'[84] His attention was brought to them walking 'about the house in an unbecoming manner' with 'a lot of men got round them'.[85] On another occasion, they were observed leaning out of their box 'lasciviously ogling' the male occupants of the stalls.[86] They made chirruping noises to gain the attention of fancied men in the audience.* Due to their provocative behaviour, Boulton and Park were thrown out of the Alhambra Music Hall on more than twenty occasions. At the time of their arrest, detectives had been observing them for a year. It is possible that they were used as a warning and example to other 'men in petticoats' who cruised the streets and theatre foyers and were seen as a public nuisance. Wherever they went, Fanny and Stella attracted male admirers, which brings into question the presence of men in the audience who favoured transvestites. This question is particularly relevant considering the large number of admirers who attended their performances on the stage as 'actresses'.

Boulton's appearances in 'his wonderful impersonation of a female character' gained him a great reputation in London and the provinces. Sometimes he received as many as fourteen bouquets at one performance, all from gentleman admirers. The *Illustrated Police News* reported that after their provincial touring performances, they were invited to the country houses of 'gentlemen', which they attended dressed as women. In every town, 'their rooms were for weeks inundated with gentlemen (including clergymen)'. So-called 'burlesque' love-letters were written to them, addressed to 'My darling Stella' or 'Dearest Fan'. It was even suggested that these after-show visits involved sexual activity.[87]

The trials of Boulton and Park had all the elements of performance. The courts were crowded with their admirers for the hearings. *Reynolds Newspaper* noted the eagerness of a fashionable public to gaze on the prisoners and hear all the 'filthy details' related by witnesses. Several well-known actors attended the hearings and, according to the *Reynolds* reporter, 'a noble Lord' surveyed the prisoners through his opera glasses—as if watching a performance in the theatre. Many of the spectators appeared to be 'in the know'. They reacted to the proceedings as they would at a theatrical performance. There was audible sympathy with 'any revelations that appeared to tell in the favour of the defendants'. However, there was also a tendency to laugh at disclosures

---

* Chirruping' was a ploy used by Victorian prostitutes to attract punters.

'which filled several people with disgust' and this inclination was 'repeatedly checked by officers of the court'.[88]

Boulton and Park could not cease performing, even in the courtroom. During the trial, they repeatedly changed their costumes and appearance. They first appeared at Bow Street in women's clothes, but later they stood in the dock as fashionably-dressed young men about town, carrying light-coloured gloves. They grew facial hair in an effort to appear more masculine. On the final day of the trial, the pair were in sober mood: 'they were quietly dressed; they did not display their light-coloured kid gloves as on former days and the familiar bouquets were dispensed with.'[89] Their acquittal could be likened to the conclusion of a stage performance. On hearing the verdict, Ernest Boulton fainted—like a heroine in melodrama. Meanwhile, the spectators greeted their acquittal with applause, cheers and shouts of 'Bravo', as if they had attended a stunning piece of theatre. Their acquittal has been seen by recent commentators to represent a wilful ignorance of a sodomitic culture by men from the upper classes and 'respectable' middle class society. But it is more likely, as H. G. Cocks has pointed out, that Boulton and Park together with their former lovers John Fiske and Louis Hurt, escaped justice because of a skilful defence and an unusually sympathetic judge.*[90]

For a man to appear in female attire in public provoked amusement and hostility—it was a threat to accepted standards of masculine behaviour. At the time of their arrest, Fanny and Stella had become too visible; they were going too far against the confines of strict behavioural codes. The 'swell' could create a nuisance in the theatre, usually without risking arrest. Similarly, a female prostitute could ogle and proposition men in the audience without being ejected. But because Boulton and Park transgressed the boundaries by cross-dressing and indulging in deliberately provocative behaviour, they were punished by being put on trial and made to suffer indignities.†

---

* Another of the accused, Stella's lover and 'husband', Lord Arthur Clinton, had died before the case came to court, probably by suicide. For a more recent coverage of Boulton and Park, see McKenna 2013. —*Ed.*

† The Boulton and Park scandal was not completely forgotten. There were obscene rhymes about the pair, while the notorious *Sins of the Cities of the Plain; or Confessions*

Oscar Wilde and wearers of the green carnation

The dominant queer presence in late-nineteenth-century British theatre is that of Oscar Wilde. This may be a clichéd statement, but Wilde remains the one homosexual figure of the Victorian age to have earned iconic status. His talent and presence dominated the fashionable London theatre until his disgrace and downfall in 1895. Prior to this, he had openly visited the theatre in the company of his circle of queer and artistic friends. However, as Alan Sinfield has pointed out, Wilde's dandified appearance and 'effeminate' manners would not necessarily have been recognised by contemporaries outside of his circle as being 'homosexual'. The effeminate dandy or bohemian aesthete was a fashionable figure, regularly encountered in the lobbies, stalls and dress circles of the West End theatres favoured by Society. The question of Wilde's homosexuality was not established until the trials.[91]

In the early 1890s a previously sublimated queer coterie was making itself visible. Yet since all homosexual acts had been rendered illegal by the 'Labouchère Amendment' to the Criminal Law Amendment Act 1885, this visibility would only have been apparent to those 'in the know'. Nevertheless the promotion of Uranianism in art and literature encouraged a more overt gay life style among groups of artistic, wealthy and well-connected young men. A cult of masculine beauty came into vogue, based on Hellenistic ideals, in direct opposition to the public school imperative of rugged physical manliness. Fashionable gay men wore well-cut expensive clothes and had distinctive hairstyles.

The cultivation of a mode of life following Greek paederastic ideology was apparent in the promulgation of love between older and younger men, and in the giving and receiving of gifts. An exclusive gay lifestyle, centred on wealth and privilege, came into being. Well-to-do gay men went abroad to fashionable resorts, and cities with queer connections, such as Paris, Monte Carlo, Naples or Algiers. They could be observed

---

of a Mary-Ann (privately printed in London, 1881) describes their supposed sexual exploits in vivid detail. Oscar Wilde possibly alluded to Ernest Boulton in the title of his comedy *The Importance of Being Earnest*—as well as in the jokes referring to the name of 'Ernest'. In the same play Lady Bracknell's reference to 'dear Lady Bolton' is another probable allusion.

dining together in exclusive London restaurants like the Café Royal, Wills's or the Savoy. The lifestyle of indolent upper-class young men in the 1890s, with its emphasis on gifts, clothes, dining and entertainment, intermingled queerness with consumerism.[92] It could also be viewed as a form of protest against paternalistic insistence on masculine productivity.

But behind the façade of elegance lurked the fear of the law and blackmail, liaisons with male prostitutes and the risk of familial disgrace. Upper-class men of this circle were vulnerable to the sexual attraction exerted by working-class men and boys. In fact, homosexuality was one of the few areas in which working-class men were capable of holding upper-class men in their power, through prostitution and blackmail.

Oscar Wilde became the undisputed leader of this group of wealthy gay men. His own public life was a series of self-promoting appearances, culminating in the final, tragic performance of the courtroom. For the four brief years leading up to his arrest, Wilde with his circle virtually monopolised the two most fashionable playhouses of the West End—The Theatre Royal, Haymarket and the St James's in nearby King Street. Between 1892 and 1895, these theatres performed the four society plays that confirmed Wilde's reputation as a dramatist.

The opening nights of Wilde's plays were 'like brilliant parties', according to Florence Alexander (wife of George Alexander, actor-manager of the St James's Theatre): 'Everybody knew everybody, everybody put on their best clothes, everybody wished us success.'[93] These were the affluent spectators in the stalls and dress circle. Nor should it be forgotten that Wilde's plays attracted a wide spectrum of society. On the opening night of *Lady Windermere's Fan*, George Alexander noticed that the pit and gallery were as full as the more expensive areas of the house.[94] The gallery spectator could observe both a society audience and its mirror image in Wilde's play.

On opening nights an intimate, exclusive atmosphere was created, presided over by the presence of Wilde himself. He was 'able to play the parts of host and master magician at the same time'. At the end of the play he would appear on stage with a cigarette in his hand as if he was in his own drawing room.[95] These curtain-call appearances, wearing a green carnation, his mauve-gloved hand holding a slender cigarette, gave out an aura of decadence, which his more conservative contemporaries, such as

Henry James and Clement Scott, found outrageous.⁹⁶ At the height of his success, Wilde attended his first nights surrounded by his entourage. For the opening performance of *Lady Windermere's Fan*, he went as far as he dared in revealing a gay identity. Wilde teasingly suggested a covert gay presence in the audience and on the stage. He persuaded members of his circle to wear green carnations in their buttonholes.

Figure 13. Oscar Wilde

On stage, Ben Webster*, who played Cecil Graham, was the only actor to wear a green carnation. When asked what all this meant, Wilde replied, 'Nothing whatever, but that is just what nobody will guess'. He found delight in the suggestion of a mysterious Masonic-type brotherhood binding an actor in the performance with certain members of the audience. The green carnation gave a hint of a secret, decadent world known only to a covert few.†⁹⁷ The result was as showy as the self-

---

* Grandson of the actor-manager Benjamin Webster —.*Ed*
† Traditionally, the shape of the carnation symbolised the anus, while the colour green was thought to be favoured by homosexuals. See Robb 2003: 151. The green carnation was an artificial, chemically enhanced creation—a fin-de-siècle example of nature turned

display of the Uranian aesthete. As Morris B. Kaplan has pointed out, Wilde's public appearances 'surrounded by admiring young men' recalled the promenading of Fanny and Stella in the 1860s.[98] There is also evidence that some of his followers may have dressed as women or 'cavorted' with cross-dressers.[99]

Figure 14. John Gray

According to Marc-André Raffalovich the appearance of many of Wilde's disciples was effeminate. They wore make-up, painted their lips, had an effeminate way of styling their hair, and swayed their hips when they walked.[100] A satirical article in *Punch* also mocked the effeminacy of 'the Decadents' who 'nightly gathered at any of the theatres where the plays of Mr WILDE were being given. Nightly, the Stalls were fulfilled by Row upon Row of neatly-curled Fringes surmounting Button-holes of

---

to artifice. A paragraph in *The Artist* describes how the white flower is given the hue by plunging its stem into a malachite green dye. See *Artist and Home Journal*, 13 (1 April 1892): 114–115: 'From Month to Month, a Summary (The green carnation to which we have referred.)'. [*The Artist* was known for its homosexual readership, particularly during the editorship of Charles Kains Jackson —*Ed.*]

monstrous size.'[101]

A few weeks after the première of *Lady Windermere's Fan*, the green carnation made another appearance, at the first performance of a rather precious little play, *The Kiss* by John Gray (a translation of *Le Baiser* by Théodore de Banville). Gray, who had probably been one of Wilde's lovers, was claimed to be 'the original' of Dorian Gray.[102] The performance took place at the Royalty Theatre, on 4 March 1892, under the auspices of J. T. Grein's Independent Theatre. Wilde filled a box with 'a suite of young gentlemen, all wearing the dyed carnation which has superseded the lily and the sunflower'.[103]

A rival box was taken opposite Wilde's by the Irish novelist George Moore, who was 'another convert to Wilde's charm'.[104] This suggests friendly competition between bohemian and queer circles. Wilde however was not without his enemies, and one of them was Gray's future lover Marc-André Raffalovich who was critical of Wilde's followers and wrote a sonnet deriding the green carnation.*[105]

The conspicuous wearing of the green carnation at the performance of a play by a fellow queer author marks its significance as a symbol of Uranianism. To the public at large, the artificial flower was a symbol of the aesthetic movement. Only those who were members of exclusive queer circles were aware that this was the distinctive emblem worn by homosexuals in Paris. Through utilising the symbolism of the green carnation, Wilde, in the theatre, created a counter-performance. He made the audience take on a role that bemused, teased and annoyed it. Wilde, by showing off the green carnation, had enjoyed a private joke, created within the framework of a queer exclusivity. The green carnation buttonhole was a frivolous taunt to the late-Victorian earnestness embodied by the more sober gentlemen of the audience.[106] The buttonhole on the lapel of a jacket was a point of penetration in the rigidly militaristic tailoring of late nineteenth-century menswear. Wearing a dyed flower gave a feminised note of frivolity to an otherwise sombre appearance of masculinity. By 1910, C. D. Wilton, writing in the journal *Modern Man*, noted that wearers of the green carnation had 'brought the

---

* For a discussion of Gay and Raffalovich's joint play *The Blackmailers* see page 284. For the novel *The Green Carnation* see page 295. —*Ed.*

inoffensive buttonhole into grave disrepute – so much so that our tailors to-day make no proper provision in dress suits for a floral decoration.'[107]

Oscar Wilde was perhaps the last overtly dissident male presence in the Victorian theatre. With his arrest and disgrace, issues had been brought into the open which society would have preferred to remain hidden. The scandal surrounding Oscar Wilde, Boulton and Park, and others brought to trial in the latter part of the nineteenth century, reveals that society could only tolerate a certain amount of transgression. It did not want to be forced to confront controversies that opposed codes of behaviour laid down by the status quo. For the majority, homosexuality was not only confusing and threatening; it was contrary to the ideal of a pure, strong heterosexual manhood.

Dissent and gentrification

Despite threats of punishment, disgrace and condemnation, nineteenth-century masculinity harboured elements of dissent. Groups such as 'dandies', 'swells' 'aesthetes' and 'Mary-Annes' liked to display themselves in places of entertainment. By making themselves as visible as possible, they deliberately flouted convention. Places for performance made ideal venues for showing off. Lobbies, boxes, auditoria offered a socially fluid, permeable space for performance. 'Toffs' and 'swells' drew attention to themselves by rowdy, infantile behaviour—arriving late, creating disturbances, chattering during the performance. The cross-dressed 'Mary-Annes' created further confusion by displaying themselves as an alternative to norms of both femininity and masculinity. In the 1890s the Wildean cult of the green carnation caused speculation over a queer presence in the audience.

Attention-seeking display by these dissident male groups deliberately set out to annoy, confuse and provoke respectable members of the audience. Such carrying-on was capable of diverting attention away from the stage performance. This created a rivalry between stage and spectator that bridged the proscenium divide. Performances in the audience could be as clearly seen as those of the actors on the stage. The theatre became a space for total diversion—not only from the stage, but in the auditorium as well. Being a place of illusion, it allowed for a departure from social and moralistic strictures. Ideals of manhood may have been reiterated in countless melodramas, but the behavioural patterns of many men in the audience deliberately flouted those ideals. This applies as much to the working man shouting down from the gallery, as to the upper-class man-about-town lurching drunkenly into the West End circle in the middle of a performance.

The behaviour of men in the audience changed with the gradual rise in the status of the theatre. In the early to mid nineteenth century, theatre going was an intensely communal experience. Varied, colourful entertainments crossed barriers of class. However, theatrical illusion tended to be intruded upon by the social clamour of the world outside. It was possible for the middle-class *paterfamilias* in his box to survey dissolute members of the aristocracy in the stalls and dress circle, while in the 'gods' above hovered the aggressive, restless, disenfranchised man of the lower classes. The cramming together in one space of men, women and children of many different social levels allowed for the expression of class feelings and aggression.

This meant there was a great deal of physical activity among audiences—fighting and shouting in the gallery, protests from the pit, chatter and inattention in the stalls and dress circle. Verbal and physical rivalry between the gallery and stalls was often apparent. Performances were liable to be disturbed by the activities of ushers, box keepers and sellers of refreshments. Stamina was often needed to queue for long hours for tickets, as well as for the push and shove to enter and leave the building. The sheer physicality of the theatre is also apparent in its function as a venue for masculine voyeurism and sexual pleasure: prostitutes could be encountered; assignations with actresses or ballet girls could be arranged; beauties of both sexes could be viewed through opera-glasses.

The spontaneity of audiences began to subside with the gradual 'gentrification' of the theatre from around the 1850s. Managements catered to the tastes of the more affluent classes and deliberately marginalised the lower-income groups. Finding themselves confined to the uncomfortable pit or gallery, their behaviour subdued by class-conscious managers, working-class audiences drifted to the music hall. It was here that vestiges of vociferous audience behaviour remained. Gentrification of the theatre also saw changes in the demeanour of wealthier men in the audience. The loud-mouthed, boisterous upper-class swell was replaced by the restrained and elegant dandy. The 'New Drama' of Wilde, Pinero, Shaw and Jones used a more literate dialogue to reflect society and its problems. It demanded a higher degree of concentration from its audience. Seated in a darkened auditorium, the spectator became a passive viewer. The time to be seen and admired was during the interval, or on entering or leaving the theatre. However the bored, indolent man-about-town leaving before the final curtain could still disrupt performances:

> When half-past-ten is turned, you feel the very air becoming tense with expectancy of something that is to happen. Crush-hatted men in evening dress appear in the street, singly or in pairs, with fair companions who trip beside them ... the later items in the music hall programme were not attractive enough to keep them; the play bored them, and they have left before the end.[108]

The gentrification of the theatre corresponded with the growth of the middle classes and bourgeois ideals. The middle-class man about town was catered for by managements providing cleaner, smarter theatres with tastefully decorated interiors, better amenities and higher standards of comfort. The gulf between the affluent middle-class man in the stalls and the working man seated in the gallery had widened.

There was also a gradual decline in men attending theatres alone or in homosocial groups, as women became increasingly independent. By the turn of the century, greater emancipation was accompanied by better transport. Women were able to come into the West End for the day, to shop in department stores and attend theatres. Matinée performances drew a predominantly female audience. In 1908, the Italian journalist, Mario Borsa, noted that London theatre queues comprised numerous women from 'feminine' employment: 'shopgirls, milliners, dressmakers, typists, stenographers, telegraph and telephone girls, cashiers, and thousands of other girls whose place on the social scale is hard to guess or define'. It was women, now participating in the formerly masculine exclusivity of the *flâneur*,

> who avail themselves of the liberty ... and coldness of the English masculine temperament to wander alone at night from one end of London

to another, spending all their money on gadding about, on sixpenny novels, on magazines, and above all, on theatre.[109]

By 1935 audiences had undergone 'one great change'—'There no longer appeared to be a breed of enthusiastic theatre-going men, who would, without fail, scramble for a seat at a first-night performance.' The average 'first-nighter' was either a man taking his fiancée out for the night, or a woman alone or with companions: 'The steady increase in the feminine element is altering everything in the theatre'.[110] The 'swells', 'johnnies' and other masculine elements that had dominated nineteenth-century audiences had long departed, to be replaced by a predominance of emancipated women.

Chapter Two:
Men before and behind the scenes

THIS CHAPTER considers the role of men connected with the labouring and constructive aspects of the theatre, including scene painting, carpentry, wardrobe and lighting. But the chapter begins with a section on the theatre orchestra, an area that was not strictly part of the backstage world, being placed between the audience and performer. Yet this was another space in which employees were usually men and in which a male hierarchy predominated. It is also an important and somewhat neglected area in theatre histories. As we shall see, its rank and file players were as low paid and suffered as bad conditions as lower-grade backstage staff.

Musicians in the theatre orchestra

On entering the theatre before the performance began, spectators would find themselves divided from the acting area, not only by the lowered curtain, or the frame of the proscenium arch; another division was created by the orchestra pit situated below and in front of the stage. Since music was part of nearly every genre presented on the Victorian stage, the orchestra was a necessary component of the performance. As well as playing overtures and *entr'actes*, it underscored moments of high tension in plays, both serious and comic. The combination of spoken drama with music meant that all theatres employed an orchestra, or at least an instrumental ensemble. Even in the humblest theatres a few musicians would accompany the play.*

---

* For instance, the German author, Theodore Fontane, visiting the Soho Theatre in 1855, noted that the 'band' consisted of 'a pianist ... accompanied by a bass, a cello and a fiddler on his right and a drum, trumpet and Turkish drum on his left'. See Fontane 1999: 10. [The Soho Theatre was a short-lived name for the Royalty Theatre, Dean Street —*Ed.*]

The personnel of theatre orchestras were almost entirely male; this included musicians, leaders and conductors. Research has shown that during the period 1750 to 1850, only two female instrumentalists were employed in theatre orchestras as against 508 males.[1] Even by 1911, when female musicians had become more acceptable, 201 women were playing in British theatre orchestras, compared to 2,219 men.[2] Although so-called 'ladies orchestras' performed during the nineteenth century, it was not considered proper for 'respectable' women to play orchestral instruments. So far as theatre orchestras were concerned, the lack of female musicians was possibly due to prejudice, both from the public as well as from a predominantly masculine workforce.

There was however, a great deal of employment for male musicians in theatre orchestras throughout the British Isles. Not all of these musicians were British; many were foreign, and most theatre orchestras contained a mixture of nationalities. For instance, in 1896 the orchestra of the West End's Criterion Theatre comprised four Englishmen, two Italians, two Austrians, two Dutchmen, one German and one 'Servian'.[3] The employment of so many foreign musicians created a certain amount of xenophobia. This is apparent in a comment on non-English players in the orchestra of Her Majesty's Theatre, that as 'it has been frequently proved [they] are incapable of the effect gained by British performers'.[4] One of the main reasons for the denigration of players in British theatre orchestras was the number of foreign musicians in their ranks.

Generally, theatre orchestra players were under a one-season contract that had to be re-negotiated for the next season.[5] Their wages varied with the type and location of the theatre that employed them. The highest paid engagements were with the opera or in concert halls. In the 1840s a rank-and-file player at the Royal Italian Opera, Her Majesty's Theatre, could earn from seventy to eighty pounds a year, while his counterpart at Drury Lane or Covent Garden earned 'from fifty to sixty pounds a year as the price of nine months' severe servitude'.[6] Considering the long hours and amount of playing required, pay was extremely low. In mid-nineteenth-century London weekly wages for theatre musicians varied from twenty-five to thirty-six shillings a week for playing for drama and thirty-two to forty-two shillings for playing for *opéra bouffe* or burlesque.[7] Very often the theatre musician earned little more than one pound per week.

However, he was marginally better off than other subordinates in the theatrical hierarchy. Supernumeraries were paid around one shilling to two shillings and sixpence per performance; the lowest paid ballet dancers earned between twelve and eighteen shillings a week; the weekly wage of aspiring actors was from about thirty shillings.[8]

The musician was in a similar position to the subordinate actor who survived on low pay and long hours. As late as 1895 an orchestral player complained that from their meagre salaries, he and other musicians had to 'keep a roof over our wives and children, pay for clothing, taxation and doctor's bills'.[9] The novelist and dramatist Charles Reade, in his obituary for Edwin Ellis (musical director at the Adelphi and the Queen's Theatres,* who died in 1880), was outraged that so accomplished a musician should die in poverty: 'he had a family and so small an income that he could not keep up the insurance. He has left a wife and children utterly destitute and could not possibly help it.'[10]

The theatre musician worked under conditions that ensured he lived in penury. He was obliged to attend rehearsals for which he received no payment, no matter how long or frequent.[11] While the actor was supposed to supply at least some of his own costumes, the orchestral player had to wear evening dress for every performance. This could mean extra expenditure out of a low wage on items such as shirts, collars and cuffs, cleaning bills and perhaps an extra outfit (probably bought second-hand). Possibly to save on wear and tear, some musicians, thinking that their lower portions could not be seen 'when the band was half underneath the stage', wore everyday trousers with their evening dress shirts and jackets.[12] The purchase and replacement of musical instruments was another major financial consideration. Prices varied considerably for new instruments—violins were cheaper than cellos, while trumpets cost less than woodwind instruments.† Second-hand instruments could be bought cheaply, but with technical improvements in new instruments they were usually out of date.[13]

---

* Actually the Queen's Theatre, Liverpool —*Ed.*
† In 1854 flutes cost £3 and clarinets ranged from £4 to £12. By 1883 oboes were £6, clarinets £2.14.0d, bassoons £15 and trumpets £5. Violins cost between £5 and £15, cellos from £9 to £27. From advertisements in the *Musical Directory*; see Ehrlich 1985: 101.

Some theatre musicians tried to take on other forms of employment, such as teaching music, to provide an additional income. But with the long hours there was very little opportunity for extra work outside the theatre. For example, in the early nineteenth century, the Italian Opera, at Her Majesty's, performed several nights a week, not counting rehearsals. Covent Garden and Drury Lane usually gave performances five or six nights a week during the season (thirty-five weeks or 200 nights) with rehearsals during the day. The heavy workload of the theatre orchestra, with a great number of performances and rehearsals, was, as one musician pointed out in 1843, 'incompatible with any considerable amount of private business. In the years that are past, many have resigned even at the Opera on this account.'[14]

With long hours and low pay, performing in the theatre orchestra could be very stressful. The life of a theatre musician, like that of the actor, was beset by insecurity. While some retained their positions in theatre orchestras for a considerable period, there was no guarantee of regular employment. The least deviation from the rules might be followed by instant dismissal.

Players knew they could be easily replaced by hundreds of new applicants. An orchestral player could lose his job through illness, or because of competition from other players, or the financial problems of theatres.[15] There was also the risk of the theatre manager reducing the orchestra for economy's sake. Dismissed orchestra players received a week's notice, without compensation for rehearsals.[16]

The responsibility for hiring players for theatre orchestras rested solely with the musical director or conductor. The rank-and-file player was completely under his power. Some conductors were lenient while others were tyrannical. Being on a low wage themselves, conductors were not always honest in their dealings with the orchestral personnel. In certain theatres the conductor was allowed by the manager to pay the musicians out of the fee for the orchestra. This practice, known as 'farming out', resulted in a great deal of contention between players and conductor, particularly if the latter was suspected of dishonesty.* It was

---

* At one 'old established' West End theatre in the 1890s, the conductor was caught out when a musician discovered that the orchestra should have been paid a shilling more

not unknown for an unscrupulous conductor to 'regulate' the wages bill so that the balance went into his own pocket. Such fraudulent practices caused 'even the best and most upright of conductors' to be looked upon with suspicion by theatre orchestra musicians.[17]

A theatre musician's job was also fairly specialised. Accompanying actors in melodrama could be very exacting. If an actor missed a cue, a brother actor would help out and the play would proceed. But if the orchestra for want of a precise cue omitted 'the chord, or hurry, or march, or dance required, the drama gets into wild, and sometimes inextricable confusion'.[18] Accompanying melodrama could be as exacting as playing for opera or in the concert hall. Music had to be loud when 'the actor works in silence' and promptly subdued as soon as the actor spoke his lines. It was supposed to enhance the action 'without drowning a spoken word'. The musical director had to 'watch the stage with one eye and the orchestra with another, and so accompany with vigilant delicacy a mixed scene of action and dialogue'.[19] But despite the specialist nature of his profession, there was scant respect for the theatre musician.

Theatre orchestra players did not have a high social status. They were considered as artisans, not as creative artists. Because they occupied a low status, nobody (including audiences, stagehands, actors and managers) held them in high regard. Theatre managers were inclined to view the orchestra as a 'necessary evil which they would do without if they could'. Actors regarded themselves as 'superior to any musician'; they were 'loath to impute any part of their success to music, even in a piece where the two arts are equally combined'.[20] Despite the almost incessant use of music in the theatre, the orchestra was not generally thought to be central to the entertainment.[21] Few spectators recognised the contribution of the musical director, and the same attitude applied to the hard-worked rank-and-file players.[22] Music in the theatre was considered as little more than background:

---

than they received. The conductor agreed to pay back each man 'between four and five pounds sterling'. As the piece they were playing for ran for over 200 nights, the conductor was still left 'fairly well on the right side of the transaction'. Given a month's notice he pleaded that the manager would not pay him for music prepared and copied. Also as a foreigner he claimed not to be acquainted with the customs of the country. See 'Caught Red-Handed', *The Orchestral Association Gazette*, May 1897: 49–50.

the average playgoer absolutely refuses to listen to either overture or *entr'actes*, being occupied in finding his seat or exchanging commonplaces in a loud voice with his neighbours ... the very idea of courtesy whether to the composer or to those who may wish to hear the music never enters his head.[23]

The 'buzz' in the audience every now and then had to be hushed down by the conductor before the performance began.[24] During the intervals, orchestras had also to contend with chatter from the stalls and dress circle, talking in the pit and quarrels in the gallery.[25] During the interval at lower-class theatres and music halls, the musicians were in danger of being the object of target practice from the gallery—an occupational hazard supposedly to be borne with good humour.[26]

Such low regard by audiences was undoubtedly galling to the orchestra, which was possibly the most overworked and exploited sector of the theatre. They were in constant demand at performances and rehearsals, subject to the whims of actors who, for the most part, despised them. It is hardly surprising that these disdainful attitudes resulted in low musical standards at most theatres, and orchestras did not attract the best musicians. While instrumentalists were easily recruited, high standards of playing were rarely expected or appreciated. Managers even sometimes tried to save money by employing amateur players.* Musicians were allowed to send in deputies 'whenever they choose'.[27] Such practices made it almost impossible to give a competent performance. In 1897 *The Stage* remarked that when incidental music in plays was 'inexpertly or irregularly given, situation after situation may be utterly spoilt ... a thoroughly dejected orchestra scraping and blowing fitfully and vilely' could ruin performances.[28] Bad playing often resulted from the boredom and indifference of the orchestra. Musicians also had to fight against the tedium of 'waits' between numbers, particularly in musical comedy. The journalist Dutton Cook noted the 'almost indecent alacrity' of musicians

---

* In 1895, J. F. Runciman, writing in the *Monthly Musical Record*, complained of the 'scratchy din' made by the orchestra on the first night of George Bernard Shaw's *Arms and the Man*. Evidently, it consisted of 'a few violins, a flute or so and an exceedingly tinny grand-piano'. Runciman complains that theatre bands are 'usually much too small to do anything decently'. They would be better if managers and audiences paid more attention to the theatre orchestra. See Runciman 1895: 169–171.

who ignored the happenings on stage when they were not playing and preferred gazing at the audience.[29] At other times the orchestral players' swearing and comments about the performance could be heard in the audience. They were capable of making 'derisive interjections', laughing aloud at jokes, or audibly sneering when one of the actors made a slip or forgot his lines.[30] At one theatre, musicians in the orchestra were observed playing chess on pocket boards while waiting for the next cue.[31]

As well as suffering poverty, abuse and indifference, players in theatre orchestras often had to put up with uncomfortable and unhealthy conditions. Inadequate lighting, cramped seating, excessive heat, draughts and insanitary backstage 'facilities' were the common lot of musicians in the orchestra pit.[32] Being placed 'underneath the boards of the stage' meant lack of fresh air and inhaling the impure atmosphere of the theatre. An article in *The Orchestral Association Gazette* described one particular band room as 'a pigsty', with an accumulation of unswept dirt, and subject to the stench 'which often pervades the room from the close proximity to places of convenience of workmen'.[33] With their long unsocial hours, subject to arbitrary change, irregular meals and often too much drink, the health of theatre musicians often suffered. They were prone to muscular ailments that threatened their livelihood. The environments in which most of them worked were also perfect for the spread of tuberculosis.[34]

A further problem occurred with late-nineteenth-century efforts to hide orchestras in theatres. The musicians were to be kept as separate as possible from the sight of the audience. In some cases, the orchestra pit was sunk several feet below the level of the stalls, with a barricade between. When Marie Bancroft (née Wilton) embarked on her scheme of improvements to the Prince of Wales's Theatre in 1865, one of her first priorities was to implement her 'pet project'—the abolition of 'the ordinary position of the orchestra'. This, she claimed, 'was the first time the orchestra had been so placed as to be hidden from the sight of the audience'. With the musicians out of sight, the former orchestra pit was 'filled by rockwork with running water and a fernery'.[35]

When her husband, Squire Bancroft, became manager of the Haymarket Theatre in 1880, he followed his wife's idea. The musicians were placed in an area beneath the stage 'owing to the necessity of finding extra room in the stalls'. This plan was not without its critics. The *Theatre* noted that once the band was removed from sight 'economy diminishes the strength of the music, the performers are indifferent or careless, and it appears too much trouble to play any *entr'acte* music at all'.[36]

Percy Fitzgerald found 'something painful, if not unpleasant, in the spectacle of these hard-working musicians cribbed, cabined and confined in a sort of cellar below, where they are seen labouring through bars, or narrow openings—a heated unhealthy den'.[37] J. F. Runciman, in *The Monthly Musical Record*, referred to the area as a 'quaint cellar or coal-hole'. He saw Bancroft's innovation as a misguided imitation of the ideas of Richard Wagner; a small band of ten or twelve players were 'shoved away into a cellar under the stage in a way that has all the disadvantages of Bayreuth'.[38] These conditions were seen to have a degrading effect on the Haymarket orchestra and its musicians.

Significantly, Bancroft, in the autobiographies he wrote in collaboration with his wife, dwells at length on the other innovations he introduced at the Haymarket, but he does not mention placing the orchestra beneath the stage. Concealing the orchestra in this way showed scant regard for the dignity and comfort of its players. Like the removal of the pit it was done for both snobbish and financial reasons. It enabled extra rows of seats to be placed in the stalls and 'foreign' musicians kept as far as possible from the sight of the well-to-do patrons.

By the late nineteenth century conditions in the orchestra pit were marginally better in some theatres. Henry Irving, for example, was very much aware of the importance of music in his productions. Among his innovations was the improvement of musical standards in the 'serious' theatre. Although Irving had no technical knowledge of music, he did have an instinctive flair—as he also had for stage lighting and production. While in most theatres the orchestra was used as a background to the situations of a play, Irving ensured that it became a vitally important element in the production.[39]

Nevertheless the Lyceum orchestra was subject to over-work and injustices. For instance, in 1897 a dozen players were removed from the orchestra for Irving's production of Victorien Sardou's *Madame Sans-Gêne*. In April of that year, the *Orchestral Association Gazette* remarked that the Lyceum orchestra had had 'a hard time of it this season' with 'no fewer than fifty-six rehearsals' since the preceding September.[40] According to a former musician the band could be summoned at any time in the morning if Irving wanted 'any particular piece of incidental music or suitable extract to go before a certain scene'.[41]

Figure 15. Mr Irving considering the incidental music: the Lyceum Theatre orchestra

Despite these difficulties, Irving treated his Lyceum orchestra with more respect than many other actor-managers. Musicians in many other theatres remained at a low level. The appalling conditions they endured fostered the need for a trade union. Unrest had manifested itself in small ways, but morale seems to have been so low that most theatre orchestral employees accepted their down-trodden status. Occasionally there were confrontations between orchestras and managements, but very few of these have been recorded. It was not until 1893 that an attempt was made to organise theatre musicians into a union. In that year both the Orchestral Association and the Amalgamated Musicians' Union were formed.*[42]

---

* The *Orchestral Association Gazette*, December 1897 (page 143), reprinted a handbill from Wigan and District Trades and Labour Council warning 'all Trade Unionists' to

Even with the formation of unions, the rank-and-file musician endured playing in a cramped, sweaty, uncomfortable pit, with little room for manoeuvre. He was forced to survive on low pay without due recognition of his artistic talents. A life of financial insecurity and a low social status ensured he remained at an artisan level.

Despite these humiliations, the theatre orchestra attracted male musicians of all grades and levels, while its employment of women was virtually non-existent. It is paradoxical that such a vital and necessary ingredient of Victorian theatre should have been held in such low esteem.

The backstage labour force

Moving from the orchestra pit to behind the scenes, we discover an army of labouring men whose conditions were little better than those of the theatre musicians. Stage illusions were achieved through the sweated labour of those at the lower end of a complicated hierarchical scale. Armies of backstage workers were under the charge of the heads of the various departments of the theatre, such as the master carpenter, the chief scene painter, the head machinist, the gasman, and the property master. Each of these was ultimately responsible to the stage manager, who had overall control of the technical and backstage staff, and was responsible for allocating their duties. He was also responsible for hiring specialist staff such as a 'super master' to rehearse the supernumeraries, or singing and ballet masters for pantomime. Preparation for a production therefore involved a whole range of skills—from artisan manufacturers to craftspeople. The theatre drew on nearly every trade of the Victorian era. Its workers and suppliers included armourers, property-makers, scene painters, tailors, boot and shoemakers, wig makers, carpenters and joiners.

For certain items, contracts were made with tradesmen from outside the theatre—bill printers, publishers, ironmongers, basket workers, glaziers, silver and gold leaf appliers, and fancy goods suppliers. This mixture of trades and skills gave the nineteenth-century theatre an industrialised aspect. Industry merged with the theatrical world in the operation of machinery, ropes and counterweights, with the use of gases

---

keep away from the Wigan Theatre Royal 'until the dispute between the Old Band and the Management is settled'.

to make limelight,* the mixing of chemicals to create spectacular effects, and, late in the century, the introduction of dynamos and switch stations for lighting by electricity.[43]

Strong men were needed as carpenters, scene painters, and for general labour. Outside the stage area, other male employees had the supervisory responsibilities of stage door keepers, porters, firemen and watchmen. Boys were also employed to call the artists on stage from their dressing rooms. All this activity did not exclude distinctive jobs for women, both behind the scenes and in the front of house. However the opportunities for female backstage employment were extremely limited, compared to the range of jobs available for men.

In certain areas women shared the same responsibilities as their male counterparts. In the front of house, for instance, both men and women were employed as door-keepers, check-takers or ushers. Backstage, there were sections in which the roles were divided by gender. For instance, male dressers worked with actors, while female dressers worked with actresses. Women were predominant in the wardrobe department as seamstresses, but certain tasks, such as tailoring male costumes, were the prerogative of men. Male employees outnumbered women in skills such as property making, hairdressing and prompting.[44]

As in the theatre orchestra, there was a great deal of insecurity among non-performing theatrical employees. Many workers were hired on a casual basis, supposedly 'auxiliary to some entirely independent trade pursued during the day'.[45] Most of the backstage labour force—'your carpenters, scene-shifters, property-men, gas-men and limelight men'— were under contract. But there were 'speculating master-carpenters and machinists' who would make a bargain with the theatre management 'for so much a week'.[46] Master gas and limelight men supplemented their earnings by accepting consultancy engagements at other theatres. Because of the increasing insecurity of working behind the scenes, stage hands often had jobs in other locations when theatre work was scarce.

Backstage employment was further affected by the contracting out of jobs to specialist firms, and by increasing technological advances. From the mid nineteenth century, many jobs belonging to specialist depart-

---

* For more about limelight, see page 70 onwards. —*Ed.*

ments within the theatres were placed in the hands of outside suppliers, as a result of the need for greater profits, as well as the disappearance of the stock system.* These included wardrobe, scene making and painting, together with related trades such as shoemaking, hosiery, armoury, and wig-making. Managements used specialist, independent firms to help streamline the work done inside the theatre itself. Routine tasks were divided out so that less preparatory work was needed and more assembly occurred at a later point in the production process.[47]

Figure 16. Behind the scenes at Drury Lane: in the flies

The changes and developments caused by sub-contracting affected male and female labour in different ways. Tasks associated with construction and maintenance (such as scenery or wardrobe) moved outside the theatres. Simultaneous developments in theatre technology saw an increase in the numbers of employees needed to run the performances. The two main areas of masculine labour, lighting and scene shifting, gained in importance. Because these were jobs performed

---

* The stock system is another name for the old repertory system, in which a theatre (or 'stock company') would put on a new play every week. —*Ed.*

inside the theatre, men remained closest to the production process. This made it relatively easy for the male labour force to organise into trade unions. Women mainly worked outside the theatre, which made it difficult for them to form unions. Those working in theatres as dressers or seamstresses were further inhibited from organising themselves because they were contracted singly, and did not work in a team like men.[48]

Advances in technology also saw the gradual erosion of manual tasks. As with the earlier introduction of machines into factories, a large theatrical labour force was taken over by technology. By the end of the century, ten men working ropes could be replaced with a four-horsepower motor. It was now possible for one person standing in the prompt corner to change a set in a few seconds 'without the slightest assistance from anyone in the flies'. The savings to the theatre management through using machines instead of hand labour was enormous.[49] The result was that by the early 1900s, a great many of the men who laboured behind the scenes were out of work.

Shifting the scenery

Until the technological improvements of the late nineteenth century, working backstage involved machinery that was heavy, complicated and often dangerous. Behind the scenes was a labyrinth of galleries, bridges, ladders, trapdoors, ropes, pulleys and weights.

Touring a theatre in 1851, the journalist George Augustus Sala* noted 'windlasses, capstans, ropes, cables, chains, pulleys innumerable,' as well as 'huge counterweights and lines' to work the curtain and act drop.[50] Almost all scene shifting involved lifting heavy materials. Operations such as raising and lowering the scenery by pulleys were performed manually. Counterweighting was used extensively to give stagehands some mechanical leverage and to make tasks humanly possible.[51] This was 'men's work' requiring strength and stamina from an under-paid, over-worked labour force. Like those who slogged in mines and factories, the backstage worker was exploited. Yet the 'world behind the scenes', with all its colour and activity, would have offered a more varied workplace than the grinding monotony of the factory.

---

* See page 27. —*Ed.*

The men involved with this necessary, but heavy, work were looked down upon: 'the generic name in theatrical parlance' for scene shifters was 'labourers'. They were 'maligned' and had to work in semi-darkness and 'under many other circumstances of disadvantage'.[52] Scene shifters were also among the lowest-paid theatre workers. Even by the end of the century they earned as little as two shillings a night in both 'first rate' and 'minor' theatres.[53]

The stage 'labourer' may have been relegated to a lowly position, but the theatre depended on his expertise for the smooth running of a long programme. He needed 'considerable accuracy of eye and dexterity of hand to adjust the different parts of scenery exactly in place with the minimum of noise and the maximum of speed'. Furniture and fittings had also to be carefully placed in the exact positions assigned to them at rehearsal.[54] In addition, many preparations had to be made for an evening's performance. In the mid nineteenth century these duties included blackleading the grooves for the scenery, greasing the trapdoors, making sure that all the 'sinks', ropes and pulleys 'and other theatrical gear and tackle' was in working order. If these little matters were not 'rigidly and minutely attended to ... such trifling accidents as mutilation or loss of life are not unlikely to happen'. Sala somewhat euphemistically maintained that 'such casualities' were a rarity because of the 'microscopic care and attention' the backstage workers gave to 'every inch of their domain behind scenes'.[55] However accidents were a regular occurrence:

> Lives have been lost, or limbs shattered, by mere accident on the stage, mishaps of a purely mechanical kind, with which the mental exertions of the performer have had little or nothing to do. Ropes, trap-doors, springboards, planks, scaffolding, ladders and so forth, are naturally the cause of disaster, if not properly adjusted and used.[56]

Accidents were blamed on the carelessness of backstage workers. For instance, at the Alhambra in 1870 one of the moveable sections of the stage came adrift because a joining rod had not been replaced. This resulted in the injury of a number of ballet girls. A newspaper report claimed that the accident was the fault of a menial backstage labourer: 'One of the men to whom the arrangement of the bracing irons was entrusted had neglected his duty, and had not observed his omission when the performance commenced on Tuesday evening.' There is no mention of the culprit having been caught, but such carelessness could result in the loss of a job for a man who had a family and could not afford to be unemployed.[57]

Figure 17. Lifting a fairy: stagehands operating a 'trap' at Drury Lane

Without the advantages of an advanced stage technology, large numbers of men were needed to make elaborate and cumbersome scene changes in as short a time as possible. With the mid- to late-nineteenth-century onset of realism, scenery was 'constructed so solidly, and with so many details, that without minute division of the work, and almost military precision in the movements of the workmen, "waits" would become intolerably long'. For Irving's 1880 production of *The Corsican Brothers* 'no fewer than ninety carpenters, thirty gas-men and fifteen property men, in all 135 persons' were permanently engaged 'in the mere task of arranging and conducting scenes'.[58]

The militaristic precision demanded by scene changes is exemplified by Percy Fitzgerald's description of the construction of the temple scene in Tennyson's *The Cup* at the Lyceum in 1881. 'No sooner has the drop-scene fallen' on the previous scene, than men emerge from every side. In three or four minutes the hills, banks, pedestals of the previous scene are hoisted up into the flies and 'long rows of jets are unfastened and carried away'. The 'three long, heavy frames or beams' that form the pediment of the temple descend.

> Soon busy hands have joined these three great joists by bolts and fastenings; the signal is given and it ascends again. Meanwhile others have been bringing out from the scene dock the pillars and their bases, ranging them in the places marked in the ground for them. ... In a few moments everything is fitted and falls into its place with martial exactness. ... We have glimpses in the galleries aloft of men hauling at ropes and pulleys or turning drums; other men below are bearing in the altars and steps with the enormous idol at the back over twenty feet high.[59]

Setting up the scene has an industrialised aspect. Different teams of labouring men are needed for various jobs requiring strength and precision. All of this has to be achieved in a limited time. Fitzgerald's description demonstrates that the nineteenth-century theatre was as labour intensive in creating illusions as was the factory in manufacturing goods for everyday use.

Fitzgerald also notes how 'Everything is fitted and falls into its place with martial exactness.' Writers of articles were fond of comparing the backstage workforce to an army. For instance, Augustus Harris, manager of the Theatre Royal, Drury Lane, claimed that the spectacular effects in his pantomime productions were 'the result of the efforts ... of an army of workers talented, trained and proficient in their respective arts, acting under the guidance of one competent man, who, like a general in the field, should have risen from the ranks, and consequently be thoroughly acquainted with the technique and minute details of the various branches of the services he is called upon to command'.[60] The masculine dominated backstage workforce is thus equated with two of the most important controlling factors of Victorian Britain—industry and the army.

The lighting men

Lighting was another labour-intensive sector of the nineteenth-century stage. The changes in stage lighting, from candlelight to gas and then to electricity, exemplify the technological advances affecting the theatre. Improvements in stage lighting meant the creation of better effects and illusions. However, the nineteenth century remained a most combustible time for the theatre. Gas had been introduced in 1817, and during most of the Victorian era it was the principal method of illuminating the stage. Lighting the stage with gas was extremely hazardous, both for audiences and employees. Gas jets were as dangerous as candles and many theatres burned to the ground. Details of deaths through costumes catching on naked flames are well documented.

Operating gas lighting was also a dangerous and complex process. Its numerous fittings required a great deal of maintenance. In an average sized theatre, the gas supply to the stage and auditorium consisted of thousands of jets. On stage, these jets were arranged on a series of battens covering each portion of the stage from front to back. The stage was divided for working purposes into measured distances which were a continuance of the grooves in which flats were pushed on or off in the days of oil and candlelight: These areas were numbered, and as Bram Stoker* wrote at the turn of the century: 'All stagehands understand No. 1, No. 2, No. 3 and so on.'[61] The battens had to be regulated during the performance at the gas plate fixed to the wall where the mains supply came in on the prompt side of the stage. The gasman with his key regulated the jets according to the stage manager or prompter's instructions. Before the pilot light was invented around the middle of the century, all gas instruments had to be lit manually.[62]

Lighting up both stage and auditorium before the performance could be a risky and cumbersome process. The enormous central chandeliers in the auditorium (such as the one at Covent Garden in the 1850s) were lit by hand. This was a particularly perilous job. It was thought to be sufficiently dangerous for an assistant gasman to be accompanied by one of the theatre firemen.

The Covent Garden chandelier could not be raised or lowered and the

---

* Irving's stage manager, also author of *Dracula* (see Chapter Three) —*Ed.*

gasman had to risk his life by leaning out into the flue—there were planks 'to prevent persons from falling into the shaft'. Eight hundred jets were lit by means of a twelve-foot long bamboo rod, twisted around the end of which was a cotton-like substance dipped in alcohol. The gas supply was controlled by one or more stop cocks near at hand, secondary to the principal control at the plate.[63] This primitive and hazardous method of lighting chandeliers persisted even after pilot lights were introduced for the stage.

A wide range of duties was expected of the gasman, and he had to be adaptable. In the late nineteenth century the increasing use of box sets made new demands on equipment intended for the use of flat scenery. A gas man might be called upon at short notice to make a light fitting adapted to some unforeseen situation, such as eliminating objectionable shadows in built-out scenery. He was also responsible for the supervision of the gas equipment in the theatre. Workshops were required for repairs and jobs such as cutting lengths of pipe and bending sheet metal.

Lighting the set was a particularly delicate operation. Once the lighting plot had been decided for a production, it was the job of the gas man to ensure that all the necessary fittings could be easily and conveniently connected to the nearest fixed gas points. Then he had to light them. For the points within his reach this was easily done by means of his spirit torch. The pilot light had to be lit by means of a long pole, similar to that used for lighting the auditorium chandelier. If there were no pilot lights the gasman had to carry his torch along every jet unless they were placed close enough to ignite one another.[64] The chief gasman then gave instructions to the lighting men for more or less light as well as for positioning the all-important limelight.

The advantage of gas over the earlier use of oil or candlelight was that it was brighter and could be regulated, but there was no way to project and focus a beam of light until the introduction of limelight. By the 1850s limelight had become an indispensable part of stage lighting.[65] It was more flexible than gas battens, but its operation involved a great deal of risk.

The limelight operator controlled his lamp by hand. He adjusted the lines to the separate oxygen and hydrogen jets by turning the cylinder of lime* in the flame or by a rotating wheel outside the box containing the apparatus. Oxygen and hydrogen were stored in leather bags at his feet. Weights were laid on these bags to release the gas, and sometimes the operator stood on the bags to obtain the desired amount of pressure.[66] This was a dangerous, unhealthy operation. While turning the cylinders, operators had to cover their mouths and noses with damp cloths to prevent the inhalation of lime-dust—'such inhalation causing much irritation and well-nigh unbearable thirst'. Occasional explosions were another danger, the result of gases becoming mixed together in the bags. 'Delicate handling' was necessary for the 'safe use of prepared material'.[67] In his manual *Theatre Construction and Maintenance*, James Buckle warns that on no account should limelight bags be manipulated on the stage or in the fly galleries. He stipulates that the tanks containing the gases for 'oxy-hydrogen' light should not be placed within the building. They should be fitted up in 'an open area or room specially constructed and the gases forced by water pressure through metal pipes into the theatre'.[68]

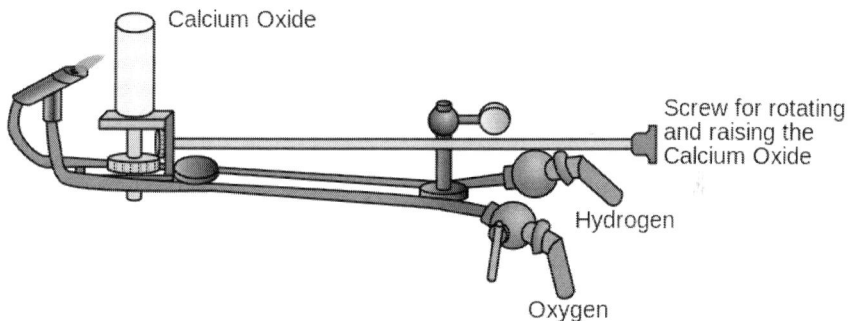

Figure 18. Limelight equipment

The limelight operator usually had a vantage point in the fly-gallery. Limelights were also operated from perches on either side of the proscenium opening or from other positions backstage or from the wings if possible.[69] By the late nineteenth century, many different kinds of limelights were in use, 'the lenses being in such variety that a skilful operator can select that best adapted to a special occasion'. The operator

---

* Quicklime (calcium oxide). —*Ed.*

with his 'limes' could create magical effects or use 'the convenient ray' to follow the hero about the stage 'so that the audience may never forget that he is present, and nearly all such aids to the imagination of the spectator are produced in this way'.[70]

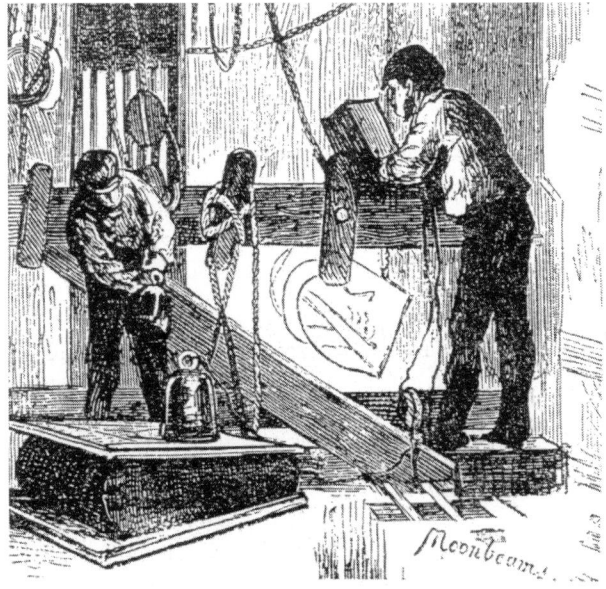

Figure 19. Limelight men in the fly-gallery

Limelight was considered to be the most important form of stage lighting because it highlighted star performers, confirming their status, making them stand out from the supporting cast. For this reason, each individual limelight operator 'had to be coached in the special requirements of the working of the play'.[71] Co-operation between the limelight operator and performer was essential. The operator, invisible and anonymous, made his presence felt by training his beam of light onto the star 'name'. His position on his perch in the flies gave him a certain power. Any deviation of the beam would take the focus away from the 'star', merging him or her into the background with the supporting cast.

There was no satisfactory way in which an operator could simultaneously handle more than one lime. For this reason, limelight gave employment to extra manpower at a time when the backstage labour force had diminished due to the system of contracting out. 'Fresh men in ever-increasing numbers became trained to the work.'[72] The skills of limelight operators continued to be required long after the introduction of electricity in the 1880s.

In a production, decisions on lighting were in the hands of the heads of the gas, limelight, and eventually electrical departments, and then taken after consultation with the scenic artist, stage manager and theatre manager or actor-manager. Lighting rehearsals could be long and exhausting. Henry Irving was apt to hold lighting rehearsals late at night, 'or rather early in the morning'—generally long after the evening's performance had concluded. The lighting men, with their daytime, as well as performance duties, must have had an inordinately long working day. However Irving's manager, Bram Stoker, claimed not to detect any signs of discontent among these overworked men. He maintained that Irving's staff were very loyal to him 'and very willing to carry out his wishes, using for the purpose their natural abilities and the skill which they had evolved by labour and experience'.[73] However, any dissent would have meant instant dismissal and the loss of income. Nor were theatrical working hours protected by unions.

In rehearsing the lighting of a scene, Irving always sat in the stalls where he could see the effects better. A large number of men from the various theatre departments were present 'especially at the experimental stages of lighting'. The gas engineer, the limelight master, the electrician all had their staffs ready.[74] When arrangements were completed, the backstage hierarchy moved into operation. The masters of the gas and electrical operators came under control of the prompter, who took his orders from the stage manager. Actors were only present at lighting rehearsals when a special technical requirement demanded their presence.[75]

Irving lit all his productions with gas, even after the establishment of electricity. The introduction of electricity meant reductions in the teams of operators for gas lighting. Not only were fewer staff required, new demands were placed on the scene painter and his staff. Electric light was whiter and colder than mellow gas light. It revealed deficiencies in settings which gas did not. Audiences complained of glare and excessive brightness and it took theatres time to come to terms with the possibilities of electric stage lighting.[76] The challenges of electricity led to the creation, early in the twentieth century, of a new role in the theatre—that of lighting designer.

The scene painter's shop

Stage design was an area where those in charge of scenery and costume exercised considerable control while enjoying a measure of artistic freedom. In a theatre dominated by scenic and visual effects, the art of the scene painter was of primary importance—particularly with the increasing demand for realistic stage presentation. The nineteenth-century scenic artist designed the settings himself and painted the scenery with his team. His studio not only had a strict hierarchical structure, it was also dominated by patriarchal and familial concerns. Victorian stage design was virtually ruled by two long-lived scene-painting dynasties —the Grieve* and Telbin† families. Members of both families worked for the most illustrious theatres of the day. Very often design techniques were handed down from fathers to sons.

Until late in the century, when scene painting began to be contracted out to specialist studios, theatres employed resident scenic designers; but by 1889 only two theatres in London retained a resident team of scenic artists. The contract system also saw an increase in the power of the scenic designer. The influence of the theatre manager decreased and, according to William Lewis Telbin, the chief designer became a manager 'on a small scale'. Renting a 'vast studio' with bills for gas and 'colour' as well as wages for 'assistants and servants' meant heavy expenses for the independent scenic designer.

---

* John Henderson Grieve (1770–1845) worked at Covent Garden from 1794 to 1845, latterly with his sons Thomas (1799–1882) and William (1800–1844). They were renowned for their spectacular scenery and special effects. Thomas Grieve became one of Charles Kean's chief designers at the Princess's Theatre in the 1850s and his son Thomas Walford Grieve was also a scene painter. William Grieve was principal scenic artist at the King's Theatre (later Her Majesty's) from 1833 to 1844. Like other members of the Grieve family he was renowned for portraying romantic, moonlit landscapes. See Finkel 1996: 177–178.

† The Telbin dynasty was long-lived, working well into the twentieth century. William Telbin (1813–1873) was part of the design team at Kean's Princess's Theatre. He collaborated with Thomas Grieve in creating the panorama *The Route of the Overland Mail from Southampton to Calcutta* for the Gallery of Illustration in 1852. William Lewis Telbin (known as Telbin the Younger) was possibly the best-known member of the family. Born in 1846, he did not die until 1931. He was noted for his work at the Lyceum where he designed sets for *Faust* (1885) and Tennyson's *Becket* (1893). See Finkel 1996: 181–182.

The system also brought about changes in the relations between designers. Telbin maintained that before contracting out, when 'few theatres existed', there was a feeling of brotherhood between the 'gregarious' scene-painters. Now that there was a greater demand for designers, there was no longer the same intimacy, and rivalries increased.[77]

Figure 20. The scene-painter's studio, Drury Lane: painting 'the trans' (i.e. the transformation scene for a pantomime)

The scene-painter received a commission for designs from the theatre manager. Before he commenced work in his studio, a mutual consultation took place. According to Telbin the younger: 'Some managers can graphically illustrate their requirements, others ... give the key to the idea and requirements of the situation by word of mouth.' Other managers could only explain the situations and 'practibilities' of the production, leaving the designer 'absolutely free-handed, reserving to themselves the right of alteration when they have a tangibility before them, either in the scene itself or in the model'.[78]

The composition, lighting and colouring of the settings was worked out on a scale model of the stage. After the model had been duly inspected and approved by the management, the master-carpenter came to inspect it with an eye to the construction of the full-scale set. He also noted the chief designer's suggestions regarding setting and striking it 'in something like reasonable time'.[79]

By the end of the century, a scene painter was sometimes on the permanent staff and sometimes engaged for the job. 'In the latter case he is paid by the piece, according to agreement'. If he was permanently employed he earned around three guineas per week in a first-rate theatre and was entitled to a week's notice. However, since some scene painters were really artists, 'their pay would no doubt be on a higher scale'.[80] William Telbin, in 1889, maintained that the income of 'the most successful scene-painter is certainly very much smaller than that of a very second-rate cabinet picture painter or even of a tolerably successful draughtsman for the chief illustrated journals'.[81]

Whether work was done inside or outside the theatre, a large studio was necessary for preparing and painting scenery. Here, the scenic designer would work with a team of male assistants. Conditions in the studios or 'paint rooms' could be as bad as those in dressing rooms for actors or band rooms for theatre orchestras. Fire was a constant peril as all scene painters smoked pipes. There was a nauseating smell of glue and size. Scenic designers and their assistants wore hats to protect their hair from paint dripping from those working above.

The studios were lit by gas and fiercely heated in order to dry the paint. Thinly-clad apprentices had permanent colds from leaving the tropical atmosphere for wintry conditions outside. It was not uncommon for old or failed performers to earn a pittance through fetching and carrying for the designer and his assistants.[82] Nevertheless, there appears to have been a certain amount of camaraderie in the paint rooms. Scene painters looked after their less fortunate colleagues. According to Joseph Harker, who was an apprentice in the late nineteenth century, 'the underdog was never allowed to be down for long at a time'. The weekly salary was often postponed. When this happened, the men would have a whip-round to help a co-worker in difficulties, such as a colour-mixer confined to bed after an accident and unable to earn money.[83]

Hours could be very long. The scene painting staff often had to work non-stop to reach a deadline. On such occasions meals were brought into the paint room from outside. Sala, in 1851, noticed the backstage staircase at Drury Lane 'blocked up with frantic waiters laden with chops and stout' for the scene painter and his assistants working throughout the night on a pantomime.[84] Later in the century, Joseph Harker recalled meals being brought into the paint-room 'in order to save time on busy days'. These meals were prepared and cooked by one of the labourers.[85]

In a setting reminiscent of the Renaissance painter in his studio, the chief designer presided over his team of assistants, each of whom had an allotted task. The mechanics of the studio could be very demanding: 'The physical strain in covering so large a surface, and in walking backwards and forwards from one end of the room to the other to judge of the effect, is exceedingly severe.'[86] Scenery was painted on a frame (usually 40 feet high and 25 feet wide). This held the wood and canvas scene and could be winched up and down through a gap in the floor, leading to the stage below; alternatively the frame could remain stationary while the artist worked on a platform that could be raised or lowered.

The painting of complicated sets was too great a task for one man. Jobs were allocated to a scene-painting team. First of all, the cloth had to be 'primed' before it could be painted. This was a time-consuming process. At the Lyceum for instance, it took the scenic designer Hawes Craven four hours, with the help of two assistants, to prime one cloth ready for painting.[87] The initial outlining in charcoal and ink, and finishing difficult or complicated areas, were tasks reserved for the chief designer. He would 'hastily scrawl' the outline of the scene onto the 'well primed' canvas, using a long pole, into the 'cleft end' of which was stuck a piece of charcoal. Then, with his assistants he would draw in the finished outline using a 'small brush and common ink, which darkening as it dries, allows the outline to shine through the first layers of colour'.

Each of the scenic designer's assistants would then perform their various tasks. A colour man would grind and mix the colours, purchased as solid blocks or as powder. The 'white-washer' using 'huge brushes', painted in 'the great masses of colour, sky, wall, foreground &c'. Shadow effects would be 'picked in' by assistants. Two more assistants were required, one at either end to tightly hold the string for creating lines, such as those of a cornice. For glittering pantomime effects involving gold stencil work, 'half a dozen assistants rush forward' with books of Dutch metal* and 'three-fourths' of the scene 'is covered in a trice with squares of glittering dross'.[88]

The painting and preparation of scenery, with the designer presiding over a team of subordinate men whose labour was divided into specific areas, demonstrates one aspect of the nineteenth century theatre's combination of creativity with industry.

The carpenters' shop

The wooden frames for the canvas flats were made in the carpenters' shop, usually located 'close to the roof of the theatre'. Here teams of carpenters hammered and sawed under the control of the head carpenter. He had to be a practical workman, as well as 'a man of initiative and resource, who can be relied on to carry out his instructions without supervision'.[89] Because of his responsibilities, the stage-carpenter earned a fairly high wage—four to five pounds per week in a first-rate theatre in the late nineteenth century. He was expected to give his whole time to the job and was not paid overtime. His principal task was to make and fit together the different parts of the scenery, to be painted afterwards by the scene-painter. He was supplied with a detailed list of the scenery required and it had to be made by himself and his assistants. He also had to provide, and sometimes devise and make, contrivances for effects such as 'a fall of crockery, a pelting hail-storm or a roaring hurricane'. The stage-carpenter usually had an assistant, and beneath them were 'jobbing carpenters' who went from theatre to theatre whenever they heard that men were wanted. Their casual work was very uncertain. For a few days or a week or two they had 'as much work as they can get through', and then, for weeks, they could be without a job. In the 1890s they were paid around 8½d. per hour. This was a penny less than the pay of the ordinary carpenter, but the work was 'of a rougher and less finished description'.[90]

---

* A form of brass sold in very thin sheets, used to imitate gold leaf. —Ed.

Besides framing the scenery in his workshop, the head carpenter supervised putting it up on stage, and had to be on hand to make insertions or alterations 'found to be necessary for the faultless representation of the piece'.[91] Setting-up was a time for collaboration between the men in charge of theatre departments 'who have never yet worked together'—the chief designer, the master carpenter, the lighting man, as well as the numerous assistants who worked below them.[92] Preparations for an elaborate production, such as a pantomime, could last all night. According to George Augustus Sala, stage carpenters usually worked from six in the morning until six in the evening, but when a new production was in preparation it was not unusual to work from seven in the morning until close of performances.[93]

Figure 21. The carpenters' shop, Drury Lane: 'profiling' a mermaid
(i.e. shaping a piece of scenery to fit the painting)

High above the theatre, the carpenters' shop was a world apart from the rest of the workforce. In 1851, Sala ascended to a theatre carpenter's shop. Here he was confronted by the noise 'of sawing, and chopping, hammering and chiselling'. In a large area, the size of the stage underneath, a substantial number of carpenters were labouring: twenty or thirty men constructed the wooden frames for the scenery and covered them with canvas. Others were making the long cylinders or rollers used for 'drops' and 'cloths'. Some worked on their knees, following with a hand-saw 'the outline of a rock or tree, marked in red lead by the scene-painter'. According to Sala, they evidently sang as they worked—'bits of Italian operas or melodramatic music'. The carpenter's shop was a hive of industry and the master carpenter constantly needed more labour. He continually gave orders for 'more nails' and 'more hands'. Sala claimed that the carpenters 'preserve admirable discipline' and obeyed the master carpenter 'implicitly'.

Sala saw the stage carpenters as a separate category from the rest of the theatre staff—a 'curious race of men' with their own traditions, operating in an area set apart from the main body of the theatre. They probably lived in the vicinity of the theatre (like other theatre workers) and they were full of the 'traditional lore' of Drury Lane and Covent Garden. Sala thought they were from families with stage connections: 'probably their fathers and grandfathers were theatrical before them'. He claimed it was rare to find a carpenter from 'ordinary life' working in the theatre or vice versa.[94] The carpenters provide an example of labouring men whose families had followed the same trade in the theatre for generations. However there were other workers, such as stage-hands and scene painters, whose families also had a theatrical tradition. It was not unusual for backstage labourers to marry lower grade performers, such as ballet girls. These unions resulted in a number of family members working behind the scenes.[95] Sometimes the 'offspring of the stage carpenter or the gasman' appeared on the stage in children's roles.[96]

Wilhelm: masculine influence in costume design

While the lighting, carpentry and scene painting sections had an all-male staff, the wardrobe department employed both men and women. Teams of seamstresses sewed and repaired costumes, while tailoring was mainly in male hands. Either a wardrobe master or a wardrobe mistress oversaw workers in the costume department. On his tour of a theatre, Sala found a number of seamstresses under the control of a wardrobe master, known as 'Mr Baster'. All were frantically working in restrictive conditions. Their workroom was not very large 'and movement is rendered somewhat inconvenient ... by a number of heavy presses, crammed to repletion, with the costumes of the establishment'. In this crowded area, 'Mr Baster' overhauled his stock, deciding which costumes can be used again 'and what is really wanted new'. Meanwhile his female team of seamstresses was to be found 'stitching for dear life'.[97]

The theatrical seamstress was as hard worked and endured as bad conditions as her sisters in the fashion trade. Lower-paid workers of both sexes involved with making theatrical costumes endured ill health and poverty. The enormous amount of labour involved with costume spilled out not only to private contractors, but also to specialists who wove and stitched alone at home. Male outworkers tended to perform tasks that necessitated the use of a machine in their dwelling place. An article of 1885 describes the plight of an elderly man in a lonely room weaving the fringe for costumes in pantomime on a dilapidated loom. He works 'far into the night' in his garret where 'furniture was conspicuous by its absence' and 'two of the cheapest of candles' supplied the only light—a marked contrast with the glittering effect of his woven fringe on spectacular fairy costumes in the pantomime.[98] Outworkers using inadequate machinery risked injury. The same article depicts another man who wove theatrical tights in a small, low ceilinged room near Drury Lane. His fingers took the place of a shuttle as he drew thread across a row of horizontal 'J-shaped' needles. He worked with the constant whirring of the machine 'as row after row of thread was added'. All this noise in a small space 'set one's teeth on edge in anything but a pleasant manner,' and probably affected the hearing of the worker.[99]

In the theatre, men predominated in the design of costumes for spectacular productions, such as pantomime. Once the costume designer had designed the costumes, they were either made up in the wardrobe department, or contracted to outside workers; the designer usually worked in an advisory capacity, suggesting materials to be used and advising how his ideas might be made up. He also communicated with suppliers over the right accessories for his designs.

The difficulties encountered by a male designer when dealing with female employees are exemplified by the career of Carl (or C.) Wilhelm (the pseudonym of William J. C. Pitcher). He was one of the most influential British designers of the late nineteenth century, and was especially noted for his fantastic costumes for Augustus Harris's pantomimes at Drury Lane.

Figure 22. C. Wilhelm: 'A Burmese Phantasy':
costume designs for Drury Lane

In a two-part article for the *Magazine of Art* in 1895, Wilhelm claimed that design for ballet, pantomime and 'extravaganza' called for 'a special skill in device other than historical drama requires, and in addition to a very necessary and correct judgement of all the possibilities of combination of colour'. It was also necessary to have a knowledge of 'the modes and manners of the various periods'.[100]

Wilhelm's technique, with his harmonisation of colours and fabrics, was an attempt to create an ordered stage picture at a time when presentation was often haphazard. He was well aware that the 'scheme' of his costumes 'costing months of labour in detail and research, and quite a fortune in expense' could be 'utterly ruined by a discordant and pretentious set'.[101]

For this reason, Wilhelm insisted on almost total control over his visual effects. Apart from designing, he regarded his responsibilities to include the supervision of lighting, general design and choreography. Wilhelm's quest for perfection was combined with a Ruskinian concern for the harmony of colour and detail. This is apparent in his description of his costumes for the ball scene in the Lyceum's 1893 production of *Cinderella*:

> The palest primrose, ranging to citron and bronze; mahogany, paling into apricot tones; symphonies of orange and lemon; maize colour, cinnamon, ivory—all were pressed into service. Tiger lilies and *Gloire de Dijon* roses, sunflowers and narcissus; fawn and leopard skins; leather and the sheen of gold, copper and brass; rich embroideries, and every conceivable fabric, entered into the design. Sumptuous brocades were woven expressly, and the costumes of the leading characters being carefully chosen in heliotrope, faint sea green and *vieux rose*, no jarring note was present.[102]

His manipulation of fabrics to represent plants and flowers is similar to the *fin-de-siècle* literary metaphor, which replaces Nature with artifice.* Parallels with his voluptuous description may be found in 'decadent' *fin-de-siècle* novels such as J-K. Huysman's *À Rebours* (1884) and Oscar Wilde's *The Picture of Dorian Gray* (1890):

---

* Wilhelm was extremely interested in the natural world. In his obituary, *The Times* stated that Wilhelm's 'knowledge of flowers and plant-life was only equalled by his knowledge of costume' ('Obituary "C. Wilhelm": Mr Pitcher's Art', *The Times*, 3 March. 1925: 18). His articles for *The Magazine of Art* included two entitled 'Flowers and Fancies—from the Garden to the Stage' (*The Magazine of Art*, LXXXIII, January 1898, 187 and November 1898, 1). His posthumous entry in *Who Was Who* included 'contemplating beauty in Nature' among his recreations.

And now and then the fantastic shadows of birds in flight flitted across the long tussore-silk curtains that were stretched in front of the huge window, producing a momentary Japanese effect.[103]

Wilhelm's artistry and delicate use of colour produced similar effects on the stage. His aesthetic approach to design was far removed from the usual glare and glitter of the electrically-lit late nineteenth-century pantomime. To fulfil his ideals, Wilhelm utilised an apparently co-operative female workforce. He praised costumiers who devoted patience and skill to his designs, 'notably Miss Fisher' (Miss Mary Elizabeth Fisher of Bedford Street).[104] He wrote that her 'enterprise in carrying out daring suggestions, including the actual fabrication of material in sundry experiments' deserved 'all the acknowledgement that can be implied on these lines'. But the costumier did not always 'grasp the full scope of one's idea', so that

> one must always be prepared with a technical suggestion for the practical solution of some artistic problem: such as simulating in a hanging sleeve of silk the enfolding undulations of a lily-of-the-valley leaf, or casting about for the best method of representing ... the gossamer plumage of a bird of paradise.[105]

Wilhelm's complicated designs created problems for the women who made them up. But he was always ready to advise with an almost feminine expertise on the construction of his creations. He claimed that the costumiers who made up his fantastic and often complicated designs gave him their fullest co-operation. Difficulties were encountered with the performers, both male and female, who were to wear the costumes. Wilhelm, with his artistry and perfectionism, was an intruder in the equally rarefied world of the 'fickle and inconstant' ballet girl and her 'effeminate' (usually imported) male counterpart.* With his advanced ideas he had intruded into a territory where certain conventions were maintained.

Whereas in other areas of the theatre (notably Irving's Shakespearean

---

* While Wilhelm had a low opinion of female performers, he was positively scathing when it came to the male dancer: as 'a votary of Terpischore he falls under the same spell' (as temperamental ballet-girls) 'and has it badly'. The *danseur* when 'not engaged in assisting the ... *prima ballerina assoluta* ... to assume some painfully wobbly position at an awkward angle ... spends his time as a sort of spring-heeled Jack or in tee-to-tumming aimlessly round the stage.' See Wilhelm 1895: I, 14.

productions at the Lyceum) innovation was welcomed, dancers in the pantomime were bound by both convention and their own egoism. They were resistant to the new ideas instigated by a talented designer. Once Wilhelm's costumes had emerged from the studio, they were at the mercy of the wearers 'who cannot, or will not, carry them properly'.[106] Dancers resisted wearing costumes that toned in with the stage picture and were appropriate to the characters they were portraying. It was not so easy for them to 'stand out' and be recognised by their admirers in the audience.

It was not only the lower-ranked *coryphée* who opposed Wilhelm's costumes. His harmonised colour schemes were viewed with distrust by leading ladies, who wanted to be noticed, regardless of the harmony of the stage picture. Despite being assured that 'the colours assigned to the chorus and supernumeraries are arranged … to accentuate or lead up to *her* costume, which is naturally chosen to display her to her best advantage,' she persisted in 'a feminine method of argument' and 'when condescending to discuss the matter at all, does so on the lines that she supposes she is to be sacrificed to the rank-and-file'.[107]

Wilhelm was undoubtedly a designer of genius, in advance of his time. In its obituary, *The Times* claimed that he was a precursor of the prominent early-twentieth-century stage designers Leon Bakst and Claud Lovat Fraser.[108] He was determined to keep up the struggle for a more unified stage design in order to 'prove the courage of one's convictions, and to stamp out the smouldering, menacing fire of what is more often than not an expression of obstinate and unintelligent caprice'.[109] He exemplifies the dominance of a male creative force in the theatre, exerting his will over the women who constructed his fantastic and complicated costumes and whose dexterity was responsible for bringing his designs to life. He also had to exert his will over female performers to wear his costumes for the delectation of an audience expecting novelty, colour and spectacle in the Drury Lane pantomime.

The invisible army

The workforce in the Victorian theatre provides an example of masculine dominance and submission within a hierarchical structure. At the top of the scale was the stage manager, who supervised the men in charge of the various theatre departments. They in turn controlled numbers of subordinate workers—both skilled and unskilled. This subjugated workforce was predominantly male, with women working in certain areas. Men of lower rank, labouring backstage, were often maligned and totally under the control of those in charge. They had to carry out heavy duties with militaristic precision, obeying the orders of men who had often risen through the ranks themselves. The backstage labouring force represented a subordinated masculinity dependent on team work and, like an army, reliant on camaraderie.

The Victorian theatre was therefore heavily dependent upon manual labour, with every man in every unit aware of his duties in putting a show together. However creating the theatrical illusion was extremely arduous. Hours were long and employment could be uncertain. These conditions particularly affected men with families. Until the end of the century, there were no unions to protect the backstage worker. Backstage work was dangerous, especially in areas such as gas lighting, with its naked flames and the use of chemicals for limelight. The machinery of the theatre was often heavy and difficult to operate, while changes of scene demanded speed and an almost militaristic precision.

For all his labour, the backstage employee remained unseen. Audiences viewed performers acting, singing or dancing on the stage. They could also observe musicians playing their instruments in the orchestra pit. But men who laboured behind the scenes were supposed to be invisible. They should, according to C. H. d'E. Leppington, keep themselves 'modestly in the background, so as to leave the spectator no trace of their existence'.[110] The results of their labour, the construction and setting of costumes and scenery, would appear as if by magic.

The 'invisibility' of the stage worker reflects the social divisions found in society at large. Backstage labourers should accept their lower status by remaining 'modestly' in the background. Like the orchestral musicians who were hidden from public gaze by Bancroft at the Haymarket, they should keep themselves from the sight of more affluent members of the audience. Nevertheless, the labouring presence was apparent from the noise of set changes, and even through on-stage accidents that could be blamed on some hapless stagehand.

It is perhaps a well-worn cliché to say that the gorgeous effects achieved on the nineteenth-century stage were the product of sweated labour. Nevertheless, all the evidence points to this as a fact. Behind the euphemistic tone of articles by journalists such as Sala and Fitzgerald may be discerned the hard labour, long hours and exploitation of the masculine backstage workforce.

Chapter Three:
Men on the stage

THE NINETEENTH-CENTURY BRITISH ACTOR had to work hard to promote an image of respectability. His career was supplemented by a constant striving for social acceptance. Anxieties over self-esteem were reinforced by the low regard held for the acting profession, particularly by the middle classes. While the morality of actresses was a perpetual concern, with the male actor questions arose concerning not only moral issues, but also his place in the prevailing masculine ideology. Prejudice and suspicion was fed by his seemingly unconventional lifestyle. A theatrical career necessitated alternatives to the accepted codes of masculinity.

An actor's life with its precariousness, odd hours, and touring to different places, was the antithesis of the conventional employment of the middle-class male. Actors seemed to conflict with masculine codes of earnestness, self-restraint, thrift and industry. They worked irregular hours that did not appear to allow time for the enjoyment of a settled family life. Nor did they have the same opportunities for security of employment. It was not until late in the century that actors began to have the advantages of professional or other benefits.

A theatrical career lacked the stability supposedly found in normative middle-class masculine employment, such as working for a reputable firm. Nor was an actor hidden in the office of a 'respectable' work place. His work involved displaying himself to the public gaze. Furthermore the contained and artificial space of the stage moved masculinity into a world of make-believe. Performing within this space caused the male actor to indulge in activities that could be considered 'unmasculine'. He dressed up in costumes of different periods and nationalities, which gave him a colourful appearance; he wore make-up, spoke with an inflated voice, and used extravagant gestures. He acted out high emotional states, subverting expectations of manliness in 'real life'. Emotionalism was considered a female prerogative; men were supposed to be more internalised and thoughtful.

Figure 23. Sir Squire Bancroft

Because actors were outside the norm, they were, in certain quarters, the objects of moral and religious disapproval. They were also considered as being intellectually inferior to other men following artistic professions, such as artists, writers, architects and high-ranking musicians.[1] 'According to some,' wrote H. B. Irving in 1900, 'the performance of the actor is hardly to be dignified by the name of art, or if it is, an art so paltry and unintellectual as wholly unworthy to be ranked with its sisters.'[2] But the actor did have his defenders. In 1851, George Augustus Sala wrote that people were 'rather too apt to call theatres sinks of iniquity and dens of depravity, and to set down actors as a species of diverting vagabonds, who have acquired a knowledge of their calling without study and exercise it without labour'.[3] The truth was that most actors worked very hard—with long hours, roles to learn, rehearsals and performances:

> If a little more were known of how hardworking, industrious and persevering theatricals, as a body, generally are—of what has to be done behind the scenes of a theatre, and how it is done for our amusement—we should look upon the drama with a more favourable eye, ... with a little more charity and forbearance.[4]

Although he had his defenders, the actor was, for most of the nineteenth century, part of a minority group—like the Gypsy. The insecurity caused by this situation led, particularly in the case of the male actor, to the cultivation of distinctive characteristics. Through his dress and manner he deliberately advertised himself as being 'theatrical'. Like the 'swell', the 'Mary-Anne' and other male groups allotted a deviant status, the actor responded to the *status quo* by cultivating an appearance and manner that set him apart, while drawing attention to himself.

Henry Irving, with his long hair, monocle, wide-brimmed hat and fur-collared coat, epitomised the West End actor-manager. Similarly, Squire Bancroft was distinctive with his swagger-stick, top hat and eye glass. An overtly theatrical manner gave an air of flamboyance or eccentricity. Actors were also aware that the attention gained by their theatricality and bohemianism was the best means of self-advertisement.

Most actors realised they had chosen an uncertain career, but there was always the hope of success and high financial rewards. Yet even the most successful performer could easily sink through a number of factors: by falling out of favour with audiences, or through drink, ill-luck, sickness, or sheer lack of talent. It was easier to fall down the hierarchical scale than it was to climb up it. The precarious life of the theatre was a sharp contrast with the successful man of commerce in the world outside, who ideally should be in a settled position within a firm, with a steadily rising income. Instead of nights spent in draughty theatres, insanitary dressing rooms and uncomfortable digs, he would have a warm home, with a wife and family to return to in the evening. The actor's life could not always conform to this settled pattern.

Actor-managers: at the top of the hierarchy

The actor-manager dominated the British theatre during Queen Victoria's reign. He occupied a position similar to that of other male figures presiding over contained, hierarchical spheres such as the church, education and industry. The difference lay in the esoteric nature of the theatre. It was the antithesis of the earnestness and sanctity associated with academic and ecclesiastical institutions.

Figure 24. Sir Henry Irving

The church, industry and education were predominantly male preserves. The theatrical workforce, on the other hand, comprised both men and women, who worked in close proximity. This was a situation viewed in some quarters as not entirely respectable. Leaders of industry, the church and education were men who earned respect and were readily accepted into society. The actor, meanwhile, had to struggle for social acceptance. There were also considerable differences in the class backgrounds of actors. Nevertheless, the stage was one area in which a man of humble birth could gain power and influence through his own initiative. Attaining social acceptance was another matter. During the early years of Victoria's reign, even the most successful found themselves barred from the higher levels of society. It was only from the 1850s with the gradual 'gentrification' of the theatre that the social character of the actor began to change. Aspirants from the upper classes began to enter the profession, while the knighthood of Henry Irving in 1895 seemed to confirm the social elevation of the successful actor-manager and other members of the theatrical profession.

Actors as managers both acted in, and had the overall responsibility for running, theatres and companies. To become a manager, an actor required 'strong motivation as well as capital'.[5] Also needed was a charismatic personality as well as qualities of character and self-help. Managing a theatre gave a chance not only to be independent, but also to gain the utmost public attention. However, managerial duties were so varied and arduous that it must have required enormous energy to combine them with learning and performing a role.

Very often actors managed theatres with the cooperation of their wives, or had a theatre manager who acted as an assistant. Despite the sharing of a heavy workload, there were many duties for the actor-manager to attend to. He had to select not only actors, but administrative, backstage and front-of-house staff. He had to decide on the plays to be performed and schedule them, frequently cutting and re-arranging texts to meet the capabilities of the company, often with an eye on the central role for himself. A whole production had to be superintended, including the moves of actors at rehearsals. His attention could be diverted to a host of minor matters, both administrative and artistic. Although theatre management could be financially risky, it was a position of authority, giving the chance for self-assertion. The post, with all its responsibilities, conformed to Smilesian notions of self-help and masculine industry.

Working their way up the theatrical hierarchy led to the display of ambition, aggression and competitiveness—characteristics also associated with men of business and industry. Their position allowed some actor-managers to become great innovators who changed production methods in the nineteenth century. They were also capable of exhibiting qualities of benevolence that belied their autocratic status. Actor-managers may have been criticised for their egoism and snobbery, but nearly all tried to relieve poverty and distress among the less fortunate members of their profession with the founding of organisations such as the Actors' Benevolent Fund in 1882.* The benevolence of those who had become successful ensured the survival of the players who supported them as juvenile leads, comedians, utility men or supers.

Figure 25. Sir Herbert Beerbohm Tree

In common with other male leaders, actor-managers exerted control and demanded obedience from those whom they employed. They inspired

---

* Henry Irving, John Toole and Squire Bancroft founded the Actors' Benevolent Fund in 1882. This provided a number of services for actors and actresses. It helped those stranded by bogus managers; it gave free medical services; it made grants or loans to players who were sick or temporarily unemployed; and provided funds for performers who were incapacitated to go into hospitals or nursing homes. The Actors' Association, founded in 1891, was part of a move toward unionisation [and a fore-runner of Equity —*Ed*.] Like the Actors' Benevolent Fund it campaigned against bogus managers and bad sanitation in theatres.

awe and respect, as well as fear, resentment and criticism. They commanded large public followings. They were kept before the public eye through innumerable engravings, photographs and postcards. Portrait painters depicted them in their most famous roles. Articles about their private lives and reviews of their performances appeared in newspapers and journals. They even contributed to the new technology. Among male actors, the voices of Beerbohm Tree, Lewis Waller and Henry Irving were captured on wax cylinders and early gramophone recordings. The performances of stars such as Beerbohm Tree and Johnston Forbes-Robertson were preserved in the silent films of the early twentieth century.

Despite their achievements, actor-managers came under increasing attack. Their power and egoism were seen as stultifying forces. Dramatists alleged that they only chose plays so they could star in them, and then mainly from established, popular authors. Aspiring actors resented the lack of opportunity under an authoritarian regime. Actor-managers, such as Charles Kean in the 1850s, or Beerbohm Tree in the 1890s, were attacked for allegedly debasing public taste through their extravagant expenditure on 'realistic' scenery and costumes.[6]

One of the main problems with the extravagances of actor-managers was the need to conform to the popular demands that sustained their positions of power. Their sway also influenced the economic and social divisions within the theatre, which were analogous to the differences of class and wealth in the world outside. Actors lower down the scale worked and rehearsed for longer hours, were paid less, had to put up with inferior dressing room conditions, as well as enduring a life of rented rooms rather than a St John's Wood mansion. They were in the thrall of the star actor-manager who usually ensured the centrality of his performances.

Some actor-managers used 'despotic' tactics, particularly toward other performers who might appear promising. F. G. Tomlins, in *A Brief View of the English Drama* (1840), cites a tragedian who deprived 'a very worthy brother actor' of the opportunity to play several important roles at Drury Lane.[7] Nor were actor-managers averse to cutting the lines of secondary characters in order to shift the focus to their own interpretations. By doing so, the star actor, according to Tomlins, threw a 'false glare' on his own performance[8] as well as altering the carefully crafted balance of the play. Another way for an actor-manager to focus attention on himself was by heading a company consisting of 'a crowd of non-entities utterly incapable of understanding or interpreting the words of the author'.[9]

By the 1880s, audiences were no longer content 'to see one part well played and the rest murdered'. The journalist R. K. Hervey thought that the actor would be more human if he did not insist that other members of the company were subordinate to himself.[10] In the 1890s, Beerbohm Tree, at Her Majesty's Theatre, was one actor-manager who realised the importance of giving opportunities to the actors surrounding him. Unlike Irving, he did not cut the texts to centralise his own performance, but let himself be 'played off the stage' by an array of equally strong actors. At the same time he was acutely aware that a company of good actors helped to create an increase in profits.[11]

The late nineteenth century saw increasing criticism of the power and influence of the actor-manager by critics such as Clement Scott.[12] In an article published in the *International Monthly* in 1900 he criticised the self-centeredness of 'the great actor-manager' Henry Irving: 'The actor-manager is, and must be, a star. ... The theatrical star is adept at looking after number one; and number one is the first consideration.'[13] In this and other articles actor-managers were accused of being inordinately vain, of looking after themselves 'in the first instance and their pockets second'. They produced plays only for self-advancement, and employed inferior players in their companies because they feared rivalry. They tried to crush the talents of ambitious young actors. They were the main cause of: 'a dearth of good British plays. ... A great author will not condescend to write down to the order of a monopolist who does not ask for his best work.'[14]

Clement Scott advocated the replacement of the actor-manager's control with a 'company-run' syndicate system like that of the Comédie Française in Paris. This idea was dismissed by the other great actor-manager of the period, Beerbohm Tree. Meanwhile the conservative playwright, Henry Arthur Jones, maintained that a 'commonwealth of players' would not work in Britain: 'The playgoing public likes to make its own heroes and heroines and loves to support them loyally.'[15] Jones and other actors, writers and journalists leapt to the defence of the actor-manager system. The so-called 'inordinate vanity' of actor-managers was 'nothing more than their necessary acceptance of the public appreciation of their powers'.[16] But, as Beerbohm Tree commented, 'it would be absurd to contend that an actor' (as manager) 'is always free from personal ambition'.[17] An actor became a manager 'through his popularity with playgoers—a popularity earned generally by personal qualities and hard work'.[18]

Nor was the influence of the actor-manager always destructive. He could set an example whereby the beginner learned valuable lessons in technique from watching and performing with him. Far from destroying a young actor's career, he could offer advice and encouragement. However the aspiring actor was in danger of assimilating worn-out tricks and mannerisms, and opportunities for assuming important roles could be limited by the actor-manager's overriding dominance and tendency to play all the leading male roles himself. His control not only dominated those with whom he performed on the stage, it also extended to mesmerising the spectators who had placed him upon a pedestal where he could be both admired and reviled.

Matinée idols and the cult of manliness

The heroic Victorian actor needed more than the ability to act. He had to project a charismatic presence and possess the combination of a handsome physiognomy, a good physique and a sonorous voice. There was, however, a dichotomy between physical and intellectual expectations. Men on stage were considered to possess more 'intellect' than mere physique. This supposedly placed them above perceptions of the frivolity and sensuality of womanhood. Percy Fitzgerald, writing in 1878 on the physiognomy of actors, concluded that the 'well-cut features', 'intelligence' and 'expression' of certain leading men were qualities lacking in actresses—'Of pretty faces there are plenty, but how few of expression or intelligence!'[19]

Comments like these ignore the existence of actresses who were as, or even more, intelligent than their male counterparts on stage. Because of this emphasis on his 'intellect' rather than his physicality, the sexual appeal of the male actor was more subtly apparent than the blatant exposure of female sexuality. This was especially the case in the musical theatre. Women in music hall, burlesque or musical comedy were expected to maintain an attractive appearance, largely for the benefit of the male spectator. Good-looking female 'artistes' were an essential economic source. Men in the audience liked to see pretty girls and their presence could draw in the crowds.

Figure 26. 'Hence, horrible shadow! Unreal mockery, hence!' (*Macbeth*) (illustrating early-Victorian 'historical' costume)

Male performers in the chorus were not considered with the same sort of emphasis on their physical attributes. Writing at the turn of the century, the journalist George R. Sims maintained that men were taken on more quickly than women for the chorus, because there was less regard for their physical appearance. So long as he had a good voice, a man could be engaged 'whether he was short or tall, plain or handsome'.[20] Male stage costume tended to be less revealing than female: since less of the male body was revealed, emphasis was placed on a handsome physiognomy and masculine bearing. These attributes were essential to actors who played the heroic romantic lead.

The early- to mid-nineteenth-century historical or 'exotic' costume typically consisted of a long tunic reaching to the thighs, ensuring the genital area was well covered. Below the tunic, legs were encased in woollen tights and occasionally knee-high boots. Pantaloons were also sometimes worn and there were variations with period styles and national dress. This type of costume was worn by actors in performances of Shakespearean and period plays.

Until the late nineteenth century, actors' legs, and sometimes their arms, were encased with flesh-toned coverings. Exposing too much flesh was not considered decent. When Sir Frank Benson played Macbeth with his legs bare, he was censured not only by provincial audiences, but also by one of the older actors of his company who considered bare legs 'a disgusting indecency'. For most of his career he would have seen the limbs of actors 'clothed in pink fleshings'.[21] Away from the legitimate theatre, semi-naked men could be viewed in the music hall or circuses—in the Hellenistic tableaux of 'Living Picture' shows; as strong men covered only by a loincloth; or as 'Graeco-Roman' wrestlers.

In the late nineteenth century, the erotic appeal of leading men became more widely publicised. Male sexual allure on the stage was largely fostered by an increasing independent female presence among audiences. This was mainly due to the new-found freedom for women to come into the West End of London from areas outside, such as the emerging outer suburbs. Their excursions were encouraged by improvements and developments in rail travel and the enlargement of the underground system. Visiting the West End, they shopped in department stores and visited the theatre—alone or in the company of other women. Very often, with an early return to the domestic sphere, it was convenient for them to attend afternoon (or 'matinée') performances to see their favourite actors. While in the evening, husbands, brothers or sons gazed at ballet-girls in the Alhambra or Empire music halls, women, often at matinées, enjoyed the charismatic presence of handsome leading men in comedies, musicals and melodramas.

The late-Victorian matinée idol cultivated an image that accorded with ideals of bravery, muscularity, physical prowess, chivalry, morality and sportsmanship. A strong media emphasis was placed upon his heterosexuality and middle-class respectability. Nearly all matinée idols were married men with families. Their wealth and success enabled them to live in affluent London areas such as St John's Wood or Bedford Park.

Actors became part of the late nineteenth-century cults of manliness and muscular Christianity. They were continually adjectivised as 'manly', both in private life and in performance. For instance, Arthur Goddard, in a series of monographs on well-known late Victorian actors—*Players of the Period* (1891)—repeatedly describes his subjects as 'manly'. William Terriss has a 'romantic and manly style';[22] Henry G. Neville is 'manly and dashing';[23] Wilson Barrett has a 'manly, frank, winning personality'.[24] The reiteration of 'manly' in describing male performance on the stage becomes a kind of mantra. It confirms a heterosexual status, while expunging any notion of feminising theatricality, dandyism or homosexuality.

The notion of manliness meant that greater emphasis began to be placed on the physical attributes of the man on stage, especially if he was charismatic, popular and handsome. In 1895, for instance, *The Era* gushed over the forthcoming appearance of the immensely popular actor William Terriss in a new 'military melodrama,' describing him in terms that would have been previously reserved for an actress. As a lieutenant in a Highland regiment, 'the beauties of his form will be more fully displayed than they have ever been before' by a 'picturesque costume' which includes 'the airy and becoming kilt'.*[25] Ideals of manliness frame the career of William Terriss—an early example of the so-called 'matinée idol'. After appearing at Irving's Lyceum, he was manager of the Adelphi Theatre from 1885 until 1897.

Terriss's successful career ended in tragedy—when Richard Prince, a deranged subordinate actor, fatally stabbed him outside the Adelphi stage door.† Terriss's biographer, Arthur Smythe, noted that he combined 'the

---

* This role was Lt Dudley Keppel in the patriotic melodrama *One of the Best* by Seymour Hicks and George Edwards, produced at the Adelphi in 1895. [See Chapter 5 —*Ed.*]

† William Prince had been employed as a supernumerary at the Adelphi Theatre. and had made demands on Terriss and other members of the company for money. On his arrest, Prince claimed that he had murdered Terriss out of revenge, because he had prevented him from obtaining employment and had blackmailed him for ten years. In January 1898, Prince was sentenced to be detained for life as a 'criminal lunatic' at Holloway

frank recklessness of the sailor with the daring of the impulsive discoverer'.[26] He also demonstrated Smilesian principles of independence and self-help. His daughter, the actress Ellaline Terriss, wrote of him: 'He had reached his high position by his own efforts—and nobody boosted him into popularity—his talents did it for him.'[27]

Before he made his professional stage debut in 1868, Terriss, like many other young men who took up stage careers, had led a 'roving, adventurous life'. Apart from studying medicine, he had been a merchant seaman, a sheep farmer in the Falkland Islands, a horse breeder in Kentucky and a tea planter in Assam—all jobs which were the preserve of men, requiring a toughness and dominance which would prove useful in theatre management.

At the Adelphi, he was immensely popular playing a series of military and naval heroes in a string of jingoistic melodramas. These roles gave every opportunity for the display of Terriss's physical prowess. His on-stage exploits—scaling the sides of ships, rescuing distressed heroines from cliff-tops, escaping from villains by swimming around a ship—exemplified a masculine sense of adventure and bravery. That these episodes were supposedly based on the past experiences of Terriss's adventurous life made them all the more 'vivid' and 'true'.[28] Through his portrayals of brave British officers Terriss became a symbol of patriotic late-Victorian British manhood, and gained an enormous popular following. He was, according to one critic, 'truly the people's hero of melodrama'.[29] His 'frank, buoyant manner' and 'cheery style of address' were often commented on, and earned him the popular accolade of 'Breezy Bill'.[30]

Terriss's self-display on the stage was accompanied by a consciousness of his good looks. He took good care of his health and was 'proud of his clear-cut face and his slim, manly figure'.[31] Terriss shared the vanity of other actor-managers, and like other performers specialising in heroic roles, he had an image to consider, one which not only made him popular, but which brought financial gain. The critic William Archer thought that his 'fatal gift of beauty' hampered him as an artist. 'He was always self-

---

Prison. See *The Times* 17 December 1897, 11; 21 December 1897, 7; 14 January 1898, 5. A detailed account of the case appears in Rowell 1987.

conscious and always cold. ... In some parts which lately came his way he acted with real sincerity and impressiveness. In a work of higher order, a lack of sincerity was his stumbling block.' However Archer does concede that 'of our heroes of melodrama, Mr Terriss was not only the most popular, but also by far the most agreeable'.[32]

Figure 27. William Terriss, c.1880

Terriss retained his good looks and youthful appearance to the end of his life. In 1894 the *Sketch* commented that 'despite the fact he is in the prime of life, he looks, upon the stage, scarcely older than his own son'.*[33] When he died at the age of fifty, Terriss's masculine beauty had hardly diminished; he 'retained to the last' his 'handsome countenance' and 'lithe, graceful figure'.[34] The death of a handsome actor-manager at the height of his popularity and beauty had the makings of legend, and Ellen Terry likened his appearance to that of 'a beautiful youth, a kind of Adonis, although he was fifty years old'.[35]

The image Terriss projected had an erotic potential that appealed to both sexes in the audience. After his appearance in *The Harbour Lights*, portraits of him in naval uniform 'appeared in every shop window' and

---

* Tom Terriss (1872–1964) who became a successful actor and director of silent films in America.

'men and women alike spoke rapturously of him'.[36] For men in the audience, Terriss exemplified ideals of manliness and bravery associated with men serving in Queen Victoria's army and naval services. For women he personified dreams of a romantic manhood. According to his biographer, infatuated ladies sent him rings, and 'bunches of flowers had been thrust into his hand on his way to the stage door by servant girls'.[37] Young girls copied romantic lines he uttered in the plays he performed into their autograph books.[38] Postcards depicting him as the heroes he portrayed, in their various uniforms, were avidly collected and swapped by adoring fans. In 1886 a photograph of him as Lt David Kingsley in *The Harbour Lights* was issued as a Christmas card.[39] Like other matinée idols, Terriss was, for his fans, an unattainable object of desire, to be viewed performing on stage behind the proscenium arch, or to be gazed upon in photographic images. His unassailability was further sustained by an evidently happy marriage and a tranquil, middle-class home life enjoyed in Bedford Park, an affluent new suburb of outer London.[40]

However an element of controversy surrounds this family idyll, over the relations between Terriss and his leading lady, Jessie Millward. In her biography Millward refers to him as her 'dear friend and comrade'.[41] They played together at the Adelphi for more than twelve years and their stage partnership developed into a close personal relationship. However great pains were taken to advertise the platonic nature of their friendship. According to George Rowell, Terriss's wife, Isobel, accepted their partnership without jealousy; realising its professional advantages; she and the children 'welcomed Jessie as a friend'.[42] Nevertheless, Terriss spent a great deal of time with Jessie. He installed her with her faithful maid Lottie in a flat in Hanover Square. This he used as a West End base. Together they gave 'Dramatic Costume Recitals', which included poetry and scenes from Shakespeare, at fêtes, bazaars and other such events. Evidently a portrait of Jessie graced the drawing room mantelpiece in Terriss's family home at Bedford Park.[43] It was in Jessie's arms that Terriss died after he was stabbed outside the Adelphi stage door.[44] In a codicil to his will, Terriss bequeathed to Jessie his leasehold cottage in Berkshire with all its contents.[45]

Whether they were physical lovers or not is difficult to ascertain. As with other Victorian relationships, a veil of silence surrounds any suggestion of sexual intimacy. Quite apart from the fact that Terriss was a married man, the two popular actors had their careers and reputations to consider. Denial of anything more than a working partnership would have given some sort of protection. Nevertheless their relationship does raise questions. If they were lovers, as has been suggested, would they have appeared so openly together, and would Terriss have displayed her portrait in his family home? Did all this provide a smokescreen for a clandestine physical attraction, or was it simply a 'brother and sister' working partnership?

Jessie defied protocol by insisting she attend Terriss's funeral. Her presence at the occasion 'clothed in deepest black' caused much comment. Victorian funerals were usually all-male occasions, with grieving wives and daughters waiting dutifully at home.[46] Henry Irving and Terriss's son-in-law, Seymour Hicks, escorted Jessie to the funeral.* She later recalled the comfort she had received from Terriss's daughter Ellaline and other members of the family, but she did not mention further contact with his widow, who died almost a year later.†[47] Jessie's presence and display of grief at the funeral brought into question the true nature of their relationship, particularly as his wife was not present.

William Terriss presents an example of a leading man who projected an image that conformed as much as possible to middle-class ideals of masculinity. On the stage he was patriotic, brave and adventurous, setting an example for British manhood of all classes. His private life showed him to be living well through his own achievements, with. a respectable home, wife and children. Yet his carefully honed image of respectability is cast into disarray, not only because of his murder by an insanely jealous supernumerary, but also through the questions raised by his long-term relationship with his leading lady.

Among his sporting and adventurous achievements, Terriss had also been 'a remarkably clever and capable half-back in Rugby football'.[48]

---

* There were two other women at the funeral who were not family members. One of these was the wife of the theatre critic Clement Scott, who attended with her husband. See 'The Funeral of Mr Terriss', *The Times*, 22 December 1897: 6, Col C.

† In her autobiography, William Terriss's daughter Ellaline makes only one reference to 'Miss Jessie Millward' in connection with an American tour. She does not mention Jessie's presence at her father's funeral. See Terriss 1955): 65.

Sportsmanship indicated purity of mind and body, a spirit of masculine competitiveness and the eradication of physical or mental weakness. It moved an actor from the 'dandification' of the theatre into realms of male competitiveness and gamesmanship associated with the public school. An actor who played sport could not possibly be 'decadent' or homosexual.

Figure 28. F. R. Benson

The noted touring actor-manager, Sir Francis Robert Benson, better known as Frank (or F. R.) Benson, was renowned for his passionate interest in sport and for encouraging the actors of his company in healthy masculine activity. Noted for his Shakespearean productions, Benson toured the provinces with his company from 1883 until the late 1920s. He was physically tireless and demanded the same kind of energy from his cast. At every opportunity he encouraged his male actors to play sport. As the theatre historian Hesketh Pearson noted, an actor like Benson 'who would break the ice and enjoy a swim between a matinée of *Hamlet* and an evening performance of *Richard III* seemed to be the epitome of a securely heterosexual masculinity.

Benson's sportsmanship appealed to respectable middle-class audiences who equated physical fitness with manliness: 'Everyone felt that Shakespeare was safe in the hands of one who could play cricket, tennis, football and hockey so well, who went in for rowing and running and water-polo'.[49] Benson believed that an actor should be in sound physical condition. If his body was not fit, and 'nervous and muscular energy not kept up' he could be neither 'quick, nor graceful, nor powerful, nor natural, nor anything else that may become an actor and a man'.[50] He imparted his own enthusiasm for sport to the male members of his company. In doing so he took on a role similar to that of a father or headmaster encouraging boys to play games. The male members of the company played in cricket matches, as well as hockey, soccer and rugby, during a strenuous schedule of rehearsals and performances.[51] Matches were played not only against the teams of other companies, but also against local men in provincial towns. This helped to create a rapport between Benson's players and the communities in which they performed.

The actors had to bridge the dichotomy between the sheer physical effort of sport and the combination of intellect and physicality involved in a stage performance. It must have been difficult to find the stamina to perform on stage after a day playing cricket or football. Physical fitness is essential for the actor (witness the numbers of present-day actors who go to the gym) but in Benson's company was there too much emphasis on sport? J. C. Trewin has written that: 'The company was by no means a group of cricketers and amphibians. It knew what acting ought to be; it criticised itself and others as bluntly and as brashly as young men have always done.'[52] Trewin's comment excludes the women of the company, as does an earlier reference by the actor Henry Ainley* to 'our Bensonian brotherhood'.[53] This heavy bias toward masculinity seems to have marginalised the actresses Benson employed, who apparently cheered on their sporting male colleagues from the sidelines.[54] However both sexes

---

* Three times married, with a number of children, but said to have written explicitly homosexual letters to the young Laurence Olivier. —*Ed.*

enjoyed cycling, which was 'much in vogue in the Company'.[55] According to Lady Benson, participation in sport was an effort by the entire company: 'We could put together a very respectable team in most games' and 'most of us' (presumably both men and women) played golf.[56] Nevertheless, within the company a masculine exclusivity appears to have been created, engendered by Benson's emphasis on sport and masculine camaraderie. This alignment of the middle-class obsession with male physical fitness and the sensual appeal of theatrical performance allowed Benson's classical revivals to gain a healthy respectability among a largely middle-class following. Lady Benson, in her autobiography, rather ingenuously claimed that Benson had 'a weakness for sportsmen' and was inclined to engage actors who said they could play games.[57] Benson's obsession with male physicality may have contained an undercurrent of homoeroticism. Nevertheless he can be viewed as a pioneer of the concept of physical fitness for actors.

By contrast with Benson's ruggedness, Sir George Alexander, manager of the St James's Theatre from 1891 until 1917, presented a more urbane, 'dandified' image. In dramas by Wilde and Pinero he depicted a more genteel form of masculinity, portraying the attitudes and manners of late Victorian high society. Nor were his performances always described in overtly masculine terms. Hesketh Pearson remembered his movements as being as graceful as they were 'decorous', and he had an 'admirably modulated' voice.[58] W. A. Lewis Bettany, writing for *Theatre* magazine in 1892, compared Alexander to a cat, commenting on his 'feline grace' and 'purring manner'. Bettany thought that his 'air of ease and distinction' did not make him suitable for 'tragedy and the more vigorous drama'.[59] George Alexander may have been renowned for his appearances in society plays, but, according to his biographer A. E. W. Mason, he also had 'a wide range from farce to tragedy'.[60] With his elegant, gentlemanly appearance, Alexander set the style for his male admirers. Just as women copied the gowns worn by actresses, men of fashion would study George Alexander's clothes before ordering their own from their tailors.[61]

Alexander was a shrewd, if ruthless, businessman and a punctilious, efficient theatre manager, who promoted a number of important plays of the *fin de siècle*. He also provides an exception to the egocentric style of management favoured by many actor-managers. Hesketh Pearson claimed that his 'precision and punctuality' were unique in the theatre of his time. He further claimed never to have known Alexander 'to attempt to bully anyone', to lose his temper or 'to be sarcastic at another's expense'. Pearson found him to be 'always considerate, fair-minded and helpful'.[62]

Figure 29. Sir George Alexander as Aubrey Tanqueray in *The Second Mrs Tanqueray*

Alexander was possibly ahead of his time in purporting to see himself as part of an ensemble and not the star. Nor did he supposedly reserve roles for himself like other actor-managers. But this did not prevent him from being the leading man in most of the St James's productions. His concern for the welfare of his company meant that rehearsals, which began promptly, lasted for only three hours, from eleven a.m. until two p.m. This gave Alexander and the cast time to rest before the evening performance. He believed that a longer rehearsal time was unprofitable.

Alexander's 'ensemble' included actors who appeared time after time in his productions. This meant that he controlled what amounted to a fairly exclusive stock company, specialising in plays aimed at an affluent high society patronage. For all his advocacy of ensemble performances and concern for his performers, it was undoubtedly Alexander's relentless determination that enabled him to remain in total control of the St James's Theatre for nearly twenty-six years.

It was possibly his ruthlessness, together with the need for self-preservation, which caused his obstructive behaviour at the time of Oscar Wilde's arrest. In order to avoid becoming ensnared in a legal quarrel over Wilde's homosexual conduct, he withheld evidence against Lord Queensberry after he tried to force his way into the opening night of *The Importance of Being Earnest* on 14 February 1895.[63] Together with Lewis Waller, who was appearing as Sir Robert Chiltern in *An Ideal Husband* at the Haymarket, he refused to stand bail, despite the pleas of Lord Alfred Douglas.[64] Wilde's name was taken off the bills at the St James's Theatre.* This all may seem like cowardice, but an impending sex scandal, especially one involving homosexuality, created a dilemma for an actor-manager with the reputation of George Alexander. To be seen to support Oscar Wilde could mean the loss of his position in a theatre whose audiences had once applauded, and now condemned, the hapless author.

Alexander's behaviour at the time of Wilde's arrest and trial demonstrates the fears over disgrace and loss of reputation engendered in high-powered men who had contact with the author. Nevertheless, Alexander, who must have been well aware of the homosexual coterie among audiences at his theatre, appears to have acted very swiftly to withhold his support for Wilde. Although he is reputed to have snubbed Wilde on visiting France in 1898, Alexander did later try to make

---

* In his 1935 biography of George Alexander, A. E. W. Mason attempts to justify his behaviour at the time of the Wilde trials. See Mason 1935: 85–86.

amends. He acquired the acting rights for *The Importance of Being Earnest* and *Lady Windermere's Fan*. Visiting poverty-stricken Wilde in Paris, he offered voluntary payments on these plays. He later bequeathed the rights to Wilde's estranged sons.

With the post-Wildean decline in Aestheticism the heterosexual appeal of the leading man intensified. The prime attributes of the matinée idol seemed to combine in Lewis Waller. With his Mediterranean good looks, a vibrant voice, virile acting ability and gentlemanly appearance, he was probably the first actor to engender a cult-like following. His popularity coincided with the movement of women toward a greater freedom and their agitation for more rights.

Waller had a stage career of thirty-two years, playing about 200 parts, and reputedly never missed a performance. Like other matinée idols, he appeared in Shakespeare, and he played Sir Robert Chiltern in Wilde's *An Ideal Husband* at the Haymarket in 1895. But it was in a series of romantic costume melodramas that his appeal to women in the audience increased. Waller's female fans voiced their adulation with extrovert enthusiasm. They rapturously received Waller's appearances as romantic French heroes such as d'Artagnan* and Monsieur Beaucaire.†

Playing these historic and romantic heroes, Waller's masculinity was eroticised, enhanced and even feminised by period costume. Posing in the medieval robes of Henry V at the Lyceum in 1900, a jewel encrusted belt dangles phallus-like between his legs.[65] As Monsieur Beaucaire, he is bedecked with frills and wears an elaborately curled powdered wig, in accordance with the contemporary view of eighteenth century French dress.[66] Historic costume removed him to periods of time associated with masculine valour and romantic encounters. It increased his erotic potential as an unattainable object of desire, separated from adoring fans by the artificiality of stage and performance.

---

* *The Three Musketeers*, adapted by Henry Hamilton from the novel by Alexandre Dumas père. First performed at the Metropole Theatre, Camberwell, on 12 September 1898, then at the Lyceum Theatre, on 3 November 1900.

† *Monsieur Beaucaire*, adapted by Evelyn Sutherland from a story by Booth Tarkington. Opened at the Prince of Wales Theatre, Liverpool, on 6 October 1902, transferred to the Comedy Theatre, London on 25 October 1902. The play had a long run of 430 performances.

Figure 30. Lewis Waller as Henry V: Lyceum Theatre, 1900

Jacob Grein, reviewing *The Three Musketeers* in 1898, noted how Waller's 'fine, manly presence, his glorious voice, his unflagging energy rendered [the audience] breathless'. His 'delightful impetuosity fired the audience to frantic applause.'[67] Evidently on Waller's first and last nights, women in the pit and gallery 'went completely mad'. His first entrances caused 'such a storm of shouts and yells and hand clapping and foot stamping that the action was held up for several minutes'. His fans banded themselves into a club vulgarly known as the K.O.W. (Keen on Waller) Brigade and packed out the pit at nearly every performance.[68]

Waller became a cult—'he was more like a god than an idol. ... It was blasphemy to suggest that he was not perfect, profanation to imply that there were other gods than he.'[69] Waller, in coping with his frenzied female following, found himself in a similar position to the actress harassed by overt male attention. He is reported to have cried out: 'Will no one rid me of these turbulent priestesses?'[70] His sexual appeal made him the target of women emerging from decades of moral and domestic repression. The worship of a male idol on stage encouraged them to throw aside restraint and voice their long suppressed desires through their Bacchanalian shouts and yells. Their behaviour foreshadows the twentieth-century adulation of iconic male figures such as pop and film stars.

That masculine physiognomy and physicality could be a cause of uninhibited frenzy introduces a disturbing aspect into the glamorised image of the matinée idol. Waller, for instance, became an object of ridicule through 'the puerile nature of the plays he put on and the adolescent behaviour of his female admirers'. According to Hesketh Pearson this prevented more discriminating audiences from taking him seriously as a 'superb' Shakespearean actor.[71] Ultimately, Waller was left to the mercy of his fans and his performances became moribund and stilted.

So far as the matinée idol was concerned, the journalistic insistence on his manliness, morality and heterosexuality was supposed to mask any trace of deviance in his private life. But popularity carried a price—it could make him the subject of speculation and gossip. The moral image promoted by the press and publicity was in danger of being shattered by inferences of marital infidelity, or of 'deviant' conduct. Success, handsomeness and assurance could make him the subject of envy, culminating in the extreme of being the victim of a stabbing by an insanely jealous subordinate player.

Yet the matinée idol fulfilled a need. To men in the audience, he provided examples of manly chivalric conduct and physical prowess. For the liberated woman, he became the means of an eroticised escapism, and seemed to be part of newly emerging freedoms. The glamorous *fin-de-siècle* matinée idol exerted an ambivalent appeal that transcended boundaries of class and gender. The combination of good looks, a fine figure, and a resonant voice with illusory middle-class moralistic ideals, aided his promotion to a god-like status.

Conviviality and rivalry: Charles Dillon

Away from the adulation of audiences, complex relations were formed between male actors. Working in the theatre, with all its uncertainties, could make temperaments highly strung, causing aggression, fear of rivalry and profound feelings of jealousy. At the same time, the theatre was also capable of bringing men together in comradeship.

As in other walks of life, homosocial bonds gave an alternative to the feminine centrality of the domestic sphere. Male actors socialised together, gave one another support. They met and worked together in companies, often for long periods of time. They shared dressing rooms and when on tour shared digs together. The peripatetic and often chancy life of the theatre helped to create a certain amount of camaraderie between actors, especially those struggling at the bottom of the scale. In these circumstances they often formed long-lasting friendships, which could prove useful in the advancement of careers.

Outside the theatre, one way in which actors could maintain contact was through drinking in the pubs and bars of major cities. The public house was a traditional space where men gathered to socialise. Drinking in the pub with colleagues offered good fellowship in a precarious and overworked profession, where there was very little time for enjoyment when not performing on the stage.

For the actor, the pub served functions other than mere socialising. It was also a means for gathering news and gossip, as well as of being alerted to forthcoming productions and vacancies with theatrical companies. It could also provide 'a delightful modulation' after the 'strain and excitement of the first night, when every nerve was quivering and it was difficult to transpose from the high key of the theatre to the lower one of home'.[72] All this conviviality contributed to the popular notion of the actor leading a bohemian easy-going life, regardless of hard work and the uncertainties of a theatrical career.

Some actors were attracted to an easy-going, bohemian life of drinking and homosocial conviviality, to the detriment of their careers. One such example is the mid-nineteenth-century actor and manager, Charles Dillon. Fellow actor-manager John Coleman wrote of him: 'No actor of our time had so many chances, and no actor ... ever so stupidly neglected them.'[73] According to the American dramatic critic William Winter, Dillon was 'a man of extraordinary talent'. If he 'had not been afflicted by a propensity for drink' he could have reached 'a foremost position in the contemporary theatre'.[74]

Physically, Dillon was the antithesis of the idealised heroic actor. Coleman gives him

> the appearance of a Gothic monster: an 'abnormally ugly young man' with a 'huge cavernous mouth, with protruding and irregular teeth, a corrugated nose, snake-like glittering eyes, a head of long, lank glittering hair growing very low on a broad but receding forehead, over the brows of which two great bumps projected.[75]

Figure 31. Charles Dillon as Othello, 1856

He later grew 'a huge black moustache' which hid 'his cavernous mouth'.[76] Coleman, on first seeing Dillon acting in a melodrama called *The Dog of Montargis*,* at a minor theatre near Portman Market, lost sight of his 'plebeian appearance' in admiration of his ability. Dillon moved 'with ease, grace and distinction ... his sword-play was magnificent; his pathos and passion alike were admirable.'[77] Dillon went

---

* Various English versions of this appeared by different hands, based on a French original by René Charles Guilbert de Pixérécourt, which ran in Paris from 1814 to 1834. —Ed.

on to tour the provinces and make appearances in London. He managed the Lyceum for two seasons—from 1856 to 1858. His acting in tragic and Shakespearean roles was very much admired. Coleman thought him 'one of the most distinguished precursors of the modern school of acting'.[78]

Unfortunately Dillon's promise and talent became dissipated by a lack of discipline, unreliability and his fondness for alcohol. John Coleman claimed that off the stage he was never happy unless 'loafing around the nearest bar with congenial companions who swallowed histories ... and his libations with equal avidity',[79] As a manager he lacked judgment and was continually in debt. In 1860, chased by creditors, he embarked on a lengthy tour encompassing North America, Australia, New Zealand, Peru and Chile. He might have 'amassed a fortune' from this tour but, according to Coleman, 'He was so erratic, so undependable, that he never gave himself the ghost of a chance.'[80] Nor did Dillon's marital life adhere to the ideals of bourgeois norms. He abandoned his ailing wife Clara, taking a rival actress, Eliza Webb, to star with him on his world tour. When playing in Australia between 1862 and 1864 she was billed as Mrs Charles Dillon, but there is no evidence they were ever married. Eliza died of typhoid fever not long after their return to New York in December 1865. Dillon stayed on in America until late 1866 and returned to England early the following year.

Dillon's later years exemplified the decline of an actor who had dissipated his talents. His voice began to lose its power and he could no longer effectively play emotional nuances. He made his last appearances touring the provinces; according to Coleman, these were mainly 'fit-ups' around Wales.[81] Performing with stock companies in badly appointed venues affected his health. In 1881, while on tour, he died of a stroke in the street in Hawick, Roxburghshire, after drinking with friends.[82]

In many ways the career of Charles Dillon subverts the masculine ideals to which other leading actors of his time aspired. He was physically ugly, rather than a model of classical handsomeness. Yet his innate ability overcame his lack of conventional male beauty. At the same time his considerable acting talent was thrown into disarray by lack of discipline and an attraction for drink and disreputable male company. His career was made further insecure by his inability to handle money; his attempts at management were hampered by debt, and creditors continually pursued him. He destroyed the fabric of a secure marital life by leaving his wife and giving her position as leading actress to a rival performer, who happened to be his mistress. Dillon provides an example of a Victorian actor whose career was destroyed by his inability to adhere to the principles of self-discipline, thrift and moral purity which constituted the 'ideal man' and which provided the basis for the success of many other actor-managers.

Bonds of male friendship: Irving, Toole and Stoker

Despite the rivalries and uncertainties of the theatrical world, platonic friendships were formed between actors that could be viewed as adhering to nineteenth-century terms of manly love. These were tenets based on ideals of Hellenism, evangelical Christianity and a reverence for medieval chivalric codes.[83] Whether in the theatre or in the world outside, platonic male friendship was supposedly above the physical expression of male-to-male desire. It could parallel, or even rival, the relations between men and women. The complexities of Victorian male friendship are evident in the relations between Henry Irving and the two men who were closest to him professionally—Bram Stoker, his manager, and the fellow actor, John Laurence Toole.

Irving's career-long friendship with Toole exemplifies the devotion and attachment which could accompany close male-to-male relations in the nineteenth century. Like many other Victorian male friendships, it is tinged with unabashed emotionalism.

Irving believed he owed much of his success to Toole. At the beginning of their careers they had acted together.* In 1869, when Irving was a struggling young actor, rejected by managers, Toole gave him work with his company, 'insisting he should be engaged and paid well, keeping his name constantly before the public'.[84]

Irving looked upon Toole like an adopted brother. Bram Stoker wrote of their friendship that 'to the last day of Irving's life' it 'never flagged or faltered' and that 'such a thing as jealousy never entered into the heart of either'.[85] But then there could have been little scope for rivalry since their talents lay in opposite directions—Irving was principally a tragedian,

---

* See also Read 2008: 11–25.

while Toole excelled in comic roles. The friendship between two egotistical actors flourished partly because there was no way in which one could intrude into the firmly entrenched professional position of the other. They certainly were devoted friends, although it may be suspected that Toole, with his unrestrained emotionalism, was subservient to the iconic status of the 'great' Henry Irving.

Figure 32. John L. Toole

According to Stoker, they kept in touch every day and wrote to each other while on tour. Evidently Irving sent Toole flowers which he kept 'till they had faded and dropped away; even then the baskets and bare stalks were kept in his room.'[86] When he learned of Irving's death on 13 October 1905, the distraught Toole is said to have ordered his servants to recover from the wastepaper basket the last words which Irving had written to him—a note of his address on a wrapper round a newspaper article.[87]

For Irving, Toole was a close male friend, a 'rock', in whom he could confide. He spoke only to Toole after the failure of his marriage. The mutual comfort they could offer each other was evident with Irving being supportive of Toole after the tragic losses of his wife, son and daughter.* Toole was so badly affected by the loss of his family that his health broke down, and he eventually had to retire from the stage.

After Toole's retirement, Irving, whenever he had the opportunity, would visit him offering support and comfort. Clement Scott wrote of their friendship: 'There has ever been something pathetic in the deep and earnest attachment between these two literally brother actors, and the public at large has appreciated it to the fullest extent.'[88] There do not appear to have been any major differences or complexities to mar their relationship. If the views of Scott and Stoker are to be taken for granted, it was a deep platonic friendship, based on reciprocal devotion, empathy and support, untrammelled by professional rivalry. More complex is Irving's professional and domestic relationship with Bram Stoker, which was mostly concurrent with his kinship with Toole. From their first meeting in Dublin in 1876, until Irving's death in 1905, Stoker was not only Irving's theatre manager, but also a close friend and companion. Like other nineteenth-century masculine friendships, it raises the inevitable questions regarding homosexual desire. Their relationship is also interesting because of the parallels that may be drawn with Stoker's famous Gothic novel *Dracula* (1897). The vampyric Count Dracula draws the lifeblood out of his victims turning them into his creatures. Similarly, Irving was capable of exerting a mesmeric hold over those close to him, making them subservient to his egoism.

From the outset Stoker demonstrated a high degree of submission and emotion in his dealings with Irving. In his *Personal Reminiscences of Henry Irving* he wrote of their first meeting: 'In those moments of our mutual emotion he too had found a friend and knew it. Soul had looked

---

* Toole's son, Frank, died on 4 December 1879 aged 23; his daughter, Florence, died from typhoid fever on 5 November 1888, aged 22; his wife, Susan, died three and a half months later on 20 February 1889.

into soul! From that hour began a friendship as profound, as close, as lasting as can be between two men.'[89]

Figure 33. Bram Stoker

Stoker's rhetoric, in describing his almost life-long friendship with Irving, could be seen to show the influence of Walt Whitman and his celebration of comradely love.* However same-sex relations in the Victorian era did not always slot into binaries of hetero and homosexuality, or, indeed, of physical or non-physical expression. Close friendships could be fairly flexible in combining the platonic ideal with an undercurrent of sensuality, which may or may not have been physically expressed.†

The position of Stoker in his relationship with Irving is made more complex by his apparent emasculation. His subservience to the demands

---

* Stoker, like his contemporaries John Addington Symonds and Edward Carpenter, was a follower of the great American poet. Irving and Stoker visited Whitman in Philadelphia, at the house of a mutual friend, on 20 March 1884, while they were on an American tour. See Ludlam 1962: 68; Belford 1996: 167. [Oscar Wilde had paid a similar visit to Whitman in 1882. —*Ed.*]

† See Smith-Rosenberg, 1986: 53–76; for a discussion of her concept related to male love, see also Robertson, M. 2008: 214–216.

of the actor placed him in a position lacking the 'manly' qualities of dominance and independence. Even Ellen Terry tapped into Stoker's 'unmasculine' involvement with nurturing and domestic matters when, in 1888, she sent him a photograph of herself inscribed 'To my "Ma"—I am her dutiful child.'[90] Stoker was Terry's friend and adviser at the Lyceum for twenty-five years. Underlying the fondness of her inscription is the teasing assignment to Stoker of a drag role, like that of a pantomime dame. Furthermore, almost from his first encounter with Irving in Dublin at the age of twenty, there are aspects that seem to undermine Stoker's masculine potential. At the time he was employed as a clerk, not considered a 'manly' position like one of more authority.[91] This lack of 'manliness' is further underscored by his hysterical outburst when Irving collapsed after reciting Thomas Hood's poem *The Dream of Eugene Aram*. Even Stoker was disturbed by this over-emotional reaction. He swore that he was 'no hysterical subject ... no green youth'. He claimed he was 'as men go a strong man, strong in many ways'.[92] Hysteria was generally thought of as being a humiliating female affliction. In men it was associated with weakness, timidity and fearfulness. These were feminine values that caused psychoanalysts to view male hysteria as a physical manifestation of homosexuality.[93]

There were also ways in which Irving did not completely conform to an idealised masculinity. His performance as Hamlet in 1878 had been called 'unmanly' by at least one critic.[94] He had thin legs, a strange gait, and a notoriously individual pronunciation. Furthermore he was estranged from his wife and therefore did not enjoy a normative home life.

So far as Stoker is concerned, there has been the rather unlikely suggestion that Irving induced a hypnotic crisis in the young man. Certainly Stoker became indispensable to Irving, and, as manager of the Lyceum, was at his beck and call, night and day. Aside from his managerial duties, he drafted many of Irving's letters and speeches. He often filled the lonely actor's empty hours by sitting up with him until dawn.[95] He shared Irving's bohemian bachelor life of dining in clubs, drinking wine and enjoying masculine conversation. He may have found giving companionship to Irving rewarding, but that he was not rewarded in kind was the disappointment of his life. Irving's pride prevented him from giving credit to anyone, except perhaps Toole, whose ideas had helped his career.[96] Stoker, in his *Personal Reminiscences of Henry Irving*, places their friendship in a domestic sphere in which he seems to take on the role of 'wife' to Irving. He claims that, after many years together, the two became so close they were able to read each other's thoughts. This was a capacity which he had 'sometimes seen ... in a husband and wife who have lived together for long and who are good friends, accustomed to work together and to understand each other'.[97] Their relationship did indeed take on the aspect of a marriage. They holidayed together, drove out together every day, dined together and visited friends and celebrities. For Irving, Stoker possibly filled the need for companionship after his bitter estrangement from his wife. For Irving's sake, Stoker ignored and neglected his own wife, also called Florence.* Also, because of Irving's demands, Stoker's son (christened Irving Noel Thornley, named after the idolised actor who was also his godfather) was deprived of his father's attention during his formative years.

Irving was said to be capable of exerting a messianic control over those close to him. Certainly Stoker appears to have been highly susceptible to Irving's demands. His working and personal relations with Irving aroused intense feelings, as is evident from his reminiscences of his friend and employer. Their relationship demonstrates the control which one man could exert over the other, particularly if his ego could be satisfied by the near-homoerotic adoration of his submissive partner. There may have been a homosexual undercurrent to their relationship, but any question of physical desire was possibly dispersed into the ambiguity of their feelings toward one another. Stoker wrote that he and Irving 'understood each other's nature, needs and ambitions, and had a mutual confidence, each toward the other in his own way, rare amongst men'.[98] His glowing and intense depiction of their friendship was published in the year after Irving's death. This adulatory biography is silent about the difficulties which Stoker and others at the Lyceum may have found when dealing with Irving's demanding personality.

Despite Stoker's relentless praise of their relationship, doubts remain. Was Stoker really content to be continually at Irving's beck and call? Furthermore, the relationship appears to have been almost entirely on

---

* formerly Florence Balcombe, she had been engaged to Oscar Wilde.

Irving's terms. The great actor's mockery of his friend and manager, especially over Stoker's support for home rule in Ireland, gives a disturbing aspect to their relationship, and Stoker was very sensitive to ridicule from Irving.[99] He also resented not being sufficiently rewarded for his continual efforts to please his friend and employer. Indeed, his novel *Dracula* has been viewed as a product of Stoker's resentment, subconscious or secret, at the way Irving drained the life from those surrounding him.[100] On the other hand, Irving had removed Stoker from a fairly humdrum life in Dublin. His association with Irving and the Lyceum allowed Stoker to meet celebrities of the day and be received by the highest levels of society. Being employed by Irving gave him the security and protection that he desired.

The relations between Irving, Toole and Stoker form a triangle of close male bonding, with Irving, as he was in all else, the central pivot. Bram Stoker, despite his possible homoerotic obsession with Irving, does not appear to have been jealous of Toole. He dedicated his biography of Irving to him and in the book describes his own close relations with Irving's life-long friend. Both Stoker and Toole were capable of a high degree of emotion and theatricality in their adoration of Irving: examples include Stoker's hysteria after the reading of *Eugene Aram* and Toole's melodramatic reaction to news of Irving's death. Irving performs the role of catalyst for the devotion of his two friends.

Homosexuality among actors

Close platonic friendship raises questions regarding the concealment of homosexual desire. But what of the Victorian actor who was homosexual? Havelock Ellis maintained that together with the artist, the singer and the painter, the actor was 'more exposed to influences out of which sexual differentiation in an abnormal direction may arise'. While there were those 'who were certainly made abnormal by nature, others, out of this sympathetic artistic temperament, may become so through their sympathies plus their condition of life'.[101] As we have already seen, there was a close affinity between deviant lifestyles and the sense of liberation offered by the theatre.

Despite the promulgation of a resolutely heterosexual image, homosexuality appears to have been fairly widespread among male performers. However, the indulgence of same-sex desire among actors, especially those of immense popularity, would have been especially problematic. The need to maintain a respectable image, along with the likelihood of arrest, prosecution or blackmail, is a major contribution to the silence that surrounds 'inversion' among nineteenth-century British theatrical performers. Furthermore homosexuality was condemned by society at large, as it transgressed middle-class ideologies regarding the healthy male body and sanitised mind. Nevertheless there was a good deal of speculation regarding theatrical performers. Around 1850, *The Yokel's Preceptor* remarked on the presence in the theatrical profession of 'many fellows' who followed 'beastly pursuits' but 'who have yet been considered respectable members of society'.[102] It threatens to 'mention the names of several', but 'out of compassion only' will withhold them. *The Yokel's Preceptor* uses quasi-Biblical terms such as 'beastly' and 'abominable' to sensationalise same-sex desire. At the same time it invites speculation by its nodding winks toward unnamed actors and managers who it claims indulge in homosexual activities. This was at a time when sodomy was still on the statute books as a hanging offence.*

It seems that, despite anxieties over punishment and exposure, same-sex desire continued to be part of British theatrical life throughout the nineteenth century. In the 1890s Havelock Ellis wrote that one of his correspondents 'had long been struck by the frequency of inversion among actors and actresses'. He even claimed to know 'an inverted actor' who had gone on the stage because it would enable him to indulge his 'proclivity'.[103] In some nineteenth and early twentieth-century writings on 'margeries', 'inverts' and 'Uranians' there are tantalising references to homosexual actors. Their anonymity avoids action for libel and supposedly protects reputations. For instance, Xavier Mayne, in *The Intersexes* (1908), claims that many of the *fin-de-siècle* matinée idols so admired by women had leanings toward homosexuality. These include 'a dozen stars of the English stage' particularly 'one of an unusual popularity and beauty'.[104] These comments appear in a privately printed work, intended for a small, specialised readership.

---

* The penalty was reduced to life imprisonment by the Offences against the Person Act 1861. —*Ed.*

For actors who may have been 'inverts', the vagaries of British law and the need for self-preservation meant that evidence had to be well hidden. Among the trades and professions of men prosecuted for male-to-male sex, named in police records and press columns throughout the Victorian period, actors and stage performers are conspicuously absent. No actor was implicated in the two major homosexual scandals of the late nineteenth century—the Cleveland Street affair and the Oscar Wilde case. H. G. Cocks, in his study of nineteenth-century British homosexuality, *Nameless Offences*, has only one doubtful 'actor' listed in his table of cases of offences reported in the press from 1800 to 1900.[105]

Evidence of prosecutions of male stage performers for indecency during the Victorian era is virtually non-existent. This suggests that members of the theatrical profession who may have indulged in homosexual activities proceeded with extreme caution. Their proclivities seem to have been contained within the boundaries of an enclosed backstage world. Also it was not unusual for those arrested for indecency to give a false name and profession.[106]

Throughout the nineteenth century, a number of areas in London and other major British cities were known as gathering places for homosexuals. These included male brothels, parks, pubs, railway stations, Turkish baths and 'iron lung' urinals.* Stage performers frequenting these venues would have mingled and cruised with other men from the world outside the theatre—from every class, trade and profession.

For an actor to be seen in such notorious places there was always the problem of recognition. He was usually well known in the community and easily recognisable from stage appearances or from photographs. As with other sexual misdemeanours, such as an extra-marital affair, discovery for a major actor could spell the loss of reputation and the ruin of a career. An actor who was homosexual would therefore have inhabited two worlds on the outer edge of Victorian society—the contained, but extrovert sphere of the theatre as well as the hidden world

---

* The circular cast iron urinal outside the Connaught Tavern in the East End was referred to locally as 'the iron lung'. The urinal was Victorian but the nickname presumably dates from after the widespread use of 'iron lung' respirators to treat polio patients in the 1920s. —*Ed.*

of the 'invert'. If he was married, he was part of another world—that of the home and family. He would have suffered not only the prejudices against his profession, but the stigmas attached to being an 'invert'. For the homosexually inclined actor, it would have been vital to maintain a cover of masculine and domestic conformity. It was also claimed that some matinée idols cultivated 'a wide female worship for advertising or social convenience'.[107] As it was, suspicion over the morality of theatrical performers was a major concern throughout the nineteenth century. It is also likely that members of the enclosed theatrical profession protected one another when the dangers of exposure for homosexual conduct were imminent.

The silence or innuendo surrounding homosexuality extends to moral warnings and guidelines for aspiring young actors. Young women intending to go on the stage are repeatedly warned of moral dangers, while for young men about to become actors, the subject of homosexuality is not specifically mentioned. The ineffability of same-sex desire meant that its presence could only be hinted at in coded terms. There are warnings about dissolute groups providing moral temptations for young actors but the aspirant is left to draw his own conclusions. For instance, the tract *Tempted London* (1888) speaks of 'the highly objectionable people' with whom a novice performer was likely to come into contact, the 'looseness' of backstage conversation, as well as 'the impertinence of managers'. These combine to hedge a theatrical career round with 'dangers both for man and woman'.[108] The suppression of any discussion of homosexuality resulted in ignorance of the subject and veiled hints. Behind moralistic warnings lay the assumption of the homosexual corruption of young male actors by older performers, managers or even admirers from the audience. This would have posed as great a moral danger for the male aspirant as the equally widespread notion of the seduction of the novice actress by the theatre manager.

Male transvestism on the stage

While a homosexual presence remained fairly well hidden, other male gender alternatives, such as effeminacy and cross-dressing, were blatant on the Victorian stage. While there were aspects of the work of an actor that could be perceived as veering toward the 'unmanly', his public persona did not usually cross the binary divide into overt effeminacy. The concept of effeminacy, or 'unmanly' behaviour, was relevant to performers such as male ballet dancers, chorus boys and female impersonators.

The journalist George Augustus Sala claimed never to see a male ballet dancer 'without feeling a burning desire not only to hiss, but to throw something hard and hurtful at the befrilled, belaced, berouged, besilk-tighted creature'.[109] The male dancer with his frilly costume, make-up and feminine-seeming movements presented an extreme alternative to rigid masculine ideology. He reached toward the outer edge of male theatricality where the social definitions of masculinity and femininity merged together. The androgynous presence of the male dancer on stage was confusing and disturbing to the heterosexual male. From around the 1870s, maligned male ballet dancers in leading roles were replaced, in theatres such as the Alhambra, by female performers appearing *en travesti*.[110] Apart from an occasional foreign import, principal men in British ballet were relegated to mime and character roles.

The backstage life of the chorus boy or ballet boy probably paralleled that of the lesbian ballet girl as described in 'a note from a friend' addressed to Havelock Ellis. Girls 'cooped up' together in crowded dressing rooms in a state of inaction and excitement with 'a wait of perhaps two hours between the performances,' are given every opportunity for the expression of lesbian sentiments. In most of the theatres there is 'a little circle of girls, somewhat avoided by the others ... who profess the most unbounded devotion to one another'. Certain girls are never seen without their particular 'pal' or 'chum', who 'if she gets moved to another theatre, will come round and wait for her friend at the stage-door'.[111] While they may have encountered social stigma, queer nineteenth-century women did not have to face being sentenced to hard labour for indulging their proclivities. For this reason, there appears to have been a more sheltered queer space for men in the theatre.

Like their female counterparts, ballet boys or male choristers were crowded together in the intimate proximity of the dressing room. Together they dressed and undressed, put on wigs and make-up, and shared in gossip. It was a milieu that positively encouraged queer behaviour. While there may have been amorous relationships between young men in the theatre, there was more likely to have been a high rate of male prostitution, which was 'by no means rare among the more mercenary adonises of the theatre. ... Young actors often profit by the passions of rich male adorers.'[112] An attractive low-paid ballet or chorus boy was as vulnerable as the female performer. In exchange for his body, he could easily accept money, gifts or promises of career advancement from the higher-paid actor, manager or wealthy man in the audience.

It is paradoxical that, while androgynous ballet boys provoked hostility, men wearing women's clothes were popular in circuses, burlesques and in the music hall. Male cross-dressing was quite widespread on the Victorian stage. In all-male student and college productions young men dressed up and played women's roles. Boulton and Park toured around giving semi-amateur performances, appearing as 'actresses'. In the professional theatre the cross-dressed actor was accepted as a non-threatening figure of fun. Played by actors who were to all intents and purposes heterosexual, comic versions of mature, dominant women were staples of pantomime, farce, and burlesque. Pantomime dames were comic travesties of women dominant in the family hierarchy such as the mother, the stepmother, the mother-in-law, the aunt, or the ugly sister. There was however a binary divide between the down-to-earth pantomime dame and the female impersonator who was usually a parody of the fashionable woman, exaggerating her feminine foibles to comic and even grotesque proportions.

While men could be mocked or prosecuted for going about in public dressed as women, on the stage they won considerable acclaim. Boulton and Park, for instance, were thrown out of the Alhambra for behaving like women, while performing as 'actresses' they were applauded and admired.[113] The men who dressed as women belonged to a sphere that was on the perimeters of Victorian society. But the theatre, with its affinities to alternative life-styles, offered protection to the cross-dressed male performer. During a time of repression, dressing as a woman allowed for a form of self-expression on the stage. A male performer in women's clothes did not threaten normative male sexuality in the same way as the androgynous dancing boy. A male actor dressed as a glamorous woman who sang comic songs and appeared in comic plays was, for most of the public, an object of mirth. However, if he was attractive with a convincing female disguise, he could, like Boulton and Park, attract male admirers from the audience and be the recipient of gifts and favours.

Female impersonators mainly appeared in popular forms of entertainment—the burlesque, the circus and the music hall. Their theatricality, combined with a desire for self-display, made many of them extremely skilful actors, dancers, singers or trapeze artists. Many of these performers were extremely versatile. For instance, during the 1870s Henri de Melvin was billed as 'the Wonderful Baritone, the Wonderful Soprano, the London Star'. He won wide acclaim singing duets with himself, in two different ranges (soprano and baritone) while dressed as a woman. In 1872 *The Era* commented that neither by 'word, look or gesture' did he overstep 'the bounds of propriety'.[114]

In the circus, the female guise of male trapeze artists benefited from a homosexual undercurrent. Admiration for the muscular masculine form and professional reliance on one another's strength and skill made most trapeze artists scornful of women—they sought sentimental attachments among other male performers. A man dressed as a woman was preferable to a female as a member of their troupe.[115]

Renowned among cross-dressed trapeze artists was 'El Niño Farini' who appeared, aged sixteen, as 'M'lle Lulu' at the Royal Holborn Empire and Circus in 1871. Purporting to be a 'great Female Gymnast' he sang a song with the refrain 'Wait till I'm a man' while descending from trapezes and ladders.[116] His astonishing feats made him 'the eighth wonder of the world'. The theatre manager John Hollingshead remembered his appearance as that of 'a well made-up girl who went through some clever catapultic gymnastics'.[117] Photographs show Farini as an androgynous youth, looking very like a slim young girl, with long blonde ringlets falling over slender shoulders.[118] 'Lulu' had been a boy with the Flying Farinis acrobatic troupe and kept up his gender deception for years. He was fêted throughout Europe and America. His true male identity was revealed when he was 25 and an injury required a doctor's examination. This caused considerable embarrassment to 'royalty, commoners, peers and plebeians' as well as to the many men who had sent him love letters. Nevertheless El Niño Farini continued to perform in woman's dress even after his true gender was discovered. According to Hollingshead, 'when the proper time came' he 'resumed his manly character' and retired from the stage 'to go into business'.[119] Eventually he grew a beard and moustache and married a relative of his stepfather.

Figure 34. El Niño Farini as 'Lulu'

Impersonating a woman in the circus or on the stage involved a degree of public deception. In the case of 'El Niño Farini' this imposture becomes further involved with the invention of a stage persona. His utterly convincing female appearance creates the belief that 'El Niño Farini' is a young woman. At the same time a further deception is being perpetrated. 'El Niño Farini' is not really of 'exotic' Spanish origin as his name would suggest, but is actually Samuel Wasgate, born in Maine, USA in the 1850s, the adopted son of the Great Farini, the renowned tight rope walker and leader of the troupe—also born in America. Cross-dressed as Lulu, 'El Niño Farini' is hardly ever seen away from the stage. He speaks only to his stepfather who accepts gifts from admirers on his behalf. 'El Niño Farini' (aka 'M'lle Lulu') creates confusion by deceiving over his origins as well as over his gender. This double deception defies the masculine virtues of honesty and openness. It equates 'El Niño Farini' with notions of female duplicity. His traversal of the binaries between masculine and feminine brings into question the extent to which his male admirers were actually deceived over his gender. As with the Boulton and Park case, how many of the love letters come from those who are aware that this is a young man 'personating' a woman? This brings into question the desires of men in the audience: do they fall for the image of a young woman, or for a girlish male body decked out in feminine accoutrements? In other words, what is the true orientation of the numbers of men who attend performances by 'M'lle Lulu' and other cross-dressed entertainers?

The gender deception practiced by the stage 'personators' of women brings the male performer into areas normally reserved for femininity. It also reveals the Victorian theatre as being a space for alternative interpretations of sexuality. A convincing female appearance which could often be mistaken for that of a 'real' woman, complete with elaborate gowns, wigs, feminised gestures and vocal patterns, not only traversed gender divisions, it complicated the hegemonic masculine dominance of the theatrical sphere. Most actors assiduously avoided any hint of effeminacy that would bring a maligned profession into further disrepute. At the same time, a minority of male performers courted popularity by appearing on stage dressed as women. Yet they remained an offshoot of the predominant masculine structure. Meanwhile, for 'real' women who entered the male dominated theatrical sphere, there were complexities to be encountered that were related to the divisions between genders.

Men versus women on the stage

The extent of the equality between the sexes in the nineteenth-century theatre has often been debated, particularly by twentieth-century theatre historians. For instance, in 1978, Michael Baker exclaimed that the Victorian actress achieved a position 'unique to her sex. ... In no other trade or profession were women treated on such favourable terms in relation to their male colleagues.'[120] While this is true to a certain extent, there were some areas into which the actress could not intrude. Gender differences meant that she could not compete with him for the same roles—although there were several cross-dressed female interpretations of Hamlet; nor was it unusual for child actresses to perform leading Shakespearean male roles.*

However an actress did not pose the same threat to a star actor as an up-and-coming male 'juvenile' filled with ambition. Respectable actresses did not go to the bars and clubs where male actors gathered for convivial drinking and to exchange news of engagements. When on tour, there was strict separation of the sexes. Male and female performers occupied separate railway carriages. On reaching their destination, unmarried men and women had segregated accommodation: 'It was an unwritten, but perfectly understood law that no single gentleman ever occupied apartments in a house in which any single lady of the company was located.'[121]

While not always equal, male and female performers shared the vicissitudes of theatrical life. Actors and actresses generally earned the same amount of money, although in subordinate areas, such as the chorus, women earned less than men. Both sexes enjoyed the triumphs of a successful performance, as well as suffering the disappointments of failure. As aspirants, both faced the dangers of becoming prey to bogus agents and managers. They equally endured long and hopeful waiting in agents' offices.

Nor did appalling backstage conditions spare either sex. While theatres provided a glamorous façade for audiences, actors and actresses endured dirt, dinginess, damp and draughts. For both sexes there was the danger of catching pulmonary diseases from insanitary dressing rooms. On the stage, they were forced to perform in a gas-tainted or 'otherwise vitiated' atmosphere which could affect their vocal powers.[122]

---

* For example, fifteen-year-old Ellen Bateman appeared as Richard III at the St James's Theatre on 25 August 1851. See Varty 2008: 81.

While the actress appeared to be equal with the actor in many respects, there were ways in which her male colleagues attempted to keep her under their control. Managers of stock companies provided some costumes for actors, but there was no provision for the actress. With a far more extensive wardrobe, she had to pay for additional costumes out of her own pocket. As Daisy Halling and Charles Lister pointed out in 1908, this practice made her so-called 'equal' wage 'convertible'.[123] An actor did not have the additional expenditure of a whole wardrobe, although he had to provide his own make-up and certain items such as 'boots, shoes, buckles, silk stockings, hats, feathers, swords, canes, wigs, modern dress, long hose, gloves, military costume'.[124]

The economic divide between the sexes was made worse by the notion that actresses tended to have shorter careers than actors: they mostly retired 'when they have lost their youth and looks',[125] although quite a number of actresses continued to appear on stage well into old age. Male actors were supposed to be able to continue their careers and perform important roles well into their mature years.[126] The disparity between male and female performers is also apparent in the fact that there were fewer opportunities for actresses on the Victorian stage. Cast lists reveal a preponderance of roles for men while there are usually far fewer female characters. For instance, the popular melodrama, *The Ticket-of-Leave Man* by Tom Taylor (1863) has eight male speaking roles and four female, one of which is a boy role, played *en travesti*. Meanwhile on the musical stage, numbers of women appeared in the choruses and corps de ballet of extravaganzas, burlesques, pantomimes and musical comedy for the enjoyment of men in the audience.

The attempted exertion of power by the actor-manager over his leading lady has been well documented. Very often it was difficult for an actress to assert herself when performing with a dominant and 'despotic' male co-star. Helen Faucit, acting with Macready at the Theatre Royal, Covent Garden in the 1830s, found him 'merciless to feelings'.[127] She maintained that his 'strong masculine mind had in it but little of the feminine element. ... Any remonstrance or objection was met by reasons or arguments so broad and strong—you were earnestly reminded of your duty to sacrifice yourself to the general good and furtherance of the effort he was making to regenerate the drama.'[128]

Figure 35. William Charles Macready as Henry IV

Macready worked his actors hard because he wanted to invigorate the stage by ridding it of ingrained conventions. He aimed for a unity of style that was usually absent from early-nineteenth-century staging. Emphasis was placed on the ensemble, and in order to create a unified company it was necessary to become a despot. Macready therefore stage-managed his productions on militaristic lines, referring to it as 'drilling' the players, constantly correcting his company over interpretation, speech and acting.[129] Faucit found his militaristic approach made him 'always somewhat too anxious' to give 'direction' to his leading lady, while her tendency to undervalue herself made her 'yield more than was for [her] good'. She also maintained that Macready took exception to everything that she did which was 'not in accordance with his own notions'.[130] Although his treatment of her seemed calculated to crush any individuality, he could not entirely make her surrender her own conception of any character she was called upon to play.[131]

Macready was well aware of Faucit's talent. His seemingly harsh treatment was aimed at honing the technique of a highly promising actress. He gave her encouragement and was concerned about her career. He hoped that he 'may yet be able to advance her in her profession, and to see her happy and respected'.[132] Despite the problems of their working relationship, Faucit and Macready remained friends until the end of his life.

Faucit managed to outrival the dominance of a powerful actor-manager, but it could be argued that many women with stage careers deliberately maintained the subservient status expected of Victorian womanhood. This appears to have been the case with Ellen Terry, arguably the greatest actress of her generation, and her relations with Henry Irving. Terry overcame the inconsistencies of her private life—three marriages and a liaison with the married architect E. W. Godwin—to become the stage epitome of the Victorian feminine ideal. With her notions of an idealised womanhood, she appeared willing to accept her place as being subservient to Irving. She considered it her 'duty' to obey Irving's orders even if she privately disagreed with them.[133]

Whether Irving deliberately tried to ensure that Terry could never be his equal on the stage is a subject for debate. Their partnership at the Lyceum was immensely popular—it lasted for twenty-five years, from 1878 until 1903. But, as Jeffrey Richards has argued, differences in their acting styles, rather than gender issues, could have been a contributing factor in the subjugation of Terry.[134] It was difficult for her to develop her range and technique when the idiosyncrasies of Irving's performance style had to be considered. Her admired performance as Beatrice in *Much Ado About Nothing* was subjected to Irving's 'rather finicky deliberate method' as Benedick. Although she could never find the 'right pace', she dared not contradict her male star partner.[135] Irving's acting was sacrosanct and there does not appear to have been any allowance for discussion of differences in stage technique.

The other difficulty for Terry in the Lyceum productions was the necessity of finding suitable roles for Irving. This was often done at her expense, and as is well known, was the reason she never played Rosalind in *As You Like It*. Irving always had to be the central focus—there was no part in *As You Like It* (not even Touchstone) that gave him this opportunity. Consequently Terry did not appear in a role for which she would have been ideal: she had been hindered because there was nothing in the play considered to be of sufficient stature for Irving. The obstructions placed on Terry's career by the actor-manager system infuriated George Bernard Shaw. He saw Terry playing second fiddle to Irving, and thought her career at the Lyceum was 'a heartless waste of an exquisite talent'.[136]

Figure 36. Dame Ellen Terry in 1886

Terry's relationship with Irving exemplifies the problems of nineteenth-century female dependence on men. But could she have left Irving's company and, like Helen Faucit, found her opportunity elsewhere? While she was at the Lyceum, Terry was almost totally dependent on the influence of Irving. He gave her a living at a time when she had to support herself and her two children. Being employed at his theatre gave her freedom from financial insecurity. So far as Irving was concerned, their joint appearances increased the profits of his theatre. Off the stage, she was useful to him as a mediator between himself and his company, his audiences and his sons. She acted as a hostess to celebrities and personal friends visiting Irving.[137] On occasion, she advised on 'pictorial matters' such as design, costume, lighting and casting.[138] There is also the much-debated question as to whether Irving and Terry were lovers.[139]

These two examples of actor/actress relationships refute the notion of equality between men and women on the nineteenth-century British stage. The advancement of the actress was, to a great extent, dependent on the demands of the actor-manager system. It gave her many opportunities and could propel her to a celebrity status, but could also bring disappointment, and she often had to fight hard to maintain her ideas and position in a masculinised sphere. She was caught in a system that placed greater emphasis on masculine charisma. Surrounded by public adoration, the actor-manager had his position to consider. He always had to be the central focus. An equally popular co-starring actress was financially useful, but the actor-manager usually took care that she did not overshadow his performance. Some actresses, such as Ellen Terry, seemed to accept this subservience to male domination, while earning approbation in the roles the actor-managerial system allowed them to play. Others, like Helen Faucit, battled to maintain their position against male dominance.

Husbands and wives in the Victorian theatre

Almost all nineteenth-century actors had wives and families. It was essential for a successful actor to present an image which conformed to the bourgeois norms of home and family, even if the demands of theatrical employment prevented the stability of a settled family life. Leading actors were constantly portrayed as family men in biographies, newspapers and journals. An optimistic picture of their family life was painted, with a happy home, a supportive wife and adoring children.

Families were important in the administration of the Victorian theatre, and family companies were a familiar sight as they toured throughout the British Isles. The family name was often used to proclaim these itinerant theatre troupes. As the actor Jerome K. Jerome* noted, 'They had, some of them, been born in the company and had been married in the company

---

* Better known as the author of *Three Men in a Boat*. —Ed.

and they hoped to die in the company.'[140] Family touring companies became associated over several generations with a specific circuit. Some troupes even managed to achieve a status of respectability within local communities, transcending the stigma attached to strolling players: 'They took an interest in the towns and the towns took an interest in them and came to their benefits* Even the lodgings which family troupes returned to again and again were considered a home 'or as near to a home as a country player could ever expect to get'.[141] These close family ties contributed to a strong sense of solidarity.

Because of the unconventional requirements of a theatrical career, marriages among actors tended to depart from the bourgeois tradition of the *paterfamilias* returning from a day's work to his waiting wife and family. Many wives in the theatre did not remain at home. They were often employed alongside their husbands—as actresses or in the co-management of theatres. For the husband and wife who rehearsed together by day and performed by night in a stock company, it was almost impossible to conform to a conventional family life. The result was that theatrical marriage provided an alternative to normative bourgeois marital patterns. It was one reason why intermarriage between those employed in the theatre was far more common than marriages between the staff of other trades or professions. An actor marrying outside the community was an exception—the pressures on such a marriage with the odd hours, travel and other conditions of theatrical life would have been very great.

Keeping marital life within the boundaries of the theatrical world also resulted in the prominence of husband and wife partnerships. Most of these were long lasting, and in this respect at least, conformed to middle-class expectations. Divorce was rare among stage couples, mainly because it carried a stigma that could be detrimental to the reputations of prominent actor-managers. Well-known stage couples almost invariably presented an image of complete devotion to their public, while in biographies and articles they were shown to be exemplary examples of wives and husbands. Marital difficulties or other family problems were discreetly hidden away from public view.

---

* Special performances to raise funds for the benefit of particular actors. —*Ed.*

Husband and wife managerial and acting teams such as the Keans, the Bancrofts and the Kendals worked hard to promote images of bourgeois marital respectability. Charles and Ellen Kean were extolled as an example of an ideal theatrical marriage. They married in 1842, and remained together for twenty-six years, until Charles Kean died in 1868. He referred to his wife as a 'solace in the hour of trouble and counsellor in the hour of need'.

Figure 37. Charles and Ellen Kean in *Macbeth*

Ellen may have given an appearance of subservience, but she was a dominant force in their union, considered his equal in the running of the Princess's Theatre. According to Charles Kean's adulatory biographer, John William Cole (who was also a member of his company): 'It has seldom happened that an actor of Mr Charles Kean's celebrity has been supported by a partner equal in ability to himself. This rare union gives them an exclusive advantage.'[142] Ellen Terry, who acted in their company as a child, remembered Ellen Kean as being equal to her husband: 'joint ruler' of the Princess's Theatre and 'not a queen consort'.[143] Clement Scott, on the other hand, described Ellen Kean as never being made unduly prominent 'though she was a capable actress by her husband's side'.[144] Publicly at least, she was at the service of her husband, tirelessly supporting him and promoting his interests.

Ellen Kean was certainly a tireless worker. As a wife and mother she was a source of solace and support. Behind the scenes she had to deal with a man who was extremely sensitive, quarrelsome and insecure.[145] His rigid exterior concealed a multitude of anxieties including the burden of a famous father,* physical and emotional weakness, self-pity and a continual demand for attention.[146] Nor did he conform to the physical ideal of a heroic actor. He 'laboured under the disadvantages of a small insignificant person, a voice unmusical and harsh in sound, and sometimes entirely unmanageable'.[147] His basic insecurity caused Charles Kean to be extremely vain, to imagine rivalries, pick quarrels, and make enemies of friends.[148] Ellen helped to smooth over these difficulties. As a talented actress, she partnered her husband, playing leading roles in his Shakespearean revivals at the Princess's. Backstage, she superintended the wardrobe—an enormous task, as 'no less than five hundred dresses have to be designed and arranged for the Shakespearean plays'.[149] She also performed duties usually assigned to the male stage-manager—such as sorting out problems at rehearsals, or instructing actors.[150]

Kean tended to view his energetic wife in masculine terms. He praised her as his aide-de-camp, and 'never had a commander one more able and indefatigable'.[151] In his production of *Henry V* in 1859, he went even further by assigning her the role of the Chorus. The gender of this role is not specified in the play, but it was traditionally played by a male actor dressed as 'Time'. Mrs Kean opened the play in female costume, as Clio 'the Muse of History'. She wore an 'ancient Greek' *chiton* but destroyed her husband's concern for historical accuracy by insisting on wearing her crinoline underneath it.† Kean's experiment in replacing the traditionally

---

* See page 140. —*Ed.*

† Mid-Victorian actresses did not usually perform in historic costume, whatever the period, without the modesty of wearing a crinoline. [See Figure 37. —*Ed.*] This could be viewed as a feminine stance against masculine domination in the theatre.

male Chorus by a female figure was generally considered a failure. The *Literary Gazette* called it 'a palpable mistake'.[152] Kean was viewed as violating Shakespeare's intentions—he had turned his wife into a vulgar attraction and underestimated the sensibilities of the audience.[153] For all this, Ellen remained a devoted wife, with seemingly inexhaustible energy.

Unusually for a period in which large families were the norm, the Keans had only one child—a daughter named Mary, to whom Charles wrote long letters during their American tour in 1859. In common with many other Victorian patriarchs, Kean also had a ward, Patty Chapman, who was Ellen's niece. She was also an actress and accompanied the Keans on their final American tour playing ingénue roles.*

Charles and Ellen Kean's paternal and maternal instincts extended to their concern for the welfare of their company at the Princess's. According to John Cole, they showed an 'almost domestic and affectionate care' for their employees. They watched over 'their morality and their happiness' and 'attended to their health'. The Keans made the Princess's 'more like a great domestic establishment than a public institution'.[154]

This caring attitude is likely to have concealed concerns over economic and financial viability. Actors in poor health or with domestic problems could prove a drain on financial resources. A strong and healthy company performed well, enhanced the reputation of the theatre, and drew large audiences. Victorian theatrical companies could became the equivalent of extended families, with the managers and their wives attending to the needs of their employees as if they were their own children. An organisation run like a family unit gave actors and actresses a sense of solidarity, especially at a time when their status was uncertain. This managerial concern for actors' welfare did not, however, extend to all theatre companies. There were many instances of demoralised players, overworked and underpaid, performing in atrocious conditions.

The support of an indefatigable wife, such as Ellen Kean, was necessary for the actor-manager. Assistance was needed for an onerous workload which involved not only performing, but also the overseeing of

---

* John Ripley's article ' "We are not in little England now" (Ripley 2007) is concerned with Charles Kean's correspondence regarding his American tour.

productions and the day-to-day running of the building. Several theatrical wives assisted their husbands as co-managers of theatres. Occasionally, like Sarah Lane at the Britannia in Hoxton, a wife became sole manager on the death of her spouse. The duties of the so-called 'actress-manageress' gave a wife near-equal status with her husband. Theatre management, like acting, was one of the few areas where a woman could work with men and assert herself, just as other nineteenth-century women assisted their husbands in the management of small businesses, shops or cotton mills.

Theatre management was also an area where husbands could find themselves under the domination of wives. The position of co-owner or manager gave them an opportunity to exert control over their husbands, even if it was away from public gaze. Stage partnerships therefore allowed wives an authority denied to women in other spheres. For instance, Leonora, the wife of the actor-manager Alfred Wigan, appears to have exerted considerable power over her husband. They both acted with Charles and Ellen Kean at the Princess's, as well as managing the Olympic and various other London theatres. Leonora Wigan was, according to John Coleman, 'a very clever helpmate ... a very pushy, sagacious, active, indefatigable woman'.[155] A great deal of Alfred Wigan's success as an actor was due to her subtle influences. She made him believe that he was acting 'of his own volition when in point of fact he was carrying out her wishes'.[156] Like other theatre wives it was also her support, 'care, energy and taste' which helped to advance his success, especially his highly popular management of the Olympic Theatre from 1848 to 1849.[157]

However great their influence behind the scenes, and however much they tried to exert their independence, wives in theatrical partnerships were viewed as 'partners' or 'helpers' to husbands who held administrative and managerial charge. Women in theatre management, as in other spheres of business, were restricted by masculine domination. A woman could lease a theatre, but she could not own it. It was often difficult for her to raise capital. Nor was she welcome in the pubs and clubs where men could make business contacts. For women, even in partnership with husbands, the responsibilities of theatre management would have proved very difficult.

Marie Wilton (later Lady Bancroft), like many of her male counterparts, found the work 'very hard' when she took over management of the Prince of Wales's in 1865: 'Day after day I was in the theatre from ten in the morning until late at night, eating when I could, for I had rehearsals to attend, to direct the dresses for the new burlesque ... to look after the painters and decorators, and to study my own part.'[158]

Figure 38. Marie Effie Bancroft (née Wilton)

A woman managing a theatre on her own needed masculine attributes, such as drive and determination to be successful. Although she may have been restricted in the commercial and financial dealings of the business, an 'actress-manageress' could exert power through giving advice and guidance, or by introducing improvements to the theatres which they managed with their husbands.

The surrender of the independence of a female manager once she was married is evident in the 'joint' biography of Squire and Marie Bancroft.

From the time of their marriage in 1867, Squire Bancroft takes over the narrative, reducing his wife to a subordinate position. Yet before they married, Marie Wilton had single-handedly introduced radical changes to Victorian theatre practice when she ran the Prince of Wales's Theatre (albeit in partnership with the dramatist H. J. Byron). The innovations that she introduced to the theatre she managed have been well documented, and her intuitive economic abilities must have been of inestimable value to her husband. Squire Bancroft may have been an actor of limited range, but he was 'a sound practical business man'.[159] Marie Bancroft was undoubtedly a more versatile performer and had an intuitive business sense. The combination of their acting and managerial skills created a formidable team.

Yet in their much-vaunted partnership there is an indication of a struggle for supremacy on both sides. In their biography, Squire Bancroft, while praising his wife as a partner, writes of her 'self-abnegation' to his management policies and her 'perfect confidence' in his judgment.[160] There are, however, suggestions of dissent between them. He claims that she accepted his opinion 'in nearly all important matters, even when ... it chanced to be at variance with her own'.[161] She was also nervous about his scheme to abolish the pit at the Haymarket: 'more than once she asked if even a little tiny pit were possible.'[162]

Bancroft seems to mock his wife by giving her request a child-like tone, while he, who knows better, goes ahead with his plan. As it happened, Marie's fears were well founded. On the opening night of their management of the Haymarket in 1879, the removal of the pit caused disruptive and rowdy protests in the theatre from the 'pittites' who had been forced to vacate the area to make way for more expensive stalls seats. Bancroft gives himself credit for the other innovations he made at the Haymarket—the picture frame stage and hidden footlights. According to him, Mrs Bancroft's sole contribution to the refurbishment of the theatre is 'ivory coloured satin curtains'.[163]

In public at least, women claimed deference to their husbands. A case in point is the other notable theatrical marriage of the late nineteenth century—that between William and Madge Kendal. In her autobiography, Madge wrote: 'My husband was never my leading man, I was always his leading lady.'[164] She promotes herself as a subordinate and dutiful wife in their stage partnership, and carefully explains that 'Until we retired, I always drew a strong line between my position as his wife and that of a member of the company.' For this reason she 'never went into the theatre through the front of house but by the stage door, like every other actress'.[165]

Figure 39. William and Madge Kendal in
W. S. Gilbert's *Pygmalion and Galatea*, 1872

A highly talented actress, who was not afraid to openly express her opinions, seemingly places herself in a subordinate position to the husband who partnered her on stage and with whom she shared in the management of theatres. Yet, for all her professed subservience, she was a formidable power behind the scenes. As an actor, William could not match her abilities. Performing together in a series of comedies and melodramas, he was usually a foil to her talents. He had a gift for light comedy, but tended to be stilted in more serious roles. Like his contemporary Squire Bancroft, William Kendal's real abilities were in theatre management. In this sphere he had his wife's support and encouragement. Both he and Madge, in conjunction with John Hare, successfully ran the St James's Theatre from 1879 to 1888.

The actor Seymour Hicks, who appeared with their company, found William Kendal to be 'a man of peculiarly imperturbable temper', a kind-hearted man who, nevertheless, was difficult to know and 'kept himself very much aloof from the members of the profession'. This was in contrast to his lively wife who 'took an interest in everyone ... even in their most intimate private affairs'.[166] The Kendals made strenuous efforts to promote an image of bourgeois respectability, and, like the Bancrofts, were held up as a model couple in a profession which was striving to be socially acceptable.

Actors and fatherhood

Fatherhood for the Victorian actor posed similar problems to those of being a husband. The requirements of a theatrical career often made it difficult to comply with the accepted role of the *paterfamilias*. For many actors who were touring, managing theatres, rehearsing and performing, limited time could be devoted to their offspring. Actors higher up the scale, who could afford to maintain an affluent home life, attempted to conform to a normative patriarchy. But many male performers, particularly those in family-run stock companies, had children who also appeared on the stage. The Victorian stage was arguably the most prolific employer of child labour after industry. Like the factory, it was an area where parents and children could work together. Numbers of children performed in theatres as actors, dancers or acrobats, or were part of the backstage labour force.* For children who toured with a family as a troupe, there was very little opportunity for a settled home life and a full education.

Where children of actors were not employed in the theatre, but enjoyed a 'normal' childhood, they were not always immune from prejudice. Alfred Wigan, for instance, was 'outraged' when his children

---

* For children and the Victorian stage see also Varty 2008; Foulkes 2005; Davis, T. 1986.

were 'grossly insulted' at their school because he was an actor. He immediately removed them from the school and evidently 'administered a wholesome public flagellation' to the offenders.[167] An even greater difficulty for an actor raising a family was the danger of childhood illness and the frequency of infant mortality. Like other Victorian parents, performers were certainly not spared the grief of losing a son or daughter. The death of a beloved child could deeply affect the performances of an actor. William Macready dealt with his grief over the death of his daughter, by relating his feelings to Virginius mourning the loss of his daughter in James Sheridan Knowles's tragedy of that name. When playing the role in 1851, he moved audiences to tears at the expression of his inward grief. Macready had not only to deal with the deaths of each of his beloved children, but also the demise of his wife Catherine, through an hereditary consumptive illness.[168] Later in the century, Squire Bancroft wrote of his grief over the death of his infant son, George Pleydell Bancroft, born in 1868. The boy's death through a 'child-illness', 'interfered with' his duties as an actor.[169] (The feelings of Mrs Bancroft over this loss are not mentioned in their joint biography). Yet however great the 'interference' of grief, actors had to continue performing regardless of their innermost feelings. A public image had to be considered as well as the necessity to continue earning money.

William Kendal and his wife Madge experienced another form of loss when they became estranged from their children. Although in her biography Madge proclaimed a happy relationship between herself and William, their marriage was 'far from happy in respect of their five children'. The Irish playwright St John Ervine asserted that Madge Kendal's character was 'too firm ... for family affection to survive'.[170] Their eldest daughter, Margaret had to have her marriage annulled and she died at the age of twenty-one.[171] Madge Kendal claimed her husband's death in 1917 was caused by a broken heart and wounded pride over their children's behaviour. He was particularly upset by the conduct of their youngest daughter, Dorothy, who married against his wishes at a registry office, and subsequently divorced her husband. For a father who had made every effort to conform to Victorian respectability, marrying outside the church and then divorcing was disgraceful conduct. Although he and his wife had 'given up all hope of any sign of affection from our family' he did leave an annuity for their four surviving children.[172] But his paternal control over his children was thwarted, particularly as they did not conform to his standards of bourgeois respectability. After all, it was his strict maintenance of those standards which confirmed the acceptance of the Kendals in respectable society.

The desire for social acceptance and respectability among leading actors extended to a strict control over their children. For the sons of actors belonging to the theatrical elite, every effort was made to educate them as 'gentlemen' and prepare them for professional careers outside of the 'disreputable' world of the theatre. Some sons of actors were sent to public schools. William Macready's actor father sent him to Rugby. Charles Kean spent three years at Eton, before he was forced to leave due to the pecuniary difficulties of his erratic father, Edmund. Henry Irving did not have a public school education, but he educated his sons to be gentlemen and he wanted them to follow the professions of gentlemen: Henry Brodribb (Harry), the elder, to be a lawyer and Laurence, the younger, to be a diplomat. However being raised in a theatrical environment meant that offspring were likely to want to follow in their fathers' footsteps. It became a kind of tradition for the sons of actors to face patriarchal opposition when seeking a stage career. The middle-class practice of a son obediently following his father into the family firm was challenged in the environment of the theatre. While children of lower-scale players often appeared on stage with their parents, star actors tended to discourage their sons from entering the theatre. They did this for several reasons: they knew the hardships of a theatrical life; they had educated their sons to be 'gentlemen'; or they feared a talent that might outshine their own. Theatrical fathers had the same concerns as parents outside the theatre over their children taking up stage careers. Yet sons and daughters nearly always opposed their fathers in the matter of going on the stage.

For some sons of actors, going on stage was a matter of economic necessity. After his father had removed him from Eton, Charles Kean was given no financial assistance and he had to consider his own welfare.[173] He soon found that having a famous father created further difficulties for a son wanting to pursue the same career. Charles Kean had to come to terms with being the son of Edmund Kean, the idol of the early nineteenth-century stage. According to Westland Marston, he considered his father's fame a 'damaging legacy'—if it had not been for this he would have been accepted by the public 'twice as easily'. Early in his career he had to fight against being called an 'imitator' of his father.[174]

The case of Edmund and Charles Kean supports the idea that genius in the father is seldom passed to his son. George Henry Lewes considered that Charles Kean had been subject to 'overshadowing comparison' with his father. Like Edmund, Charles was endowed with great physical force. He had more personal discipline than his father and elaborated 'every scene to the utmost power'. But whereas Edmund was 'a master of passionate expression' his son was without 'subtlety or sympathy'. He was 'rigid' and 'stolid'; he had 'none of those unforgettable looks which made his father terrible to fellow-actors no less than to spectators'. His voice sounded harsh and rasping in contrast to his father's 'marvellously musical' lower range.[175] Charles Kean's real genius lay in theatre management and promoting his would-be educational, historically 'accurate' revivals of Shakespeare. These were areas in which his undisciplined father would probably not have excelled.

The problems besetting the offspring of a talented father are also evident in the careers of the two sons of Henry Irving. Like Charles Kean and William Macready, they defied their father's wishes by going on the stage. Apart from the fact that he wanted 'gentlemanly' careers for his sons, Irving also thought that his name would be a handicap in making a stage career.* Both sons had also to overcome the problems of being raised by their embittered mother, Florence. For most of their boyhood, she was separated from Irving and had a pathological hatred of him. She taught them to regard their famous and successful father with ridicule and contempt.[176]

As it was, neither son could be said to have inherited Henry Irving's mesmeric power or genius. Henry, calling himself H. B. Irving, formed his own company in 1906 and attempted to follow in his father's footsteps by playing his most famous roles. This was an almost

---

* In 1882, at the ages of 11 and 12, Harry and Laurence Irving appeared as Charles and Joseph Surface in a performance by children of the screen scene from Sheridan's *The School for Scandal* at Wellington Barracks. At least one 'discerning critic' was eager to note that the boys showed 'hereditary talent'. See Brereton 1908: I, 361.

impossible task, since he could hardly emulate the qualities that made his father unique as an actor. The artist W. Graham Robertson recalled that 'he followed his father as closely as possible and, aided by a strong personal resemblance, produced an exact copy up to a certain point. But all the wonder, the terror, the fascination of the original lay beyond that certain point.'[177] Those expecting to see a replica of his father's performances were disappointed. Hesketh Pearson claimed that, as Hamlet, he 'had no notion of the music of the verse, which he delivered in a drawling and meaningless monotone. ... If his name had not been Irving the critics might not have been so polite.'[178]

W. Graham Robertson wrote of the acting of Irving's younger son, Laurence, that 'He was awkward, ugly, stagy in the worst sense.'[179] But in the role of Earl Skule in Ibsen's *The Pretenders* at the Haymarket on 13 February 1913, he appeared to Robertson and Ellen Terry to be the image of his father. They 'could not recognise Laurence. Henry Irving was before us—with his mesmeric personality, his strange pale beauty, his atmosphere of romance and mystery'.[180] *The Times* critic seemed aware of Laurence's similarity to his father when he commented that he made 'a strange, moody, dreaming, thoroughly "soul sick" figure ... always fixing your attention'.[181] It would seem that Laurence had more successfully brought back memories of his father than his elder brother with his attempts to keep alive their father's repertoire. Irving, at Ellen Terry's instigation, also tried to encourage Laurence's talents as a playwright. Tragically, Laurence's career was cut short when he was drowned with his wife in a shipwreck when sailing home from Canada in 1913. Neither H. B. nor Laurence Irving qualified for entries in the *Dictionary of National Biography*, as did their father.[182] Whatever their failures or their successes, the sons of Henry Irving remained in the shadow of their late father's talent.

It is paradoxical that Irving, the first actor to be knighted and promoter of the social status of the actor, did not adhere to the marital ideal. He had deserted his wife, Florence in 1871, after she mocked his performance in *The Bells*. He never spoke to her or met with her again. They never divorced, but there was a legal separation. A divorce would have compromised not only Irving's career, but also his life-long commitment to promote the respectability of the actor. Irving continued to support his estranged wife and their sons for the rest of his life.[183] Despite this marital non-conformity, Irving achieved his aim in reaching the heights of respectability and social acceptance.

Social acceptance: the actor as a 'gentleman'

Irving was exceptional. For most actors reaching a higher social rank was precarious. If he was to succeed, it was essential to adhere to the ideal of the successful, self-made man. He had to avoid any hint of scandal—or at least to keep up the appearance of marital fidelity. Despite the non-conformist pattern of theatrical life, he was obliged to cultivate middle-class respectability. This meant he had also to overcome the difficulties of reconciling his profession with that of a 'gentleman'. Edmund Yates, writing in *Temple Bar* in 1863, applied the Smilesian principle that an actor's social position was in his own hands. The status of a gentleman could be reached if an actor gave up his egoism and his eccentricities 'of dress, manners and monetary matters'. If he was modest, avoided 'any uncalled for public display' and led an honourable life, he would, according to Yates, be accepted into society.[184] In other words the actor would have to conform by shedding the 'bohemian' characteristics of his profession and become an imitator of the society that so often rejected him.

In the early and middle years of the nineteenth century, William Macready and Charles Kean, reaching the top of their profession, enjoyed something approaching a higher social status. Yet although both had received a public school education, they were not fully accepted by the highest levels. Macready entertained several members of the aristocracy, as well as celebrities from the worlds of art and literature.[185] He aspired to be accepted by the upper classes, but wining and dining the aristocracy was mainly for professional purposes. At the same time his position as a leading actor placed him on closer terms with luminaries from the worlds of art and literature.[186]

The desire to be accepted at a higher social level became an obsession with many actors. Some actually felt guilty and despised working for a profession that was held in low regard. Being an actor stigmatised them and hindered social advancement. Charles and Ellen Kean had repugnance both for the stage and for other actors despite the success and financial reward a stage career had brought them. Charles Kean wrote to his daughter that he did not want her to come in contact with theatrical people. He avoided meeting other husbands and wives who were actors, and avoided them as much as possible outside the theatre.[187] Because of their theatrical connections, Kean and his wife were unable to be accepted at the desired higher social level, and had to content themselves with friends of lower rank.[188]

Efforts made by well-known actors to give the appearance of belonging to a higher social class could provoke ridicule and scorn. St John Ervine noted that William Kendal's 'cult of respectability' may have 'earned appreciation for him and his far abler wife' but it 'made both of them disliked because of the ostentation with which the respectability was displayed'.[189] Like Charles Kean, William Kendal kept himself 'very much aloof from the members of the profession'.[190] Outside the theatre, he and Madge tried to avoid the society of other actors. In private life, they assumed his real family surname of Grimston. This rather formidable name suggested upper-class respectability and seemed to eradicate the theatrical bohemianism associated with their more famous name of Kendal.[191] William Kendal's attempts to cover up the source of the fame and affluence of himself and his wife seem ludicrous, particularly as the Kendals (or Kendal Grimstons as they were also known) were viewed as models of theatrical respectability and widely accepted by polite society.

The gradual social acceptance of the actor from around the 1850s resulted from the return of middle- to upper-class audiences to the theatre and the entry of actors from a higher social level into the profession. According to Percy Fitzgerald, when Irving became manager of the Lyceum in 1871, it was a time when 'the stage was purified very much from the impurity attached to it before. Traditions of good breeding and high conduct were not confined to special families like the Kembles,* but had spread over the whole profession'. Families of 'condition' were ready to allow their sons, after a university education, to choose to enter the dramatic profession.[192]

---

* The actor and theatre manager Roger Kemble (1721-1802) had twelve children, several of whom became actors, the most famous being Sarah Siddons (1755-1831) and John Philip Kemble (1757-1823) —Ed.

It was the knighting of Henry Irving, on 18 July 1895, which symbolised the social acceptance of the actor and supposedly removed 'any remaining prejudices against the drama'. Ironically, Irving's knighthood was announced in the same week that Oscar Wilde was sentenced to two years hard labour for gross indecency.[193] The stigma against the acting profession was seemingly removed by the touch of the Royal sword.* At the same time prejudices against moral deviancy remained insurmountable. Nor was the bias against the acting profession completely removed. Only those who had reached the top of the scale, whose behaviour appeared exemplary, were accepted into society. Henry Irving optimistically stated to the Actors' Association in 1895 that players were no longer patronised, they were 'courted and welcomed'. A man of good family no longer lost 'caste' when he became an actor. However recognition of the status of the actor came mainly from upper-class society audiences. A stigma still survived with middle class and provincial attitudes. Irving called for 'recognition' to be extended to 'that huge middle class, and especially the upper portion of it, which, to so large an extent, rules public opinion in this country'.[194]

By the late nineteenth century, the apparent respectability of the theatre resulted a remarkable upsurge in the number of 'civilian' newcomers to the stage. A new breed of actors came from families representing a broader cross-section of society than had previously been drawn to a theatrical career. Military men and the sons of military men went on the stage, as did the sons of civil servants, engineers, journalists, writers, lecturers, educationalists and artists.

The respectable backgrounds of actors were widely publicised in journals aimed at a middle- to upper-class readership. For instance, in 1899 the *English Illustrated Magazine* carried a brief report on the character actor Arthur Bouchier. He is extolled as 'one of Society's gifts to the stage'. Emphasis is given to his education at Eton and Oxford, as well as his military background—his father being a captain, his uncle a

---

* It is significant that the second actor to be knighted by Queen Victoria (in 1897) was not a leading contemporary figure. The recipient was Squire Bancroft who had long since retired from the stage and by the 1890s was considered to be 'a historical personage'. See Schoch 2004*b*: 183.

colonel and his grandfather a general in the Army.[195] The social standing of an actor could be more important than his talent. Society audiences in the 1890s liked to see actors on the stage with whom they could identify on a class basis.*

Off the stage, the successful actor was taking on the appearance of a gentleman. He became a 'well-dressed man, and as little anxious to obtrude his profession as an officer or a barrister'.[196] The lifestyle of top-ranking actors bore witness to their absorption into upper-class levels of society. Their former low status was confounded by their intimacy with influential members of the establishment. In 1885, the journalist Thomas Hay Sweet Escott found that 'London theatrical hosts and hostesses are on the increase.'[197] Actors and actresses reciprocated the hospitality of their hosts in London's high society. The Bancrofts gave 'frequent dinners to their numerous admirers at their residence in Berkeley Square'. Wilson Barrett was famous for 'suppers which are banquets' and occasionally gave 'dinner parties on Sundays'. But the 'most prodigal and magnificent of theatrical hosts' was Henry Irving: 'whatever he does is done on a great, even a grand scale, and done without ostentation, without violating any of the laws of good taste. Whatever the entertainment he has devised for his friends is the best of its kind.'[198] In the Beefsteak Room at the Lyceum, Irving's 'ordinary hospitalities' were 'simply endless'. Here he entertained 'the whole social scale' to dinners—from the Prince of Wales 'to the humblest of commoners'.[199]

T. H. S. Escott also noted the contribution of the men's club to the social acceptance of the actor. The club, formerly the bastion of masculine and class exclusivity, had done 'a great deal to bridge over the gulf that once existed between the classes'. It had 'brought representatives of different orders of men into close and friendly intercourse'. The

---

* In his novel *The Tragic Muse* (1890) Henry James, describing Basil Dashwood's acting technique, mocks the amateurishness and inexperience of many upper-class young men who went on the stage: 'he never got out of rehearsal. He uttered sentiments and breathed vows with a nice voice, with a shy boyish tremor, but as if he were afraid of being chaffed for it afterwards; giving the spectator the sense of holding the prompt-book and listening to a recitation. He made one think of country-houses and lawn tennis and private theatricals; than which there couldn't be ... a range of association more disconnected from the actor's art.' (Book Fifth, XXX,. 307–308)

homosocial conviviality of the club undoubtedly appealed to an actor after the rough and tumble of stage life. His extrovert character made him 'of all others a clubbable man'. The odd hours he was compelled to keep made club life 'particularly convenient'. Becoming a member of a gentleman's club gave the actor respectable status. He found himself 'in a circle which includes men with whom thirty years ago it is not very likely that he would have been on speaking terms'.[200] Like the pub, a club became a place of refuge, where male companionship could be enjoyed after the rigours of performing in the theatre. Since many clubs excluded women, they offered an escape from wives and families, from the demands of co-starring actresses or even those of mistresses. The club could therefore be a refuge for actors who were bachelors as well as those who were married. In his club an actor could enjoy the society of men from other walks of life, as well as smoking rooms, billiards, cards and even the attention of manservants.[201] Theatrical clubs, such as the Garrick and the Green Room, provided a space for relaxation and socialising before going to work in the theatre: 'At the Garrick ... many of the most famous lights of the present-day stage may be found of an afternoon, chatting together and enjoying a rubber at whist before the time comes for an early dinner and the call-boy's summons to duty.'[202]

Becoming a Freemason was another way of finding male companionship while achieving respectability. Freemasonry with its secrets and rituals was a brotherhood totally excluding women. It was one of its 'inviolable rules' that 'none but males can be admitted'.[203] Freemasonry forged links between middle and upper class men. Its leaders were from the aristocracy and royalty—in 1878 the Prince of Wales was installed as Grand Master of English Freemasons. For those in lower ranks, being a member of a lodge helped to establish middle-class status. It was a condition of Freemasonry that 'none but worthy men may be admitted to the craft.'[204] This did not prevent the formation of lodges whose members were in marginalised professions, like the stage. For the actor, joining a lodge seemed to establish a respectable status. The theatrical nature of Masonic rituals, accompanied by dressing up in robes and regalia, undoubtedly appealed to performers. A lodge was founded in Drury Lane Theatre and some notable actors and managers were Masons—including Henry Irving, William Terriss, Edward Terry and Sir Augustus Harris.[205]

Paradoxically, Freemasonry attracted prejudices similar to those encountered in the theatre. Its secrecy and exclusivity caused speculation, suspicion and religious condemnation—especially from the Roman Catholic Church. Possibly the fame of an actor such as Irving was hijacked to confer acceptability on 'the brotherhood'. However Irving seems to have been ignorant of such a motive. He, like other successful actor-managers, became a Freemason as part of a move to achieve respectability. The parallel rise in status of the actress was largely due to the social acceptance of the male actor in environments such as these, which previously had been confined to the upper-class men of commerce and industry, and which largely excluded women.

By the end of Queen Victoria's reign, the successful actor-manager enjoyed a bourgeois life-style similar to that of the affluent man of commerce or industry. The home life of a popular actor-manager is described in an article in *The Harmsworth Magazine,* August 1901. It concerns Lewis Waller, who is shown with his wife (formerly the actress Florence West) and their small daughter living in domestic comfort in the well-to-do London suburb of St John's Wood. The article emphasises Waller's status as an affluent family man, equating him with successful men in other spheres. Like other middle class men, he has a study 'lined with bookcases and emphatically built for one!' Waller, in the privacy of his study, 'reads his plays and studies his parts'. This sort of work, according to the article, 'demands freedom from interruption'. The study is a masculine space for retreat, private work and learning—a wife would usually have to knock to be admitted. Waller, like other men of business, has had to fight hard to gain his position in the theatre against keen male competition—'A man who has won a place has his work cut out to keep it.' Away from the theatre, Waller indulges in 'manly' pursuits—he is fond of outdoor recreations such as golf, but his ultimate status symbol is the ownership of a motor-car, one of the latest advances in technology. This vehicle has 'won his affections' and he drives it to and from his work in the theatre.[206]

Ownership of a house and garden in St John's Wood, a 'home-loving' devoted wife, the beginnings of a family, driving a motor-car—these are significant of the rise in status of the eminent late Victorian or Edwardian actor, whose wealth and success has allowed him to become part of an upper-middle-class milieu. By the early twentieth century, the theatre was a flourishing social institution, patronised by all classes and even by royalty itself. The standard had also improved immeasurably. It would seem that the actor had rejected his former outcast status and had now become the equal of that level of society that once had turned its back on him. However, it was only the few actors at the top of their profession who formed a kind of theatrical aristocracy enjoying the privileges of wealth and status. The mass of struggling, underpaid subordinates still persisted, while a handful of powerful leading male actor-managers continued to dominate the theatrical hierarchy.

Chapter Four: Plays and playwrights: the struggle for control

MASCULINE DOMINANCE in the nineteenth-century British theatre extended to the writing of plays. Not only was there a preponderance of male playwrights, men were also in control of other areas related to the playwriting profession. These included the important post of Lord Chamberlain whose office wielded inhibiting censorship over the efforts of dramatists, both male and female. This chapter discusses the masculine-driven agitation against censorship, as well as the struggle by Victorian dramatists against constraints placed upon their creativity, and their attempt to achieve a higher social and professional status.

The Victorian dramatist was not held in the same sort of regard as the star performer, particularly during the early years of the era. While some actor-managers and 'actresses-manageresses' wrote and performed in their own plays, the jobbing dramatist tended to occupy a more lowly position on the hierarchical scale. This was despite the fact that he was the very person upon whose work an actor depended for his performance, as well as for the economic success of his theatre. Not only was the dramatist considered secondary to the performer, he was not as highly regarded as the poet or novelist. Furthermore, audiences were usually attracted by the name of a star actor, rather than the author of the play in which he was appearing.

This situation gradually changed, but mainly in areas of the theatre that had become 'gentrified' or attracted specialist audiences. During the 1860s and 70s the comedies of T. W. Robertson attracted a middle-to-upper-class following. In the 1890s the names of Wilde, Pinero and Jones were a draw for followers of 'progressive' drama. Nevertheless, the average dramatist continued to be subservient to the actor-manager. His subservience was exacerbated by the demands of managers, performers, scenic and technical staff, by the need to conform to public taste, and above all by the constraints of the Lord Chamberlain's censorship.

Throughout the century, dramatists had a constant struggle to protect their creative output from interference and intrusion. Yet despite these restrictions, a great many men and a smaller number of women wrote for the stage.* Playwriting, like acting, was an area of nineteenth-century theatre whose conditions affected both sexes. But despite a female presence, writing for the stage was primarily seen as a masculine pursuit. Handbooks for would-be dramatists refer solely to the male gender, totally excluding the possibility of aspiring female playwrights. For instance, in *How to Write a Good Play* (1892), the actor Frank Archer expresses the view that a good dramatist must 'above everything else' be a man. He should also possess a variety of masculine attributes, which according to Archer, are of greater importance than mere creative ability. He has to be 'a politician, a historian ... an orator ... a man of action and thought. ... Above all, he must directly and publicly impress a crowd of other men.'[1] Playwrights were seen as men of the world, 'who, in addition to their literary ability have mixed much with all classes, and experienced the ups and downs of life'.[2]

Even William Archer, champion of the New Drama, held the same sort of misogynistic views. He maintained that in the future the 'best plays' would be written for, and by, men.[3] It is significant that, although he campaigned for theatrical reform with a missionary zeal, Archer marginalised or ignored female dramatists.[4] His commentaries on a number of plays published in *The Old Drama and the New* (1923), totally exclude works by female dramatists.[5]

Male misogyny was a prime reason for the obstructions faced by nineteenth-century female dramatists.† They had to overcome a number of gender-related prejudices. Masculine pseudonyms were sometimes

---

* Allardyce Nicoll in *A History of English Drama* Volumes IV (1800–1850) and V (1850–1900) (Cambridge: CUP, 2009) lists 427 female playwrights out of a total of 3,486 dramatists writing in the nineteenth century. According to his listings the highest percentage of plays written by women occurs during the 1880s and 1890s. There is also the possibility of 'hidden' female playwrights since women sometimes wrote under masculine pseudonyms. They could also be among those listed who are anonymous, unknown or identified only by surname or surname and initials. See Booth 1991: 141–142.

† For more on nineteenth-century British women playwrights see Newey 2005; Davis and Donkin 1999.

used to ensure their works were performed, or to avoid damage to reputations. As with female managers, the help of men was needed to negotiate legal, business and contractual matters. There was also the widely-held view that women could not write plays as well as men. This was possibly due to the perceived limitations of their experience of life as implied by male critics and commentators.* The plays of female dramatists were constantly compared with those of their male counterparts. For instance, in 1894 Constance Fletcher used the male pseudonym of 'George Fleming' to get her play *Mrs Lessingham* produced at the Garrick Theatre. William Archer reviewed the play as written by 'George Fleming,' while subscribing to the common knowledge that it was the work of a woman. At the same time, he praised her: 'I do not deny that this lady has luck on her side, but her first and greatest piece of luck lay in her ability to write a strong, moving and eminently actable play.' However, behind his praise lay a somewhat patronising tone: 'I fancy it would be a very keen critic who should detect a feminine hand in the workmanship.'[6] Archer implies that this appears to be the work of a man rather than the writing of a woman. It is exceptional for a woman to be capable of writing such a 'strong play'.

Despite the performances of several notable plays by women authors during the 1890s, playwriting continued to be defined as a masculine province.[7] In the *Era* review of Henry James's unsuccessful *Guy Domville* the failure of the playwright is compared with the supposed inadequacies of women dramatists:

> Mr James's perceptions are clear and strong enough for any man. But he has a feminine love of half-tones and a feminine shrinking from 'scenes', strong denouements and vigorous measures of any kind. ... Women cannot write plays for the same reason that Mr James cannot write them. But women can and do write charming novels. A really pathetic thing is

---

* For instance, the early nineteenth-century dramatist James Robinson Planché wrote that his wife, Eliza, 'had amused herself' by translating and adapting French dramas. Despite his wife's evident 'considerable success' and the fact that she wrote nine plays performed at the Olympic and Haymarket theatres, Planché views her playwriting as an activity to occupy her spare time. Furthermore this information appears as a footnote in his account of his own career, *Recollections and Reflections* See Planché 1872: 246 footnote.; see also Newey 2005: 78.

that both ladies and super-dainty novelists are often attacked by the plague of playwriting.[8]

James's subtle style, relying more on finely tuned sensitivities than high-flown melodrama, seems 'feminine' to the reviewer. He emasculates James, equating him with 'inferior' or inexperienced female playwrights. Ideally, a 'masculine' playwright should produce stronger, more balanced work than James's 'feminizing' subtleties. Apparently, James lacks the 'architectural ability' defined by Frank Archer as part of an analytical mind not usually associated with women.[9] It is interesting to note that the review for *Guy Domville* appears beside a less than complimentary one for a play by a woman—Dorothy Leighton's *Thyrza Fleming*, presented by the Independent Theatre Society at Terry's Theatre.*

The homosocial world of the male playwright

The marginalisation of women dramatists extended to their virtual exclusion from the homosocial, 'bohemian' world inhabited by their male counterparts. This masculine exclusivity was reinforced by gatherings in all-male clubs and literary groups.† Coteries of theatrical and literary men met at regular intervals in informal masculine venues, such as pubs, for discussion, drinking, smoking and eating.

The young Dion Boucicault,‡ after the success of *London Assurance* in 1841, became part of an all-male circle of semi-bohemian, influential writers. They gathered regularly at the public house behind the Olympic Theatre—run by Mark Lemon, who later became editor of *Punch*. The group discussed the theatre, literature and world affairs.[10] Like other such gatherings it was not exclusively theatrical—its members came from a

---

* Several women playwrights had to be content with publishing unperformed plays, a notable example being Augusta Webster, whose Roman tragedy *The Sentence* was highly praised by reviewers when published. For a somewhat different view of women playwrights see Scullion 1996. Thanks to John Stock Clarke for this suggestion. See also page 181 note. —*Ed.*

† There were some upmarket clubs that admitted women before 1880, such as the Albemarle, the Nineteenth Century and the Russell, but they excluded actresses. The Pioneer and New Century Clubs only admitted actresses after the turn of the century. See Tracy C. Davis, 'Edwardian management and structures of industrial capitalism', in Booth and Kaplan 1996: 113.

‡ See pages 177 onwards —*Ed.*

CHAPTER: FOUR: PLAYS AND PLAYWRIGHTS: THE STRUGGLE FOR CONTROL 161

diversity of professions, including journalism and dentistry. Conviviality was intermingled with earnest debate on a wide variety of subjects. This proliferation of clubs, coteries and societies allowed men of all professions and callings to make contact, to learn about each other and not be confined to their own occupational circles.

The interior of one of these all-male establishments was remembered by the dramatist and journalist, George R. Sims. The Unity Club, 'half-way down Holywell Street,' was situated in 'a long, rather low-ceilinged room comfortably furnished with easy chairs and a big sofa and filled with tobacco smoke and the clamour of voices. ... The company consisted chiefly of actors, authors and journalists and their invited guests.'[11] For many a young journalist or dramatist such an environment was very useful for making contacts. It was from the Unity Club that Sims received introductions to the worlds of newspapers and the theatre.[12] Outside clubs and literary societies, dramatists (especially in the second half of the century), mixed with both men and women prominent in literature, art and science at levées and soirées held at the homes of wealthy and successful celebrities.[13]

The dramatists who met at soirées and in all-male bohemian clubs came from a variety of social backgrounds. Their origins were often reflected by the status of the theatres for which they wrote their plays. Many of those churning out melodramas for minor or transpontine theatres came from lower down the social scale, while those writing plays for fashionable West End theatres came from mainly professional backgrounds, such as journalism or the law. A number of dramatists were from middle-class families, while others were of humble origin, or were self-educated. Very few of the prominent nineteenth-century dramatists came from theatrical backgrounds. An exception was T. W. Robertson who was born into a family of provincial actors with whom he toured around the Lincoln circuit, and whose sister was Madge Kendal.[14]

Several dramatists were connected with the theatre in another capacity such as management. Administrative duties were often combined with a prodigious output. Alfred Bunn, noted for a number of plays, adaptations and opera libretti, was manager both at Drury Lane and Covent Garden during the 1830s and 40s. Edward Fitzball, author of at least 150 melodramas, comedies and libretti, was Reader of Plays at Covent Garden from 1835 to 1838 and at Drury Lane from 1838 until 1851. James Robinson Planché, who wrote numerous plays, extravaganzas, burlesques and opera libretti, was also a designer, antiquarian and musician.

Tom Taylor, author of the highly successful melodrama *The Ticket-of-Leave Man*,* is an example of a man who combined playwriting with other varied activities. As well as writing sixty-nine plays, he was Professor of English at the University of London, a barrister, Assistant Secretary to the Board of Health in London, and art critic and editor of *Punch* from 1874 until his death in 1880.[15] His variegated career pattern exemplifies the professional freedom granted to Victorian middle-class men of energy and talent. The prodigious output of many dramatists, combined with a demanding administrative workload, shows that men who wrote plays perhaps needed more drive than genius. This may be compared with the lot of female dramatists, many of whom were denied the same educational opportunities as men and unless (like Sarah Lane at the Britannia in Hoxton) they managed theatres, were forced to combine their playwriting activities with supervising a home and family.

Demands on the dramatist

In 1863, an article by the critic and dramatist, George Henry Lewes, on 'The Miseries of a Dramatic Author' advised the aspiring playwright: 'You must mould your work not according to your conceptions of art and nature, but according to the capabilities of actors, or the prejudices of the stage.'[16] When a play had been accepted by a theatre, the dramatist's work came under the control of management, actors and backstage staff. All of these factions made considerable demands on the playwright, whether male or female. But the fate of the dramatist was ultimately in the hands of the theatre management. The manager had the power to accept or reject a play and to make substantial alterations if it was accepted:

> The work which has cost him [the dramatist] so much anxious thought, every exit and entrance having been pondered with severe attention, every speech polished ... with fastidious care, has to be altered, as if it had been put together by a carpenter.[17]

---

* See pages 247 onwards. —*Ed.*

For the manager the practical and technical possibilities of staging had to be considered. This was particularly the case with a first-time dramatist who lacked the necessary theatrical know-how. It is more than likely that his play would need pruning and re-arranging to make it performable. As a young, relatively inexperienced dramatist, Dion Boucicault gratefully accepted alterations made by Charles Mathews and his wife, Madame Vestris,* to his successful comedy *London Assurance* (Covent Garden 1841). In his 'Preface' to the first edition of the play he expresses his gratitude to Vestris for her 'judgement, taste and valuable suggestions with regard to alterations of character, situation, dialogue, expunging passages and dilating others, to her indefatigable zeal'.[18] As a beginner, Boucicault was eager to accept suggestions that would improve his play. Later, with more experience, he would think otherwise.

Authors may have complained, but managers also had problems. They had to read a great number of plays, many of which were sent in by inexperienced authors. Larger theatres employed a Reader of Plays for the task of reading and selecting. Alfred Bunn, who did this job along with other duties, complained that, with hundreds of pieces submitted 'the task of deciding, to say nothing of reading, is quite harassing enough'.[19] The difficulty was not with established dramatists, but with beginners and would-be authors: 'those who are candidates for the glory of seeing their works on the stage and themselves in print'. Out of hundreds of works 'sent promiscuously by unknown writers' to Drury Lane Theatre in 1840, there was, according to Bunn, only one 'deemed fit for representation'. Among plays submitted by 'men of note' many were found to be 'fraught with danger and dismissed accordingly'.[20] Literary plays (including verse dramas by well-known poets) were especially 'unactable', and according to George Henry Lewes, 'suitable only for the study'.

The theatre manager could not afford to spend money on 'a romantic scheme of elevating the drama'. His concern was with making money by catering for popular taste: 'His business is not a romantic one but a commercial one.'[21] According to Lewes, in order to get his play performed, a dramatist should concentrate on action rather than words.

---

* The actress/opera singer Lucia Elizabeth Vestris, née Elizabetta Lucia Bartolozzi —*Ed.*

Managers had 'contempt' for the words of a play. Instead they laid 'the greatest stress on its construction, on situations and "parts" for the actors'. If a manager 'finds a play lags ... or is unintelligible in any parts' he is, according to Lewes, 'justified in altering the piece'.[22] Lines often had to be altered to suit the principal players, new scenes had to be added and others omitted. The result was that there could be inordinate delays in waiting for a play to go into production.

While some managers may have offered practical help to dramatists, there were others who made changes such as cutting or altering scenes without consulting the author. These men were often far less educated than the dramatists whose plays they commissioned. Managerial 'interference' with a dramatist's work caused a great deal of aggravation. Dion Boucicault was one dramatist who vehemently expressed his opposition to the power of managers, most of whom he perceived as being ignorant. In 1877, he wrote scathingly of 'the commercial manager':

> This person in most instances received his education in a bar room, possibly on the far side of the counter. The more respectable may have been gamblers. Few could compose the bill of the play where the spelling and grammar would not disgrace an urchin under ten years of age. These men have obtained possession of our first-class theatres, and presume to exercise the artistic and literary functions required to select the actors, to read and determine the merit of the dramatic works and preside generally over the highest and noblest efforts of the human mind.[23]

Although the status of dramatists was supposed to have improved by the end of the century, evidence shows they were still regarded by some managers as subordinate. In 1895, the journalist and dramatist Arthur à Beckett wrote that he felt 'the greatest repugnance in dealing with theatrical managers, having to dance attendance on them, and to "look the other way" when they have been guilty of discourtesy'. He had known 'authors of the highest standing submitting to treatment from managers to which they would never have been subjected by editors or publishers'.[24]

The playwright, in his eagerness to have his work performed, could be subject to the dominance of another man, not always as honest or intelligent as himself. He could also be subjected to the feminine power of an 'actress-manageress'. Clever women managing West End theatres, such as Madame Vestris or Marie Bancroft (née Wilton), proved more astute than some of their male counterparts in promoting dramatists. Vestris helped to launch the career of Dion Boucicault by presenting his comedy *London Assurance* at Covent Garden in 1841, while Marie Wilton successfully presented the influential comedies of T. W. Robertson at the Prince of Wales's during the 1860s.

Although an actor-manager would often produce (or stage-manage) the play himself, the production was more likely to be in the hands of the stage manager, usually another source of masculine control.* A 'Handbook for Would-be Dramatic Authors', published by *The Stage* in 1888, warned that 'the fortunes of the play depend much upon the stage manager' who was a gentleman 'born and bred in the theatre' and 'imbued with theatrical ideas'.[25] An aspiring dramatist therefore needed 'all of his tact' at rehearsals of his play. He was advised not to quarrel with the stage manager; it was better to let him have his own way 'than set him against you and your piece, and he will do far more good than he will do harm to it'.[26]

An author was often required to alter his play 'to cut one scene here and write another there, to shorten this part and "write up" that'.[27] If the play starred a leading actor-manager, the author could find that the leading role would need a lot of alteration, or 'writing up' as it was colloquially termed. This usually meant expanding a role with extra lines and scenes and reducing supporting roles to give the star performer central focus. Actors in secondary roles could also request their parts to be 'written up', often regardless of the plot.

It was considered usual for the dramatist, once his play was accepted, to encounter difficulties with the actors, both male and female. George Henry Lewes claimed that a person without experience of the stage could not understand 'the galling trials which the dramatist has to endure from the sullen, silent opposition of the actors'.[28] Problems usually arose from the time of the initial reading of the play by the author to the cast. A leading actor 'who was at first full of hope' feels that his role is

---

* Play production was not exclusively masculine. Ellen Kean helped with stage-management, while Madge Kendal was cited by Seymour Hicks as 'one of the very finest stage-managers. ... She rehearsed every part in the play if necessary and taught men, women and children their job perfectly.' See Hicks 1939: 47.

'ineffective' or thinks that the role allotted to a rival actor is 'becoming too effective'. The principal actress feels that her role is not long enough, she finds that she is 'too long absent from the scene' or has to be on stage while others 'make long speeches to her, which she has to feed with interjections or feeble enquiries'. No sooner are 'such discoveries' made by the actors 'than you can read the discontent in their faces'.[29] There are also continual demands for 'exit speeches'—'No actor willingly quits the scene without a point, or something to raise a laugh.' It does not matter whether the speech bears little relation to 'the business of the scene'; the one 'imperious desire' of the actor is to have an exit speech.*[30] Some actors would even offer to help with the 'reconstruction' of the play. Naturally, the dramatist would want to 'maintain' and 'carry out' his own ideas, but if he wanted his play performed he dare not 'offend the stage manager, or differ with the [theatre] manager, or quarrel with the actors'.[31] All this undoubtedly proved most frustrating for dramatists.

Dramatists were not only subservient to the requirements of leading players and managers. In a theatre increasingly reliant on scenic effects, they also had to consider the needs of the technical staff, as well as the audience's demand for spectacle and sensation. Some considered action more important than literary merit. George Henry Lewes, for example, maintained that the words of a play were of 'secondary importance' and should be left until after 'the plot has been fully conceived and planned into acts and scenes—and these have been made complete by the addition of action—every deed elaborated, every movement understood.' The words should 'spring' out of the action.[32] However, elaborate scenic effects and action were inclined to force the literary content of a play into a subordinate position. The dramatist often had to contend with his name on the playbill being eclipsed by those of the scene-painters and

---

* The veteran actor, William Farren, insisted on being given the final moralistic 'tag' speech of Boucicault's comedy *London Assurance* when it was first performed at Covent Garden in March 1841. This was regardless of his role being that of the roué Sir Harcourt Courtly. Farren refused to act the part unless he was given the concluding lines, which were assigned to a more moral character. When Boucicault protested that the speech would sound 'rather strange in the mouth of Sir Harcourt Courtly' Madame Vestris replied that the public would not find it strange and that the actor to whom the speech had originally been given 'approved'. See Boucicault 1889a: 461.

descriptions of the scenes they had painted. Occasionally the scene-painter's name was in larger, bolder type than that of the author.[33]

Edward Mayhew in *Stage Effect* (1840) wrote that 'Nothing is more common than to sacrifice the author rather than inconvenience the carpenter.'[34] However an author should construct his play so that *flats* and *set scenes* might alternate each other.[35] Mayhew also advises the prospective playwright to hold on to his ideas; he should never 'sacrifice his feeling to suggestions from the management, for cutting this effect, or elongating that' and 'above all, he should never write what are called *carpenters' scenes*'.[36] Yet so-called 'carpenters' scenes' (usually played downstage) were necessary for a swift transition as they allowed the setting-up of the next major scene. Sensational, exciting effects were memorable for an audience; the scenic artist and stagehand became more important than the dramatist. As Frank Archer advised in *How to Write a Good Play* (1892) 'A play with sensation scenes is not necessarily a poor one' but it would not 'stand the test of time. The class of audiences that is the main support of such productions is one for which realism and spectacle have the greatest charm. ... Finished dialogue in such pieces would be wasted labour.'[37]

The dramatist who wanted to survive by writing plays not only had to exercise tact with actors and management, he also needed to be extremely versatile. If attached to a minor or popular theatre, he had to be able to write or adapt at great speed and to turn his hand to such diverse genres as melodrama, comedy, burlesque, or opera. The public demanded novelty, and there were constant calls from managers for new works. Playwriting became highly competitive—numbers of dramatists were waiting to be performed and wanted their fees.[38] With the constant demand for new and original work, the dramatist had to work at great speed. A large output was also essential because financial rewards were low: a number of plays had to be provided for one or more managements in order to make a living wage.

Dramatists attached to theatres had different methods for working speedily. For instance Charles H. Hazlewood (well known for his 1863 adaptation of *Lady Audley's Secret**) used a 'cut-and-paste' system for

---

* Based on the 1862 'sensation novel' by Mary Elizabeth Braddon —*Ed.*

providing plays for the Britannia. He took his plots, and often the dialogue, from sensational reports in newspapers or from 'penny dreadfuls'.[39] With the aid of assistants, he would 'run through periodicals jotting down the main incidents in stories ... scissoring out here and there'. Cuttings were 'docketed' alphabetically and when Hazlewood was commissioned to write a play he or his assistants 'would take down from the shelf sundry envelopes'.[40] Not all playwrights 'pigeon-holed' their creative ideas like Hazlewood. But a fast turnover meant a dramatist could have over a hundred plays to his credit.

Many dramatists wrote plays in addition to performing other tasks in the theatre, such as administration. In 1840 Alfred Bunn wrote of the great demands made on his time while trying to write plays as well as being manager of Drury Lane: 'I have over and over again, after rising at six, writing till eleven, attending rehearsals of three and four hours duration, superintending the ordinary duties of management, ... had to sit up the greatest part of the night to complete a project.'[41] Playwrights could also be as difficult as managers and actors. Managers were anxious to obtain the best new plays as soon as possible, but writers who were short of money often provided only the first acts of plays and the managers sometimes had to wait years for the second and third acts. There was also the danger to the manager of rejecting a play, only to find the author had given it to a rival who had a great success with it.

Dramatists tried to complete work in the shortest possible time, knowing that a fee would be paid for each act received by the manager. Before the typewriter came into general use in the 1880s, they painstakingly wrote plays with quill and ink, very often in bad lighting and in conditions that made production of work extremely slow. If a play was accepted there was the task of making copies for the management and especially for the scrutiny of the Lord Chamberlain. Professional copyists often took on the job as a sideline to legal copying. This appears to have been a predominantly masculine task. Evidently there were also networks of copyists, often working within families. An overload of plays, or parts of plays, was passed around to other outside copyists—usually male. The need for all this transcribing by hand was greatly relieved by the invention of the typewriter. With the introduction of the typing pool in the 1880s, the copying of plays became a mainly female task.[42]

The difficulties faced by nineteenth-century dramatists in getting their works performed largely arose from the masculine domination of the theatre. Many dramatists were forced into a position of emasculating subservience to managers, actor-managers and stage staff. Their creative output was in the hands of controlling men apt to make changes which would satisfy the demands of a system more reliant on star performers and technical effects than on authors. The average dramatist was therefore forced to subsume his creativity to the exigencies of managers, both male and female, and to the whims of actors and actresses, as well as scenic demands. There was also the need to produce work almost incessantly in order to survive, and perhaps support a family, on comparatively low income.

However, with the gradual disappearance of the stock system* from around the 1860s and the introduction of longer runs, conditions for dramatists improved immeasurably. They had more leisure to write: at home in the study, or by going out into the tranquillity of the country or seaside. West End dramatists of the late nineteenth century, like Henry Arthur Jones or Arthur Wing Pinero, were under far fewer external pressures than their earlier counterparts. They were able to pace their work in order to fit in with longer time scales for rehearsals and performances. The early-nineteenth-century theatre had consisted of variegated bills that changed every few days. Now (largely thanks to the innovations of the Bancrofts) a single production could occupy a theatre for an extended run. Theatre managers began to plan the production of a new play in terms of months and seasons, rather than rushing it on in a couple of days.[43] Successful dramatists, like actor-managers and novelists, could live the comfortable lives of affluent family men.

Originality versus adaptations from the French

For dramatists struggling on low fees, churning out work under pressurised conditions, it was often quicker and more remunerative to adapt a foreign play. Throughout the nineteenth century, French literature and drama provided ideas for a number of British plays. The reasons for this lack of originality were largely financial. Managers found it more

---

* See Page 64. —*Ed.*

economical to commission adaptations of French successes than to pay the full fee for an original play. As a beginner in 1841, Dion Boucicault had received £300 from Charles Mathews and Madame Vestris for his comedy *London Assurance*. Three years later when he offered a new play to the Haymarket, the manager, Benjamin Webster, stated he would only pay £100 for it. In reply to Boucicault's objection, Webster remarked that he could go to Paris and select a 'first-class comedy'. A translation would cost him £25. Why should he give £300 or £500 for a play whose success was uncertain? Boucicault sold his original play for £100 and accepted a commission to translate three French plays at £50 a piece: 'The English dramatist was obliged either to relinquish the stage altogether or to become a French copyist.'*[44]

By the middle of the century, the submergence of a hitherto original British drama into a plethora of adaptations proved problematic. The question of whether to adapt French plays or produce original drama greatly concerned male commentators, including Dion Boucicault and his circle. Since there was no copyright to protect dramatists, nothing could be done to prevent writers taking the plots, ideas and characters of others. This practice was encouraged by managers who would rush out several versions of a popular play at rival theatres. Boucicault and his friends came to the conclusion that just as Shakespeare had borrowed from the Italians, so nineteenth-century British dramatists should borrow from the French. Dramatists soon found that they could increase their productivity and earn more money through translating or adapting French successes, rather than producing an original British drama. The best of these adaptations improved on and developed the French original, even making it seem like an original British play.[45]

The dearth of original playwriting was exacerbated by authors turning to other spheres. For male authors in particular, there was the necessity of earning enough to maintain homes and families. Many preferred the camaraderie of the male-oriented sphere of journalism to the difficulties

---

* In Dickens' *Nicholas Nickleby*, the actor-manager Vincent Crummles asks Nicholas to supply a new play 'by Monday'. When Nicholas protests at the short notice Crummles gives him the script of a French play and says 'Just turn that into English, and put your name on the title-page.' —*Ed.*

of dealing with actors and managers. When a great deal more money could be made through journalism or by writing novels, few continued to write for the stage. In 1876, the theatre manager John Hollingshead complained of the lack of new playwrights. While new theatres were being built, both in London and in the provinces, 'no one is building a new author'. There was 'a small and devoted band of six dramatic authors (more or less)' writing regularly for the stage. But one becoming a manager had diminished even this figure and another, 'the most fruitful and original of our authors,' had returned to acting. The constant revivals and French adaptations could not go on forever: 'The playgoer will not always be fed upon hashed mutton.'[46]

Hollingshead was writing in a period of transition. The modest innovations of Tom Robertson in the 1860s continued to influence, but the following decade would herald the appearance of a group of dramatists who strove for a new, original British drama. Yet, even here, the influence of the French *pièces bien faites* remained strongly discernible. As Michael Booth has pointed out, this influence could be beneficial—it helped with skilful plotting and more credible situations.[47] However, by 1893, Henry Arthur Jones could write that: 'We have almost ceased to translate and adapt from the French, and to-day it is as unusual for our leading West-End theatres to play French adaptations as fifteen years ago it was unusual for them to produce original English plays.'[48] At the time Jones was writing these words, the Garrick was the only leading West End theatre where a French adaptation was being performed.*

The financial position of the dramatist

For most of the nineteenth century the average British dramatist was not highly rewarded financially. Like other theatre employees, the earnings of the dramatist were affected by the various economic fluctuations of the Victorian era. His income could suffer a decline, with managers (at both major and minor theatres) becoming bankrupt. Nor could he obtain adequate remuneration until managers entered into fairer contractual agreements.[49] A dramatist's earnings also fluctuated in accordance with

---

* This possibly relates to *A Pair of Spectacles* by Sydney Grundy. See note on page 180
—Ed.

the location and type of theatre for which he was writing. Higher fees were paid to authors whose work was accepted for London's West End theatres than to those who wrote for the suburbs or provinces.

Regardless of the location of the theatre, payments were not made for revivals. It did not matter how successful or how long a play ran, the author received one payment and not a penny more. However, a fee might be increased if the play ran longer than a specified number of nights, negotiated when the manager bought the play. But with the demand for novelty and rapid changes of the bill, very few plays reached the required number of performances. The author's only hope was that if his play was successful, his power was increased for the next round of negotiations with the management.[50]

In comparison with the high earnings of star performers, as well as high profits often earned by managers, the remuneration of the dramatist seems grossly unfair. Even after Lord Lytton's protective copyright legislation of 1833*, he was exploited. While an actor could earn as much as £50 to £60 a night, the dramatist was paid a flat fee for each play. This was usually around £50 to £100 per act. A manager could make a small fortune from a smash hit while the author received a pittance. For example, the well-known dramatist Tom Taylor was paid a mere £200 for his highly successful melodrama *The Ticket-of-Leave Man*, which, in 1863, had a record run of 407 performances at the Olympic Theatre. Worse still, his hit comedy *Our American Cousin* ran for a year at the Haymarket in 1861 and brought the manager, John Buckstone, a profit of £20,000 while Taylor received a fee of only £150.[51] Tom Taylor, as already noted, was involved with other spheres than the theatre. Many writers whose plays had brought financial success to the theatres that employed them, struggled on a fraction of a leading player's salary. Meanwhile star performers were criticised for making money at the expense of writers.[52]

Like actors, nearly all male Victorian dramatists were married. They had to increase their output or take subordinate employment in order to support a family and live in comfort. The mid-Victorian dramatist

---

* The Dramatic Copyright Act 1833, promoted by the novelist and playwright Edward Bulwer-Lytton, then an MP, later Baron Lytton —*Ed.*

surviving on fees of £150 to £200 was in a far less secure position than a middle-class *paterfamilias* with a steady job. Around 1858, the annual income for a professional man was £250 to £300; by the 1860s it had risen to £500 per annum. A professional upper-middle class family man with two or three children could earn from £800 to £1,000 a year.[53] By comparison, the average dramatist's earnings were probably not much higher than those for entrants to the Civil Service who, in the mid nineteenth century, earned around £80 to £90 per annum.

Low financial rewards made it impossible for the mid-Victorian writer to live comfortably by only writing plays. Prominent dramatists such as Douglas Jerrold, T. W. Robertson and W. S. Gilbert worked in other spheres such as journalism to earn a sufficient income. Bulwer-Lytton, despite the success of plays such as *The Lady of Lyons* (1838) and *Money* (1840), turned to the far more lucrative trade of writing novels. More could be earned from fiction, because publishers could offer large advances. A theatre manager was not usually in a position to offer a substantial advance for a play.[54] In comparison with the dramatist, the average novelist was financially more secure. As an anonymous 'novelist' explained to the *Pall Mall Gazette* in 1892:

> A novelist writes to earn his daily bread. He deals in an article for which he can get a fairly regular price. On that he can often manage to live in a tolerable condition of lower-middle-class comfort. Why, then, should he waste his time in writing plays as a speculation? And where would he look for food, lodging and clothing for himself and family, while he was engaged in preparing this doubtful and dangerous bid for popular favour?[55]

This letter was in response to *The Pall Mall Gazette*'s series 'Why I Don't Write Plays'. Well-known writers and novelists were invited to answer questions regarding the divorce of the novel and the stage, which had been the subject of recent discussions led by William Archer. Typically, the majority of the writers contributing to the debate were male. They included Thomas Hardy, R. D. Blackmore, A. T. Quiller-Couch, George Moore, George Gissing and Frank Harris. Two female novelists also contributed: Mrs Margaret L. Woods and Mary Elizabeth Braddon. The answers from the group of writers are, as John Stokes has pointed out: 'remarkable both for their apparent ignorance of recent events in the theatre and for their instinctive hostility to the dramatic form'.[56] Thomas Hardy, for instance, blamed the conditions imposed by theatrical presentation for the divergence between literature and the stage:

> In general, the novel affords scope for getting nearer the heart and meaning of things than does the play: in particular, the play as nowadays conditioned, when parts have to be moulded to the actors, not actors to the parts; when managers will not risk a truly original play; when scenes have to be arranged in a constrained and arbitrary fashion to suit the exigencies of scene-building although spectators are absolutely indifferent to order and succession, provided they can set before them a developing thread of interest.[57]

Although Hardy wrote plays himself, he obviously found the technicalities of the stage a hindrance to creativity. Playwriting, with its restrictions due to theatrical practicalities, did not allow the freedom of time and place enjoyed in composing a novel.

Apart from the anonymous 'novelist' cited above, none of those who replied mentioned the financial differences between writing for the page and the stage. After all, this was the era in which the financial position of the dramatist had vastly improved: 'In defiance of reason, the playwright today is better paid than the novelist, just as the preacher is better paid than the journalist.'[58] Nevertheless, throughout the nineteenth century, successful novelists, and even poets, could earn extremely large profits. Tennyson negotiated an annual fee of £5,000 from his publishers. Both Disraeli and George Eliot were offered £10,000 for novels. In the 1860s, Charles Dickens, by far the most successful Victorian novelist, received £11,000 and £12,000 for his final novels. His writings (including back sales) produced from £10,000 to £13,000 per annum.[59] When high sums such as these could be earned by writing novels, it is hardly surprising that many dramatists either deserted the profession or wrote plays as a sideline to other professional or administrative activities.

Those who tried to subsist by solely writing plays often faced penury. The various economic shifts of the mid nineteenth century caused reductions in fees, particularly those of dramatists writing for minor theatres. For example, supplying pantomimes and melodramas to the Britannia Theatre earned £3 a piece in the late 1840s, but by 1850 this sum had been reduced to £2. Many writers for East End and transpontine theatres drifted down the financial and hierarchical scale, taking hackwork wherever they could find it. A sad example was Charles Somerset. He had supplied the Surrey, Adelphi and Olympic theatres with melodramas throughout the 1830s. By the end of the 1840s he was reduced to writing 'canine melodramas' for Sam Wild's portable theatre, and finally earned a pittance doing hackwork for the lowly Bower Saloon and the Grecian Theatre. According to the playwright and manager, Edward Stirling, Somerset was last seen standing before the Mansion House 'with a printed label round his neck inscribed thus: "Ladies and Gentlemen I am starving." '[60]

Figure 40. Edward Bulwer-Lytton, Lord Lytton

Nor were copyright laws of help to dramatists. The Dramatic Copyright Act of 1833, instigated by Edward Bulwer-Lytton, was intended to give the dramatist more control over his output. It gave dramatists property rights over unpublished works, exclusive rights to benefit from stage performances, as well as copyright protection for printed dramatic texts. Managers could no longer perform a play without paying a fee and obtaining the permission of the author. Without his written consent, the theatre manager was 'liable to a penalty of not less than forty shillings for every offence, or an action for damages'. However, there were managers who used dishonest practices in order to escape 'the payment of a few shillings to a poor dramatist'. Portable theatres or booths were opened alongside theatres owned by respectable managers. Unscrupulous managers 'played for nothing pieces the others honestly paid for, frequently anticipating their production at the regular theatre, and therefore diminishing their attraction'. It was very difficult to police the offenders since they were often 'gone before a writ could be served upon them'.[61]

The Bulwer-Lytton Act did not entirely protect the dramatist from dishonest managers or publishers. New plays were printed in cheap acting editions designed largely for performance by amateurs. Some unscrupulous publishers paid authors only a few pounds for copyright and profited by collecting the performance fees for each play on their lists, keeping them for themselves.

Another attempt to protect dramatists came from the Dramatic Authors' Society, also founded in 1833, following the Royal Assent to Bulwer-Lytton's Copyright Act. This was founded by a group of seven male dramatists led by James Robinson Planché who met at the Albion Tavern opposite the stage door of Drury Lane Theatre. These men recognised that legislation alone would not sufficiently protect dramatic copyright. They aimed to ensure the payment of fees to dramatists for stage performances of their works. Their society struggled to close loopholes in the law, including the collection of fees by publishers rather than authors.[62] This was the first society set up solely for the interests of dramatic authors, rather than performers or managers. It introduced a scale of fees for the performance of different dramatic genres. It was not long before most London playwrights had joined the society and on the title pages of their published plays they were designated 'Member of the Dramatic Authors' Society' which served as a warning to scheming managers. A play could now be regarded as the exclusive property of an individual author.[63]

The Dramatic Authors' Society provides an early example of masculine-driven reforms to the working conditions of nineteenth-century British dramatists. Although membership was predominantly male, a few women writers were admitted as honorary members, including Eliza Planché, Felicia Hemans and Mary Russell Mitford.[64] The Society was for the protection of dramatists of both sexes, but as Jane Moody has pointed out, women were probably given honorary membership without the benefit of 'professional sociability'. It is also likely that they were excluded from the society's meetings.[65]

The society did not become fully efficient until around 1860 and many popular playwrights refused to join. These included F. C. Burnand* and Dion Boucicault who maintained they could do better for themselves by looking after their own interests. They would not even allow their plays to be placed on the society's lists.[66] Boucicault, in particular, was able to combine an aggressive business sense with writing plays. It was due more to his efforts than those of the Dramatic Authors' Society that financial conditions for dramatists began to improve from the 1860s—around the time the Society became fully operational.

Dion Boucicault: raising the status of dramatists

Dion Boucicault was one dramatist who was not afraid to confront managerial power and agitate for fairer conditions. From his position, as both actor-manager and playwright, he demanded that managers share profits with authors rather than pay for each act received. Of all the nineteenth-century British male playwrights, he was the most business-like and arguably the only one capable of exerting power over other men of business in the theatre. He was convinced that no-one could look after his interests better than himself. Through promoting his own plays with their immense popular appeal, he turned them into desirable commodities.

Although this was primarily an exercise in self-promotion, Boucicault profoundly influenced the economic status of the British playwright. He reversed the relationship between author and manager by his ability to rake in a larger share of the profits than had previously been awarded to the dramatist. His skills at negotiating paved the way for the lucrative West End theatre of the 1880s and 1890s.[67]

---

* Sir Francis Burnand, playwright and contributor to *Punch*, nowadays best known as the librettist for Sullivan's *Box and Cox*. —Ed.

As early as 1848, Boucicault had attempted to introduce a royalty system for British dramatists. This was based on the practice in France whereby authors received a ten per cent royalty on box office takings, rather than a straight fee. But he could not convince fellow British dramatists and his proposals angered managers and actors. It was not for another twelve or so years that Boucicault was able to introduce a royalty system. This was to have a profound effect on the status of the British playwright.[68]

Figure 41. Dion Boucicault

Following the immense success of his melodrama *The Colleen Bawn* at the Adelphi Theatre in 1860, Boucicault joined forces with the manager, Benjamin Webster. They signed an agreement by which all profits and losses were to be shared equally between the playwright and manager. However, the stage and all departments of the theatre gradually came under the control of Boucicault. Webster, one of the most prominent Victorian theatre managers, was forced to take a back seat in his own theatre and to have no say in its artistic policy. For the first time, a dramatist had wrung from a theatre manager an agreement strongly in his favour, giving him the right to control the presentation of his plays. A British dramatist could now earn a nightly royalty payable upon performance of his work and take a share of the box office profits. This made it possible for him to earn his living solely through writing plays. At first other managers resisted the new demands of playwrights, but gradually, thanks to Boucicault's tenacity, the acceptance of a flat fee by the dramatist became a thing of the past.[69]

Boucicault was so confident in his own talent that he was able to exploit the lucrativeness of theatre management. Working both in England and America, he applied lessons learned in one country to the other. The system he brought to the London stage was mainly founded on his experience in America. The immense success of *The Colleen Bawn* in New York in 1860 meant that Boucicault could own two houses and live ostentatiously. By the mid 1860s, he had become the dramatist with the largest pecuniary interest in the theatre. Never before had a nineteenth-century British author earned so much money from his own plays, nor enjoyed such a high standard of living.

Boucicault created a system that allowed for maximum profits. In London, his plays were put on at one or more theatres, in different districts (one in the West End and one in the East End), while he received a share of the box-office earnings. When his plays were on tour, he also received a 'clear half' of the net profits from provincial theatres. This made Boucicault a promoter of his own output—combining the roles of playwright, manager and actor. So popular were his sensational melodramas that he was able to create and take advantage of competition between rival managements.[70] Boucicault provides a supreme example of masculine ingenuity and business acumen. It was largely due to his efforts that substantial profits began to be made by both male and female dramatists. At the height of his powers in the 1860s and 70s, Boucicault himself was capable of earning £1,000 to £1,500 in a week. By the late 1870s, a playwright could earn more than a novelist.[71] As we have seen, Tom Taylor, in 1863, had received only £200 for *The Ticket-of-Leave Man*, whereas in the 1880s Henry Arthur Jones made over £18,000 from his highly successful melodrama *The Silver King*. Nevertheless it proved difficult for older dramatists who had subsisted on low fees to reconcile themselves with the greater earning capacity of the new generation of playwrights. In 1888 the veteran dramatist James Robinson Planché was amazed to learn that F. C. Burnand had received £800 for his successful burlesque of Douglas Jerrold's *Black-Ey'd Susan*, while earlier in the century Planché himself had never received more than £100 for his 'Lyceum pieces'.[72]

By the end of the nineteenth century, the position of the dramatist was more secure than previously. Copyright reforms resulted in an author's proprietorial rights being protected with greater safety. He was paid rates reflecting the commercial value of a successful play. More impetus to produce original work was given by the Berne Convention of 1886, which stopped the pilfering of French and German plays.* In 1891, Dion Boucicault contributed to the establishment of new copyright laws in the United States, which prevented trans-Atlantic piracy.†[73] As copyright became more effective, the dramatist was also assured of a substantial income from the reading public.[74] From around the 1890s, plays began to be published in a more durable and presentable form. They were easier to read than the earlier flimsy paperback series with their small print, such as Dicks's, Dunscombe's, Lacy's and early Samuel French editions. A higher standard for the publication of plays encouraged British dramatists to aim towards a reading public, as well as those who came to see their plays in the theatre. Turn of the century playwrights, such as George Bernard Shaw, Harley Granville Barker and J. M. Barrie included lengthy, involved and highly detailed stage directions in their works,

---

* Adaptations from the French continued. For instance, Sydney Grundy's popular comedy *A Pair of Spectacles*, which was produced at the Garrick in 1890, was a version of the Parisian success *Les Petits Oiseaux* by Labiche and Delacour. [Grundy was a prolific playwright, largely basing his plays on French originals, but later choosing his own plots, notably in *The New Woman*. —Ed.]

† Ironically, Boucicault had himself been guilty of trans-Atlantic plagiarism. He evidently stole the idea for the sensation scene in his melodrama *After Dark* (Princess's 1868) from *Under the Gaslight* by the American dramatist and manager Augustin Daly. The sensation scenes in Daly's melodramas were regarded by the author as an essential element and were subject to copyright. Daly took out a successful action against Boucicault and received a royalty for every performance of *After Dark*.

partly for the benefit of those reading their plays away from the theatre. By 1900 the successful stage author could enjoy a more secure life than his predecessors, largely thanks to the efforts of Dion Boucicault.[75]

The dramatist as director of his own plays

With his increasing financial and social status, the dramatist began to direct his own plays. Although 'stage management' (or directing) was an almost exclusively male preserve, some women dramatists were involved with producing the plays they had written.* Replacing the stage manager as superintendent of rehearsals gave the male dramatist a patriarchal control over his output. For a play to be advertised as being 'under the personal direction of the Author' asserted a previously denied authority. The dramatist's professional integrity and independence were increased; his subservience was diminished. Instead of the actor exerting his demands over the dramatist, it was the author who now had almost total power over the actor. However, there were dissenting voices among actors and managers. The actor-manager Wilson Barrett claimed that dramatists were 'mistaken' in expecting to direct entire productions themselves 'without reference to scenic effect and many other things which go to make the success of the play'. He thought that 'people who do the work of production can often help the author very much after he has invented his motive or mainspring'.[76]

Nevertheless, dramatists such as Dion Boucicault, T. W. Robertson and W. S. Gilbert possessed an intimate knowledge of theatrical technique, which they utilised in their productions. Dion Boucicault led the way for authors to produce their plays themselves, rather than entrusting them to the stage manager. Stage management was part of his strategy to give more power to the playwright and eliminate subjugation to managers and star performers.[77] Boucicault began directing his own works in 1855 in America, when he managed the Gaiety Theatre in New Orleans.[78] As a director, he was determined to ensure that everything was done the way

---

* For instance, Sara Lane, manager of the Britannia Theatre during the 1870s and 80s, produced and performed in a series of melodramas written by herself. See Powell 1997, 125, 131. Marie Bancroft directed her own one-act play *My Daughter* at the Garrick, where it had several performances in 1892. (British Library Playbill 343).

he wanted. He was a strict disciplinarian and worked ruthlessly to get the right results, often with little regard for personal feelings or sensibilities.[79]

In 1915, Townsend Walsh, Boucicault's first biographer, claimed to have 'pumped dry' every actor he had met 'in the last twenty years' who had appeared with the great playwright and actor-manager.[80] Boucicault as a director may have been 'an exacting martinet' but, according to Walsh, 'his every word of direction was obeyed with childlike docility'. However, he had 'a vast number of enemies' among actors: some were envious of his talent and success, others were intimidated by his 'hot, hasty Irish nature'. Yet, according to Walsh, they all acknowledged him as being 'a masterful stage manager'; his instructions were carried out with 'enthusiasm and admiration'. Leading actors 'obeyed implicitly and without a murmur the dogmas of the dramatist, sometimes given harshly and always imperiously'.[81]

Boucicault also had the ability to spot talent among actors and to see what was wrong with a scene and make it work. In his methods of staging, Boucicault was, according to Ernest Bradlee Watson, 'careful, insistent and extremely inventive'.[82] The famous Polish-American actress, Helena Modjeska, remembered how he 'took infinite pains teaching most of the people not only how to say their lines, but what to do, how to bow, how to enter or exit, even how to hold a snuff-box and how to brush off with a graceful gesture the snuff from their ruffled frill'.[83] Boucicault may have been a disciplinarian with his actors, but ultimately he was intent on winning his public with 'sensational' stage effects. These were designed to excite audiences, bring crowds into theatres and increase the profits of the entrepreneurial author.

Contrasting with Boucicault's sensational melodramas were his friend Tom (or T. W.) Robertson's attempts at domestic realism at the Prince of Wales's Theatre. This small venue on the periphery of London's West End (in Charlotte Street, near Tottenham Court Road) *was run by the talented 'actress-manageress' Marie Wilton with her husband, Squire Bancroft. The theatre (seating 814 in 1866) had been deliberately revamped to accord with the tastes of an upmarket audience. Its elegant interior, complete with white lace antimacassars on the seats, giving the

---

* Previously the Queen's Theatre, now the Scala. See note on page 5. —*Ed.*

feeling of a middle-class drawing room, perfectly accorded with the 'genteel' comedies of T. W. Robertson. The conventional values of his plays matched those of the middle- to upper-class audiences who flocked to the Prince of Wales's Theatre during the 1860s and 70s.[84]

Figure 42. Thomas William Robertson

Robertson's success was due to the support of a woman manager. Between 1865 and 1870, Marie Wilton presented Robertson's series of comedies in which he attempted to show 'real life' on the stage. Today, these plays may seem conventional, but in his time, Robertson was considered to be extremely innovative. He rejected the mannered acting and sensationalism of melodrama, replacing it with naturalism and restraint. His plays attempt to reveal ordinary people in ordinary, everyday situations. Their deliberately non-rhetorical dialogue demanded a restrained style of acting. Similarly, scenic effects were not spectacularly decorated but were as realistic as possible.

Nearly all of the plays have one-word titles hinting at the theme, rather than blatantly advertising it: *Society*, *Caste*, *School*, or *Ours*. The sensational aspects of melodrama are replaced by moments of rather banal domestic realism, such as portraying a fully equipped tea party.[85] It was the tea and sandwiches scene in Act I of *Caste* that caused his plays to be popularly referred to as 'cup-and-saucer drama'. Despite his attempted realism, Robertson did not completely overthrow conventions. His characters are very human, amusing and likeable, but he proceeds with extreme care. At the outset, he may introduce themes of considerable social significance, yet he does not resolve or develop them. In his best-known play *Caste*, the serious question of relations between social divisions becomes subverted into a pleasing fantasy aimed at a society audience. This restraint characterises his plays as much as it did the man.

Robertson was the antithesis of the sheer power and energy of Dion Boucicault. Marie Wilton remembered him as being of 'a highly nervous temperament ... biting his moustache and caressing his beard'.[86] Yet, despite their different natures and styles of dramatic writing, Robertson and Boucicault were the first nineteenth-century British dramatists to significantly influence the staging of their plays and the performances of actors.[87] At the Prince of Wales's Theatre, the Bancrofts gave Robertson a position of total artistic control over his plays. He accepted leadership, but, as Bradlee Watson has written, he 'chose to cooperate rather than dictate'.[88] However, he also possessed the gift of imparting his ideas and 'making vivid to the actors the characteristics they were to impersonate'.[89] The Bancrofts found working with him 'a labour of love', claiming that the ideas of the author were in perfect accordance with those of the actors. Marie Wilton wrote of rehearsals for *Society* in 1865: 'My views on acting so entirely agreed with Mr Robertson's that we encountered no difficulties whatever, and everything went smoothly and merrily.'[90]

It seems extraordinary that, as the Bancrofts assert, a play could be rehearsed and performed under the conditions of the nineteenth-century theatre, without any signs of temperament or dissent. Their claim may be questioned, but the complete abandonment of a group of actors to the development of a new, realistic manner under the guidance of one man was unique for its time.[91]

Robertson's would-be naturalistic comedies fell out of favour, but he was not forgotten. In 1884, Henry Arthur Jones wrote of 'a distinct vein of Mr Robertson's influence' running through almost every comedy and almost every melodrama produced since his time. But, as Jones acknowledged, his school was 'passing away' and 'the next step forward in

English drama does not lie in that direction'.[92] Nevertheless, Robertson created a distinctive style amid all the adaptations and stock melodramas of the mid-Victorian theatre. His radical influence foreshadowed the 'realism' in late nineteenth-century society drama.*

W. S. (William Schwenck) Gilbert claimed that stage management, as it was then understood, was due to Robertson's innovations. In directing his own plays and comic operas, Gilbert proved to be as innovative as Robertson and as demanding and autocratic as Dion Boucicault. William Archer maintained that he was the only English author to possess enough force of character to impose his conceptions on 'an autocratic stage manager'.[93] Gilbert's passion for control over every aspect of the production of his works arose both from his aggressive temperament and his view of the condition of the Victorian stage.[94] Like Boucicault, he was determined that authors should assert their rights. He maintained that a manager had no right to interpose between the author and the realisation of his ideas. To ensure the absolute authority of their written text, authors should see that their works had adequate and proper rehearsals. New plays should not be thrust on the stage after a few days preparation, as was usual in stock theatres. Gilbert insisted that the success of a play depended on the time spent rehearsing it.[95] He insisted that the author had absolute authority over every aspect of his play, including advising on casting and costume.

Gilbert's mission was to wrest the control of his plays from the interference of actors and management. By usurping the traditional function of the stage manager, Gilbert cast aside haphazard production methods and introduced a more disciplined approach. His direction of the Savoy operas for the D'Oyly Carte Company was increasingly militaristic. The cast had to be obedient to his every command. He created a model stage for blocking the action, in which the actors were represented by small pieces of wood.[96] At rehearsals, Gilbert would adhere strictly to these blockings, drilling his actors in every movement and gesture, every

---

* Pinero, in his comedy about the 1860s theatre, *Trelawny of the 'Wells'* (1898), famously paid a fictional tribute to Robertson, in the character of Tom Wrench. In the last act of the play he clearly demonstrates that he saw Robertson as the instigator of direction by the author, rather than by the stage manager. See Bratton 1995: note, 326.

inflexion of speech. When these had been perfected, he would spend long hours practicing facial expressions and the smallest movements of hands and feet. He was prepared to go over every scene, or section of a scene, twenty, forty or fifty times if necessary.[97]

Figure 43. W. S. Gilbert as 'Ironmaster at the Savoy'

Producing the Savoy operas in the 1880s allowed Gilbert to perfect his techniques. His ultimate aim was for the performance to be as close as possible to his own conception. The rigid discipline that he enforced to achieve this aim was perfectly acceptable in the late nineteenth century. Gilbert had a militaristic belief that 'The principle of subordination must be maintained in a theatre as in a regiment.'[98] The actor George W. Smalley remembered his 'Procrustean rules' for training actors 'to which all natural gifts must be made to bend. ... So many steps to a particular spot; such a gesture to express such an emotion; the arms to be moved in accord with a settled theory of plastic effect; the tones of the voice to be such as the master thought most likely to come over the footlights.'[99]

Although he has been criticised for reducing the D'Oyly Carte Opera Company to 'a troupe of mimicking marionettes', there is evidence that he collaborated with players to create 'business' and sometimes incorporated their ad-libs into the text. It has even been recently argued that Gilbert was capable of a more psychological approach to characterisation. This was probably 'a fundamental part of his coaching of experienced and trusted actors'. The 'mimetic' approach was possibly reserved for those actors who had yet to be moulded into Gilbert's 'preferred shapes'.[100] However, Gilbert made no compromise on adhering to the text as he wrote it. An actor who introduced an unapproved gag might be fined half a week's salary.[101]

Gilbert's contemporaries, such as Arthur Wing Pinero, followed his methods by directing their plays as a non-divergent rendering of their work exactly as they had conceived it. Mrs Patrick Campbell, for instance, complained of the 'awful fatigue' of rehearsals for *The Second Mrs Tanqueray* (1893). Pinero imposed upon the actors 'every piece of characterisation—every inflection'.[102] However, the actor Cyril Maude, in his autobiography, claimed that Pinero rehearsed the cast with 'extraordinary care and attention'. Sitting close to Mrs Patrick Campbell, 'he taught her every word and look'. According to Maude 'She bore it like a lamb.'[103] Yet she appears to have given more understanding to Pinero's fallen woman, Paula Tanqueray, by resisting his emphatic, melodramatic stage directions. Instead, she subtly indicated a woman of sensibility with a refined upbringing. This conflicted with Pinero's indication of the lurid past of a courtesan.[104] Mrs Patrick Campbell's resistance to the restrictive direction of a male author resulted in her great success in the role of Paula Tanqueray. Yet late-nineteenth-century playwright directors, such as Pinero, were extremely protective of their work. The stage was a space for playing out the drama exactly as written, with little allowance for innovation by the performers. Producing his own plays now gave the male dramatist an opportunity for the exertion of power over the actor.

The stage producer, as distinct from the author as director, has generally been acknowledged as a twentieth-century development.

However, there is evidence to suggest that the equivalent of the modern producer (as opposed to the 'stage manager' or author) existed from at least the 1880s. An anonymous article entitled 'A Few Words from the Unseen' appeared in *Theatre*, May 1889. It reveals the existence of an individual in overall control of the stage production, separate from the stage manager or the playwright. Probably written by a producer, the article takes its cue from the words on West End playbills: 'Produced under the direction of —' The article claims that 'these few words' have appeared 'lately on the bills of many a London theatre'. However, the producer is 'generally passed over unobserved by the play going public' and the critics often ignore his efforts.[105] By the 1890s, the producer was gaining more attention and his name appeared prominently on the bills. Some actor-managers also advertised themselves as producers. Paul M. Potter's dramatisation of Du Maurier's *Trilby* was 'produced under the personal direction of Mr Tree' at the Haymarket in 1895.[106] Not only did Beerbohm Tree manage the theatre and famously star in the role of Svengali, he directed the play as well.

Censorship and the call for reform

By the end of the nineteenth century, the British dramatist had gained greater control over his output. He could direct his own plays. He earned more money and enjoyed a higher social standing. Yet his creativity and freedom of expression was still greatly curtailed by the restrictions of censorship. He was forced to conform to the demands of two sources of policing—the Lord Chamberlain's office and a conservative public opinion. These powerful forces combined to inhibit the fruition of a mature British drama, unafraid to portray controversial issues. Instead, the Lord Chamberlain exercised a paternalistic control over artistic expression. This amounted to a male empowerment over authors and theatres. Not only was censorship under masculine control. The debates it provoked during the latter half of the century were led by influential men of letters, such as William Archer and George Bernard Shaw.

The Theatre Regulation Act of 1843 had abolished the patent theatre monopoly* and allowed spoken drama in all theatres. However, gaining

---

* See page 5. —*Ed.*

the right to perform any type of drama tightened the censorship of what was performed. All theatres had to submit any piece to be acted 'for hire' to the Lord Chamberlain. He had absolute authority to forbid the performance of the whole or any part of the play. These restrictions applied to all dramatists, whether male or female.[107] The Lord Chamberlain's authority was delegated to the Examiner of Plays. This functionary was also the licenser of theatres. But by far his most important duty was to observe the Lord Chamberlain's legal instructions regarding subjects suitable for the stage. This ensured that the dramatist could not give free expression to many contemporary problems. Overt representation of religious, political, or moral matters was forbidden. Official censorship ensured the absence from the stage of open discussion of sexual problems. Furthermore, the views of the Lord Chamberlain were reinforced by conservative public taste. The majority of playgoers, managers and even dramatists agreed with official control over subjects for theatrical representation.

There was concern for the protection of women and children from unsavoury subjects. In 1853, George Henry Lewes protested against the licensing of an English translation of the fallen woman play *La Dame aux Camélias* by Dumas *fils*. The life of a courtesan was 'a subject not only unfit to be brought before our sisters and our wives, but unfit to be brought before ourselves'.[108] It was men who decided on the subject matter suitable for women to see. Lewes's protest is also hypocritical in suggesting that the fallen woman theme was 'unfit' for his own sex. Many upper class men kept mistresses and furtively participated in the so-called *demi-monde*.*

In 1899, George Bernard Shaw wrote in an article for the *North American Review*: 'I can say that few things would surprise me more than to meet a representative Englishman who regarded my desire to abolish the Censor otherwise than he would regard the desire of a pickpocket to

---

* While Dumas' *La Dame aux Camélias* was banned from the British stage for over twenty years, Verdi's operatic adaptation *La Traviata* was performed in Italian, at Her Majesty's Theatre, in May 1865. An English version of the opera, called *The Blighted One*, was licensed for the Surrey Theatre in the same year. There seems to have been a difference between the suitability for audiences of opera and spoken drama. See Stephens 1980: 104–105.

abolish the police.'[109] In other words, Shaw's 'representative Englishman' felt safe to visit a theatre, where thanks to censorial control, he was guaranteed protection from shock or outrage, where he would not be confronted with uncomfortable truths, where the accepted standards of decency, decorum and respectability would be upheld. The patriarchy of the Lord Chamberlain ensured his comfort.

The dramatist who wanted his plays performed had to be careful not to offend his audience or the censor. The vigilance of The Examiner of Plays had to be constantly borne in mind. Passages containing alleged or actual political, sexual or religious allusion were struck out of an otherwise acceptable script. But this censorship created confusion among authors and was highly hypocritical. Some plays were rejected entirely, while adaptations of risqué French comedies could be passed on the grounds that they were frivolous and therefore relatively harmless. On the other hand, works of literary merit by British authors (such as Wilde's *Salomé*) were subject to vigorous censorship.

William Archer saw 'the very existence' of the Lord Chamberlain's office as 'a perpetual menace to dramatists'. Its interference either silenced them or frightened them off from tackling any but perfectly 'safe' themes. A dramatist could 'spend a year of his life in the construction of a serious work of art which may be annihilated at a single stroke' by an overzealous censor.[110] With the creativity of the dramatist being inhibited by the ever-watchful eye of the Examiner of Plays, there seemed to be little hope for the cultivation of a serious British drama relevant to the important questions of the day.

The Lord Chamberlain was hardly challenged until the 1890s. Indeed, most of the support for his censorship came from within the theatre itself. Victorian managers and playwrights found it advantageous to have the boundaries of their subject matter laid out for them. In 1892, at a time of intense debate on censorship, the American dramatist Arthur Goodrich wrote in *Theatre* magazine that

> The duty of the Censor is to reject the immoral and protect and encourage the moral. Therefore all the dramatist has to do is to conform to regulations which, personally, he may object to, but he has no right to set aside.[111]

In effect, a dramatist became his own censor, taking care to avoid subjects which might be considered offensive and, at the same time, bearing in mind the fact that a rejected play meant loss of income. Similarly, a manager knew better than to seek a licence for a script that could be considered anarchic, blasphemous, or immoral. It is relevant that out of nearly 3,000 plays submitted to the Lord Chamberlain between 1852 and 1865 only nineteen (less than 1 per cent) were refused licenses.[112]

The plight of the dramatist may be compared with the difficulties faced by novelists over the restrictions placed upon them by publishers and circulating libraries. These organisations exercised a form of censorship similar to that of the Lord Chamberlain in the theatre. The high purchasing power of Mudie's Circulating Library (founded in 1842) gave it tremendous influence over the publishing market. Its founder and director, Charles Edward Mudie had strong views on the proper moral tone he considered fiction ought to take. Like the Lord Chamberlain with drama, he had the power to consign a book to failure. Although Mudie's censorship was not official, it was an example of the power exerted by the opinions of one individual. He was frequently attacked by both authors and publishers angered by his censorious selection and exclusion of books. When Mudie's finally closed its doors in 1937, one source of censorship vanished, but the control of the Lord Chamberlain over drama remained firmly in place.

The dramatist confronted a more powerful, officially sanctioned form of censorship than the novelist. Until the action taken by William Archer, George Bernard Shaw and other progressives in the 1880s and 90s, remarkably few voices spoke out against the power of the Lord Chamberlain. Some mid nineteenth-century dramatists even expressed gratitude for the advice of the Examiner of Plays.[113] According to the Report of the 1866 Select Committee on Censorship, Charles Reade and Dion Boucicault were two dramatists who 'expressed no objection to the existence of censorship, if only it were accompanied with a right of appeal, probably to the Home Secretary'. Boucicault was also convinced that 'the English public, like that of the United States, is perfectly fitted to be its own Censor'.

Two men of the theatre who opposed censorship were John Hollingshead, manager of the Gaiety and the dramatist, Tom Taylor. At the 1866 Select Committee, they 'maintained in unqualified terms the futility of the office' of the Lord Chamberlain.[114]

In the 1870s a challenge to censorship came from W. S. Gilbert. He wrote a letter to the editor of *The Era* in which he defiantly stated that he considered himself to be 'quite as well qualified to judge of what is fit for the ears of a theatrical audience' as William Bodham Donne, the current Examiner of Plays. Gilbert 'systematically declined to take the slightest notice of Bodham Donne's instructions'.[115] The following year, he deliberately baited the Lord Chamberlain's office with his political burlesque *The Happy Land*, first performed at the Court Theatre on 3 March 1873. Defying the rules against the portrayal of living political figures on the stage, Gilbert turned Gladstone and two of his ministers into cartoon characters. He satirised their policies and personal mannerisms without any pretence at disguise. The burlesque attacked the Government's bungling attempts at reform by a thinly disguised trio of mortal politicians provoking similar chaos in Fairyland.[116]

Bodham Donne had licensed *The Happy Land* claiming that it contained legitimate general satire. However, at the first performance, it became apparent that not only did the text contain specific political gibes; the three main characters were made up to look exactly like their real-life political counterparts. Having attended the first performance himself, the Lord Chamberlain notified Marie Litton, the female manager of the Court Theatre, that the licence would be revoked unless the subversive make-up was removed and the offensive text modified. The play was performed that night in defiance of the Lord Chamberlain, but continued in a sanitised version.[117] The 'objectionable masks' (i.e. make-up) were retained when the burlesque went on tour in the provinces 'where political feeling certainly runs quite as high as in London'.[118]

The action of the Lord Chamberlain exemplifies the hypocrisy his censorship engendered. The political satire in *The Happy Land* was no more harmful than that which appeared regularly in the articles and cartoons of journals such as *Punch*. William Archer maintained that 'the only rational excuse' for the Censor's 'act of authority' was that 'the political prejudices of the audience' might be aroused 'to endanger the public peace'.[119] The stage was supposed to remain silent on all controversial matters. There was an underlying fear that satires like *The Happy*

Land could provoke anarchy such as had been recently seen in Europe. Gilbert's political stage burlesque challenged these notions. *The Happy Land* was successful—it ran for over 200 performances and led to further experiments in the same vein. Gilbert's next challenge to the authorities came in his farce *The Realm of Joy* (1873) where he referred to the Lord Chamberlain as 'The Lord High Disinfectant'.[120]

Figure 44. Henry Arthur Jones

Regardless of the attempts of censorship to exclude serious contemporary debate from the stage, the decade from 1885 to 1895 was termed 'the Renascence of English Drama' by Henry Arthur Jones. It was the era in which all of Wilde's dramatic output was performed (before he was disgracefully silenced). The best work of Jones and Pinero appeared during this period, as did the early plays of George Bernard Shaw. Above all loomed the widespread, if controversial, influence of Ibsen, giving an impetus for a more realistic, outspoken drama. This was a period of intense debate in the theatre, instigated by William Archer, George Bernard Shaw and Henry Arthur Jones. In innumerable articles and addresses they argued for necessary reforms to the British theatre. But the main thrust of their campaign was against censorship. Without the removal of the Lord Chamberlain's powers British theatre could not progress.

The clash between conservatism and progressiveness resulted not only from censorship, but also from the self-imposed limitations of dramatists. Ideally they should have been able to break away from censorial constraints. Yet the majority continued to be inhibited, not only by the Lord Chamberlain, but also by their own innate conservatism. Most West End dramatists held reactionary views and came from the same respectable backgrounds as their audiences in the stalls and dress circle. Any attempt to approach daring or controversial themes was ultimately diverted by giving the play an expected, stereotypical denouement.

A successful dramatist did not want to risk having his work suppressed before an audience could make its own judgement. In an article on censorship, William Archer suggested there was a stigma attached to the suppression of a play. The author could be consigned to obscurity by having his work pronounced unfit for public presentation. His reputation could be tarnished and his subsequent work might not be performed at all. If his play was banned the dramatist had 'no means of stating his case or setting himself right with the public'. He would be seen as 'the vendor of immoral wares ... for the public does not draw that distinction between serious art and ribald frivolity which the Censor is so careful to draw.'[121] It was argued that censorship reflected the views of the majority of the public, whose voice was listened to attentively by the Lord Chamberlain. Theatre was a popular art form. Censorship could control its power to influence opinions, encourage imitation or mould behavioural attitudes.

Unfortunately, censorship severely restricted the so-called Renascence (or Renaissance) of British Drama, especially as dramatists were denied the freedom to deal with serious contemporary issues.[122] At a time when British drama could have made more worthwhile contributions to the world stage, it had to suffer the prejudices of Edward F. S. Piggot, the Examiner of Plays who succeeded William Bodham Donne. His inhibitive censorship accelerated the campaigns of William Archer, Henry Arthur Jones and George Bernard Shaw. But they found themselves in a minority as they were opposed by numbers of critics, managers, actors and dramatists—all of whom who supported the Examiner of Plays.

Archer was further isolated through his defence, in 1892, of Oscar Wilde over the suppression of the London production of *Salomé*. This was to have starred Sarah Bernhardt. The play was fully in preparation, when, to Bernhardt's surprise and annoyance, the British censor stepped in. Piggot banned *Salomé*—not only because of its Biblical characters—its theme of incest also gave offence. Wilde attacked the Examiner of Plays for pandering to 'the vulgarity and hypocrisy of the English people, by licensing every low farce and vulgar melodrama', while suppressing his poetic treatment of desire.[123]

Archer's defence of Wilde's *Salomé* was especially courageous, considering there was almost universal support for censorship. Archer was the only witness to advocate its abolition when he appeared before the Select Committee's 1892 enquiry. All the other witnesses, led by veterans such as the actor-manager Henry Irving, the reactionary critic Clement Scott and the dramatist Comyns Carr, spoke strongly in favour of the Lord Chamberlain and Piggot.[124] The anti-censorship campaign became a battle between opposing male factions. An army of Piggot supporters ultimately defeated Archer, Shaw and their supporters.* Archer seemed undeterred by this powerful support for Piggot. He continued to express his concerns over the 'destructive influence' of censorship. Unless it was abolished, 'near-pornographic' comedies and melodramas approved by the Examiner would continue to fill theatres, while important plays by Ibsen, Pinero and Jones might never reach the stage.[125]

Piggot is a paradoxical figure in the late nineteenth-century debates on drama. He retired in February 1895 and died about a month later. He provoked strongly partisan feelings between opposing reactionary and progressive forces. Estimates of his worth depended on where a man (or woman) stood in the debate.[126] To his supporters he was a tolerant, beneficent censor, encouraging high moral standards in drama, 'reflecting the feeling of the English public through all its alterations and inflections'.[127] Piggot's detractors saw him as tyrannical, bigoted and responsible for the retardation of British drama. Shaw wrote for the *Saturday Review*: 'It is a great pity the Censorship cannot be abolished

---

* Although they had opposing ideas, Clement Scott, toward the end of his career, was complimentary about Archer's abilities. He writes that Archer was a 'learned and accomplished critic and student'. Drama received 'full value of his careful and meditative method'. (Scott 1899: I, 542, 554). Scott evidently had the ability to differentiate between performance and the play. He seems to have admired Archer as a writer and thinker, while resisting his progressive ideas on Ibsen and censorship.

before the appointment of a successor to Mr Pigott [*sic*] creates a fresh vested interest in one of the most mischievous of our institutions.' Sharing Archer's concerns over censorship, Shaw was almost hysterical regarding Piggot's relationship with the 'higher drama'. This was: 'one long folly and panic, in which the only thing discernible in a welter of intellectual confusion was his conception of the English people rushing towards an abyss of national degradation in morals and manners, and only held back on the edge of the precipice by the grasp of his strong hand'.[128] To give him his due, Piggot had the difficult task of censoring drama at a time when many of the accepted values were being overturned and psycho-sexual issues were being widely discussed.

Jacob Grein, an 'unconventional' foreign influence

Because of censorship, playwrights continued to portray dubious subjects in a coded form or to have their plays performed in private theatre clubs. The first and arguably most important of these venues was the Independent Theatre Society, founded by the Dutch journalist and entrepreneur Jacob Thomas Grein. Born of a Jewish family in Amsterdam, Grein brought a foreign influence into the conservative British theatre. He had moved to London in 1885, where he worked both in commerce and journalism. According to his wife, Alix (who wrote under the masculine pseudonym of Michael Orme), Grein, despite his Dutch Jewish origins, made life in England 'definitely his own'.[129] But it was not until 1895 that he became a naturalised British subject. In London he started his own periodical *The Comedy: a Fortnightly Review* (it later became *The Weekly Comedy*). However his reputation increased with the founding of the Independent Theatre Society in 1891.

Possibly it was Grein's Jewish heritage that contributed to his energy, enthusiasm and financial acumen. While progressives such as George Moore and William Archer continually debated the necessity for a 'British free theatre' modelled on André Antoine's Théatre Libre in Paris, it was the foreigner, Grein, who was prepared to put the idea into action. The Independent Theatre Society was intended to be an alternative to the commercial theatre. Grein's idea was to present plays of a high literary and artistic value rejected by commercial managements, or, more importantly, banned by the censor. Emphasis would be placed on the author rather than star actors and scenic innovators. In order for such a venue to function legally it had to be a subscription society for members and guests. In this way, productions would be 'private' and the Examiner of Plays could have no censorial control over the plays presented. By flouting the Lord Chamberlain in this way, Grein was advocating a typically British compromise. He was able to present unlicensed plays by running the Independent as a club, but, as we shall see, he was prevented from entirely fulfilling this aim.

Figure 45. J. T. Grein

Like other avant-garde ventures, a minority supported the Independent. Although the controversial initial production of Ibsen's *Ghosts* in 1891 had 3,000 applications, throughout its existence the Independent never had more than 175 members.[130] By comparison, the London private theatre clubs of the 1950s and 60s had memberships of tens of thousands. The paradox of private club performances (usually on Sunday nights) would continue virtually until the abolition of censorship in 1968. As a rule, Independent productions appeared only twice, once for members and once for the general public.[131] The organisation survived on a financial shoestring. Grein maintained that its income was never more than £400 per annum. Despite these low returns, he remained convinced that progressive drama could not flourish on the commercial West End stage. It belonged to the small private theatres with minority audiences.[132] Having subsidised the Independent Theatre himself, Grein withdrew from management in 1895. He remained attached to the Society, but concentrated on his business interests in the City.[133] The Independent then became a limited company and struggled on until 1898.

Grein usually described himself on playbills as 'Founder and Sole Director' of the Independent.[134] Although he presided over the venture, he had the support of his lifelong collaborator and friend Charles W. Jarvis, who was, for a time, secretary. There were also a number of helpers backstage and in administration. Initially Grein appointed a committee, which apart from the novelist, Julia Frankau, consisted of several outspoken men, including George Moore and Frank Harris. The aim of the committee was to find a permanent home for the Independent. But this was not to be, mainly because rent was a prohibitive factor. There was also a foreign (mainly Dutch) male influence in the society's administration. A. Texeira de Mattos, born in Holland, was a secretary for the organisation and translated into English plays by Zola and the Belgian symbolist Maurice Maeterlinck. Another Dutchman, Herman de Lange, not only acted in, but also produced, most of the plays presented by the Independent. He was, according to Grein's wife 'an autocrat ... but many actors remember much of "the business" they learned under his austere, paternal guidance'.[135] In 1894, the female dramatist and author Dorothy Leighton joined Grein as co-director, bringing a temporary prosperity and helping him with the incorporation of the society.

Grein's venture only lasted for a few short years—from 1891 until 1898. His management was inclined to be contradictory. Changes of policy beset the Independent from its controversial first production of Ibsen's *Ghosts* at the Royalty Theatre on 13 March 1891, until its final performances (of *Blanchette* by Eugene Brieux) in 1897. Grein's contrariness resulted partly from the difficulties of finding suitable plays, and partly from his own moralistic stance. Like the Parisian Antoine, he wanted to promote 'realism' in the work of new dramatists, but it was to be realism of a 'healthy kind'. At the same time he was opposed to what he saw as 'the immorality' of the plays performed by Antoine's troupe.

He also thought a lot of modern French drama was 'simply filthy'. According to his wife 'his tastes were quite unaccountable'.[136] He championed Zola and Ibsen but was 'horrified to the soul' by Shaw's comic diatribe on the economic necessity of prostitution, *Mrs Warren's Profession* (1893). Yet the play he chose to launch the Independent Theatre Society was Ibsen's *Ghosts*, concerning the taboo subject of hereditary disease.

The sad fact was that no suitable play by an 'unconventional' British dramatist, containing a 'healthy' realism, could be found. Grein rightly thought *Ghosts* a great play that should be seen. He decided he would circumvent the Lord Chamberlain's ban by giving it a club performance. The ensuing furore (led by reactionary critic Clement Scott, with whom Grein had a life-long feud) is well known, and it is sufficient to say that *Ghosts* brought both fame and notoriety to the Independent Theatre. Yet Grein was forced into a position where he had to retract on presenting uncensored plays, and subsequent productions were licensed.*

The dichotomy between Grein's desire for a liberated theatre and his innate conventionality seems to reflect the uncertainties of an era when the open discussion of social and morally relevant matters was only approved to a certain extent, before it was restrained by middle-class mores.

Grein also 'ignored the risk of being mistaken for one of his grandfather's race'[137] at a time of anti-Semitic prejudice in certain circles of British society. Nevertheless he was an alien Jew whose productions of controversial and foreign plays upset members of a parochial and xenophobic mainstream theatre. This was especially the case with his production of *Ghosts*. Even worse, his venture was in 'imitation' of Antoine's 'notorious' French theatre that supposedly performed plays of a dubious nature.

The powerful Henry Irving was vehemently opposed to Greins's policies. He railed against the Independent Theatre and its promotion of

---

* This paradoxical situation was exemplified by the performance of William Archer's translation of the Danish drama *A Visit* by Edward Brandes at the Royalty Theatre on 4 March 1892. Archer, furious at the censorship of his translation, had the full text, with the suppressed dialogue in brackets, printed out on leaflets and distributed to the audience. See Schoonderwoerd 1963: 118.

literature 'absolutely foreign to British codes of morals, manners and social usage'.[138] Meanwhile Grein was critical of Irving for his lack of interest in new British drama at the Lyceum. He was also highly critical of the British theatre in general—its plays, management and actors. Some of this criticism was published abroad in French, Dutch and German journals. Grein also gave praise where it was due and offered his services as an intermediary between Dutch theatre companies and British authors, suggesting English plays suitable for production in Holland.

In many ways, Grein was the antithesis of the usual late Victorian theatre manager. He had been a dramatic critic and playwright in his native Amsterdam, but he was an amateur regarding theatre management. He did not act or produce and he rarely attended rehearsals. Nor did the Independent perform any of his own plays. He did not develop a permanent company or have a permanent theatre like Antoine in Paris. Venues, usually on the periphery of the West End, such as the Royalty Theatre in Soho, were hired for performances—usually at matinées.[139] These were theatres that were either about to close, or had seen better days, and were inexpensive to hire.

Although Grein supported the company with his own funds, productions were as economical as possible. Elaborate West End scenic realism was conspicuously avoided. Grein maintained that 'elaborate scenery and eminent actors were for a bad play'. More important were ample rehearsals and good stage management. The scenery used was often from the stock in the theatres where the Independent performed. Casting was always a problem, especially as finances had to be considered. Amateur actors were used with variable results, while professionals sometimes appeared gratis or for a small fee. They considered it worthwhile appearing at the Independent because of the publicity it attracted. While Grein promoted some well-known actors, his haphazard system meant that he never formulated a distinctive method of acting, as found in Antoine's company. Grein also seemed to be unaware of the ascendancy of innovative directors in Europe, such as Stanislavski in Moscow, Reinhardt in Berlin and Copeau in Paris. The Independent productions ignored experiment and did not promote any radical new British director.

Grein did, however, attempt to encourage new British dramatists, even if the results could be disappointing. He advertised the Independent as 'a literary theatre' but this aim was never quite fulfilled, despite his intention to 'stimulate the production of a native unconventional school, and to give a hearing to those who strive to foster the undeniable *renaissance* in drama'.[140]

George Bernard Shaw wrote that Grein's search for 'native dramatic masterpieces' was pursued 'with the ardour and vigour of a foreigner'[141] but no real masterpiece came to light. The difficulty was, as Shaw admitted, that most aspiring dramatists were attracted by the possibility of fame, money and success in the commercial theatre: 'No author whose play strikes, or is aimed at, the commercially successful pitch, will give it to Mr Grein.'[142] Another problem was that Grein promised his subscribers half a dozen new plays each season. This meant that new plays had to be found, whatever their quality, and most presented were, according to Shaw 'indifferent'.[143]

Grein also claimed that plays had been 'promised by writers of distinction'. These either did not materialise, or were failures due to the author's lack of theatrical expertise. This was the case with George Moore's *The Strike at Arlingford* (Opera Comique, 1893). *A Question of Memory* by the female partnership known as Michael Field* (also presented at the Opera Comique in 1893) proved they were better poets than they were dramatists. Most of the other 'native' writers were minor talents, or were without theatrical experience. Grein, with varied success, presented the first and only plays of writers known in other spheres, such as Arthur Symons†, James D. Vyner and Dorothy Leighton. He also promoted the first plays of John Gray and Marc-André Raffalovich, both of whom had tenuous connections with Oscar Wilde and his circle.

George Bernard Shaw was the only British dramatist of real talent and lasting fame to be staged by the Independent, and then the society only presented his first play, *Widowers' Houses*, in December 1892 at the Royalty Theatre. Grein with his contrariness turned down Shaw's next play *The Philanderer* (1893) and positively rejected *Mrs Warren's Profession* (completed 1893). Yet it would have taken Shaw a great deal longer to be accepted without Grein's support. He later told Grein that it

---

* Nom de plume of the lesbian couple Katherine Bradley and Edith Cooper —*Ed.*
† See page 32. —*Ed.*

was the existence of the Independent Theatre that made him finish writing *Widowers' Houses*. Grein had given him the experience of rehearsal and performance and showed him that he possessed the gift of 'fingering' the stage.[144] Lesser dramatists must have also felt the same debt of gratitude at a time when, in other spheres, controversial plays were either rejected or censored. Grein believed there existed 'a small but daily increasing number of younger authors' who wanted to convey 'real human emotion' and to show 'real human life'. The position of many of these authors was hopeless unless Grein could rescue them and obtain a try-out at one of his matinée performances.[145]

Figure 46. George Bernard Shaw

During the seven years of its existence, the Independent put on twenty-eight plays. Thirteen of these were new and original British plays, of which six were full-length, and seven were in one act. These numbers included five plays by women dramatists, which, considering the relatively small number of their plays presented commercially, was quite a substantial portion of the 'native' British drama promoted by Grein. Apart from plays by Ibsen and Zola, the Independent performed no other major European dramatists. Promised productions of Strindberg's *The Father* and plays by Maeterlinck did not materialise. The work of less significant Scandinavian, French and Dutch dramatists was presented with varying success. However Grein did at least give his audiences an idea of trends in drama outside Britain.

Grein promoted a fairly diverse range of plays. Even if they were not masterpieces, he at least gave struggling British writers and dramatists a chance to have their work performed, to see it come alive in rehearsal and on the stage. The Independent also paved the way for the establishment of other private theatre clubs promoting uncensored new drama.

A notable successor was the Stage Society (later the Incorporated Stage Society), founded in 1899 by Frank Whelen. This was a substantially more successful venture than the Independent. It offered more varied plays and its performances were better rehearsed. As well as plays by Shaw, it presented suppressed or non-commercial work by a number of notable early-twentieth century British dramatists, including Harley Granville Barker, Somerset Maugham, St John Hankin and Arnold Bennett. Among foreign dramatists, it gave the first British performances of plays by Chekhov, Gogol, Wedekind, Hauptmann and Strindberg. It had a far larger membership than the Independent—around 1500 by 1907. It also lasted far longer, surviving for almost forty years from 1899 until 1939.

Had it not been for Grein and his Independent Theatre, later organisations such as The Stage Society promoting 'unconventional' plays might not have existed. In 1909, William Archer traced the 'renovation' of British drama to the first performance of the Théatre Libre in Paris in 1887.[146] It may therefore be argued that it was a chain of foreign influences, from the founding by Antoine of the Théatre Libre and its subsequent inspiration for the Dutchman Jacob Grein, which provided the impetus for the flourishing of alternative theatre in Britain. Grein had founded the Independent Theatre Society as part of the protest against censorship and the desire for more freedom of expression in drama. His courageous attempt to release the British theatre from its restrictions gave dramatists, both male and female, a chance for the performance of polemical work.

The legacy of the Victorian era

Despite campaigns and private performances of suppressed plays, censorship remained firmly in its place. The late-nineteenth-century theatre edged toward a new freedom of expression, but was still subject to censorship and conservatism. These restraints gave rise to campaigning voices. Leading men of the theatre, critics and dramatists such as Boucicault, Gilbert, Archer, Jones and Shaw, fought to ensure that the dramatist was no longer relegated to a subordinate position. They spoke out against censorship; they confronted managerial control and challenged the power of the actor-manager; they secured financial rights; they allowed the dramatist to direct his own plays. Some, such as Boucicault, may have been acting out of self-promotion, yet dramatists gained more security and, by the end of the century, had greater control over their creative output.

Neither Shaw, Jones nor Archer, lived to see the fruition of the reforms for which they had so vigorously campaigned: a National Theatre was not founded until 1963; censorship was not abolished until 1968. In 1889, Boucicault had optimistically proclaimed that through his 'emancipation' the dramatist 'was made the star and the actor and manager relegated to the back seat'.[147] Yet six years later, Shaw wrote that: 'The strongest fascination of the theatre is the actor or actress, not the author.'[148] Dramatists had greater control of their creative output, but the theatre remained under the domination of a string of actor-managers, all at the height of their powers. Some dramatists may have been able to control actors in rehearsal through directing their own plays, but with a few exceptions such as Wilde, Jones and Pinero, the name of the author did not draw the general public like that of the leading actor.[149] By the turn of the century the dramatist earned more money than his predecessors, and had gained an increased social standing—but he continued to be ranked behind the interpreters of his creative product.

It is also paradoxical that, despite the call for a more progressive drama, a British playwright with the international influence of Ibsen,

Strindberg or Chekhov did not emerge. This is possibly because the British theatre was not allowed the freedom of expression found in the French, German, Russian or Scandinavian theatre. The legacy of late-nineteenth-century British drama is founded not so much on structural innovation or open moral debate, as on verbal brilliance. Oscar Wilde with his comic subversion of the 'well-made' situation, his wit and love of paradox, not only influenced the British drama of the ensuing century but ensured his international reputation as the representative playwright of late Victorian drama. Even so, his reputation as a dramatist rests mainly on one play—*The Importance of Being Earnest.* Other Victorian dramatists have not fared as well, although in Britain there have been recent revivals of plays by Bulwer-Lytton, Boucicault, Gilbert,* Pinero and Jones. These are all male dramatists, and it is significant that despite a number of interesting plays, no nineteenth-century woman dramatist has achieved lasting success.

---

* W. S. Gilbert survives on the 21st century stage through his libretti for the Savoy Operas. But even these masterpieces of Victorian comic opera are not revived as frequently as in former years, while comic operas by other Victorian authors and composers are no longer performed.

Chapter Five:
Masculinity in comedy and melodrama

CONSIDERING THE MASCULINE PREDOMINANCE in nineteenth-century British playwriting, how were masculine ideals reflected in the diversity of Victorian drama and its array of different masculine 'types'? How far do male characters in the plays represent the masculine ideal as projected by Victorian writers and thinkers such as Kingsley, Smiles and Ruskin?*

Men in the 'real' Victorian world were dominant in nearly every sphere. Ideally, they were supposed to be successful, honourable, chivalrous and morally upright. Victorian drama portrayed both the vindication and the corruption of these ideals. Like other contemporary art forms, its goal was to provide a moral lesson. However movements such as the Pre-Raphaelites and late-nineteenth-century aestheticism provide an important exception by turning away from rigid moral codes. This backlash was reflected to a lesser extent in the 'New Drama' of the 1890s.

The ideal framework for demonstrating the triumph of morality was the genre of melodrama. The melodramatic form dominated the nineteenth-century British stage—not only in the popular theatre. It was also a vital ingredient of 'high' verse drama and opera libretti. Its conventions were burlesqued on the musical stage, while its engagement with social reality was reflected in farce and comedy. With its influences on other genres, melodrama became a far-reaching, variegated entertainment. It was subject to many variations and could be more complex than just a moralistic struggle between hero and villain. Its form and content altered in response to the various social changes occurring throughout the nineteenth century.[1]

---

* Charles Kingsley, clergyman and novelist, epitomised 'muscular Christianity'; John Ruskin, art critic and social reformer, attacked the worst aspects of industrialisation; for Smiles, see Page 6. —*Ed.*

Melodrama's complexities reflect the variety of contemporary social concerns. Its idealised concepts of subjects such as morality, love, marriage, and the family stemmed from anxieties engendered by the revolutions in France and elsewhere in Europe. This made melodrama an important theatrical response to the challenges facing society. As a populist form it propagated patriotic and evangelistic ideals, while its outcome of virtue triumphant reflected the assertiveness and xenophobia of Victorian Britain.

While purporting to show realism on the stage, melodrama idealised the situations it represented. Good and evil, virtue and vice, were presented in sharply defined contrast. Until developments in the late nineteenth century, there was little room for subtlety or psychological representation. Complex situations were explained or demonstrated. Involvement with the narrative drive was more important than the situation of any one character.[2] Characters tended to be 'types' representing a social level or moral stance. Yet from these stylised representations, social and moral complexities begin to emerge, making melodrama a varied and vital dramatic form. The framework of virtue defeating evil allowed for variations within various melodramatic genres. But melodrama did not always stay within a specific genre and very often subjects overlapped. Nautical melodrama, for instance, was often combined with domestic melodrama and could even contain elements of the gothic.

In the complex, socially responsive world of melodrama, the opposing masculine forces of hero and villain led a continuous battle between good and evil. The archetypal hero embodied an idealised moral masculinity. He was chivalrous, brave, romantic, achieving and morally pure. He asserted his independence, and exemplified the romantic notion of the individual and his struggle against the universe. The hero was unquestionably heterosexual, although he bonded platonically with his own sex. He had his counterpart in the good and pure woman whom he defended, and who supported him in the defeat of evil and injustice. The hero was politically correct, never straying too far into controversy. He was intensely patriotic, upholding British values before everything else. His moral stance was imbued with an evangelistic fervour. He fought against injustice, false accusations, even imprisonment, and he invariably ensured a moralistic triumph by the final tableau. The neatly resolved ending with the hero marrying or winning the rescued heroine offered a comforting assurance of regeneration for the audience. His defeat of villainy symbolised the upholding of Christian principles and morality.

However, a wholly virtuous, unflawed hero would be theatrically boring. Within the melodramatic framework, there were many variations on the heroic type and his background, reflecting not only the different genres of melodrama, but also the era in which the work was written. The radical early nineteenth century, for example, favoured the proletarian hero: the sailor, the factory worker or the farm labourer. With the emergence of a more bourgeois society during the mid to late nineteenth century the hero rose in the social scale. By the end of the century, nearly all the heroes of melodrama came from the middle to upper classes. As the moral example supposedly emanated from upper-class masculinity in the 'real world', in the same way an upper-class stage hero demonstrated moralistic ethics to socially mixed audiences.

In the struggle between good and evil, the stage villain personified the antithesis of the masculine ideal. He subverted masculine ideology by rejecting its notions of chivalry, morality and steadfastness. He claimed strength through evil deeds, but usually finished in a weakened, defensive position. The male villain had his gendered counterpart in the female villain. While he subverted masculine ideology, she subverted the womanly ideal. She was neither passive nor virtuous, but personified the image of the fallen, impure or 'tainted' woman. Her 'masculine' qualities were evident in her attempts to exert power over men. Male and female villains were therefore equally active in the spread of evil. Both were the cause of their own destruction (they rarely died at the hands of the hero) and each ultimately suffered a fate appropriate to their gender. The male villain was usually brought down by forces of nature or by accidents within his material environment—a collapsing bridge, a burning building, drowning at sea or in a river, or even being struck by lightning. The demise of the female villain was more psychological—she was likely to go mad and die, or mysteriously commit suicide.

The destructive energy of the villain gave rise to the situation against which the hero had to prove himself. Paradoxically, it was usually the villain, rather than the hero, who exerted the most fascination for audiences. With his distinctive mannerisms, make-up and costume the male villain was far more memorable and indeed, popular—especially with spectators from lower class areas where crime was rife and where there was opposition to authority. The villain existed on various social levels. He was just as likely to be a lower-class landlord, or an East End thug, as an upper-class squire or indolent gentleman. That the villains of melodrama came from diverse social backgrounds demonstrated that evil with its consequences does not depend upon class—it exists in the psyche of the wrongdoer rather than his social status.

David Mayer has argued that because melodrama is set 'within exciting, threatening and disturbing environments' the villain becomes closely identified with anxieties arising from the domestic and colonial changes overwhelming nineteenth-century society. He personifies hostile elements confronted in a rising capitalist economy. When he is recognised, caught or killed the threatening circumstances with which he can be identified are reduced. This argument may overload the basic intentions of the nineteenth-century dramatist. But a feeling of relief was meant to envelop the audience once the villainous menace was finally removed. The ultimate unwinding of the problematic situation on the stage gave the spectator a momentary escape from the problems of his own life. Yet it also allowed for identification with domestic difficulties encountered in real life: greedy landlords, ambitious factory owners or harassers of women.[3]

The hero and villain are popularly viewed as opposing masculine forces in Victorian drama, but the distinctions between the forces of good and evil are not always so clearly defined. Well-intentioned young men can be led astray by other men who introduce them to the vices of fraud, gambling or drink. Not all those who are led into temptation can extricate themselves. Very often it is a good woman or close platonic friend who helps a fallen man back onto the path of righteousness. At other times good and evil can exist in one male character, resulting in complex feelings of guilt and remorse. If the leading male protagonist cannot resolve deep moral issues, then the way out is usually death. This is part of the continual pattern throughout melodrama, that however misguided a man may be, evil cannot triumph and a feeling of redemption should pervade as the final curtain falls.

What of the other variations on masculine behaviour found in Victorian society—of the proliferation of male figures such as the swell, the patriarch, the bohemian, the snob, the bounder? In melodrama, they become subordinate to the hero or villain. Lower class or eccentric male characters join the comic subplots. In comedy and farce however, outlandish male characters are likely to be the main protagonists. Whereas melodrama exemplified ideals of masculine morality, comedy and farce lampooned the accepted notions of the masculine ideal, by undermining patriarchal authority and making it an object for laughter and ridicule.

Comedy and farce, like melodrama, concerned themselves with the anxieties besetting society. Their themes reflected the core values of society—love, marriage and money. Both genres investigated and subverted assumptions underlying the notion of a well-ordered bourgeoisie. Domestic life and the harmony of the home became important comedic targets. With moves toward the emancipation of women, stronger, less submissive female characters became dominant in comedy. Usually it was the wife who was capable of extricating her errant husband from a tricky situation.[4] Comedy questioned the double life of middle-class men. Like the melodramatic villain, a straying husband was always caught and made an example, usually by a dominant female figure, such as his wife.

Victorian comedy and farce therefore both contrast and engage with melodramatic convention. In melodrama the hero encounters situations evoking horror, pity or excitement before domestic peace is restored. Comedy and farce show an anti-hero confronting situations which provoke laughter and derision before he returns to the haven of the home. Masculine ideals are therefore subsumed into laughter. However, as in melodrama, it is always ensured that by the final curtain, morality and social correctness are triumphant. No matter what difficulties are encountered between courting couples or between husband and wife, convention demands they be resolved or evaded. This could sometimes mean that promising or serious themes were jettisoned in favour of a crowd-pleasing conclusion.[5]

Defenders of the Empire: sailors in melodrama

Defending Britain's vastly expanding Empire was a prime masculine responsibility. The Army and the Navy were major employers of men, while soldiers and sailors played an important role in popular and patriotic imagery. Their exploits were reported in newspaper articles, they featured in stories, while their uniformed appearance was recorded in paintings, photographs, post cards and engravings.

And of course, soldiers and sailors figured prominently in Victorian stage entertainment. So far as melodrama was concerned, their exploits complied with prevailing moods of patriotism and xenophobia. Uniformed heroes, especially sailors, also became mouthpieces for social criticism. This was particularly the case in the pre-Victorian era when the restive decades of the 1820s and 30s engendered radical ideas. Radicalism, like so many other attempts at social reform in the nineteenth century, was largely male driven. Male working-class characters such as sailors, agricultural labourers or factory workers expressed criticism of social injustice. As befits a movement concerned with the rights of the lower classes, the promotion of radicalism in melodrama belonged to the minor theatres, many of which were located near to areas with large working-class populations.

Nautical melodrama was one of the most important stage genres to express radicalism. Not only did it promulgate patriotic British ideals, it also included situations identifiable to the audiences, especially those living close to ports and the sea—trouble with landlords, the press gang, long absences of men at sea and problems on returning home. Because its characters were mainly ordinary people, nautical melodrama was popular with audiences at the Surrey Theatre and other minor venues. Its populism made it an ideal vehicle for social criticism. The genre contained the usual stock characters such as the villain, heroine, comic man and comic woman, but the introduction of the sailor hero created a unique and individual character. Here was a figure embracing most of the ideals associated with manhood. He was brave, patriotic, chivalrous, courteous to his superior officers, and loyal to his waiting wife. He gave support to the oppressed, and vehemently opposed social injustice—condemning issues such as capitalist greed, slavery and the cruelties of British naval life. At the same time he was intensely patriotic and not afraid to openly express his emotions.

As represented on the stage, the sailor hero was a stylised figure, presenting a heavily coded image that made him instantly identifiable and set him apart from the other characters in the play. His appearance changed little from the early to the mid nineteenth century. He wore a distinctive 'nautical' costume and make-up, while he spoke in a specific maritime jargon, laden with sea-faring metaphor. His feelings for comrades, his wife or sweetheart, his ship and flag were expressed through metaphorical language filled with maritime imagery as in this example from Douglas Jerrold's *Black-Ey'd Susan* (1829):

> WILLIAM: There's my Susan! Now pipe all hands for a royal salute; there she is, schooner-rigged—I'd swear to her canvas from a whole fleet. Now she makes more sail!—outs with her scudding booms—mounts her royals, moonrakers and skyscrapers; now she lies to! [6]

Not only were the purity, bravery and patriotism of the sailor-hero offset by a defining costume and jargon, specialist actors interpreted him on the stage. The best known of these was T. P. (Thomas Potter or 'Tippy') Cooke, who starred in nautical roles from around 1825 to 1860. So great was his popularity that he was demanded at theatres catering for audiences of all social levels. He could as easily perform before lower class audiences at the Surrey Theatre in Blackfriars as for more socially mixed patrons at the Adelphi in the West End. His popularity allowed plays with a different emphasis on the sailor-hero to become acceptable.[7] Early in his career he presented a new type of sailor-hero to the public— William, in Douglas Jerrold's *Black Ey'd Susan; or All in the Downs*. This character overthrew the earlier eighteenth and nineteenth century stereotype of the swashbuckling 'Jack Tar'. He was a more believable creation.

Charles Dickens, in a letter to the painter Clarkson Stanfield, dated 24 August 1844, described T. P. Cooke as William. His costume consisted of trousers which were 'very full of the ankles'; a 'black neck kerchief' was 'tied in regular style'; the name of his ship was painted around his 'glazed hat'; he wore a red waistcoat; the seams of his 'blue jacket' were 'paid with white' (i.e. smeared with pitch or tar to make them waterproof). Dickens continues with a description of Cooke's 'business' which suggests the style of his acting:

> I lift up my eyes as far as I can ... take a quid from the box—screw the lid on again (chewing at the same time, and looking pleasantly at the pit)—

brush it with my elbow—cock up my right leg—scrape my foot on the ground—hitch up my trousers.[8]

As the *Illustrated London News* noted in 1853, William was a 'new school of sailor who could render Jack harmonious and put a soul within his senses. ... At last, we had the man—the simple, fervent, genial, fearless, self-forgetting man'.[9]

Figure 47. Mr T. P. Cooke as 'William' in *Black-Ey'd Susan*

Here was a working class 'tar' who was also the indubitable romantic hero. He was also a devoted husband who eagerly returned to his wife after three years' brave service to his country. The focus was not on exploits at sea, but on the relationship of husband and wife in a domestic setting.[10] But perhaps the most important aspect of Douglas Jerrold's new type of sailor-hero was a working class origin that allowed for radical inferences. William had to join the Navy in order to escape the poverty of a rural labourer's existence. Social relevance such as this made him identifiable to audiences at minor theatres, many of whom encountered similar difficulties in lower-class life. Identification with William's predicament was a factor that contributed to his immense appeal.[11] *Black-Ey'd Susan* was possibly the most influential of nautical melodramas. Its popularity continued throughout the nineteenth century when it was performed in various versions, and inevitably became the subject of burlesques.*.

Some plays sought to raise the social level of the stage 'tar', transforming him into an embodiment of middle-class morality. Often the obscurity of his origins was overcome by the discovery of a genteel birth or being restored to long-lost connections. For instance, Mat Merrion, sailor-hero of J. T. Haines's *The Ocean of Life; or Every Inch a Sailor* (Surrey, 1836) is elevated to officer status so that Isabella, the upper-class lady he marries, may have a husband of appropriate social rank by the time the curtain falls. The social elevation of the working-class sailor hero lessened to a certain extent his earlier position as a spokesman for social injustice among the lower orders. It was a step toward the heroic example being set by upper-class values and the relegation of lower-class characters to a secondary comedic status.

Nautical melodrama may have raised questions regarding the status of sailors, but it gave very little space to the worst excesses of naval life such as flogging, or to moral issues such as sodomy at sea. Indeed there is an almost complete avoidance of the question of maritime homosexuality. The public and the Lord Chamberlain would not have tolerated this subject. Furthermore, a sailor-hero could not possibly be involved with actions that were universally condemned and were punishable by hanging. In the navy, buggery was subject to more severe penalties than in army or civilian life. It was considered as serious as murder or mutiny.[12] While the nautical hero is never involved with sodomy, a hint of misconduct may be levelled at a villainous character. For instance, there is a suggestion of male sexual misdemeanour in the nautical drama, *The Harbour Lights* by George R. Sims and Henry Pettitt, produced at the Adelphi in 1885. The secondary villain, Nicholas Morland, has been

---

* Burlesque versions include *The Latest Edition of Black-Eyed Susan; or the Little Bill that was Taken Up* by F. C. Burnand and M. Williams (Royalty, 1866) and a *Black-Eyed Susan Burlesque* performed at the Alhambra on 30 July 1884.

dismissed from the navy for misconduct. Evidently, he had behaved 'disgracefully' before he was court-martialled. The play's strongly heterosexual hero, David Kingsley, refuses to defend him at the trial. The exact nature of the offence is not disclosed. That it is something too dreadful to be mentioned gives a strong implication of sodomy—particularly as Nicholas Morland does not show desire for any of the female characters in the play.[13]

Among the other evils besetting early nineteenth-century maritime life, the sudden appearance of the press gang was a convention of nautical melodrama. The situation of the hapless hero carried off by the gang on his wedding day undoubtedly aroused audience indignation at the unjust methods of the Royal Navy. As he is forced away from his bride by the press gang, Harry Hallyard in J. T. Haines's *My Poll and My Partner Joe* (Surrey, 1835) inveighs against this unjust system and the country that invented it, yet he ultimately resolves to do his duty 'as a man':

> What! Force a man from his happy home, to defend a country whose laws deprive him of his liberty? But I must submit; yet, oh proud lordlings and rulers of this land, do ye think my arm will fall on the foe as though I were a volunteer? No!—I shall strike for the hearts I leave weeping in my absence, without one thought of the green hills or flowing rivers of a country that treats me as a slave! [14]

Harry Hallyard's speech demonstrates the anger of the lower classes against those in high positions. Men are needed to fight for their country, and it is the working classes who suffer when husbands and fiancés are forcibly removed. Harry claims that he will fight for the honour of his friends and family, rather than a country that treats him as 'a slave', yet in the following act he goes back on his word, making patriotic statements and defending the honour of 'Old England'.

Flogging, the other great cruelty of early-nineteenth-century shipboard life, is condemned in a handful of melodramas with reformist zeal, but it is never physically presented on the stage. The sight of men stripped to the waist, tied to masts, and whipped until it drew blood, would have been too distressing for audiences, despite the violence found in a great deal of melodrama, and indeed experienced by audiences dwelling in the poorer districts of the metropolis. Graphic representation of naval cruelty would also have fallen foul of censorship by bringing the service into disrepute. *The Sea!* by Charles A. Somerset (Queen's Theatre 1834) is one nautical melodrama that speaks out boldly against a system that allowed men to be flogged. Jack Neptune, the play's sailor-hero, intervenes when a drunken crew member is about to be whipped by his captain:

> Punish him your honour, but not with that instrument of torture, the cat; it is cruel, degrading and unnatural. The man who has been once publicly whipped, if he possess one spark of manly feeling, sinks too low in his own estimation to rise; and I trust the day is not far distant when so foul a stain on our national character, as the laceration of a fellow-creature's flesh, will be blotted from old England's naval and military code forever![15]

Impassioned speeches such as this and Harry Hallyard's denunciation of the press gang made the stage a platform for reform. Naval sanctioning of cruelty and injustice tarnished the patriotic image of 'Old England'. Parading such ideas before predominantly working-class audiences could be viewed as an incitement to revolution and were a cause for alarm by the establishment.

When Victoria ascended the throne in 1837 the radicalism of melodrama was diminishing. Although he was still capable of social criticism, the sailor-hero was becoming less outspoken. A potentially dangerous working-class sailor could be made safer by cocooning him in archaism and nostalgia. He gradually became a comic character subordinate to his socially superior officers. He was also a more sentimentalised creation, reassuring audiences about the pleasanter side of a sea-faring life. Harsh realities tended to be ignored, and his ship became a haven. For a sailor to feminise his vessel as 'she' or 'her' gave it the aspects of both wife and mother. The feminisation of his vessel extends to metaphorical comparisons with wives or sweethearts. As Paul Perilous tells his Phoebe in Edward Fitzball's *False Colours! Or, The Free Trader!* (Theatre Royal, Covent Garden, 1837):

> You are my ship, my chart, my life. By day, by night—in the calm and in the storm—your image was always my beacon light—the point from which the compass of my soul never varied.[16]

In his attempts to win Phoebe, he constantly uses maritime imagery. Metaphorical language merges the love for his sweetheart with his longing for his ship and the camaraderie of its all-male crew. While at sea, his woman is a memory, and he is surrounded by the presence of male physicality. A sailor's attachment to his ship is in danger of replacing his longing for the wife, sweetheart or mother waiting for his return from sea. For instance Ben Binnacle in C. Z. Barnett's 'nautico-domestic melodrama' *The Loss of the Royal George; or the Fatal Land Breeze* (Sadler's Wells, 1840) is uncomfortable on land and anxious to return to his ship, which takes on the aspect of a welcoming female presence:

> I don't like being ashore somehow at all: 'cos when you're in a town, all the streets are so much alike, there's no telling one from t'other; and the houses are the very pickers of each other: and then when you're in the country you see trees, hills and fields, and fields, hills and trees: 'twould puzzle an admiral to tell the different bearings. Well, I'll aboard once more; I always feels as pleased to see the old ship again, as a middy does, with a well-filled locker. The *Royal George*, bless her tender heart, is the best craft on the waters.[17]

The stage sailor is no longer a threat to the establishment with dangerously radical pronouncements. He now lulls the audience with his feelings of sentiment and nostalgia.

Tom Tough in *The Minute Gun at Sea!*, also by C. Z. Barnett (Surrey, 1845), paints a positively idyllic picture of a sailor's life:

> Give me the life of a sailor. He roams the world—his ship is his home—he carries with him his apartments ready to be furnished. The world's treasures are laid bare to him, every climate, every soil, every people become familiar to him—and if he gets shot in defence of his country, his bed is ready to receive him. ... His pride is his duty—and to maintain the uninjured flag under which he serves. He has few wants beyond his grog and the girl of his heart. His purse is his shipmate's who needs it—and if the evening of his life seems lowering through his early prodigality, there rises on the distant horizon of his old age the stately towers of Greenwich Hospital—the sailor's hope, his refuge, his reward.[18]

This speech subscribes to a romantic middle-class view of the British 'tar'. This sailor does not criticise the establishment. He presents an optimistic view of life at sea. He is uncomplicated, dutiful, generous and patriotic. These were the qualities mid-nineteenth-century audiences associated with the sailor and preferred to see on the stage.

Nor has *The Minute Gun at Sea!* a contemporary setting like many previous nautical melodramas. The action takes place during the eighteenth century, in 1749. This remove in time allows for a more distanced view of some of the worst features of a sea-faring life. There is mention of flogging and the press gang carries off the hero Miles Lansdowne on his wedding day. Both of these injustices had disappeared by 1845. Setting the play in the previous century also invites a comparison between the 'improvements' of the early Victorian era and the 'bad old days'. The play is therefore imbued with a sense of nostalgia. For instance Tom Tough, the principal sailor in the play, is designated as wearing 'old fashioned seaman's dress' in the costume list. Nor does he represent working class radicalism. Instead of being the hero, he is a rather sentimental, comic figure, the sidekick of upper-class Miles Lansdowne. Tom Tough does not appeal against injustice, but reinforces the popular image of the 'jolly sailor':

> We never says a word to make folks sad or sorry—'cause, do you see, we're never sad or sorry ourselves. Whoever saw a melancholy sailor? Why it is as unlike his character as top boots would be to a dress.[19]

Tom may be lower in rank to Miles Lansdowne, but class divisions are transcended by the platonic friendship between the two men and the support which Tom gives to Miles. They serve together at sea, performing brave deeds, such as preventing the crew from getting drunk 'to quell the despair of their situation' when the ship is about to sink. Tom loves Miles 'as a brother' and, like a pedagogue, he teaches him how to perform maritime tasks:

> And I was proud on him. I first larned him to knot and splice, and he took it so kindly. ... Many an hour have I stood at the binnacle to larn him how to box the compass—and it did my heart good when he took his first trick at the weather wheel and kept her course so steady that he might have shoved the end of her flying jib boom into a musquito's eye.[20]

When Miles faces death by hanging he leaves his sister Rachael to the care of Tom and asks her to become his wife.[21] This portrayal of masculine friendship continues the theme of male bonding found in earlier nautical melodrama, particularly friendship and support between men of different ranks. Sailor-heroes remain firmly heterosexual, but this does not exclude close platonic friendships with their mates. A late nineteenth-century 'naval officer' wrote that friendships between men at sea 'tend to be much closer, more sentimental than when ashore. Everything makes for confidentiality, one is shut away from the world, and so much in pairs with friends, during watches and so on'.[22] In nautical melodrama these loving friendships almost invariably end in loss. Friends can be parted in battle, or, as in *The Minute Gun at Sea!* they can be separated by an accusation of desertion and the sentence of hanging. But the threat of separation does not last long as Miles is reprieved at the last possible moment—just as he is about to go to the gallows.

A later nautical melodrama *Ashore and Afloat* by C. H. Hazlewood (Surrey, 1864) also harks back to earlier conventions, yet its sea-going hero, Hal Oakford, belongs to a higher social stratum than previous nautical melodramatic heroes. He exhibits the flaws and virtues associated with young upper-class men. His father is a well-to-do farmer and he looks forward to receiving his inheritance, but he is a philanderer and succumbs to the vices of drinking and gambling. Yet he is also capable of performing good deeds. When Hal is reminded by his captain, after an attack on Algiers, that a prisoner must be treated with respect, Hal's response is imbued with patriotism and a British sense of fair play: 'Of *course* he must, your honour; and while England is the first to conquer her foes, she may also prove the last to ill-treat them.'[23] In this play an upper-class character is outspoken when it comes to social injustice. When Abn Ali, an escaped slave, exclaims 'Happy England, where slavery is unknown', Hal replies 'Not quite unknown for we've women who make shirts for five farthings a piece, and if that isn't slavery I don't know what is.'[24] This is a reflection on the plight of out-working needle-women. Hal also exhibits qualities of heroism that redeem him from his youthful prodigality. At the conclusion of the play he rescues the heroine Ruth who is trapped in a flooded mine, by descending into the mineshaft in a basket. This 'sensation scene' gives an example of the heroism of a nautical hero. His final ascent toward the light above, clinging to a rope while supporting the rescued heroine, typically symbolises the triumph of an idealised masculinity over forces of evil.

The sailor could also be a more complex figure than the bland chauvinism of the average melodrama suggests. He could exemplify

British working-class strength, while being potentially problematic.[25] George Soane's *The Chelsea Pensioner* (Queen's Theatre, 1835) has a sailor-hero who is jealous and violent. He poses a threat to others and his career is threatened by his problems. Frank Meaden, boatswain of the *Lion*, returns from sea to discover that his Jane has an (albeit innocent) interest in soldiers. This induces a fit of jealousy in which he tries to strike her.[26] He is xenophobic, harbouring an almost pathological hatred of the French:

> Deep sea swallow them! The French lubbers—I hate them—men, women and children; it was a French devil with her *parlez vous* that made Jane false to me—but only let me come amongst them![27]

He is capable of exhibiting the bravery and magnanimity associated with the usual sailor-hero, saving the life of his captain and returning at the last minute to claim his fiancée. However even the proverbial 'happy ending' is unsettling. Jane, thinking she will never see Frank again, leaps off a rock into the sea. No sooner is she saved by the 'idiot boy' Walter, than Frank suddenly appears and takes his unconscious fiancée in his arms. As she recovers, the stage directions call for *Thunder*. Seeing Frank, she *'laughs hysterically'* and faints.[28] While it is unlikely that a dramatist of this period would have utilised any great psychological insight, the conclusion of *The Chelsea Pensioner* seems to ask questions. Its mixture of nautical and gothic elements contributes to a disturbing departure from the usual moralistic or patriotic resolution.

H.M.S. Pinafore: parodying naval melodrama

Nautical melodrama was the subject of innumerable burlesques and parodies. But perhaps the most enduring of these is Gilbert and Sullivan's comic opera *H.M.S. Pinafore; or the Lass that Loved a Sailor* (Opera Comique, 1878). In his libretto, Gilbert mocks and subverts many of its conventions: overt patriotism, the crossing of boundaries of rank; the masculinity of the sailor-hero. He manipulates a popular genre of melodrama as the basis for a satirical debate on the subject of social equality. Through parody he demonstrates the absurdity of melodramatic conventions.[29]

The opera opens by portraying a happy, united crew watched over by a benevolent captain. The sailors are to all intents and purposes stalwart and patriotic. However, they are not the lower class, hard-drinking rough and swearing men who usually made up the crew of Victorian battleships. These sailors are more refined. They speak with the diction and vocabulary of Oxford graduates. They serve on a ship that does not take its name from a masculine symbol of British imperialism, but from a feminine domestic garment.

In the opening chorus, the sailors maintain that they are

> sober men and true,
> And attentive to our duty.[30]

But their claim is undermined by a hint of misdemeanour:

> When at anchor we ride
> On the Portsmouth tide,
> We have plenty of time to play.[31]

The pure and dutiful image projected by the stage tar is mocked by Gilbert. Sailors were not always sober, true or attentive. Their 'play' when ashore could involve drunkenness, visiting prostitutes or even an involvement with male prostitution. Although he avoids the unmentionable subject of sodomy, Gilbert's tars are highly theatrical. Their 'attitudes' may parody the melodramatics of T. P. Cooke, but they also mock the theatricality behind overt displays of maleness:

> His foot should stamp and his throat should growl,
> His hair should twirl and his face should scowl;
> His eyes should flash and his breast protrude,
> And this should be his customary attitude—(*pose*).[32]

Ralph Rackstraw, the hero, is a parody of heroic tars such as William in *Black-Ey'd Susan*. But he is not the brave and brawny figure usually associated with the 'British sailor' on stage. Instead, he is more like the softer Romantic hero of the well-made play. His romanticism is made absurd by his quasi-maritime surname which literally means 'bedding straw'.[33] His fondness for romantic rhetoric is made ridiculous through being uttered by a 'common sailor':

> In me there meet a combination of antithetical elements which are at eternal war with one another. Driven hither by objective influences—thither by subjective emotions—wafted one moment into blazing day, by mocking hope plunged the next into Cimmerian darkness of tangible

despair, I am but a living ganglion of irreconcilable antagonisms. I hope I make myself clear, lady?[34]

Figure 48. Poster for *H.M.S. Pinafore*.

At other times his language parodies the sea-faring metaphor and jargon of the sailor-hero in melodrama:

> Well your honour, love burns as brightly on the fo'c's'le as it does on the quarterdeck, and Josephine is the fairest bud that ever blossomed upon the tree of a poor fellow's wildest hopes. ... She is the figurehead of my ship of life—the brightest beacon that guides me into my port of happiness.[35]

Josephine herself takes on a task usually reserved for a male character. When lovelorn Ralph threatens to shoot himself, she appears in the nick of time to prevent him. This is a gender-reversal of the stock situation in which the heroine about to kill herself is saved by the sudden appearance of the hero. Being the captain's daughter, Josephine is a heroine who is not of the lower orders, but from a higher rank. Gilbert subverts one of the typical conventions of nautical melodrama—usually the sailor-hero loves a girl of his own class and she would be threatened by the attentions of a high-ranking villain. The love of a young man for an unattainable woman, usually of dubious morals or of higher social standing, is a convention of social melodrama. In Gilbert's satire, Ralph is a romantic hero of lower status. Josephine may be socially unattainable, but, like other 'well-made' heroines, she loves a man of lower rank and wants to marry him. Nor is she the 'older woman' of society melodrama. As Andrew Crowther has pointed out, the absurd confusion of the ending proves that if the Captain and Ralph were exchanged as babies, Josephine must be younger than Ralph and he must be older than he appears—making him the older man.[36]

Questions of social status are complicated by the appearance of a man of higher rank, Sir Joseph Porter. His outlook is strongly heterosexual and class-biased. He maintains that 'A British sailor is any man's equal, excepting mine.'[37] Sir Joseph embodies the patriotism found in nautical melodrama, but diverges from the usual pattern. In early nineteenth-century melodrama the tar exhibited xenophobic aggression toward foreign tyrants. Sir Joseph targets the tyranny of higher British Navy ranks. He demands Captain Corcoran not to fall into the temptation to take advantage of his crew just because they are of a lower rank:

> That you are their captain is an accident of birth. I cannot permit these noble fellows to be patronised because an accident of birth has placed you above them and them below you.[38]

Sir Joseph further subverts melodramatic convention through endorsing class equality. He is a member of the ruling class rather than a disgruntled 'common man'. Furthermore, he undermines the Smilesian notion of the self-made man. Through advancing himself, a man can be 'the Ruler of the Queen's Navee,' without even having gone to sea. It has nothing to do with intellect or knowledge of nautical matters.[39] Through his ironic portrayal of Sir Joseph, Gilbert pokes fun at those who have reached high positions in the Navy and other organisations—sometimes without prior knowledge or interest in the background to their post.

Sir Joseph's desire to marry Josephine casts further aspersions on the order of the ship. It will be a levelling of rank. On the other hand, Ralph Rackstraw's intention to marry her is destructive to social order. However it is a foregone conclusion that Josephine and Ralph will be united in time for the finale. This is due to the absurdities of a conclusion in which Gilbert parodies several melodramatic conventions. The swapping of babies of different classes is a convention made famous in Verdi's opera *Il Trovatore* (1853). It was, of course, later parodied by Oscar Wilde in *The Importance of Being Earnest*. The sudden, miraculous revelation of the change of status of the hero is a similar situation to that found in nautical melodramas such as J. T. Haines's *The Ocean of Life* (1836). Ranks are exchanged with the rise in position of the sailor, meaning that he can gain privileges previously denied to him—including the captain's daughter.[40] Sudden exchanges of rank have repercussions for the heroine. She is now reduced to being the daughter of a common sailor, but if she marries Ralph, she will be elevated to her former social position.

Gilbert utilises, and makes even more absurd, melodramatic conventions, in order to ridicule the notion of a class system based on birth.[41] His satire supports the existing social order, but it has an appeal for all social levels. While the gallery possibly enjoyed the jokes at Sir Joseph's expense, the intellect behind the parody would have appealed to the educated middle classes in the stalls. They would have found in the satire a way of emasculating and even debasing the sailor-hero. Differences between rank and class are a subject for laughter. For instance, when Captain Cocoran becomes a 'common sailor', the actor portraying him traditionally showed his fall in station by adopting a cockney accent and dropping his 'h's.[42] Through mocking the snobbery and differences in naval rank, Gilbert satirises the attitudes of both the working-class tar and the upper-class officer. .

Soldiers on the stage

His brave deeds, patriotism and distinctive qualities made the sailor, rather than the soldier, the popular representative of British heroism on the early-Victorian stage.

However, with the advent of the Crimean War in 1853, the emphasis temporarily shifted to the soldier. The Crimean War disrupted the comparative peace of the mid-Victorian period. This conflagration occurred far from Britain in an exotic sounding land. The British soldier being sent abroad to fight for his country aroused deeply patriotic emotions. With British and French forces combining to oppose the Russian enemy, the Crimean War forced British men serving in the forces to sail away from the motherland to fight in a virtually unknown terrain. For this reason the conflict loomed in the popular imagination, having as great an impact as the Boer War at the end of the century. Reports of the war could be read in newspapers, while engraved illustrations and photographs gave at least an idea of the reality of the battlefield. Nevertheless, for popular audiences, spectacular reproductions on the stage with living actors and scenic effects presented a greater reality than the printed word could convey. Twenty-five patriotic melodramas dealing with events in the Crimea were performed between 1854 and 1855. In London, these plays were produced in transpontine theatres, south of the river, or in the East End. They were theatres attracting a considerable lower-class patronage. Using the conventions of melodrama, the Crimean War plays portrayed contemporary events taken from descriptions in newspaper articles. An attempt was made to replace the fictional representation of military and maritime men usually found in melodrama with real-life situations.[43]

In the Crimean War melodramas, the common soldier becomes the central figure. The topical context of events elevates him from being a rather dubious secondary comic character, as he was often represented on the stage. Even so, the nationally loved figure of the British 'tar' is not far away. In most of the Crimean War plays British sailors continue to make a prominent appearance, demonstrating their customary bravery by coming to the aid of beleaguered French and British armies. But the central focus is on heroic British soldiers from the lower ranks. The emphasis is therefore on the deeds of a lower-class masculinity rather than the upper echelons, such as the generals who led their troops into battle. The common soldier as a central figure brings home the effect on the lower-class man of the horrors and turmoil of war. As with other forms of melodrama dealing with a lower-class milieu (such as 'nautical' or 'factory' plays) the Crimean War play provides characters identifiable to working-class elements in the audience. Recognisable characters on the stage helped audiences to understand and participate in contemporary events.[44]

A further attempt at authenticity was made by the introduction of regional British soldiers from Ireland, Scotland and Wales. Although the use of regional types could be seen to demonstrate the effect of war on the common man, these characters were usually comic stereotypes. In particular the Irish soldier became (according to *The Times*) 'an indispensable and often central figure' in 'every military melodrama ... the chief representative of valour and humour in the three kingdoms'.[45]

While claiming to be realistic representations of the Crimean War, these melodramas relied heavily on conventional character patterns and plotlines, no doubt because they were written in haste. However the situation and setting did allow for the introduction of new themes, particularly in the representation of foreign masculinity. French and Russian soldiers personified the popular view of foreign infantry on the stage. The French, who had tended to be despised in British melodrama, were now shown to be bold and dashing officers. Ordinary Russian soldiers were depicted as members of Slavic races, especially Poles and Circassians eager to escape Russian oppression for the freedom of France or England. All Russians were supposed to be suppressed by the Tsar and his agents who forced them to fight under the *knout*. Gallant Russian officers (often called Romanoff) express their faith in 'England's Rule' when they are rescued wounded from the field by British officers.

Melodramatic convention existed alongside attempts at an almost documentary realism in the presentation of these plays. Generals and personalities like Florence Nightingale were portrayed on the stage. Actors representing real life military leaders made rousing and patriotic sounding speeches, based on those reported in the press. Documentary realism extended to crowd scenes and the would-be faithful reproductions of battles.

The Battle of the Alma, a 'Grand Military Spectacle' presented at Astley's Royal Amphitheatre on 23 October 1854, was an example of the combination of documentary realism with theatrical spectacle. The production employed large-scale masculine forces to represent battalions of soldiers going off to battle. Not only did it employ 400 supers, but the cast included appearances by actual soldiers—the '1st Royal Fusiliers and the Band of the Coldstream Guards'.

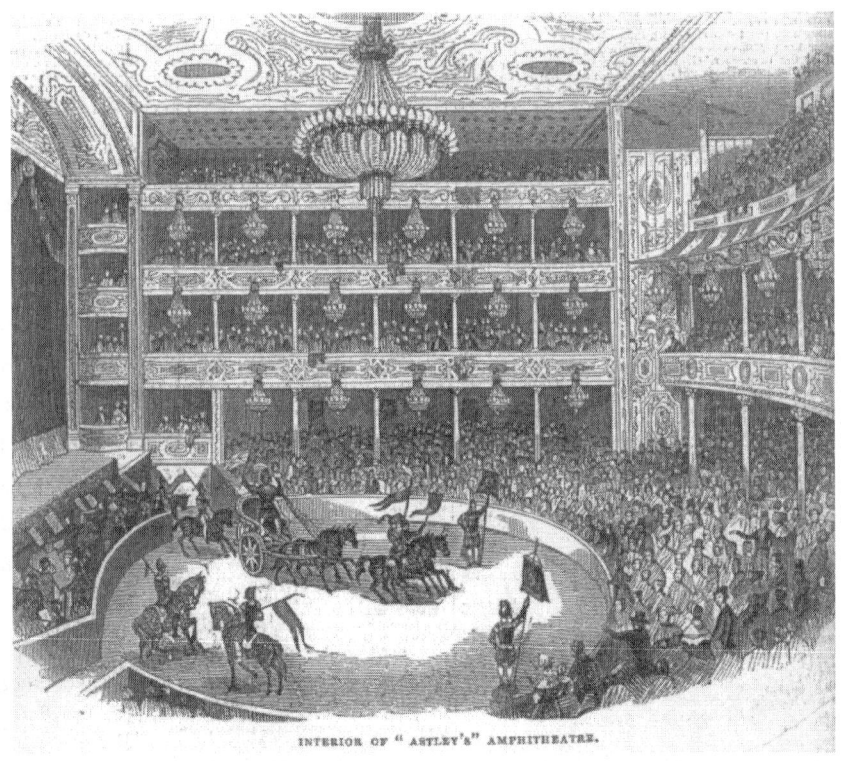

Figure 49. Interior of Astley's Royal Amphitheatre

Astley's, the home of the circus and equestrian spectacles, in Westminster Bridge Road, Lambeth, made the production as realistic as possible, giving it the utmost emotional and patriotic impact. This is evident in the opening scene in which soldiers take their leave and embark from Southampton Pier. A steamer is seen alongside the wharf. Soldiers embark while the on-stage band plays the popular song 'The Girl I Left Behind Me'.

The Times described the spectacle: 'To enlarge the field of action an inclined platform, nearly as broad as the stage itself, descends from the stage into the circle, so as to cover the whole of the orchestra' who are 'forced to take their place at the side'. In the first scene the main body of troops entered 'not by the wing, but by the circle, and then march in order up the inclined plane, till they embark in the vessel'. Soldiers rising through the middle of the audience caused 'a general excitement'. In the final battle 'the allied forces proceed through the circle, and ascend the platform ... till the Cossacks make a sally into the ring, when two conflicts take place—one on the stage, and the other below so that the whole theatre becomes a field of battle'.[46]

According to the stage directions for the final scene 'all the incidents of war must be observed'. The ultimate battle scene with its 'Grand struggle between Cossacks and Cavalry' contained realistic detail, probably gleaned from newspaper reports: 'As the English and French advance—the wounded are brought to the rear—the women of sailors attend them—bind up their wounds and carry them off.'[47] The spectacle concluded with a 'Grand Charge ... up the heights, which are cleared of the enemy and the English and French colours hoisted amidst loud cheers of God Save the Queen'.[48] Evidently the audience was 'wrought into a feverish state of excitement' by the battle scenes which they regarded 'as symbols of the real conflict abroad'.[49] Static illustrations of battle could be viewed in journals and newspapers, but the stage was able to give a living representation of the conditions of the Crimean conflict.

By 1855, as the Crimean War dragged on, patriotism had become tinged with disillusionment. Even in earlier plays flaws in the conduct of soldiers and sailors subverted the resolutely patriotic image. George Dibdin Pitt's *The Battle of Inkerman* (Pavilion Theatre, 1854) includes a traitorous British sailor who becomes the object of execration. In *The Siege of Sebastopol; or the Horrors of War* (Britannia Theatre, 1855), a comic cockney soldier confesses to being a coward, wishing he were a supernumerary soldier in the theatre, and expressing nostalgia for the London pubs.[50] Newspaper reports of the difficulties faced by men at the front were reflected in the plays. *The Fall of Sebastopol* (Astley's 1855) contains complaints about the conduct of the army, and the sufferings of the men at Balaklava during the bitter winter of 1854–55 are graphically presented. Frozen groups of British soldiers are discovered 'muffl'd up' against the cold—'Jack Frost' takes noses.[51] Sergeant Campbell describes Balaklava as a 'dirty hole. ... There's not a pigsty in the United Kingdom that wouldn't be clean compared with Balaklava.'[52] Meanwhile Miles the navvy assures the audience that anyone who has seen the suffering of the soldiers as he has would not grudge the taxes needed to support them: 'No one can see our soldiers toil, fight and suffer, as I have seen them, without feeling how worthy they are of their country.'[53] In the last scene brave British sailors are turned into beasts of burden. They are forced to haul heavy cannons by hand because the horses are weakened by bad provender.[54] The sailors perform the task with 'cheerful pluck' but there is an underlying criticism of their loss of heroic status through being reduced to taking on the tasks of animals. There is also an insistent attack on the unfairness of the British Army system of purchase and promotion, especially when compared with the French and Russian armies. As J. S. Bratton has pointed out, 'The prevailing tone of the piece reflects the less euphoric public mood.'[55]

Ten or so years later the events of the Crimean War were the subject of domestic comedy in Tom Robertson's *Ours*. This play concentrates more on the upper-class officer, while presenting the common soldier in a rather patronising light. The Bancrofts at their Prince of Wales's Theatre, which was aimed at an upper level patronage, produced *Ours* in 1866. In the play, an upper-class Scottish officer, Angus MacAlister, goes to the Crimean war 'for the sake of change', and captures the Russian colours. As well as eulogising the bravery of a Scottish soldier, this play succumbs to the convention of wives and girlfriends following their men to battle. In the third act the general's wife Lady Shendryn, together with her niece Blanche Haye and companion Mary Netley, intrude into the masculine confines of a military hut, which seems to trivialise the hardships and horrors of the Crimean war. Mary and Blanche play at being soldiers, and there is more pre-occupation with food and drink than with the off-stage skirmish between the British and Russian armies.

The play was well known for the ingenious making and baking of a roly-poly pudding on stage in the Third Act. This domestic activity diverts attention from the battle raging outside. The battle seems to last a remarkably short time before the officers return to eat with their women 'All on the alert as at a picnic'.[56] This view of domestic cosiness is far removed from actual conditions on the Crimean front. Yet the presence of women near to the battlefield is not so far-fetched as it would first appear. There is evidence that some wives did in fact travel to join their soldier husbands at the Crimean front.[57] Several of the Crimean War plays discussed earlier have wives following their husbands to battle. For instance, in *The Battle of the Alma* Paddy O'Driscoll's wife Biddy follows him to the battlefield, while Russian ladies seated 'in the carriage of Prince Menchikoff' watch the conflict from a safe distance.

Ours is one of Robertson's 'genteel comedies' so it is perhaps appropriate that its upper-class officers are shown in a fairly positive light. Only one of the soldiers, Chalcont, a commissioned officer, has been wounded. Although he has sustained an injury to his leg, he is able to be fairly mobile. While the other officers go off to battle he takes on the feminised domestic role of preparing meals 'like a squaw in a wigwam'.[58] Closer to reality is the attempt at social commentary in the portrayal of the lower ranking soldier, Sergeant Jones. His wife has given birth to twins. This means that he now has eight children to support on 'one-and-tenpence a day'. It is 'a small income for so large a family' but Sir Alick and Lady Shendryn have been 'very kind'. Jones also receives gifts from higher-ranking members of the household and lives in the hope of promotion to colour-sergeant. This may be a rather condescending portrayal of a working-class soldier by a middle-class author, yet it focuses on the not uncommon difficulties faced by a low-paid, lower-rank military man with a large family to support.

In Robertson's *Ours*, men march to battle offstage. The patriotic spectacle found in earlier Crimean War plays is downplayed. Military bands are heard in the background, their strains receding into the distance. Even the din of battle is heard from afar. These effects, novel at the time, allow the audience to feel the emotions of departure and imagine the war, without being confronted by the reality of its horrors as were popular audiences for the 1850s Crimean War plays. Robertson's sentimental representation lulls the bourgeois audiences of the 1860s into feelings of security, nurtured by the propaganda that Britain and her Empire were imperturbable.

By the end of the century, soldiers tended to be associated with womanising and the spread of venereal disease. This was particularly the case in works written by socially conscious, middle-class authors. The fact that sailors traditionally had 'a girl in every port' and could also carry infection was conveniently ignored in nautical melodrama; however the misconduct of soldiers became a common theme of drama and literature toward the end of the century. Very often there was conflict between soldiers and sailors. For instance, the Adelphi melodrama *The Union Jack* by Sydney Grundy and Henry Pettitt (1888) portrays the moralistic struggle between a soldier-villain and a sailor-hero. The soldier, Captain Morton, can 'never withstand a pretty face'. He is deemed 'not a desirable acquaintance for any lady, particularly for one who has no father or brother to take care of her'.[59] *The Times*, in its review of the play, remarked that 'It has long been an accepted convention that a blue-jacket should always champion a defenceless woman and that a red-coat should persistently endeavour to compass her betrayal.'[60]

Soldiers were not only associated with the seduction of women. A number were involved with male prostitution. They solicited themselves to well-to-do clients in large cities, like London, where there were garrisons. Payment for sex with other men was an easy way to boost a soldier's meagre wages. It could bring him 'more money in half an hour than he is likely to receive in his whole week's pay'.[61] With barracks located near to the centres of cities, soldiers were more often seen than sailors. This made them more easily 'available'. During the late nineteenth century, male soldier prostitutes could be solicited in parks, Turkish baths, music hall promenades and theatre galleries. Xavier Mayne, in *The Intersexes* (1908), described the soliciting soldier as 'almost open self-marketing. ... On any evening, the street corners or promenades of the big music halls or cheap theatres of London and other cities show one of the flower of the British soldier-prostitute, dressed in his best uniform, clean shaven, well-groomed and handsome with his Anglo-Saxon pulchritude and vigour—smiling expectant.'[62]

Perhaps it was because of this perceived immorality that it was the Scottish, rather than English, soldier who defended the Empire in melodramas inspired by contemporary events. The Scottish soldier became an idealised figure in popular culture. The Scots were seen as brave defenders of the British Empire, and their popularity was bolstered by Queen Victoria's enthusiasm. In 1854 they helped to win the Battle of Balaclava; they fought alongside English soldiers in India, Afghanistan and at Khartoum. As in painting and literature the brave Scottish soldier became a recurrent figure in mid- to late-nineteenth-century drama. He was popularly viewed as an example of loyalty, morality and bravery. But even here a flaw may be detected in his otherwise brave military character. Among the principal characters of Dion Boucicault's *Jessie Brown; or The Relief of Lucknow* (Theatre Royal, Plymouth, 1858) are two Scottish brothers, Randal and Geordie MacGregor, who are 'Officers in the English Service'. While Randal exhibits qualities of leadership and bravery, his younger brother loses his nerve and finds he cannot face the fire of battle:

> My tongue fails me—as my limbs do. ... I am a coward ... the passion of fear is on me—I cannot stir. ... I am paralysed ... it cannot be that my father's son, my brother's brother, can be so miserable, so contemptible a thing as this![63]

Feelings of guilt and remorse are overcome thanks to female encouragement, that of the working-class heroine, Jessie Brown. Geordie ultimately demonstrates the bravery and resource expected of a Scottish soldier. He helps his brother to lead the army in the fight against the sepoys* (the 'black devils') who threaten the British encampment in the Redan Fort. He is taken captive by the villainous Nana Sahib who tries to force Geordie to write to his brother telling him to surrender. Geordie appears to write the letter, but he writes in Scots Gaelic, which the Indians cannot read. Instead of telling his brother to surrender, he warns him of imminent danger. The drama reaches a thrilling conclusion with the rescue of the beleaguered British inhabitants by the Highlander regiments, whose approach is heralded by the distant sound of bagpipes coming nearer and nearer. The curtain falls on a 'Grand Tableau' depicting the defeat of the Sepoys and the triumph of the British forces.

Elements of patriotism and national certainty also permeate the series of nautical and military melodramas written for William Terriss at the Adelphi Theatre during the late nineteenth century. This matinée idol appeared as a succession of sailor and soldier heroes from 1885 until his untimely death in 1897.† Like his predecessor, T. P. Cooke, Terriss embodied British heroism. (He even successfully portrayed William in his 1896 revival of *Black-Ey'd Susan*.) The so-called 'Adelphi melodramas' in which Terriss appeared drew a large and loyal public.

---

* Indian soldiers, who rebelled against British rule in the Indian Mutiny of 1857. —*Ed.*
† For Terriss's death, see page 100.

They were popular attractions that paralleled the more serious 'New Drama'. While they reflect some of the concerns of 'New Drama', particularly in moral and social matters, they promote middle-class values while pandering to popular taste.

The naval and military characters played by Terriss promulgated late nineteenth-century ideals of masculinity. They were intensely moral, romantic, patriotic, loyal and caring. They expressed Christian principles of charity and forgiveness. They exhibited physical and moral strength. They were stoic in the face of trials and tribulations, ultimately restoring order from social chaos. In playing these roles, Terriss displayed his renowned athleticism. He scaled the sides of ships or clung to cliffs in rough seas while attempting to rescue a woman in distress; he even demonstrated his prowess as a swimmer. His physicality was an essential element in Adelphi melodrama. It helped to sustain the fantasies surrounding the melodramatic hero: his strength, his bravery, his chivalry and his undoubted heterosexuality.

The Adelphi hero, as portrayed by Terriss, confronts evil in a series of basic situations. These elaborate on, and are even borrowed from, those of earlier nautical melodrama. Falsely accused by a villainous rival, the hero faces disgrace or ruin; he is separated from a wife or sweetheart who is coveted by that same rival; after enduring extreme hardship or extraordinary danger, he is ultimately exonerated; restored to his beloved, he swears patriotic allegiance to his Queen and country. The formula however contains some radical departures from earlier conventions. The main difference is in the rise in status of the hero, a reflection of the increasing bourgeois influence on popular culture. The hero is no longer a working-class 'tar'; he is now an officer of middle- to upper-class origins. He is set apart by his class, rather than by a fancy costume and a nautical jargon. He no longer expresses overt radicalism. Instead, he reassures a British audience of its place in an imperialist environment. Middle-class spectators are made comfortable in the knowledge that this brave hero is of the same status as themselves. Class boundaries are transcended, with the upper-class officer usually emerging as the hero. The earlier convention of the common sailor rescuing his captain at sea tends to be reversed. In *The Harbour Lights* (George R. Sims and Henry Pettitt, 1885) Lieutenant David Kingsley has saved the life of a lower ranking sailor who had fallen overboard.[64] When this brave deed is recalled, David shows more modesty than many of the early nineteenth-century heroes. Instead of blatantly proclaiming his bravery, he maintains a 'stiff upper lip', like a 'gentleman'. The class emphasis is further reversed in the play's 'sensation scene'. Kingsley is rescued from drowning by the same sailor whose life he had saved at sea.

Because of the audience's appetite for realism, the late nineteenth-century nautical hero is made more credible than his predecessor. He no longer bears a name that metaphorically identifies him as a sea-farer. When maritime jargon is used, it is more discreet and less flamboyant than previously. For example, David Kingsley describes old Nelson's consent to his marriage in terms of winning a battle at sea: 'He shewed a fight at first, but I poured a broadside of love into him and he hauled down his colours.'[65]

Nor is there the confused metaphorical comparison between the sailor-hero's sweetheart and the workings of his ship. Instead the late-nineteenth-century nautical hero tends to indulge in a romantic sentimentality regarding his tangible beloved. Nor is sentiment used to create sympathy for poverty and injustice. It now advocates middle-class notions regarding love and marriage—masculine loyalty, female innocence, wifely obedience and moral purity An example of this sentimental indulgence occurs in *Harbour Lights* when David Kingsley apostrophises the engagement ring he has carried round the world:

> Little ring, I've looked at you and you've bidden me hope during many a long dark watch at sea. Now we're home again, little ring, and we're going to part. Somebody else is going to have you and to keep you forever—and you will make Dave Kingsley's sweetheart Dave Kingsley's wife.[66]

This encapsulation of the ideals of love, engagement and matrimony, as expressed by an intensely appealing actor, could not fail to create an empathy with the audience.* David Kingsley's pretty speeches accord

---

* This was a favourite passage for inserting into the autograph books of young Victorian girls. Its popularity was probably due more to the charm of William Terriss than to the literary merit of Sims and Pettitt's melodrama. Photographs of William Terriss in the role of David Kingsley were also popular on Christmas cards. See Rowell 1987: 32, 34.

with the late nineteenth-century elevation of women to the status of domestic angels. At the same time he reduces any assertiveness in his beloved Dora by giving her child-like, docile qualities. The ring for her finger is 'little'; she will be attached to him 'forever'. As his wife she is expected to be obedient and subservient. For all his avowed protectiveness and loyalty, the sailor-hero views his wife as being inferior to his masculine superiority. He wants to exert control over her words and thoughts, so that they accord with his own middle-class patriotic idealism.

Although he may view his wife as subservient, the military or sailor hero is capable of expressing social criticism. He may not be as radical as his predecessors, but when confronted by injustice he can be surprisingly unpatriotic. David Kingsley, for instance, is suddenly recalled to his ship on his wedding day. This situation shows him to be a more complex character than the usual patriotic sailor:

> What can I do? My heart should be beating high—I should be proud to go and fight my country's battles. There's a chance for the bluejackets this time, they say; instead of that, I feel as though I should choke—for the first time in my life I hate the sea.[67]

Kingsley faces a dilemma similar to that of earlier nautical heroes— such as Harry Hallyard in *My Poll and My Partner Joe* when he is press-ganged at the church door. Like Harry Hallyard, David Kingsley is being forced away. He has doubts over his sense of duty, but inevitably he embarks to go to the war in Egypt. His wife, Dora, is also a mouthpiece for social criticism. Unable to clear David's name from a false accusation of murder, she rails against 'a cruel and unjust law' that says 'a woman shall not speak the word that might save her husband's life'.[68] In early-nineteenth-century melodrama it was the rights of workers and slaves that were the main focus of social criticism. Now it is the rights of women and the different laws governing the two sexes that come under scrutiny.

Social commentary may not be as didactic as in the earlier more radical nautical melodrama. A sense of justice is part of the moralising that underscores these plays. The soldier or sailor hero undergoes a number of tribulations, usually stemming from the false accusation of a crime, before he defeats evil and goes out to perform his patriotic duty.

The evangelistic principles inherent in the Adelphi melodramas also imbue their strong vein of patriotism. Soldiers and sailors go off to restore order and to bring British Christian principles to 'heathen' parts of the Empire. This sense of duty and self-sacrifice attains an almost religious significance, as in *Boys Together* by J. W. Comyns Carr and C. Haddon Chambers :

> VILLARS: Our own happiness and comfort must be set aside when our duty lies clear before us—that we belong to our country first, to those who love us next and to ourselves last.[69]

The performance of duty is made even more forceful by the inclusion of an actual contemporary event. For instance, Villars and Ayot in *Boys Together* go to fight with General Gordon at Khartoum. Yet even this historical situation evokes criticism at odds with the play's overriding xenophobia. After the fall of Khartoum Ayot concedes that: 'England does ruin things sometimes.'[70] But being abroad also allows for comparisons between the British way of life and the exotic world into which the soldiers have stumbled. The second act setting of 'The Market Place at Abu Haraz' is an imaginary, stage version of an Oriental location, replete with female slaves and evil traders. Amidst this theatrical orientalism, the young British officer expresses a preference for the street markets in London—at The Cut in Waterloo and at Covent Garden. Upholding British superiority against a perceived inferior foreign culture would undoubtedly have helped to establish feelings of patriotic self-satisfaction among all social levels in the audience.

The desire to maintain British superiority fuels a fervent sense of duty toward Queen and country. Loyalty may be tested by wrongful accusation, but patriotism inevitably wins through. In these plays the representtation of British military and naval patriotism is sometimes influenced by contemporary events other than battles. For instance, *One of the Best* (1895) was based on the Dreyfus affair. This melodrama was a collaboration between the actor-manager Seymour Hicks and George Edwardes (later famous as manager of the Gaiety Theatre).* A Scottish soldier, Lt

---

* George Bernard Shaw labelled this play 'One of the Worst. ... The play even judged by melodramatic standards is a bad one.' However, he did concede that 'Mr Terriss

Dudley Keppel, VC, is wrongfully accused of betraying British secrets. Like Dreyfus, he is stripped of his military honours, but he refuses to part with his Victoria Cross, giving it to his sweetheart for safe-keeping. Then he goes into penal servitude shouting 'God Save the Queen!'[71]

Figure 50. William Terriss as Lt Dudley Keppell in *One of the Best*

Once freed from the injustice of false accusation and imprisonment the nautical or military hero is inclined to release pent-up emotion. He gives way to tears as fluently as William (in *Black-Ey'd Susan*) and his early nineteenth-century companions. Weeping induces sympathy for the loyal officer who has served his country and been wrongfully treated on his return. However, according to contemporary codes of masculinity, too much emotion is unmanly. This was a time when questions over masculinity and effeminacy were provoked by the Oscar Wilde trial. *One of the Best* was premiered on 28 December 1895—eight months after

---

continues to retain his fascination, even in tartan trousers.' See *Saturday Review*, 28 December 1895, repr. in Shaw 1932: III, 287, 289.

Wilde had been sentenced. Lieutenant Dudley Keppel gives 'signs of great emotion' when his innocence is proclaimed, but he soon *dashes the tears from his eyes in a quick, rough soldierly manner* exclaiming: 'Ah, this makes a woman of me!'[72] The hero is allowed a moment to weep, but he must quickly contain his emotions before his masculine image is compromised. By the final curtain, with justice restored, Keppel, a Scotsman, confirms that he is: 'proud to be once again, a BRITISH SOLDIER'.[73] This spirit of jingoism pervades all of the Adelphi melodramas. *The Union Jack*, for instance, concludes with Jack Medway, metaphorically uniting the men of both Army and Navy under one flag:

> As we began them, so let us end our lives—brothers in arms and brothers in spirit—types of the services that have ever stood, shoulder to shoulder, side by side under the Union Jack![74]

The audience is left secure in the knowledge that Britain's mighty Empire will continue to be protected by her forces. However, the Adelphi melodrama went further than mere jingoism. It continued the radical processes of the early nineteenth century, whereby the hero was engaged with issues arising from both domestic and imperialist ideology. An officer of higher rank now provided the heroic example. Sympathy was evoked for a middle-class, rather than working-class, hero. This new hero offered the audience a stirring, satisfying sense of national identity. He imparted middle-class values regarding British imperialism, intended to stir the audience into patriotic satisfaction, and remove any doubts over the rights or wrongs of British imperial expansion.

Factory Lads: working-class men in melodrama

The radical themes found in early nineteenth-century nautical melodrama also permeate the relatively small group of plays dealing with industrial unrest. The so-called 'factory plays' of the early nineteenth century focus on the struggle of the worker to win his rights at a time of upheaval.

Nautical melodrama presented an idealised portrayal of the brave man at sea. Plays about industrial unrest attempted to portray working class men with greater reality. The labourer is shown as being a victim of his circumstances. Plays about industrial unrest presented situations that were closer to home than the fantasised stage portrayal of naval life.

Factory melodrama reflected contemporary concerns. Unlike nautical melodrama it did not produce popular heroes to satisfy the popular imagination. It tended to concentrate on groups of working men who bond together to confront the power of their employers. In nearly all of the plays their problems are caused by the replacement of the workforce by machines, resulting in the loss of jobs. The need for progress results in divisions of loyalties. Often, the leading male protagonist is torn between his employer and the need to support his striking comrades. This question of loyalties tends to make the anti-heroes of factory melodrama more complex than their sea-faring brothers. They are concerned with their jobs, their wages and the welfare of their families. While often being fearful, they can also be brave, caring and humane. In some of the plays they speak in dialect, in others they are given language as formalised as that of the sailor-hero.

The semi-realistic representation of working-class men rebelling against their employers reflected the discontent felt by many working men in the audience. On the stage they saw recognisable images of working-class life and situations with which they could identify. In the early nineteenth century most of the 'factory plays' were performed at minor theatres and the majority were produced in London. Many of the minor theatres, such as the Surrey in Blackfriars, had strong radical and Chartist connections. Because of their locations, close to poorer areas, they attracted a large working-class element. It was not until around the 1860s, when radicalism had been overtaken by middle-class ideals, that plays about factory workers, or with leading working-class characters, were performed in West End theatres.

Nautical melodrama presented an imagined world of the sea with exotic locations visited by sailors. Writers of factory plays created an imagined North of England in which rural settings were contrasted with industrialised towns and cities. The stage representation of the industrial North also had a basis in reality. Dramatists based their settings on reports and sometimes on a first-hand viewing. This allowed their engagement with contemporary political events to show an immediate response to the agitation of the period.[75] The function of factory plays was not only to entertain, but also to raise questions about the effects of industrialisation. The absorption of these issues into a melodramatic framework undoubtedly gave the plays an immediate appeal to popular audiences. They could see on stage the effects of rapid industrialisation—the power and greed of factory owners, the advance of mechanisation, and a low-paid, underfed workforce agitating for better conditions.

The concept of a class struggle was central to early-nineteenth-century melodrama. Divisions caused by industrial progress are reflected in the plays—some are biased toward the factory owner and progress, while others side with the plight of the working men.

One of the best-known pre-Victorian factory melodramas, John Walker's *The Factory Lad* (Surrey, 1832), takes a more enigmatic approach. While the factory owner is the villain, Walker also makes a stand for progress. His sympathetic treatment of an unemployed male workforce contains a subtle suggestion that tragedy was inevitable. Ultimately, the workers in the play are helpless in the face of progress—facing imprisonment or the firing squad. Both the factory owner, Squire Westwood, and his men are involved with the economic dilemma pervading industrial life in the early nineteenth century. Westwood must replace men by machines for the sake of profitability. He is also up against competition from his neighbours. While Walker conveys the problems faced by factory owners, he shows Westwood as having little sympathy for the men losing their jobs. Machinery increases the wealth of the factory owner while his redundant workforce faces poverty, starvation and the workhouse.

The Factory Lad contains most of the conventions common to factory melodrama, including that of the sacked male workers bonding and conspiring in the public house. This is a masculine space where men can talk in secret, and from which wives are totally excluded. It is also a place of which wives disapprove—where money needed for rent and food is spent on drink. In a later factory melodrama, *The Foreman of the Works*, by George Fenn (Standard, 1886), a wife is removed by force when she intrudes into an all-male meeting looking for her husband. Women are excluded from the clubroom 'when the brotherhood is in secret conclave'.[76] A group of labouring men plotting to burn down a factory fuels the bourgeois obsession with the evil effects of drink on the working classes. Drinking among the lower orders is inflammatory, it leads to disorder and criminal acts, making a strong case for temperance.

From the group of conspiring men there emerges a leader who is either a villain or a hero according to the political stance of the dramatist. John Walker, in *The Factory Lad*, gives the men a leader who does not work in the factory and who lives on the margins of society. Will Rushton, a half-crazed, broken-hearted pauper, is partly a villain and partly a misguided anti-hero. Because of his outcast status, he is made the representative of social ills. Rushton has suffered almost all possible punishments meted out to working class men. As a child he was sentenced to six weeks hard labour for stealing apples. He has subsequently lost his wife and children; he has been whipped, imprisoned and transported. His sufferings have unhinged him.

Rushton's actions demonstrate the combination of radicalism and morality inherent in early-nineteenth-century melodrama. An outcast, he seeks revenge for the wrongs inflicted on him by those of higher rank. He leads a group of dissatisfied, vulnerable men to criminality. Not only does he instigate the strike and burning of the mill, he also strengthens the bonds that draw together men facing adversity. The men become outcasts, like Rushton. They swear to 'be true to each other', even if they are forced to turn to poaching. By staying tightly together they cannot easily be arrested and may avoid transportation or hanging.[77] Walker reaches back to an imagined past by equating the men with the feudal brotherhood which supposedly existed in medieval and Tudor times. He deliberately gives his working-class characters a rhetorical language, filled with archaisms. This gives nobility to characters usually portrayed as comic or servile.[78]

Ideals of brotherly love are apparent in the relationship between Will Rushton and George Allen. The literary ideal of romantic friendship usually identified with the upper classes is transferred to two working-class men—a poacher and a factory worker. Throughout the play, Rushton and Allen give support and protection to each other. They are drawn closer together by becoming outsiders. Forced to the edge of society, they lead each other into further danger. Yet it is through following Rushton that Allen encounters trouble. Crimes such as striking and burning down factories must be punished according to laws laid down by the controlling powers. But Walker does not allow for the conventional neatly resolved conclusion. He finishes the play on an enigmatic note that reflects the underlying psychological instability permeating the play. The men have been coerced by a mentally unstable leader into activities that have brought further uncertainties into their lives.[79] The final tableau shows Rushton, having shot Westwood, facing levelled military muskets. The audience is left to question not only the fate of the men on stage, but the challenges faced by workers and manufacturers in a changing, industrialised society.

Becoming outcasts, facing the workhouse, supporting starving families—these are some of the dilemmas facing men who have lost their employment through the introduction of more efficient machinery. As *The Factory Lad* demonstrates, their desperation leads to criminal acts. The men in Walker's melodrama are forced to consider becoming robbers or poachers.

In G. F. Taylor's *The Factory Strike; or Want, Crime and Retribution* (Royal Victoria, 1838) the strikers actually become a band of robbers. In this play the association between protest and crime is more obvious and damaging to the workers than in *The Factory Lad*. The striking men are led by a trouble-maker, Harris, who, in contrast to Will Rushton, is employed in the factory. He induces the men to burn down the factory building and then forces them to become an outcast robber band. They may regret leaving their wives and children, but the men have taken on a life of freedom far from the drudgery of the factory floor. They may feel some guilt, but there is also an undercurrent of jocularity. Like Robin Hood and his Merry Men, the band is united by criminal activity and the defiance of establishment rules.[80]

Not all the men go out on strike. The earlier radicalism of *The Factory Lad* is replaced by loyalty toward the factory owner. Warner, the play's anti-hero, is torn between his own misgivings about striking and his loyalty to his comrades:

> So it has come to this—a strike! Mad, infatuated fools—Harris will lead them to destruction if they strike. Can I desert them?—yet my wife and infant child must they perish? Oh, little did he, who first contemplated doing manual labour by machinery, think of the misery it would excite.[81]

Warner curses the machine, but he also believes that the workers should support the employers who 'seek to protect themselves and do justice to their honest labourers'. Although a reduction in wages has been proposed as 'a last resort', workers should assist the employers and 'not work their ruin and our own downfall'.[82] In a play produced at the beginning of the Victorian era, sympathy is directed toward the difficulties of the hard-pressed employer, rather than to the deprivation of the oppressed worker. Through supporting his employer, Warner, unlike George Allen, is cut off from his comrades. He does not participate in burning down the factory, or in the murder of the factory owner. In contrast to Rushton, whose sufferings have driven him to the verge of madness, Warner gains strength through his dilemmas. But he still blames the strike for all his troubles:

> All my sorrows, all my misery I owe to that which has raised itself up in the land like a giant and is worshipped by the working classes like a demigod. I mean a strike![83]

Strikes only bring misery, not higher wages. The strike causes his wife and child to starve. Warner cannot find work, but he refuses charity. Nor will he go into the workhouse:

> From that my soul recoils. ... Only think of poor souls being torn away from each other—to linger a few months apart, not to see each other's sufferings—sleep apart—die apart—after being together fifty years.[84]

Warner is made the mouthpiece for social criticism. Although he faces the workhouse, those above him are shown to be capable of humanity. Unlike villainous landlords in many other melodramas, Tom Nokes is moved by the plight of Warner and his family. He will try to ask for them to be given time. Ashfield, the factory owner, is also shown to be charitable. He turns out to be the victim when Warner turns to robbery. Hearing of Warner's starving family, he hands over the money. He also promises to try to help Warner because he was not involved with the strike. In this way, the play demonstrates that not all employers are evil—they will help the workers who are loyal to them. However, there is a paradox at the conclusion. Like *The Factory Lad*, the play ends on a questioning note. After being falsely imprisoned, Warner is given a last minute reprieve. Justice is restored to the worker who has opposed the strike and been loyal to his employer. Presumably, he returns to a wife and child who are dying of starvation.

In factory melodrama, the working-class protagonist faces events that ultimately he cannot control. He is defeated by the onslaught of the machine and the strength of capitalist greed. He must concede like Warner, or go under like George Allen. Honest working men are driven to commit criminal acts through the hopeless conditions of their existence.

By the 1860s radicalism in the theatre had diminished to make way for bourgeois concepts and values. Plays purportedly about factory workers and their problems were slanted toward the tastes of middle-class audiences. Dion Boucicault's *The Long Strike* (Lyceum, 1866), loosely based on Elizabeth Gaskell's 1848 novel *Mary Barton*, evades issues that may prove controversial. Instead of depicting dreadful living conditions, the urban working-class milieu is made to appear picturesque, and its inhabitants saucy or comic. Serious, complex questions of industrial unrest are largely ignored. *The Long Strike*, like other mid- to late-Victorian plays dealing with industrial unrest, is on the side of the factory owner rather than his oppressed workforce, which is shown to be misguided in striking for better conditions.

The bourgeois influence was apparent in the series of mid-Victorian melodramas dealing with working-class protagonists. The earlier complex anti-hero, torn in his loyalties toward his fellow workers and his employer, was replaced by a middle-class conception. Like the 'tar' in nautical melodrama, he lost his heroic status. Instead he became naïve and gullible, conforming to the rules laid down by his superiors. From being a mouthpiece for radicalism he was turned into a sentimental, even grotesque, figure following the paths of evangelical correctness. His morality was put to the test in a series of melodramas portraying a naïve working-class lad leaving his roots (usually in the North of England) and being inveigled into the underbelly of the London metropolis. Here he confronts forces of evil and compares the goodness of the environment he left behind with the temptations of the vast capital.

A middle-class view of lower-class life pervades Watts Phillips's melodrama *Lost in London*, first performed at the Adelphi in 1867. The plot revolves around a Lancashire miner, Job Armroyd, who comes to London in search of his wife, Nelly. She has been abducted by the upper-class villain Gilbert Featherstone and installed as his mistress in fashionable Fern Villas. The play's settings are therefore more diverse than those of earlier factory melodramas, which usually revolve around one industrialised location. Here, a contrast is made between a Lancashire mining community and the high life of London.

The factory melodramas attempted to place working-class men and women firmly within their environment, creating a feeling of identification between minor theatre audiences and the characters on the stage. *Lost in London* places its working-class protagonists on view for examination by upmarket West End spectators. Detailed stage directions describe Job and his mining colleagues as if they were Darwinian 'specimens'—belonging to a race apart. Job is described as 'a fine, rough looking specimen of his class'.[85] His fellow miners are rough, stalwart hirsute-looking fellows'.[86] They even speak a different language with their strongly colloquial Lancashire accent. But they are not shown to be downtrodden. Instead they are cheerful, loyal and optimistic, even singing a chorus as they work.

London is viewed as cruel, crowded and dangerous—it is no place for the simplistic Northern man. On the other hand Bleakmoor is a dull place for a restless wife. The only excitement comes from disasters at the pit. The dangers of the mine and the conditions of the miners are portrayed with a certain amount of discretion. Nevertheless the audience is left with some idea of the hazards of coal mining:

NELLY: But the mine ... think o' the dangers o' the mine Job. ...

JOB: The mine has its faults o'coorse. Theer's the choke damp as blots out a man's life a fore he can lift to see o' which side th' death's comin'. Then theers the fire damp, as scorches a stout lad into a cinder.[87]

As much information is given about the realities of working in the pits as propriety will allow. After all, a middle-class West End audience does not want to be made upset or uncomfortable by too graphic a portrayal of the realities of a coal miner's life.

Like the other miners Job is a stereotype. By describing himself as being 'but a slow koind o' blunderin' chap',[88] he promotes a popular view of the Northern labouring man, gullible and trusting, presenting a moralistic example with his concerns over right and wrong. At the end of the play he becomes an advocate for evangelical principles. Having rescued Nelly from a decadent life-style, he watches over her as she faces death in a humble cottage on the outskirts of the metropolis.

Her death is part of the ultimate evangelical argument, reiterated in numerous 'fallen woman' plays of the period. The straying woman has to die; she can no longer be part of a respectable God-fearing world. It is for the husband she has wronged to forgive her, and Job demonstrates Christian qualities of forgiveness. Although he had vowed never to look on Nelly's face again, hearing of her straitened circumstances, he finds work nearby to support her. His forgiveness even extends to the villain Gilbert Featherstone. When he shows remorse, Job refrains from killing him and sets him free to bear the guilt of his wrongs.

Job forgives Nelly before she expires in front of a distant view of London—the city that lured and rejected her. As she dies Job takes on the aspect of a simple, saintly man. Pointing upward with, according to the stage directions, '*a bright hopeful look*', he claims that he will find Nelly again in Heaven.[89] Adhering to convention, the fallen woman is dead. Meanwhile the villainous Featherstone, who wronged her, has survived, albeit bearing a weight of guilt. Her loyal husband has forgiven her and overcome adversity to embrace Christian ethics.

A Lancashire lad led astray

Moralism also forms the backbone of Tom Taylor's *The Ticket-of-Leave Man*. In this play the theme of a fallible Northern lad encountering the dangers of London life is developed with greater realism and flexibility. This melodrama was first produced three years before *Lost in London*, in 1863 at the Olympic, another West End theatre. Lower-class life is again portrayed from a largely middle-class point of view. Nevertheless, an attempt is made to present an extremely realistic depiction of the London underworld.

The Ticket-of-Leave Man proved to be one of the most popular and enduring of Victorian melodramas. Like many other stage works of the period, it was adapted from a French play—in this case, *Léonard* by Edouard Brissebarre and Eugène Nus. However, Taylor's utilisation of a London setting with actual locations, as well as local and provincial accents, makes *The Ticket-of-Leave Man* a specifically British melodrama.

Taylor also raises issues regarding contemporary British concerns over crime and the law. His principal theme involves the ticket-of-leave system and the prejudices against a man on parole trying to make his way in society. The ticket-of-leave system was introduced to Britain under the Penal Servitude Act, 1853. It arose from the partial abolition of the transportation of convicts to Australia. Under the terms of the Act, British convicts in prison for lesser offences and sentenced to further labour in the colonies could finish their sentences at home. The proviso was that they had to work at approved labouring jobs such as navvying. To remain in Britain and live at large in society, previously convicted men were given a 'ticket-of-leave'. This 'ticket' had to be carried at all times and presented to the police at specified intervals.[90]

Figure 51. Tom Taylor

The ticket-of-leave system raised public anxieties. What was to prevent the ticket-of-leave man from throwing away his card? How were the police to know his whereabouts? Furthermore ticket-of-leave men were associated in the public mind with a spate of muggings (or 'garrottings') carried out by organised gangs in 1862.[91] Anxieties over the ticket-of-leave system led to concerns over the licensing of Tom Taylor's melodrama. The Examiner of Plays questioned the suitability of the play's title and its performance before a respectable audience at the Olympic Theatre. Apparently his explanation to the Lord Chamberlain that the ticket-of-leave man was 'a very estimable person, fallen into bad company' allowed the play to be licensed.[92]

Taylor attempts to assuage public anxieties with the curtain line of the play: 'You see, there may be some good left in a Ticket-of-Leave Man after all.'[93] Yet he was accused of fudging the issue. *The Athenaeum*, in its review of the play, claimed that while Taylor had 'endeavoured to correct natural prejudices of society against the returned convict' he had not 'exactly fairly stated his case'. Because his hero was an innocent man, unjustly accused, he did not fully answer the question 'what is to be done with the real criminal?' Society should know whether such men could be trusted.[94]

Even so, *The Ticket-of-Leave Man* is a highly moralistic play, and the lessons learned by its titular hero, Robert Brierly, had a profound effect on its audiences. The Lancashire lad stumbles into the sphere of criminals. He is led astray and wrongfully convicted. In many ways Brierly is extremely sympathetic, capable of preaching moral truths, and ultimately helps to bring the criminal elements to justice. He also has to overcome the difficulties faced by the convict on parole. But Brierly's fortitude is not always secure and under the pressure of events he is capable of wavering. Unable to find work, he is tempted to join forces with the two villains, Dalton and Moss, who led him astray in the first place. But he sees the error of his ways and betrays them to the law.*

The Ticket of Leave Man also warns of the harmful effects of London life on young men intending to come down to the metropolis for a 'spree'. Brierly is restless—he cannot sleep, and suffers from delirium

---

* Henry Neville, who was renowned for his realistic portrayal, successfully performed the role of Robert Brierly until his retirement in 1910. Tom Taylor, in his introduction to Samuel French's edition of the play, praised Neville's 'unstaginess', and 'the force of his impersonation'. He was also impressed by the 'excellence' of his north-country dialect, which was 'essential to the proper representation of the part'. Neville also played Job Armroyd in Watts Phillips's *Lost in London*: see page 245.

tremens. Hectic London life is contrasted with the world he has left behind: 'I used to sleep like a top down at Glossop'. He can never close his eyes 'but I'm back wi' the old folks at home'.[95] His debilitated state makes him an easy prey for crooks on the look-out for 'a flat to put off the paper' (i.e. a fool to pass counterfeit banknotes).[96]

Returning as a convict on parole, Brierly becomes a far more sympathetic character than he was at the beginning of the play, where he emerges as a rather foolish young swell. On his release from prison, he exemplifies the difficulties faced by the ticket-of-leave man over employment and acceptance by society. Unlike other parolees, Brierly is not really a criminal. He is framed by the villains, Dalton and Moss, and suffers imprisonment for their misdemeanours. His innocence makes him more empathetic. His return to civilian life also marks a return to one of the themes found in early-nineteenth-century radical melodrama—that of the outcast in society. But the outsider of 1860s melodrama is not bent on revenge; he exhibits principles of self-help. He tries hard to gain respectability. Thanks to his sweetheart, May Edwards, he gets a job with Mr Gibson's City firm, but he is thwarted at every turn by the machinations of the two villains.

Under the terms of the Penal Servitude Act, a man on parole could only work manually. He would not have been allowed to work in a City office. By ignoring this fact, Taylor draws attention to the social distinctions and stigmas engendered by the Penal Servitude Act: false accusation and discovery of his past forces Brierly out of a respectable job. There is 'the convict's taint' about him. Thames boatmen draw back from him. Honest people give him a wide berth. He cannot even work as a navvy because of the fear of dangerous ex-convicts, who might be 'garrotters'.

Through its themes of criminality and imprisonment, the play also highlights the necessity for deception and disguise. The need to conceal identity affects the principal male characters, who both hide and reveal criminal activity. Brierly has to hide the fact that he is on parole. Released from prison, he pretends that he is May's brother. He has to find work low down the scale 'in some line where the work's nasty and low pay—where they don't ask questions'. Working in Mr Gibson's broking office, he is under intense pressure to conceal his past. But an 'honest face' cannot always be relied upon. Looks can prove to be deceptive—they may mask criminal tendencies.

Figure 52. Poster for *The Ticket-of-Leave Man*,
Royal Princess Theatre, Edinburgh

Disguise and concealment are also utilised in the surveillance of crime. Hawkshaw, the detective, constantly disguises himself to observe criminals—only revealing his true identity to bring the miscreants to justice. Through disguise and concealment he listens and watches for signs of wrongdoing. Hawkshaw is a representative of the plain-clothes surveillance system introduced in the early 1860s for monitoring men on parole.[97] The occupation of detective was a relatively new one. Spying on fellow citizens for signs of anti-social behaviour created distrust and suspicion among the public.

A detective in disguise is as much a threat to Brierly as he is to Dalton and Moss—especially as Brierly is arrested through police bungling and faulty observation. Hawkshaw plays a cat-and-mouse game with him before reaching a conclusion already clear to the audience—that he is innocent and has been framed. Taylor shows Hawkshaw and his forces as being slow to act and vengeful. His implied criticism of police methods propagates public suspicion and contempt for the plain-clothes man.[98]

James Dalton, alias 'The Tiger', is the real criminal. He uses disguise to avoid discovery and arrest. With his partner, Melter Moss, he subverts moral values—particularly the loyalties attached to masculine friendship. Together, they plot and plan and try to outwit each other with their dodgy deals. For Dalton, friendship, death and treachery are never far apart: 'The pal who sticks to me, I stick by him, till death. But the man who tries to double on me had better have the hangman looking after him than Jem Dalton.'[99] Dalton destroys homosocial bonds; he has caused the death of the 'best mate' that Hawkshaw ever had.[100] He proffers friendship to Robert Brierly while trying to defraud him. Seeing his vulnerability, he solicits the young man to become his 'tool' and pass counterfeit banknotes. He and Moss attempt to draw Brierly into their clutches by thwarting every attempt he makes to earn an honest living:

> BRIERLY: Not content with leading me into play and drink and devilry—with making me your tool—with sending me to a prison, it's you that have dogged me—have denounced me as a convict.
> DALTON: Of course—you didn't think any but an old friend would have taken such an interest in you.[101]

The 'friendship' of Dalton and Moss is treacherous. They cannot be trusted and their double-dealing makes a mockery of the loyalties associated with the ideals of male companionship. Brierly has learned by his mistakes and is able to offer cautionary advice to young Sam Willoughby, who is about to go down the same road as he did. Bad companionship can prove injurious to a young man:

> Sam, my lad, listen to me. ... A bad beginning makes a bad end, and you're beginning badly; the road you're on leads downwards, and once in the slough at the bottom o't—oh! trust one who knows it—there's no working clear again. You may hold out your hand—you may cry for help—you may struggle hard—but the quicksands are under your foot—and you sink down, down, till they close over your head.[102]

Brierly's preaching contains a warning to young men about the company they keep, of the dangers of being led astray by other men who may be unprincipled and unscrupulous. It is the heroine, May Edwards, who most strongly exemplifies the evangelical ethics embedded in the play. Moral enlightenment is associated with the action and value of the leading female character. She offers love and loyalty while Brierly's dissolute male companions prove treacherous.

Like other working-class heroines in melodrama, May is a strong-willed woman. At first she is ill and destitute, but she gains strength as the play progresses. She begins, like Brierly, by being extremely vulnerable. Her work as a street singer may raise questions about the respectability of a young working-class girl, but she does not resort to prostitution in order to survive. Instead she exemplifies virtues of thrift, while remaining true to Brierly, and even risking unemployment for his sake.

It is May's intervention that helps to prevent crime; she intercedes in a male preserve of navvies, convicts and criminality. Like wives in factory melodrama, she tries to lure her husband away from an all-male conspiracy. In contrast to the treachery of his criminal companions, she will give true love and support to her husband:

> We are man and wife, and we'll take life as man and wife should, hand-in-hand. Where you go, I will go, where you suffer, I will be there to comfort; and when better times come, as come they will—we will thank God for them together.[103]

A strong-willed heroine is supportive of a vulnerable anti-hero. While the male characters, good and bad, observe each another, May watches over her husband like a guardian angel. It is part of the play's highly moral stance that a good woman is protective of a man who has strayed. This could be seen as a gender-reversal of the usual situation in which an untrammelled husband ultimately forgives his erring wife.

As we shall later see, a wife offering support to her erring husband was to be a major theme of 'fallen man' plays written toward the end of the century. Robert may have been injured, but he does not die. Instead, there is a seemingly optimistic ending. In the words of the *Illustrated London News* review, 'He has before him a future which abounds in promise of better days.'[104] But given his vulnerability, will he continue to resist temptation?

In Charles Smith Cheltnam's racy, if inferior, sequel, *The Ticket-of-Leave Man's Wife; or Six Years After*, first produced at the New Theatre in Greenwich in 1866, the gender bias is reversed. In this continuation of Tom Taylor's play, it is May (now married to Robert), who is falsely accused and sent to prison. Robert faces the outside world while his wife is incarcerated. He is forced to give up his ironmongery business because of 'hard-hearted creditors'. Desperate for money he faces temptation and falls once again into the hands of Dalton and Moss. Cheltnam's sequel reiterates situations from Taylor's original play. May, on her release from prison, again tries to intercede in masculine spheres of criminal activity. The detective Hawkshaw is still disguising himself and still wants to repay Dalton for causing the death of his pal 'years ago'. In this sequel Dalton dies the 'sensational' death appropriate to a male villain. While fighting with Brierly he falls from a collapsing balcony and breaks his back.

However a new and topical theme is introduced into this sequel—that of emigration. Like other young men of the time, Brierly wants to escape his circumstances and emigrate to Australia. There he and May will begin a new life. When their innocence is finally proved, the two male characters representative of commerce and industry prove benevolent. Mr Totty, the 'Railway Sub-Contractor', offers to pay their passage to Australia, while the broker, Mr Gibson, will advance a sum to stock 'a good farm' or a sheep run. Brierly will take on the traditionally masculine role of a sheep farmer, while May will be supportive as a farmer's wife. In a curtain speech which has echoes of that in Taylor, Brierly asks for the 'courage and strength' to do his best in 'that free land where none will deny me the right to labour for my bread, or stab me to the heart with fingers pointed in scorn'.[105] Earlier, in John Walker's *The Factory Lad* (1832), Will Rushton returned, disillusioned by emigration; in the 1860s, emigration to the imagined paradise of Australia offers a working man and his wife hope for a better future.

The Ticket-of-Leave Man's Wife was initially written for a minor suburban theatre, at Greenwich, where it was probably performed before a predominantly working-class audience. On 4 August 1866 it was presented at the more up-market Olympic, the theatre where Taylor's play was successfully first presented. It had a mixed reception. Tom Taylor's vastly superior *The Ticket-of-Leave Man* by comparison is a play by a middle-class author, written for a largely middle-class audience.

Like other 'metropolitan' melodramas it presents a bourgeois view of working-class life. However both Taylor's play and Cheltnam's sequel present a sympathetic portrait of a Lancashire lad unwittingly caught up in criminal activities. His subsequent sufferings place him on an evangelical path toward moral rectitude. But through making the anti-hero a moralistic example, more serious social issues, such as the question of the paroled convict, are toned down. Even in 1863, Tom Taylor was criticised for not portraying a ticket-of-leave man's life in stronger terms.

Divided self: *The Corsican Brothers* and *The Bells*

Dion Boucicault's *The Corsican Brothers* (Princess's 1852) and Leopold Lewis's *The Bells* (Lyceum 1871) are far removed from the neo-realism of metropolitan melodrama. They present a complex view of masculinity in gothic and foreign settings, involved with the supernatural and the workings of the mind. Both these plays give a pre-Freudian representation of a divided male persona. *The Corsican Brothers* presents dual masculinity by having twin heroes. In *The Bells* divisions of personality are represented in one central character. The split male personae in these plays could be viewed as a reflection of the Victorian fascination with double identities and secret lives.

Both *The Corsican Brothers* and *The Bells* were written for West End theatres and adapted from French sources. While neither could be considered a literary masterpiece,* they were popular vehicles for star actors—and wildly successful at the box office. Charles Kean, and later Henry Irving, starred in *The Corsican Brothers*. Irving's performance as Mathias made him synonymous with *The Bells*. Both plays reflect middle-class concerns such as maintaining respectability, temptation to commit a crime, and communication with loved ones. These two plays were possibly more famous for their ghostly scenic effects, than for any crude attempt at psychoanalysis. They also reflect the contemporary fascination with mesmerism and spiritualism.

---

* An anonymous critic wrote: '*The Bells* is not a good play, it is poorly Englished and poorly built. One is a good deal less interested in the remorse of Mathias than in the devices of the man who plays him.' Quoted in Bingham 1978: 83–84.

The Corsican Brothers was first performed at the Princess's Theatre on 24 February 1852. It was adapted from the 1844 novella *Les Frères corses* by Alexandre Dumas *père* and retains its foreign locations. The first act takes place in Corsica, a country associated with blood feuds, bandits and wild scenery. The setting for the central second act is Paris, a city popularly considered sexually permissive and decadent. Against these 'exotic' backgrounds a drama is played out among a group of aristocratic gentlemen who are involved with feuding, womanising and the paranormal.

The play departs from earlier melodramatic convention in several ways. It offers no developed or extended female role. Instead, women are relegated to a secondary status on the periphery of a male-dominated world. The main focus is on gentlemanly characters belonging to an upper-class milieu. This means that men of the same elevated social level play out the struggle between good and evil. The play further departs from the norm by dividing the central heroic role between the twins who are the Corsican brothers of the title—Louis and Fabien dei Franchi. Not only is the dual role intended to be played by one star actor, it merges, transubstantiates, and even triplicates.

The twin brothers are central to the gothic elements of mystery and the supernatural that remove the play from reality. They are enveloped by tricks of time, telepathy and ghostly appearances. Fabien claims that Louis and himself are one.[106] There is 'a strange mysterious sympathy' between them:

> No matter what space divides us, we are still one in body, feeling and soul. Any powerful impression which the one experiences is instantly conveyed by some invisible agency to the senses of the other.[107]

Their telepathic communication gives Fabien in Corsica feelings about his brother in France. The play's preoccupation with telepathy and time reflects mid-nineteenth-century technological developments. The telegraph was an invisible agency that could rapidly bring communication, while traversing the distance between people. Railways, with their timetables, meant a greater dependence upon clocks and times of departure and arrival. Boucicault's melodrama with its repetitive time schemes and telepathic communication seems to be caught up in the rhythms of this new technology.[108]

The play was renowned for its astounding ghostly effects. The supernatural appearances of Louis, and the visions of his death, were reminiscent of earlier gothic melodrama. These effects necessitated a new stage technology, which included the invention of a new type of trapdoor. The so-called 'Corsican trap' gave the illusion of the ghost of Louis dei Franchi gliding, descending and emerging from the ground.[109] Creating the illusions for these supernatural effects also added an extra dimension to the twin heroes. They necessitated a third Corsican brother image as a double for Louis' ghostly visitation at the end of the first act.

Doubles were used in the 'phantasmagoria shows' performed by illusionists, which were popular during the 1840s and 50s. Their supernatural effects undoubtedly influenced the ghostly appearances in *The Corsican Brothers*. Stage magic seems to have been a male-dominated sphere—nearly all of the leading illusionists and inventors of magical apparatus were men. Even the famous apparatus used for the ghostly effects in *The Corsican Brothers* was a male invention—that of Dion Boucicault himself. Supernatural appearances in the play involved the vision of a male phantom—rather than that of a female ghost, as was often seen in earlier gothic melodramas, notably M. G. Lewis's *The Castle Spectre* (Drury Lane 1797).

The division between the twin heroes is further reflected by a divergence in their interests and outlook. They represent two aspects of mid-nineteenth-century masculinity. Louis is part of a dissolute urban gentlemanliness. He inhabits the upper-class confines of Paris, with its salons, masked balls and courtesans. Meanwhile, Fabien enjoys the freedom of the open spaces of Corsica. He expresses the individualism of the Romantic hero. He sees himself as 'free and Corsican'. His eulogy to liberty and nature imitates Wordsworth's Romantic vision:

> You wonder, naturally, that any one should choose to live in such a wild and ignorant land; but I am native to the soil, like the green oak, or laurel rose. I love to explore the forest, and to rove over chasm and torrent with my rifle for companion—to sit on a mountain ledge, with the theatre of nature at my feet, and revel in the sense of liberty and boundless space. In the city I should be stifled as in a prison.[110]

While enjoying these freedoms, Fabien has forebodings about his brother. Both have fallen in love with the same woman. Louis has followed her to Paris, claiming to be studying law or medicine. Fabien, imbued with a sense of duty and having no desire to travel, remains at the family chateau in Corsica to be with their mother. His telepathic feelings about his twin bring about pathological changes. He becomes 'sad, uneasy, gloomy' and finds it difficult to conquer his depression. This anxiety is symptomatic of a mid-nineteenth-century fascination with the workings of the mind. It could also be viewed as a reflection of upper-class concerns over sons or brothers serving abroad as soldiers or civil servants. As well as conveying good news, the telegraph could invisibly carry messages of grief and sorrow.

The second act of *The Corsican Brothers* is a flashback explaining the cause of Fabien's anxieties and the circumstances of Louis's fatal quarrel in Paris. Four short scenes comprise a mini social melodrama set in the enclosed world of wealthy, indolent gentlemen. Masked balls, early morning supper parties and duels fought over trivial matters present a decadent contrast with British bourgeois respectability. Gentlemen bring women of dubious morality into this sphere for their pleasure. Liaisons are formed with 'Ladies of the Ballet' from the Paris Opera.*

The married woman, Émilie de l'Esparre, beloved by Louis dei Franchi, is lured into this contained gentlemen's world. She is humiliated by being made the subject of a wager by her ex-lover Chateau-Renaud, who is a womaniser and duellist. He forces her to attend Montgiron's bachelor supper party and compromises her honour with promises to return her letters to him. It is his protection of her honour that leads to the fatal duel with Chateau-Renaud. Louis dies because of the trivial pursuits of gentlemen. Duelling over taking a woman to a party seems as ludicrous as the feud (in Act I) between Corsican peasants over a hen.

The duel takes place in the forest at Fontainebleau, in reality the location for many notorious sword fights reported in newspapers.[111] Fighting over a woman is a competitive male ritual that can be extremely interesting in terms of stagecraft. In performance, duels turn into little

---

* The so-called *Rats de l'Opéra* were noted for their immorality. Irving, when he revived *The Corsican Brothers* in 1880, had difficulty in persuading actresses to play sinful ballet-girls. They would not behave as was required of them. Bram Stoker remarked that: 'they would have set an example at a confirmation class.' See Stoker 1906: I, 168–169).

episodes within the main action, having their own plot-line. The duel between Fabien dei Franchi and Chateau-Renaud in Kean's production at the Princess's in 1852 appeared more realistic and varied than the usual stage sword fight.

Figure 53. *The Corsican Brothers*: duel scene from the 1852 production
(from the watercolour by Edward Henry Corbould)

George Henry Lewes described how Alfred Wigan as Chateau-Renaud, during a pause in the fighting, leant upon his sword and broke it: 'Fabien, to equalise the combat, snaps his sword also, and both of them take the broken halves, and fastening them in their grasp by cambric handkerchiefs, *they fight as with knives.*' To the nineteenth-century audience 'the minute ferocity of detail ... with a truth on the part of the actors, which enhances the terror' gave an effect 'so intense, so horrible, so startling, that one gentleman indignantly exclaimed *un-English!*'[112] Broken swords are used like knives; a gentlemanly duel becomes as savagely aggressive as a vengeful fight between Corsican peasants.*

---

* Irving repeated Kean's 'business' with the broken swords in his 1880 production. In his sonnet *Fabien Dei Franchi* addressed to 'my friend Henry Irving', Oscar Wilde writes of 'the broken swords' used in 'the lonely duel in the glade'. (Wilde, 'Fabien dei Franchi' in Wilde 2003: 860) The artist W. Graham Robertson also recalled seeing

The duel between Chateau-Renaud and Fabien dei Franchi was a choreographed episode in a play full of divisions. Its episodic structure resulted partly from an unconventional time-scheme, zooming between past and present. This was further enhanced by the multiple images of the two main protagonists. The traditional hero-figure was divided—both psychologically and symbolically. These divisions needed to be delineated through the skills of a single actor. Irving, in his portrayal of the twin brothers, 'sought no aid from make-up'. According to Graham Robertson, he subtly emphasised the differences between the two brothers: 'Fabien and Louis were physically identical, yet after the first glance, no one would have mistaken them. Fabien was the noble savage, Louis the finished product of civilisation, exquisite in manners, meticulous in costume, gentle and courteous, chivalrous and charming.'[113] The twin brothers may be viewed as representing divisions in one male self, or they could represent the dualities contained in relations between men. The play promotes themes of male rivalry and competitiveness. It shows men inhabiting different worlds: a secret urban world of illicit sexuality, or revelling in the freedom of open spaces. But the play also shows the deep feelings, tenderness and concern which can exist between brothers and which is the basis of masculine friendship.

Whereas *The Corsican Brothers* has twin heroes, Leopold Lewis's *The Bells* (Lyceum 1871) concentrates on divisions of personality within a central male protagonist. It is one of the earliest plays to indulge in a pre-Freudian exploration of the dark forces within a man. Mathias is a split personality, obsessed by the memory of a past crime. He combines outward goodness with an inner evil. Because of these divisions within himself, he can't be easily categorised as either a hero or a villain. This was part of his fascination for nineteenth- and early-twentieth-century audiences. Mathias, a single outsize character, dominates the play, and none of the other characters are developed to the same extent. They act as foils to the main protagonist.*

The Bells was adapted from a French play, *Le Juif polonais*, based on

---

Irving and William Terriss (as Chateau-Renaud) fighting with broken swords. See Saintsbury and Palmer 1939: 189.

* *The Bells* was a favourite with Queen Victoria, who saw it eight times. —*Ed.*

a novel by Erckmann-Chatrian, the double-barrelled pseudonym of the Alsatian authors Emile Erckmann and Pierre Alexandre Chatrian. It was produced at the Théatre Cluny, Paris, in 1869. Lewis's English version is largely remembered for the portrayal of Mathias by Henry Irving, who by all accounts had a divided, complex personality. This probably helped him in interpreting the complexities found in the character of Mathias. The themes of an outwardly respectable man committing murder and suffering guilt and remorse in *The Bells* are similar to those found in a narrative poem which Irving was fond of reciting—Thomas Hood's *The Dream of Eugene Aram*. Like Hood's poem, *The Bells* attempts a psychological analysis of a murderer.

Guilt and remorse resulting in madness and death for the leading male protagonist had been the subject of earlier melodramas, particularly those dealing with vices such as drink or gambling. But *The Bells* attempts to dispense with their crudely demonstrative language. Instead, fears arising from the subconscious are suggested by delusions and involuntary actions that Mathias attempts to ignore, suppress or conceal. The play's mixture of guilt and remorse with the elemental and supernatural suggests Shakespearean influences—particularly those of *King Lear* and *Macbeth*. These were both roles which Irving was to play later in his career— Macbeth in 1888 and Lear in 1892. At the same time, *The Bells* with its suggestive depiction of a guilty soul looks forward to the early twentieth-century Symbolism of dramatists such as Maeterlinck and Strindberg.

The crime committed by Mathias has an even more disturbing aspect than those usually committed by mid nineteenth-century stage villains— the slaying of a Jew for his money. Mathias's prosperity arises from this long-concealed crime, which could be viewed as anti-Semitic. In nineteenth-century Britain, although progress was made toward acceptance, Jews were despised and considered outsiders. Gentile society tended to be oblivious to the realities of Jewish life and customs. Jews were traditionally seen to be involved with financial wheeling and dealing. In literature they tended to be either caricatured or shown as evil and grasping. However, the Jewish merchant in *The Bells* is a victim, rather than the usual comic or villainous character. Even so he is described in stereotypical terms—he has a large black beard, wears a green cloak and fur cap and has 'great boots covered with hare-skin'. The association between Jews and wealth is emphasised by the gold-filled 'girdle' or money-belt, which he wears around his waist.[114] For most of the play he is an invisible presence. The audience only sees him in the vision of the Bridge at Vechem at the end of Act One, where, in Irving's 1871 production, he presented a terrifying aspect as he slowly turned his 'ashy pale' face down stage and sternly fixed his eyes on Mathias.*[115]

Figure 54. Henry Irving in *The Bells*

In the third act vision, Mathias confesses to his murder of the Jew. His description has an anti-Semitic tone. He refers to the Jewish merchant as if he were an animal being led to the slaughter. His demonstration of the murder is accompanied by the cry: 'Ah! Ah! I have you now, Jew!' He pushes the body into the lime kiln with the exhortation of: 'Go into the

---

* In the French version, the first act concluded with the coincidental appearance at the inn of another Polish Jewish merchant. The physical similarity to his victim was startling for Mathias. Clement Scott, in his *Observer* review, castigated Leopold Lewis for replacing this scene with the vision of the Bridge at Vechem. He had 'for the sake of a beautiful stage picture, sacrificed the most important point in the tale' and 'given a wrench to the quietly revolving wheels of the story'. See *Observer*, 26 November 1871; repr. Mayer 1980: 100.

fire, Jew, go into the fire!'[116] In his memories of Irving as Mathias, Eric Jones-Evans recalled the 'bestial blood-lust' in the actor's face and eyes as he struck the fatal blow. He maintained that this 'went far beyond acting and mere effect'.[117] It is discomforting to note that Irving as Mathias gave a demonstration of greed and racial hatred before audiences, many of whom were ignorant of Jewish life and may have harboured anti-Semitic prejudice. In the play, Mathias is psychologically and physically punished for murder, but he is not condemned for having killed out of racial hatred.

Nevertheless, the crime that weighs on Mathias's conscience may have had a partly racial motive. Specifically, it is a Jewish merchant who keeps returning to haunt him. Fifteen years after the murder, Mathias continues to hear the bells on his victim's sleigh and sees his accusing eyes. The details of the crime haunt his mind, driving him to near-madness. Nor does he die a death moralistically framed with remorse and forgiveness. Instead, he dreams of being sentenced to death, and on waking, he feels the tightening of the noose around his neck. He dies the sordid death of a felon condemned to hang. Clement Scott described how Irving, in the final moments, presented 'the very ugly picture of a dead man's face, convulsed after a dream in which he thought he was hanged'. It was a terrifying moment that could not 'fail to be admired'.[118] Ellen Terry, in her autobiography, recalled how Irving's imagination acted 'physically on the body'. As Mathias, 'he really did almost die—he imagined death with such horrible intensity. His eyes would disappear upwards, his face grow grey, his limbs cold.'[119]

The idea of such a violent crime being committed by a man of respected position would have undoubtedly shocked and thrilled audiences. Mathias, the burgomaster, outwardly epitomises middle-class respectability—inwardly, he harbours a guilty secret. He symbolises the notion of the bourgeois male leading a double life. Secrets can lead to fear of discovery, prosecution, feelings of guilt and retribution. In this respect, *The Bells* points the way to the later 'problem plays'. But unlike many later 'problem plays' it does not have a contemporary English setting: the action takes place at a safe remove from the realities of the bourgeois world, in a picturesque Alsatian village. Nor is the period that of the 1870s. The play is nostalgically set a few decades earlier, in 1833. This combination of nostalgia and a folksy location helps to bring Mathias's state of mind into focus. A feeling of false security is induced by the village inn of the first act—a cosy, Christmas card world of warmth and hospitality, contrasting with the snowstorm outside. Eric Jones-Evans recalled that it was only when the audience saw through the window at the back 'fast-falling snow in the gathering dusk of Christmas Eve and heard the moan of the rising wind' that they felt 'a strange premonition that all was not well—that some fearful tragedy was about to occur'.[120]

Mathias enters into the protective environment of the village inn like the idealised *paterfamilias*. He presents a jovial front and shows devotion to his wife and daughter. But appearances are deceptive—the kindly father-figure harbours a terrible secret.

An attempt is made to show his inner psychological turmoil by actions that signify his mental state to the audience—such as clumsily dropping the tongs or banging down his glass on hearing mention of the Polish Jew. He also exhibits psychological symptoms associated with a guilty conscience. He has bad dreams; he talks in his sleep, has a constant thirst at night and is feverish.[121] Mathias lives in fear of betraying himself. He even stops himself from being hypnotised at the fair in case he unconsciously confesses to his past crime.

In Act Three, he locks himself away with his guilty secret. By being alone, he will not betray himself to his wife if he talks in his sleep.[122] Mathias has an almost masturbatory obsession with the deed he must keep hidden. He lulls himself into a sense of false security. Sinful secrets lead to self-betrayal; they can result in madness and perhaps death. Even by locking himself away, Mathias does not escape his sin. The vision scene in Act III conveys two unconscious states of mind. Evidently dreaming, Mathias finds himself on trial. He is regressed by the Mesmerist into a further unconscious state, wherein he re-enacts his crime. He betrays himself with this confession and is sentenced to hang. The figure of the Mesmerist preys on the Victorian fascination with hypnotism and the fear of its ability to extract secrets.

Mathias' external appearance as the archetypal *paterfamilias* is torn away by hypnosis. His outward appearance also masks his fear of discovery, but he does not exhibit remorse for having killed the Jewish merchant. When, in Act Three, he thinks he has triumphed, he speaks of his conscience being at rest.[123] but the text of *The Bells* shows Mathias as being unremorseful. It was Irving's interpretation that invoked remorse. He gave a sub-text to Leopold Lewis's drama by creating illusions which made critics see 'the effect of deep remorse' portrayed with 'thrilling truth'.[124] John Oxenford, in his review in *The Times*, noted how Mathias's conscience 'torments him in a form so palpable that it almost becomes a bodily persecution'. Irving 'works out bit by bit the concluding hours of a life passed in constant effort to preserve a cheerful exterior, with a conscience tortured until it has become a monomania'.[125]

Irving made Mathias even more of a centralised focus than he was in the text of the play. Even Etienne Singla's musical score was cut, leaving only the themes significant to Mathias and the Mesmerist.[126] Extra 'business' was interpolated which drew attention to Irving's cleverness as an actor, but also emphasised the guilty conscience of Mathias. At the end of the play, Irving held centre stage. He lengthened his part by speaking his dying words against the diminishing peals of wedding bells and struck the final line of a secondary character, Walter, from the script.[127] By focusing almost the entire play on Mathias, a respected man with a guilty secret, Irving demonstrated the destructive power of past sins, and touched on the unconscious fears of his audience.

While *The Bells* and *The Corsican Brothers* may have given cause to reflect on bourgeois concerns, they also turn male psychology into escapist entertainment. Middle-class anxieties over masculine behaviour are transferred to the safety of fantastic situations and picturesque locations. In both plays the male psyche becomes involved with tricks of time and divisions between reality and the paranormal. Boucicault's romantic melodrama of 1852 utilises new stage technology and magical illusion to illustrate the inner workings of the masculine mind. Dreams and visions are conjured up behind gauzes; ghostly figures appear and disappear through the use of mirrors, trapdoors and magical lighting effects. The main protagonists are replicated in spectral visions by the use of doubles. Later, in 1871, Leopold Lewis's *The Bells* moves towards a more internalised, symbolic representation of masculine guilt. For this production, Irving introduced special lighting and scenic effects that enhanced the inner torments of Mathias. Both these plays concern a divided masculine psyche, and attempt a 'psychological approach' through utilising the 'sensational' advances of nineteenth-century stage technology.

Challenging male supremacy: *The Magistrate*

Concerns, anxieties or feelings of guilt over masculine transgression could also be assuaged by laughter. The supposed double life of the outwardly respectable middle-class man became a subject of mockery in comedy and farce. These two genres set out to demonstrate the hypocrisy surrounding bourgeois masculinity. By evoking laughter they helped to undermine the masculine ideal.

A great many comedies and farces were topical with a contemporary urban setting—especially that of London. A recognisable, modern setting made the satire more relevant. Audiences were made to laugh at the loss of dignity suffered by respected upholders of the Victorian status quo— such as magistrates, clergymen or high-ranking military and naval officers.

The farces which Arthur Wing Pinero wrote for the Court Theatre between 1885 and 1893 exemplify this trend. The plots of these plays usually follow a pattern in which masculine leaders of the social hierarchy have their authority put in jeopardy through being led astray by a younger person about to ascend the social ladder. Through variations on this plot-line, Pinero challenges the expectations of behaviour and decorum associated with the high status of his central male characters. Through ultimately restoring this hierarchy to order, Pinero seems to remove any sense of threat. However, while everything may appear to come right at the end, masculine power remains questioned.

The Magistrate is the best-known of Pinero's Court farces. It was the first of the series and it opened on 23 March 1885. The Court Theatre (later replaced by the Royal Court Theatre) was situated in Lower George Street, Chelsea. It was close to an area which, during the 1880s, attracted a coterie of well-to-do artists, writers, actors and bohemians including Oscar Wilde, James McNeill Whistler,* Charles Ricketts and Charles Shannon. However, so great was the success of *The Magistrate* that it

---

* DHL: 'Rex Whistler'—clearly a mistake, since Rex Whistler was not born until 1905! J. M. Whistler was a friend of Oscar Wilde but they later fell out. —*Ed.*

attracted a far wider metropolitan audience than just the Chelsea aesthetes. The play 'literally took the town by storm'.[128] It was hailed as a new type of English comedy, making earlier farces appear 'extravagant and impossible'.[129] Pinero's aim in writing *The Magistrate* was, as he told the *New York Times*, 'to raise farce a little from the pantomimic level'. He tried 'to create probable characters in possible situations'.[130]

Figure 55. Arthur Wing Pinero

The play ridicules the upper-middle-class masculine front of respectability by reverting and subverting normative bourgeois social traditions. In a situation which overturns patriarchal authority, the magistrate of the title, Aeneas Posket, is led astray by his stepson, Cis Farringdon, a youth of 19 whose mother represents him as a boy of 14.

Posket represents the typical fifty-year-old, professional middle-class man. He lives comfortably in Bloomsbury and belongs to a gentlemen's club. While he is kind and exceedingly philanthropic, he can also be pompous, gullible and easily led. Furthermore the comical alliance of his Virgilian first name, Aeneas, with the ludicrous surname of Posket helps to reduce his stature as a man of high position.

Posket is unable to comprehend the precocious behaviour of his stepson or the liberated attitudes of his young wife, Agatha. He is deceived by both of them. Agatha, whose first husband died in India, claims she is five years younger than her real age. This also necessitates reducing the age of her son, Cis, who is forced to play the role of a fourteen-year-old, while behaving like a young swell of nineteen. A major theme of the play is Agatha's desperate efforts to prevent Posket from finding out her deception.

The name Cis (short for Cecil), sounds feminine—although Pinero, with a hint of irony, describes him as being *a manly youth*. From his first appearance there is a disturbing sexual ambiguity about him. In fact, Pinero was insistent that the role be played by a male actor and not by an actress, as was customary for boy's roles.[131] He was most concerned about the representation of this character on the stage. In a letter to the American manager Augustin Daly, prior to the New York production, he wrote that Cis Farringdon 'must be quite a boy—pleasant in appearance and fresh and ingenuous in manner. He must *look* but 14 and *act* like a young man of 20.'[132] Had Cis been played by an actress he would have appeared too effeminate and would have had a different kind of appeal for the audience. The comedy arises from a young 'manly' man of nineteen behaving like an adolescent boy.

Cis certainly seems to be the subject of a great deal of physical attention from both sexes. It is somewhat disturbing that his immature appearance should make him the subject of bisexual attraction, particularly as he is dressed in an Eton jacket, the attire of an adolescent boy. Was Pinero subtly satirising the Uranian/Hellenic/paederastic idealisation of the ephebic young man, or could he even be hinting at a more sordid interest in juveniles? Agatha describes how her husband's friends 'are always petting and fondling and caressing what they call "a fine little man of fourteen".'[133] His boyish appeal causes women to chase after and to 'mother' him. He encourages female attention, and Agatha thinks 'It's very awful to see these innocent women fondling a young man of nineteen.'[134]

Cis offers conflicting signs regarding whether he is a boy or a man. Like a boy of fourteen, he receives pocket money and cracks nuts with his teeth. But he also manages to lead the life of a swell. He gambles, tells risqué stories, flirts with girls, smokes and swears. He even has a private room at a notorious late-night establishment—the Hotel des Princes in Meek Street. By making a supposedly fourteen-year-old boy behave like a grown-up swell, Pinero mocks a young bachelor's life of sprees, drinking, gambling and womanising.

It is to the less than respectable venue of the Hotel des Princes that Cis lures his stepfather in the hope of having his debts paid off. This situation subverts the normative relations between father and son. In upper-middle-class circles it was customary for a father to initiate his son (or even his stepson) into the 'man's world' of gentlemen's clubs and business interests. Instead Cis introduces the elderly Posket into the world of the houses of pleasure and the *demi-monde*. It is not without a hint of irony that Cis extols the inestimable benefit to a youngster in having 'someone always at his elbow, someone older, wiser and better off than himself'.[135]

Pinero inverts the Platonic ideal of an older man protecting and advising his *ephebe*. In this case, it is the younger man who leads the older man astray. Cis, by coercing his stepfather out into the *demi-monde*, makes him deceive his wife. There is even doubt over his past behaviour. Cis watching him write a note excusing his absence and pinning it to a curtain, exclaims: 'Hallo, Guv, hallo! You're an old hand at this sort of game are you?'[136] Nevertheless Posket insists that he wants to help his stepson, to rescue 'the child from his boyish indiscretion'. In his eyes, Cis is a delinquent boy, not a youth of nineteen. In this comically ambivalent situation, a young man, dressed like a boy, attempts to lead an older man into temptation. The question of money is also involved: a wealthy older man is to settle a younger man's arrears. Cis's extortion of money from Aeneas Poskett carries a whiff of blackmail.

In the second act, Cis takes Posket to the Hotel des Princes. Its fancy French name is indicative of a place frequented by arrogant young swells out for pleasure. The location in 'Meek Street' is an ironic reflection on the pretensions of its clientele. Pinero tries to keep within the bounds of propriety by not being too explicit about the nature of the establishment.[137] A 'rather gaudy' room in the hotel turns out to be a toned-down version of the dubious locations for adulterous carryings-on found in French farces.* That this is a venue for illicit pleasures is broadly hinted at. Such West End establishments were not entirely unrespectable, but had overtones of raffishness, being used for drinking, gambling and more covert night-time activities. Pinero's Hotel des Princes is a space where men dine together, or furtively entertain their mistresses in private rooms. Previous clients having scratched their names on the mirrors is an indication of its dubious status. Such a venue attracts a range of male visitors, many of respectable position, but it is not the place for 'respectable' women.

Posket enters the Hotel des Princes 'nervous and reluctant'. He imparts a respectable bourgeois fear of discovery of impropriety. In such an environment he must conceal his identity—he poses as 'Mr Harry Skinner of the Stock Exchange'. But it is the intrusion into this location for illicit masculine indulgences by two respectable women—his wife, Agatha and her sister, Charlotte—which gives the cue for farcical mayhem. Matters are further complicated by the arrival of the police, who investigate the hotel for being open after hours. In late Victorian society, pleasures of the night were under tight legal control. The police could take names and addresses and issue summonses for being on dubious premises at prohibited hours. This meant the exposure of guilty secrets for otherwise respectable gentlemen. Cis and his stepfather manage to escape, pursued by the police. They leave behind the respectable party—Agatha Posket, her sister, Colonel Lukyn and Captain Vale—who are arrested. They are to be tried next morning before the magistrate at Mulberry Street Police Court—who happens to be Aeneas Posket!

Posket's appearance next morning, in the magistrate's room at the Mulberry Street Police Court, is 'extremely wretched'. A respected

---

* The French 'Palais-Royale' farces produced by Charles Wyndham at the Criterion during the 1870s eliminated the adulterous elements on which the plots hinged. While retaining the chases, concealments and guilty revelations traditional to farce, a safe degree of propriety was preserved for London audiences. See Bratton 1995: xiii.

magistrate has been pursued throughout the night by the law. This male pillar of society is made to appear both ridiculous and pathetic. His evening dress is 'muddy', his linen 'soiled and crumpled' and he has 'a small strip of black plaster' across the bridge of his nose'. Being chased through the London streets has removed every shred of magisterial dignity and made him a laughing-stock. *The Times*' critic wrote that: 'The idea of so grave and responsible a personage as a metropolitan magistrate occupying the ludicrous situations assigned to Mr Posket tickles the public immoderately.'[138] Like a character in a Greek tragedy, he recounts off-stage events to the audience. During his long and colourful soliloquy he takes the roles of both himself and Cis:

> Then what occurred? A dark room, redolent of onions and cabbages and paraffin oil, and Cis dragging me over the stone floor saying, 'We're in the scullery, Guv; let's try and find the tradesmen's door.' Next the night air—oh, how refreshing! 'Cis my boy, we will both learn a lesson from tonight—never deceive.' Where are we? In Argyll Street. 'Lookout, Guv, they're after us.' ... Then the fun began. We over into the square—they after us. Over again, into Baker Street. Down Baker Street. ... 'Come on, Guv—you're getting blown.' ... 'What road is this, Cis?' Maida Vale. Good gracious! A pious aunt of mine once lived in Hamilton Terrace; she never thought I should come to this.[139]

The narrative reduces Posket's masculine authority. Its comic effect is to make him appear ridiculous, pathetic and inept—definitely not a hero in the mould of his namesake Aeneas. Use of the present tense gives his narration a cinematic quality, which works upon the imagination of the audience, releasing the action from the confines of the picture-frame stage. Situations such as Posket's chase across London would have been difficult or impossible to stage. Instead, Pinero in his farces innovated long, expository reportage of events suffered between the acts. This gave an opportunity for the comic versatility of his leading player.

A heroic accolade may be awarded to Cis who has performed super-human efforts in Posket's defence. Supposedly, he ran all the way from London to Hendon, and walked back from there to Bloomsbury. From a position of weakness at the beginning of the play, he has attained the status of a classical athlete. Cis is elevated to being a hero, while Posket continues to be reduced to size. His behaviour becomes more illogical and ridiculous. In a daze, he sentences his wife and sister-in-law, her fiancé and his house guest to seven days imprisonment, 'without the option of a fine'. But he has also been part of their transgression. His actions turn him into a satirical embodiment of the pomposity and hypocrisy associated with men of high position.

Figure 56. Poster for *The Magistrate*, Royal Lyceum Theatre, Edinburgh

In the final scene, Posket's partner, Bellamy, makes a *deus ex machina* appearance to announce that he has declared Posket 'non compos mentis'. The ladies have been released while their partners, Lukyn and Vance, have been sent to a House of Correction. This is an ironic reversion of the usual melodramatic situation where women are made to suffer for male transgressions. In this case, the men are punished for supposed immorality, while the ladies go free. The so-called 'double standard' is turned inside out during Agatha's final show-down with Posket. She accuses him of having revelled in 'a dissolute bachelorhood:'

> POSKET: Hah! Whist every evening!
> AGATHA: You can't play whist *alone*. You're an expert at hiding, too! ... When you wished to conceal yourself last night, you selected a table with a lady under it. ...
> POSKET: I fancy, madam, you found my conduct under that table perfectly respectful?
> AGATHA: I don't know—I was too agitated to notice.
> POSKET: Evasion—you're like all the women.
> AGATHA: Profligate! You oughtn't to know that!
> POSKET: No wife of mine sups, unknown to me, with dissolute military men; we will have a judicial separation, Mrs Posket.[140]

However, the moment Agatha confesses to her deceit over the ages of Cis and herself, she conforms to the stereotype of the obedient wife. Having displayed wilfulness and independence, she appears to become the submissive wife of domestic ideology. But she still gives herself some leeway 'I'll never deceive you again—except in little things'.[141]

Thanks to Cis, Posket escapes punishment. Recognised by the hotel waiter as 'the man who escaped from Meek Street last night,' he desperately tries to regain his status. Cis rushes in to announce his engagement to Beatie Tomlinson. This temporarily takes attention from Posket's misdemeanours. Agatha, still seeing Cis as 'an infant' tries to forbid the marriage. But Cis, being nineteen, may, according to the law, obtain his guardian's consent. The magistrate, whose dignity has been threatened, whose pomposity and hypocrisy have been exposed, now redeems himself with his munificence. He promises Cis a thousand pounds on the day he marries and emigrates to Canada. At the same time, he is removing a corrupting influence from his life, as well as triumphing over his deceiving wife. The harmony of hearth and home would appear to have been restored. But there is still the question of a high-ranking official being able to evade exposure and scandal because of his high position.

Critics saw *The Magistrate* as a play without any of the 'objectionable immorality' of the French Palais Royal farces. *The Times*, for instance, thought it superior to all French farces 'in its freedom from grossness and fidelity to English notions of the humorous'.[142] Joseph Knight, drama critic of *The Athenaeum*, held a more reactionary view. His warned a conservative readership, many of whom were women, that 'a spice of wickedness seems all but indispensable to this class of piece'.[143]

In *The Magistrate* Pinero introduces themes similar to those in French farce: suspected unfaithfulness, secret philandering, the accidental meeting of suspects at a venue of dubious reputation. The question of obtaining money from an older, wealthier man hints at blackmail and even prostitution. This gives a disturbing ambivalence to the play, suggesting that perhaps it is even less decorous than it may have appeared to the 1885 audience.

Philanderers and profligates in the 'New Drama'

The secret lives of men in high position were a dominant theme in the socially conscious 'New Drama' that emerged during the final decades of the nineteenth century. While jingoistic military and naval heroes drew popular audiences to the Adelphi and elsewhere, fashionable spectators flocked to a group of theatres located near to the exclusive 'little parish of St James's'—the area surrounding St James's Palace and St James's Church, Piccadilly. These theatres included the St James's, which, under the management of George Alexander, saw premières of plays by Wilde and Pinero. Other fashionable venues were the Haymarket, the Garrick and Wyndham's. Society audiences attending these theatres obtained a vicarious pleasure from seeing themselves portrayed on the stage—but it was not always a flattering portrait. The so-called 'New Drama' focused on questions of upper class morality. Those who were shunned by polite society often took centre stage, particularly the fallen woman and the fallen man. Criticism was levelled toward the attitudes of society, especially the so-called 'double standard' that allowed men their peccadilloes, while the behaviour of women was severely constrained.

Many of the comedies and social dramas of the *fin de siècle* concentrate on upper-class male protagonists who are morally flawed. Most of these plays are by middle-class male authors and it was the emergent middle class that justified itself by claiming manly ideals of purity and purpose. Upper- or leisure-class men were perceived as effeminate, idle and immoral.[144] Men from aristocratic families, however, filled most of the higher executive, legal and legislative positions. Their exalted position made them particularly vulnerable to scandal—both sexual and financial. Insolvency was a disgrace and many upper-class men lived under the threat of large debts being called in. Sexual scandal emanated from issues such as illegitimacy, marital discord, adultery, bigamy, venereal disease and homosexuality. In a wealthy society sex and money were intertwined—as is suggested in Oscar Wilde's *An Ideal Husband*.[145] It is the fear of financial or sexual scandal that forms the backbone of most plays dealing with the fallen upper-class man. The scandalous results of secret financial dealing and sexual philandering become a target in the society dramas of Wilde, Pinero, Jones, and other writers of the time.

Confrontation with a past secret was a basic ingredient of plays dealing with the fallen man, as it was in plays dealing with fallen women. In problem plays it is usual for both the female courtesan and the male profligate to die, or attempt to die, by poison. Poisoning is the favoured method for expiry, possibly because it is a 'cleaner' method of dying on the stage and spared audiences the distressing sight of gushing blood. The convention of self-poisoning by the male profligate also contained a Hellenistic allusion: the philosopher, Socrates, after accusations and a trial, poisoned himself by drinking a cup of hemlock.

In melodrama the fallen woman almost invariably dies, and has to find redemption through the forgiveness of a pure man, usually her wronged husband. In the late nineteenth-century problem play, the would-be male suicide is nearly always saved by the intervention of a good woman, who sets out to reform him. For example, in Henry Arthur Jones's *The Dancing Girl* (Haymarket, 1891) the wicked Duke of Guisebury is saved from poisoning himself by female intervention. He survives to do good works on the island he has inherited in Cornwall. Meanwhile, Drusilla Ives, the 'dancing girl' of the title, whom Guisebury has corrupted, dies a mysterious and possibly sordid death in New Orleans.

Sydney Grundy's *A Bunch of Violets* (Haymarket, 1894), is a play in which the fallen man actually dies on stage. Sir Philip Marchant, a parliamentary candidate, cannot face accusations of both fraud and bigamy. He takes poison and dies in the arms of his daughter—appropriately named Violet. As in the protracted death scenes for female courtesans, there is an amount of stage 'business' for the actor playing Sir

Philip. Dying, he feels for his daughter's button-hole of violets which has fallen on the floor: '*VIOLET comes to him, picks them up, puts them in his coat and her arms round his neck.* As the curtain falls *his head falls on her shoulder.*'[146] This highly sentimentalised ending seems designed to create sympathy for a fallen upper-class man whose remorse over past misdeeds has become unbearable.

By showing men to be flawed, the position of the central male protagonist in late-nineteenth-century drama becomes considerably weakened. Strength is usually to be found in the leading female characters— the good wife who supports and forgives her philandering husband, or the fallen woman fighting against the society that ostracises her. The emergence of a flawed, if fascinating, anti-hero coincides partly with a growing interest in psychology and partly through an awareness of the plays of Ibsen. Aspects of both hero and villain are often merged into one character. Well-meaning upper-class men are shown as misguided and self-deluded, particularly in their attitude towards women. Chivalric intentions often go awry. For instance, Aubrey Tanqueray, the upper-middle-class protagonist of Pinero's *The Second Mrs Tanqueray* (St James's 1893), marries his mistress, Paula Ray. This is in deliberate defiance of society's rules and expectations. He wants to prove that it is possible for a woman who has 'never met a man who treated her well' to find happiness in marriage. Also, he is a lonely widower, seeking the companionship of a wife. By installing his mistress as his wife, Aubrey Tanqueray is making a political statement. The play argues that this is a rash act. Aubrey introduces Paula to his family and stuffy Surrey society with disastrous results. She becomes bored and restless; she finds herself ostracised. Ultimately, she commits suicide away from the view of her husband, and of the audience. The fate of Aubrey Tanqueray is not questioned, although he has, in effect, killed his wife.

Male protagonists such as Aubrey Tanqueray are the antithesis of the idealised hero. Their intentions, partly out of self-interest and partly in defiance of society, create tragedy and havoc. In *The Second Mrs Tanqueray* Pinero sets out to prove that crossing the moral boundaries laid down by the status quo can only lead to disaster.

In society or 'problem' plays, aspects of masculinity are not contained in one central character. A weak, misguided or fallen male protagonist is counter-balanced by a moral arbiter, or *raisonneur*. This is usually a highly respectable, mature, upper middle-class man, employed in a responsible position such as that of a lawyer. A stock figure of the well-made play, he mediates between masculine and feminine worlds. He comments on the action, imparts moralistic advice and tries to make the fallen man see the error of his ways. He often takes a moral stance that is ostensibly directed to the protagonist on stage, but at the same time addresses men in the audience.

An example of this occurs in Pinero's early play, *The Profligate* (Garrick, 1889). Hugh Murray, a respected Scottish solicitor, lectures rakish Dunstan Renshaw about the consequences of 'sowing wild oats':

> But what of the time when those wild oats thrust their ears through the very seams of the floor trodden by the wife whose respect you have learned to covet! You may drag her into the crowded streets—there is the same vile growth springing up from the chinks of the pavement! In your house or in the open, the scent of mildewed grain always in your nostrils, and in your ears, no music but the wind's rustle amongst the fat sheaves! And worst of all, your wife's heart a granary bursting with the load of shame your profligacy has stored there![147]

This speech has the tone of a social purity tract. Rhetoric and metaphor are used to make a social and sexual problem palatable to the audience. Pinero gives a coded warning of the effects of youthful profligacy. Underlying his moral arbiter's harangue is Pinero's anger over the irresponsibility of philandering men and his outrage at the Contagious Diseases Acts, which punished women for the results of the profligacy of their male partners. Pinero's indignation is even more vehemently expressed in *The Second Mrs Tanqueray* when Aubrey Tanqueray condemns the behaviour of Captain Hugh Ardale:

> Curse him! Yes I do curse him—him and his class! Perhaps I curse myself too in doing it. He has only led 'a man's life'—just as I, how many of us, have done! The misery he has brought on me and mine, it's likely we, in our time, have helped to bring on others by leading 'a man's life'![148]

These were courageous words to speak in a theatre favoured by high society. Pinero's admonition boldly addresses those men in the audience who kept mistresses or visited brothels. The health and lives of respectable women could be destroyed not only by their husbands' deceit and dissipation, but also by the fear and misery caused by the threat of sexually transmitted diseases. In *The Profligate* Pinero attempted to draw sympathy toward the fallen man, while addressing the problems resulting from 'sowing his wild oats'. He wrote the play in 1887, but it was not performed until 1889, when it was the opening production at the Garrick Theatre in Charing Cross Road.

Contemporary debates on ethics and the sexuality of men seem to have influenced Pinero's problem play. In *The Maiden Tribute of Modern Babylon* (1885) W. T. Stead had written sensationally of upper-class rakes corrupting innocent young working-class girls.[149] Pinero's profligate is an upper-class rake who seduces schoolgirls.

Dunstan Renshaw is 'a town gentleman who does ill in the country'. He is married off to naïve schoolgirl, Leslie Brudenell, by her guardian. Somewhat improbably, he falls in love with this unworldly, impressionable young girl. Efforts to dislodge himself from his sinful past are thwarted by the appearance, in Italy, of his ruined and abandoned mistress, eighteen-year-old Janet Preece. There is the unspoken hint that he may have infected her with a venereal disease. Learning of his past misdeeds, traumatised Leslie asks him to 'go'. At the end of the play he returns to London, sick and exhausted, wanting to reconcile himself with his estranged wife. He is filled with self-reproach and remorse.

Pinero's original intention had been for Dunstan to poison himself and die on stage. However, John Hare, actor-manager of the Garrick Theatre, thought the death of the central male character in full view of the audience would be too distressing. Pinero agreed to change the ending. He justified his action to his critics:

> Could not the moral I had set myself to illustrate be enforced without distressing the audience by sacrificing the life of a character whose sufferings were intended to win sympathy? Reflection convinced me that such a course was not only possible but it was the one which in no way tended to weaken the termination of my story, whilst it promised to extend that story's influence over the larger body of the public.[150]

In Pinero's changed ending, Dunstan Renshaw is about to poison himself when *he utters a sudden cry and holds the glass from him at arm's length.* Committing suicide will be 'the deepest sin of all my life'.[151] At this very moment, his wife rushes in and takes him in her arms. She will bear on her shoulders 'the burden of the sin you have committed'. Through her purity, she offers salvation and the prospect of starting a new life together.[152]

Figure 57. *The Profligate*, Act IV, at the Garrick Theatre: Dunstan Renshaw rejects committing suicide

This prospect of salvation through the firm foundation of a marriage assuages an audience who would have otherwise been 'distressed' by the suicide of the main character. Nevertheless, the attempt of a fallen man to commit suicide was considered to be 'utterly unconventional'. For *The Times* reviewer 'the only analogy that could suggest itself to mind' was death-scenes in fallen women plays starring Sarah Bernhardt or Mrs Bernard-Beere.*[153] By making the main protagonist a fallen man, as opposed to a fallen woman, Pinero drew attention to the problem of upper

---

* Mrs Bernard-Beere was the first Mrs Arbuthnot in Oscar Wilde's *A Woman of No Importance* (Haymarket 1893).

class male philandering. He posed the question as to whether the dissolute male could reform himself. At the same time he was addressing the sexual habits of certain men in the audience. As *The Times* wrote, the play had unquestionably the merit of dismissing the audience 'with some pregnant reflections on their minds'.[154]

A highly moralistic ending concludes a story that began with Dunstan Renshaw being portrayed as debauched, dissolute, deceitful, cynical and thoroughly immoral. On his first entrance, the stage directions describe him as 'looking not more than thirty but shewing on his face and eyes signs of the wear and tear of dissipation'.[155] Toward the end of the play when he returns ill, he 'looks old and broken, his voice is hollow and feeble'.[156] Pinero subscribes to the notion of secret sin being revealed in the face, as expounded in moral purity tracts and sermons:

> The face tells tales. Vice writes its history on the countenance, and many a man has only to look into the glass to see the history of his life graven there in many a line, carved by Satan's subtle skill.[157]

The question of a man's sins revealed in his face was to be the theme of Oscar Wilde's novel *The Picture of Dorian Gray* (1890). Throughout *The Profligate* sickness is linked with sexual transgression. According to moral purity campaigners, by following 'your animal nature ... you shall reap in a debilitated and perhaps diseased body, which, so terrible is the punishment for impurity, you may hand down to the third or fourth generation.'[158] This theme underlies *The Profligate* and seems to prefigure Ibsen's *Ghosts* (1881)—although Pinero was to deny an Ibsenite influence on his plays.*

The Profligate was the first play to apply the conventions of the fallen woman melodrama to the behaviour of a dissolute man. The idea was a complete novelty. Pinero had changed the gender roles of society melodrama. The critic in *The Times* wrote that Pinero had said to himself 'Why should not the heroine of fiction and her husband change places? Why should not the stigma of a sinful past for once be his—his also the shame and the suffering of an exposure in the eyes of the one he

---

* Throughout his career, Pinero was concerned not to be thought of as a disciple of Ibsen. He did not see *Ghosts* until it was first staged in London in 1891—by J. T. Grein's Independent Theatre, at the Royalty Theatre. See Dawick 1993: 175.

loves?'[159] The play goes as far as it can to show the results of a dissolute life-style and strongly hints at the menace of social disease. *The Theatre* summed up its moral content in one long sentence:

> What a lesson [*The Profligate*] teaches to the most thoughtless man of the world: it shows him how the consequences of self-gratification will one day rise up against him as spectres to haunt and destroy him should he not have, as in this case, a pure loving woman, who, at the same time she condemns, can pity him, and, with the aid of that pity, hold forth a hand to lead him to a better path, and guide and support him as he stumbles on his upward way.[160]

By making 'a pure loving woman' save her philandering husband, Pinero subscribes to the ideals of the social purity movement—that women were the moral protectors of the home.[161] At the same time, he panders to audience expectations of a morally satisfying conclusion. Nevertheless, William Archer insisted that Pinero had dragged English drama 'out of the toyshop and put it back in touch with adult art'.[162] *The Profligate* received excessive praise, but despite Archer's enthusiasm there was a dissenting voice from the dramatist Sydney Grundy who told Archer that he thought the play 'a fine situation set in a puerile play, written in the language of journalism'.[163]

About six weeks after the first performance of *The Profligate*, there appeared a 'social play' that would have a more profound effect on British drama. This was Ibsen's *A Doll's House*, presented by Charles Charrington and his wife, Janet Achurch, at the Novelty Theatre on 7 June 1889. Even Pinero could see that his attempts were 'clumsy and shallow compared to Ibsen'.

As William Archer wrote in his comparison of the two plays: 'Ibsen's characters stood solid in three dimensions; beside them Mr Pinero's seemed like mere cardboard profiles.'[164] Pinero had been 'daring' in raising 'the wild-oats question'. But, according to Archer, 'He approached it … from the very safest side, and handled it, or rather touched upon it, in the very safest fashion'. On the other hand, Ibsen, in tackling an equally controversial subject,

> far from taking his ethics for granted seized upon, analysed and pulverised the current … ideal of marriage. He went straight to the root of things, instead of skimming over the surface.[165]

Pinero later had to admit that *The Profligate*, the play of which he was most proud, had become out-dated in comparison with the plays of the great Norwegian dramatist.[166]

Wilde, dandyism and Uranian subtexts

Oscar Wilde, at the conclusion of *An Ideal Husband* (Haymarket, 1895), also shows the redemption of a fallen man by his puritanical wife. However, Sir Robert Chiltern has not tried to commit suicide; he has survived blackmail over a financial error and intends returning to Parliament. Gertrude Chiltern, like Pinero's Leslie Brudenell, offers the prospect of a new life together as the curtain falls. Wilde, however, was giving a more complex and deviant view of social problems than the stern, heterosexual moralising of dramatists such as Jones and Pinero.

Wilde famously said of *An Ideal Husband* that it contained 'a great deal of Oscar'. In his four society plays of the 1890s may be discerned strongly autobiographical elements; layers of sub-text point to the personal dealings, hopes and fears of Oscar himself. He allows glances toward his marital life and his alternative, homosexual life—his relations with Bosie, as well as a coterie of other male lovers, friends and blackmailers. He also may be seen to address, through hints and inferences, a queer contingent in the audience. The plays therefore contain Uranian sub-texts that cannot be ignored. They are, in fact, filled with codes that could have been easily interpreted by those in Wilde's circle.

In the late nineteenth century, homosexual desire was expressed, albeit for an exclusive minority, in Uranian verse and other writings, but it could not be openly shown on the stage. Because of the Lord Chamberlain's censorship and the possibility of public condemnation, neither Wilde nor his contemporaries could have written an explicitly 'gay' play, even had they wished to. British drama was therefore unable to challenge homophobic prejudice in the same way as, arguably, did verses published in *The Artist*, *The Chameleon*, *The Spirit Lamp* and other little magazines of the period. For the stage, a homosexual presence had to be subterfuged. As Alan Sinfield has stated: same-sex passion in the plays of Wilde 'was not ruled in, neither was it ruled out'.[167] No dramatist of the time would have written a serious play in which the central protagonist was openly shown to be a sodomite. This did not however prevent the presence of male bonding, verging on homosexual love, in plays by Wilde and his contemporaries. Several plays of the late nineteenth century deal with platonic male friendship, discreetly raising the question of same-sex love between men.

For instance, *The Idler* by Charles Haddon Chambers (St James's Theatre, 1891) focuses on the close male friendship between Mark Cross and Simeon Strong, an American millionaire. Before the play opens, the two had met as young men at a prospecting town in California. It was here that Mark rescued Simeon from drowning. This was also the place where Simeon's brother had been shot by John Harding, now an MP and the play's 'fallen' protagonist. Mark wants Simeon to forgive Harding and take him (Mark) as a surrogate brother. For this reason, in the third act he invites Simeon to his 'bachelor's apartment'. Here they indulge in typically masculine pursuits such as drinking whiskey and smoking cigars. At the same time there is a strong suggestion of physical closeness and tender concern between the two men. The stage directions indicate Mark's tactility toward Simeon: he continually lays his hand on his shoulder, and at one point clasps his hand. Mark and Simeon 'understand' each other. Simeon says that the feelings between them 'don't require to be spoken. There's a truth in a hand grip—a look in the eye—that makes you know your man, eh?'[168] That there may be 'something unspoken' between the two men is carefully diverted by Mark being in love with Lady Harding. At the end of the play he leaves Lady Harding to her husband, and sets off to lead Simeon's North Pole expedition.

The scene between Mark and Simeon is probably more concerned with portraying bonds of platonic masculine friendship than with suggesting a homosexual relationship between the two men. Victorian male friendship tended to be highly emotional and even tactile without necessarily being expressed sexually. Nevertheless *The Idler* is probably unique in portraying deep same-sex feelings between two men who are equals in age and in experience of the world.

It was more usual for dramatists such as Wilde to subscribe to Hellenic paederastic ideology by portraying the influence of an older man over a younger one. This ideal forms the basis of the plot of *The Blackmailers*, an attempt by John Gray and Marc-André Raffalovich to write a play that was more explicit about a same-sex relationship.

Nevertheless, homosexual inferences had to be encoded.

For all its faults, *The Blackmailers* takes a bold look at the complexities of queerness in the late nineteenth century. Raffalovich and Gray could be viewed as an alternative couple to Oscar and Bosie. Raffalovich even saw himself as a rival to Oscar Wilde, and their joint play is probably an attempt to challenge his success. However, it only achieved a single matinée performance at the Prince of Wales's Theatre on 7th June 1894. It had a cast of well-known actors, most of whom were associated with the Adelphi Theatre. According to Raffalovich, the cast 'mangled and mutilated' the play.[169] Evidently, the reception of 'a patient and friendly audience' was more of puzzlement than interest. However there was 'a mild demonstration at the conclusion' and a call for the authors, 'but although they were in a private box, they did not appear at the footlights.'[170]

Figure 58. Marc-André Raffalovich, aged about 16

Although the audience gave *The Blackmailers* a polite reception, the critics were less than enthusiastic. *The Era* thought it 'a depressing and dreary afternoon's entertainment'. Like many in the audience, its critic was perplexed by the play: the authors 'understood to be two very deep young men—disciples of the Ibsen cult' hinted at 'depths of iniquity which we cannot fathom'.[171] Gilbert Burgess in *The Artist* (a journal noted for its publication of Uranian verse),* thought it 'a curious play' and dismissed Gray and Raffalovich as belonging to 'the new *décadent* school of poets'. Burgess also noted Wildean influences, to the detriment of the authors: 'In many of the would-be epigrams there are traces of the trail of Mr Oscar Wilde, but his wit and wisdom are painfully lacking.'[172]

Clement Scott, writing in the *Illustrated London News*, 16 June 1894, seemed aware of homosexual inferences. He thought it was 'scarcely worthwhile to write plays in order to advertise such abnormal cases of depravity'. He went on: 'This is not holding the mirror up to nature. It is showing an unnatural monster in a very dirty and dusty looking glass.'[173] 'Unnatural' and 'abnormal' were terms applied by the press, the church and society to the sexual deviant.

The play takes a heavily ironic view of homosexuality. The two blackmailers of the title are possible male lovers. This means that gay men are covertly represented by those who caused them fear, misery and ruin. The queerness of Claud Price, the main protagonist, is further disguised by his blackmailing his former mistress—a married woman in high society. This raises another question by showing that it was not only homosexual men who were subject to blackmail—heterosexual men and women engaged in illicit affairs could be just as vulnerable.

Claud Price exerts his influence over Hyacinth Halford Dangar, a 24-year-old ex-public-school boy who practices extortion on his former schoolfellows. Claud is a 'loner' who seeks a kindred spirit. He finds in the aesthetically named Hyacinth a promising subject to influence against society. His family calls the young man Hal; significantly, only Claud uses the name of Hyacinth. The classical Hyacinthus was a youth madly loved (and accidentally killed) by Apollo. The myth was a favourite allusion in the Uranian sub-culture.† In 1893, Oscar Wilde had written a

---

* See footnote to page 46. —*Ed.*

† *The Artist*, in July and October 1889, had included Hyacinthus and Apollo among a number of suitable classical or homoerotic 'Subjects for Pictures' (see Brake 2001: 123). The sun god and his mortal lover made appearances in Uranian verse and prose. Walter Pater, for instance, retells the story in a French monastic setting in his

letter to Bosie, addressing him as Hyacinthus. This letter had fallen into the hands of blackmailers. Gray and Raffalovich would certainly have been aware of the rumours circulating about Oscar and Bosie—of their association with renters and encounters with blackmailers. Their use of the name Hyacinth, with its connotations of Uranianism and blackmail, leaves little doubt as to the underlying theme of the play.

Like the plays of Oscar Wilde, *The Blackmailers* is full of homosexual codes. Undoubtedly among those 'respectable' patrons puzzled by the play at its single performance sat a minority used to deciphering allusions. The difficulties of being a queer man in a hostile world forms one of the main sub-texts of the play:

> HAL: Only think of having to keep a watch over your face, your gestures, to be acting before one's nearest. Oh! that must be exciting, delightful, that must be knowing that one lives.[174]

Both the homosexual and the blackmailer live in constant fear of being found out. Deception creates an exciting life even if it is filled with danger. It is a situation where both the extortioner and his victim become outlaws from society. Claud Price is an outcast—he is therefore 'lonely'. His 'loneliness' equates with the popular notion of the homosexual being a sad, self-pitying, withdrawn individual.[175] In Hyacinth he finds a kindred spirit. In a passage deleted in the typescript submitted to the Lord Chamberlain, Price makes it clear that he has found another man (a male lover) to share his life with:

> PRICE: Hyacinth, don't think that my loneliness has weakened my judgement. I am not more tempted than I have ever been to share my wisdom and my gains and the excitements of my life with someone else: but until I found you again I had not discovered anywhere in anyone what I sought, what I wanted.[176]

Price is capable of exhibiting tender feelings toward Hyacinth, but the actual word 'sodomite' is never used. For example, an argument between Hal and Price in Act II rises to a hysterical crescendo, with Hal/Hyacinth denying what he really is:

---

homoerotic short story *Apollo in Picardy*, which appeared in an issue of *Harpers New Monthly Magazine*, November 1893, entirely devoted to 'degenerate' literature.)

PRICE: You know what you are, Hyacinth, don't you?
HAL: What I am? What do you mean?
PRICE: You know the name by which this sort of transaction usually goes—even amongst the unprejudiced?
HAL: No ... (*under PRICE's look he falters*) Yes.
PRICE: And it is?
HAL: Spare me! Spare me! Claud!
PRICE: Blackmail. (*HAL is silent*) What did I say?
HAL: (*Tremblingly*) Blackmail.
PRICE: And you are a blackmailer, my dear Hyacinth.[177]

The terms 'sodomy' and 'sodomite' (which would presumably have been in the audience's mind at this point) are replaced by the words 'blackmail' and 'blackmailer'. That is the irony underscoring the play; by making Claud and Hyacinth blackmailers, the authors attempt to mask the intended homosexuality of the two protagonists. At the same time the theme of blackmail reveals the strong links between sex, money and menace—all of which formed the background to the late-nineteenth-century homosexual 'underworld'.

At the end of the play Hyacinth runs away to join Claud in Paris.* This happens just after Hyacinth has been put on trial by his reactionary family. In a hysterical speech he denounces the attitudes of upper class respectability toward deviancy. He rails against the dominance of his mother, which he sees as a contributing factor to his transgressive nature. Like many other rebellious young men from the upper classes, he is threatened with expulsion to the colonies—hard work in New Zealand will make 'a man' of him. Unable to countenance such a fate, Hal, like other fallen men in melodrama, contemplates poisoning himself. But in this case, same-sex love intervenes. Just as Hyacinth is about to drink the wine into which he has poured a phial of arsenic, a note arrives from Claud, urging him away: 'I don't want to triumph without you, my pupil, soon to be my equal. Come. We understand each other now and the

---

* Paris was a congenial sphere for British sexual escapees (i.e. 'deviants'). A year later it would provide a refuge for some of the friends of Oscar Wilde and eventually for Oscar himself. After hearing of Wilde's arrest John Gray discreetly left for Berlin, where he joined Raffalovich who had come from Brussels. See McKenna 2003: 383; McCormack 2000: 183.

world.'[178] Hyacinth steals away from the family tribunal. The two 'blackmailing cads' escape justice and will presumably live together in Paris. Finding the glass of poisoned wine, Hyacinth's uncle asks the other family members: 'Do you think it would have been better if he had taken it?' In other words, those who deviate against the norm are not fit to live in a respectable heterosexual society.

Regarding this conclusion, *The Times* remarked that 'the curtain descends upon the "note of interrogation" beloved of Ibsenites'.[179] A seemingly 'Ibsenite' ending made Clement Scott, enemy of the 'New Drama', indignant. He fulminated that Hal was too much of a coward for suicide 'and sneaks off to Paris to cheat and blackmail more people, rather than glorying in his power of imitating the criminal classes'.[180] Scott missed the underlying point that Hyacinth 'sneaks off to Paris' out of love for Claud. This upbeat note to the ending goes against the notion of paederastic love always ending in tragedy—as was the case with the classical Apollo and Hyacinthus. Nevertheless by portraying Claud and Hyacinth as blackmailers, Gray and Raffalovich still subscribe to notions of degeneracy among young men who stray from the *status quo*.

The Blackmailers resembles Wilde's *A Woman of No Importance*, produced the previous year. Both plays exploit the Hellenic ideal of an experienced older man falling for and influencing a vulnerable younger man. In ancient Greek culture, *paederastia* was seen as an exalted blend of the physical and spiritual, but also accompanied by loss. This was an ideal that influenced the Uranian view of homosexual relationships not as a union of equals, but as 'the unequal and hence unnatural coupling of older man and youth'.[181] In *The Blackmailers* Gray and Raffalovich evade loss, while subverting the paederastic ideal. The older man and youth (usually the target of blackmailers) become perpetrators who use extortion as a weapon against an unsympathetic society.[182]

In *A Woman of No Importance*, Oscar Wilde also gives an ironic twist to the paederastic theme. He introduces a suggestion of incest. This further helps to disguise a Uranian subplot. If the older man turns out to be the boy's father, how could he possibly seduce his own son? Nevertheless, Lord Illingworth's interest in Gerald Arbuthnot is perhaps the most blatant expression of homosexuality in Wilde's plays. It is also the first of his plays in which a dandy is a leading character.

Like Wilde's other dandies, Lord Illingworth is given a mask of heterosexuality. But Wilde's underlying theme does not seem to have been lost on his queer contemporaries. For instance, Lytton Strachey, after seeing Beerbohm Tree's revival in 1907, told Duncan Grant that the play was: 'The queerest mixture! Mr Tree is a wicked Lord, staying in a country house, who has made up his mind to bugger one of the other guests—a handsome young man of twenty.'[183]

While the codes could be deciphered by those in the audience of a 'Uranian' disposition, other spectators were 'charmed' by Beerbohm Tree's performance in the first performances of Wilde's society melodrama. Wilde informed Beerbohm Tree, when he was about to play the role, that Lord Illingworth was 'certainly not natural. He is a figure of art. Indeed, if you can bear the truth, he is MYSELF.'[184] *The Times* review described Beerbohm Tree as having 'a carefully studied make-up' denoting 'a man who has travelled much and added an exotic touch to his profligacy. He cultivates a philosophy *à la* Oscar Wilde'.[185] 'Exotic' was a term for 'degenerates', usually aimed at queer men. Linking this terminology with a reference to Wilde himself suggests that *The Times*' reviewer was well aware of the autobiographical propensities inherent in the character of Lord Illingworth.

With Lord Illingworth and his 'exotic touch' Wilde presents the antithesis of both the traditional patriarchal figure and the stern moral arbiter found in the plays of Jones and Pinero. Like Lord Henry Wotton in Wilde's novel *The Picture of Dorian Gray*, Lord Illingworth advocates individualism. He tries to tempt Gerald with a hedonistic philosophy that reflects his own jaded view of life. He wants to mould Gerald into a dandy in his own image. His motives in luring away this underpaid bank clerk to be his private secretary are highly suspect. Lord Illingworth exemplifies the Hellenic ideal of the older man exerting a paederastic influence over youthful innocence and beauty.

Every attempt is made by Lord Illingworth to turn Gerald against the maternal influence of Mrs Arbuthnot. But through trying to free Gerald from his mother, he replaces her possessiveness with that of a thwarted older man. His passion for Gerald is not an equalised love. It is the more egoistical passion of a man whose own youth has fled. He seeks a young ideal whom he can mould into a younger version of himself. At first, he tells Gerald that the reason he made the offer to become his secretary was 'because I like you so much that I want to have you with me'.[186] When he discovers that Gerald is his son, he becomes even more attracted, because it is easier to see Gerald as a reflection of himself. That he is motivated by incestuous desire exemplifies, as Patricia Flanagan Behrendt has pointed out, the dandy's totally self-centred pursuit of novel experiences.[187]

Gerald is an ineffectual young man, caught between two incestuous passions, that of his father and that of his mother. Ultimately, he rejects Lord Illingworth's temptations and chooses possession by the two women—his mother and his (token) wife, Hester Worsley. He has been saved from the dubious (i.e. homosexual) influence of his father. Being Hester Worsley's husband will be a better career than Lord Illingworth's secretary—he will live on her money. Ultimately, Lord Illingworth experiences the loss of a desirable young man, as is usual in paederastic mythology.

Wilde however spares Illingworth the usual fate of the fallen man in society melodrama. He does not commit suicide by taking poison. Nor is he filled with guilt and remorse over his past mistakes. Instead, he retaliates by reminding Mrs Arbuthnot that she was his mistress—and his whore.[188] He is literally struck out of the family circle by Mrs Arbuthnot. Dazed by 'the insult of his punishment', he seems to evaporate, leaving only his glove behind.[189] Possibly, he goes on to continue the profligate life of a dandy elsewhere, but in Mrs Arbuthnot's estimation he is no longer of any importance. Wilde has killed off his 'fallen man' by far more subtle means than a phial of poison.

Homosexual deception also forms the undercurrent of Wilde's comedy, *The Importance of Being Earnest*, produced at the St James's Theatre on 14 February 1895. But in this play the subject is handled with greater subtlety and cynicism.* Wilde maintained that the philosophy of *The Importance* was that 'We should treat all trivial things of life seriously, and all the serious things of life with sincere and studied triviality.'[190] Through this philosophy Wilde turns the serious issues of

---

* References are to Wilde's original four-act version as reprinted in Wilde 2003: 357–419.

his personal life into a comedy about deception. At the same time he pokes fun at a society where breeding, birth, rank and wealth are more important than values of honesty, love and honour. Wilde sets his characters revolving in a farcical whirlwind through crises over identity, deception, courtship and marriage until they reach desired prosperity and an appearance of restored normality.

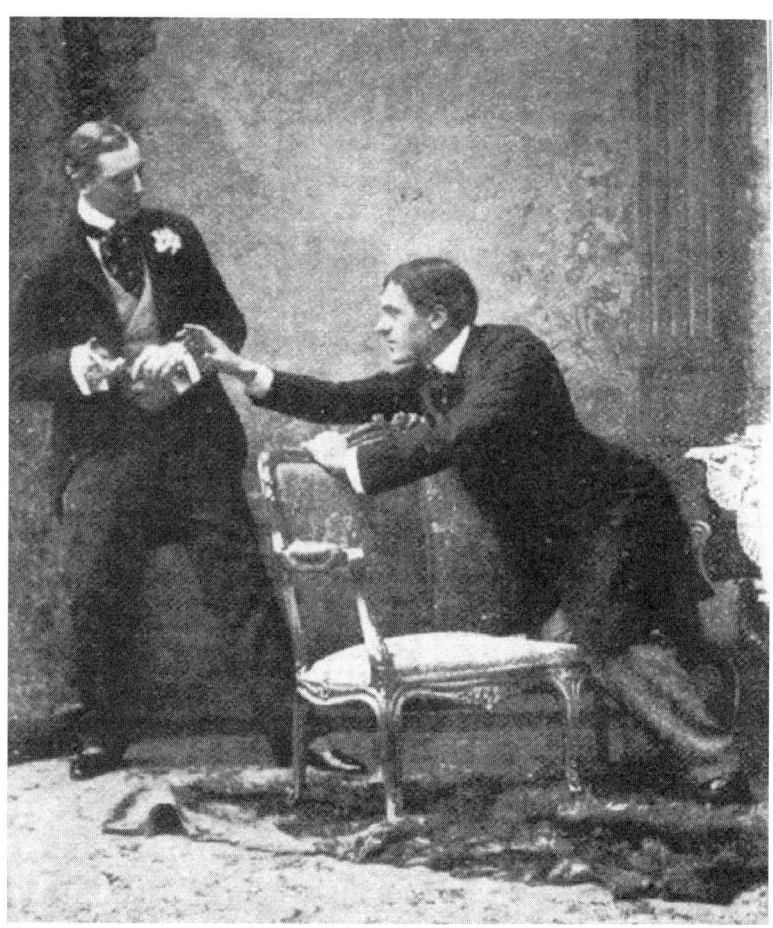

Figure 59. *The Importance of Being Earnest*: Allan Aynesworth (Algy) and Sir George Alexander (Jack) in the original production

Wilde's dandyism, his epigrams and philosophy, pervade the play. A carefully contrasted quartet of central characters becomes the mouthpiece for wit and cynicism. Having two leading male characters versus two leading female characters allows for contrasts and tricks of doubling.

There is also a possible comic allusion to Boucicault's *The Corsican Brothers** in the disparate relationship between Algernon Moncrieff and John Worthing, JP.

Unlike Boucicault's Corsican brothers, Algy and Jack are not aristocratic, nor like Lord Goring and previous Wildean dandies, are they members of the peerage. Both are part of an upper middle-class that aspires to equal the aristocracy. They are also considerably younger than the usual mature leading men of Wilde's society dramas. Algernon is an idle young man-about-town who spends lavishly on dining out, exceeding his allowance. John Worthing lives in the country, where he 'has to adopt a high moral tone on all subjects' because of his guardianship of his ward Cecily Cardew. He comes up to London for pleasure, while Algy takes his pleasures in the country.

Through creating two young male protagonists, Wilde is able to play games with notions of male philandering. He conjures with not one, but two, secret lives. Algernon and Jack invent convenient alternative personae that are the direct opposite of their real selves. Algernon, the dandified young man-about-town, has fabricated Bunbury, an invalid friend in the country who offers an escape from social duties in London society. Jack has concocted a wastrel brother Ernest, who lives in the Albany (the notorious abode of profligate bachelors and upper-class queer men) and 'gets into the most dreadful scrapes'.[191]

From a queer perspective, these invented personae may be viewed as a cover for illicit sexual activity. Prolific, coded references to Wilde's (not so) secret life are spread throughout *The Importance of Being Earnest*. The play is filled with Uranian in-jokes, often subtly conveyed. As Patricia Flanagan Behrendt has pointed out, it is established from the outset that Algernon is 'musical'. Before his first entrance he is heard playing the piano, and we later discover that he arranges the music for Lady Bracknell's parties. 'Musical' was one of a number of code words or euphemisms for being homosexual.[192] *The Times* critic seemed to be hinting at these codes when he commented that the play was 'almost too

---

* As mentioned earlier, Wilde evidently saw Henry Irving's revival of *The Corsican Brothers* in 1880 and also wrote a sonnet inspired by Irving's performance. [See page 259 footnote. —*Ed.*]

preposterous to go without music'.*[193]

The appellation of Ernest has, according to Gwendolen Fairfax, 'a music of its own'. Indeed, the play's title and its repeated connotations on the word and name 'Ernest' point to Uranian influences. It is well known that 'Ernest' was a late-nineteenth-century term for homosexuality, probably referring to the first name of cross-dressed Boulton (of Boulton and Park). It is also likely that through using the name, Wilde was alluding to a volume of homoerotic verse called *Love in Earnest* by a schoolmaster, John Gambril Nicholson, published in 1892. The poems tell of his obsessive love for a boy named Ernest. One of the poems entitled 'Of Boys' Names' contains the refrain that of all boys' names: ''Tis Ernest sets my heart a-flame.'†[194]

Uranian verse speaks of an exclusive, secretive and mysterious world of same-sex love. Wilde, aware that the mysteries of Uranianism had to be encoded for the stage, creates situations for his two main protagonists that carry suggestions of the double life endured by many gay men of his time. Algy's 'Bunburying' and Jack's 'Ernest' constitute an escape into a secluded sphere where the hidden self may be revealed. It provides an outlet from a rigid society, hostile to those who transgress its values. Algy and Jack seek contrasting loopholes for their proclivities. When Algy speaks of 'Bunburying' all over Shropshire, he could be cruising the countryside for rustic trade—not unlike Pinero's profligate. Or could this even be a sly reflection of Edward Carpenter's homosexual/bourgeois/utopian dream of a rural lifestyle, complete with his rustic lover, George Merrill?

---

* The gay inferences of the term 'musical' were made explicit (a year after *The Importance of Being Earnest*), by Raffalovich in his French treatise *Uranisme et Unisexualité*: 'As for *musical* ... I have read in the best journals of a well-bred, good-looking young man, amiable, sympathetic and *musical* who wants to be adopted by an older gentleman, or travel with a wealthy young man, or keep company with a man of the world. I have also read of a wealthy man of the world who would like to have as a secretary or travelling companion, or friend in town or country, a well-born young man, sympathetic and *musical*.' See Raffalovich 1896: 188. (DHL's translation and italics).

† Another possible source for Wilde's use of the name of 'Ernest' (and indeed that of 'Bunbury') may have been the 'Farcical comedy' *Godpapa* by Wilde's arch-enemy Charles Brookfield, written in collaboration with F. C. Philips (Comedy Theatre, 1891). See Lawrence 2009: 21; also Powell 1990: 108–204 and 126–128.

Conversely, Jack comes up to town from the country in search of more sophisticated pleasures. His invented younger brother, Ernest, seems to have the attributes of a 'fallen man'. This suggests a darker side to Jack—a 'Jekyll and Hyde' persona. He is internalised and secretive whereas Algy likes to roam free. Jack's denial that he is a 'Bunburyist' suggests a denial of being a 'sodomite'. If Gwendolen Fairfax agrees to marry him, he will 'kill his brother'. In other words, he will conform to society's demands for a 'normal' married life. But 'Ernest' and 'Bunbury' cannot easily be done away with.

Algernon says that nothing will induce him to part with 'Bunbury'. He imparts to Jack dandiacal advice that subverts the ethos of marital fidelity: 'if you ever get married, which seems to me extremely problematic, you will be very glad to know Bunbury. A man who marries without knowing Bunbury has a very tedious time of it.'[195] He promulgates Wilde's cynical view that marriage is a duty from which a man needs a release into other sexual activities. But marriage can prove 'problematic' for a homosexually inclined husband. That 'Bunbury' is really a code-word for homosexual philandering is signalled by Lady Bracknell's inferences when Algy informs her that his friend has 'exploded'. Lady Bracknell exclaims:

> Exploded! Was he the victim of revolutionary outrage? I was not aware that Mr Bunbury was interested in social legislation. If so, he is well punished for his morbidity.[196]

As well as reflecting upper-class fears of left-wing insurrection, Lady Bracknell becomes a mouthpiece for current perceptions about homosexuality. 'Social legislation' was a euphemism for the movement to change the laws for sex between men. Punishment was meted out to sexual transgressors, while 'morbidity' characterised same-sex desire in terms of disease, decay and death.[197]

Lady Bracknell also expresses popular, psychologically-based notions of homosexuality when she discovers Robert Hichens's novel *The Green Carnation* on Jack's bookshelves. This appears to be 'a book about the culture of exotics. ... It seems a morbid and middle-class affair'.[198] Apart from the fact that Wilde did not like the book, Lady Bracknell's remarks convey the view of homosexuality being outlandish and effeminate, as well as being a form of mental illness.* Algernon's reply about 'Bunbury' being 'found out' and dying seems to hint at the sorry outcome of the discovery of illicit behaviour, leading to arrest or even suicide.[199]

The less salubrious side of Wilde's homosexual life is reflected in the so-called 'Gribsby scene', which appeared in the original four-act version of the play. One of Wilde's renters, Charlie Parker, is supposedly portrayed as one half of the firm of writ-serving solicitors, Parker and Gribsby.[200] Mr Gribsby turns up at Jack's country house to arrest 'Ernest' Worthing for debts run up for suppers at the Savoy Hotel. The scene constitutes an elaborate joke revolving around sex, money and food. Wilde liked to dine out with his renters and the Gribsby scene not only alludes to one of the boys, it also equates consumption with money. As Miss Prism remarks: 'There can be little good in any young man who eats so much, and so often.'[201] The episode also reflects the duplicitous nature of many of those surrounding Wilde. Jack, in the persona of 'Ernest', has spent a considerable sum on meals. He is willing to see his friend Algy arrested for his debts. When Gribsby tries to escort Algy to Holloway, his prisoner is indignant: 'I am not going to be imprisoned in the suburbs for having dined in the West End.'[202] These words would prove prophetic. Soon, Wilde was to be imprisoned in a suburban jail, at Pentonville, on 25 May 1895—almost four months after the play's opening night. He would not have found 'the gaol ... fashionable and well-aired', but he would have discovered there were 'ample opportunities for taking exercise at stated hours of the day'[203] as he filed around and around the exercise yard.

That Jack, even if he wanted to be rid of Algy, would allow him to be arrested for his own misdeed, reveals the heartlessness at the core of the play. Wilde ridicules a society more concerned with class, wealth and position than concepts such as honour or spiritual love. Algernon represents the totally self-centred young men from the upper classes. Like other Wildean dandies, his intense interest in Jack stems from seeing a reflection of himself in his friend. Both view marriage as a means of

---

* *The Green Carnation*, published anonymously in 1894, includes a thinly-disguised portrayal of Oscar Wilde and Lord Alfred Douglas. It was withdrawn from sale in 1895, but had already been used to build up the case against Wilde. —*Ed.*

gaining material things they desire but do not possess. Without a family of his own, or any pedigree, Jack wants to marry aristocratic Gwendolen. Meanwhile, Algy, without any money of his own, becomes engaged to Jack's extremely wealthy ward, Cecily.

Marriage, for both sexes in the play, is a convenient way of gaining wealth and privilege—it is a commercial proposition. When Jack tells Algy that he has come up to London to propose to Gwendolen, Algy replies 'I thought you had come up on pleasure? ... I call that business.'[204] Gwendolen, although she is engaged to Jack, tells Cecily that she finds 'effeminate' men 'so very attractive'. She implies that by marrying an effeminate (i.e. homosexual) man, demands would not be made on her. She would have the material benefits of marriage while being free to live her own life.[205]

Any declaration of love becomes a performance, lacking deeply felt emotion. Algernon woos Cecily using verbose language which makes him appear like the ridiculous hero of a second-rate melodrama: 'I have not merely been your abject slave and servant, but, soaring on the pinions of possibly monstrous ambition, I have dared to love you wildly, passionately, devotedly, hopelessly.'[206] For Cecily, becoming engaged is also a pretence—love and marriage are products of her imagination, things she has written about in her diary. Love and marriage are a sham. According to Wilde's philosophy, the real pleasure is to be found in 'Bunburying'. It offers a man release from feminine domination and marital duty.

All the women in the play try to take control in a world where they find masculine power diminished. Cecily does not see 'any sense at all' in Algy's ludicrous declarations of love: 'The fact is that men should never dictate to women. They never know how to do it, and when they do do it, they always say something particularly foolish.'[207] Gwendolen has her mother's domineering tactics. She dominates Jack by insisting that his name is Ernest. She knew 'from the first that you could have no other name!'[208] By seeing him as 'Ernest' she has found the 'effeminate' man she desires for (in a gay reading) a marriage of convenience. Gwendolen also subverts the Victorian ideal of the dutiful daughter. She disobeys her domineering, match-making mother. With Lady Bracknell there is a blurring of gender and a hint of the pantomime dame (the role has been successfully played by male actors in drag). By arranging Gwendolen's marriage, Lady Bracknell usurps the patriarchal role and its duty of granting permission for a daughter to marry. She may also be perceived as part of the Uranian in-joke that pervades the play. Algy continually refers to her as 'Aunt Augusta'—in the 1890s, 'aunt' or 'auntie' was slang for an older queer man.[209]

The 'Uranian in-joke' also subverts a conventional happy ending, with Jack discovering he is really Ernest Moncrieff. The question remains—will he continue to be as profligate as his imaginary brother was? Or will he join forces in 'Bunburying' with his new-found brother, Algernon? In spite of his claims of 'exploding' Bunbury, Algy has sworn never to give up 'Bunburying'. Jack also has come to terms with being a 'Bunburyist'—he realises 'the vital importance of being Earnest'. In other words, he has discovered his true (homosexual) self. Being two of a kind unites Algy and Jack—both have capitulated to marital compromises which will gain them money and a title. However Wilde's cynical view of marriage as a mask for the profligate husband extends beyond the cover of a happy ending. As Wilde knew from his own experience, the marriages of Jack and Algy are likely to be accompanied by hypocrisy, deception and the fear of scandal.

The Importance of Being Earnest demonstrates that in his society plays Wilde went as far as he could in formulating a Uranian language for the stage—a subtext of codes and inferences recognisable to a coterie of queer disciples. In his plays, they saw a reflection of themselves and their attitudes. As *Theatre* remarked in its review of *The Importance of Being Earnest*: 'The new comedy ... will not fail to attract votaries of a society which enjoys nothing more keenly than an exhibition on the stage of its own weakness.'[210] With his dandified characters, Wilde deliberately subverts late-nineteenth-century codes of manliness. His dandies display a feminine concern with themselves and the image they present to the world. They proclaim a doctrine that espouses hedonism and opposes the sobriety advocated for masculine respectability. The subjects for their hedonistic doctrine are usually physically attractive younger men whom they can mould into images of themselves. Wilde's dandies (with the possible exception of Lord Illingworth) appear to have won in the end. For the sake of propriety, they also appear to conform to heterosexual orthodoxy by marrying or placing themselves under the protection of dominant women.

Despite an ultimate appearance of compliance, dandies tend to ignore, or disobey, the strictures of the older generation. As with Lord Goring and the Earl of Caversham in *An Ideal Husband* there is a continual battle against parental authority, particularly when it comes to doing one's duty by getting married. Lord Caversham claims that 'Bachelors are not fashionable any more. They are a damaged lot. Too much is known about them.'[211] Gossip and speculation surround the lives of unmarried young men with fringes, wearing green carnations in their button-holes. But dandies want to escape from a restraining, puritanical environment. They want to challenge society. This challenge is evident in their self-proclamation and highly visible presence.

Another vital part of the challenge is the embracing of an alternative sexuality—an escape into the Uranian ideals of same-sex love. Wilde dared to present this dandiacal anarchy in his plays. He challenged society by mocking and subverting its attitudes. At the same time, his plays are possibly the most autobiographical of the nineteenth century. In writing them, Wilde revealed aspects of his life while performing a deception on his audiences. Under a mask of melodramatic convention, he conveyed the concerns faced by himself and other Uranians surrounded by a hostile *fin-de-siècle* society.

The changing reflections of masculinity

Oscar Wilde's transgressive dandies form part of the reaction of the New Drama against the masculine ideal. Middle-class values are challenged by the Wildean hedonistic philosophy and the depiction of male protagonists with questionable morality. Behind this lies criticism of an indolent, non-productive upper-class world: Wilde feminises upper-class men by turning them into vain, self-centred, indolent dandies. Pinero, meanwhile, is critical of upper-class corruption and condemns the immorality of gentlemen in 'a man's world'.

At the same time, the middle-class ideal of masculinity is still upheld in popular melodrama. Naval and military dramas at the Adelphi and elsewhere promote values of patriotism, loyalty, moral purity and steadfastness. This is indicative of the strong class bias in the representation of masculinity on the nineteenth-century stage. It also reflects the changes in class and hierarchical structures occurring in the world outside the theatre.

Early melodrama features radical working class heroes. With the rise of the middle class and the gradual gentrification of theatres comes an increasing emphasis on a middle-class environment. Masculine ideals are promoted through the example of an upper-middle-class hero. The class structure also affects those who transgress against masculine ideology—the villains. In early nineteenth-century melodrama villains tend to be the men in charge: the squire, the factory owner, the greedy landlord or the stern captain at sea. Even these categories are divided by class structure. Wicked squires and landowners come from a dissipated and corrupt upper class: aristocratic men are the main seducers of lower-class female innocence and are capable of destroying the domestic harmony of the humble man. Self-made men who have risen from the lower ranks to positions of power—factory-owners and landlords—are viewed as destructive and villainous. Villainy points to flaws in the masculine psyche such as dominance and aggression. Soldier and sailor heroes are often capable of brutality—particularly in defence of those in distress. The middle class may associate the aristocracy with dissipation, but also sees the working man as a potential criminal. Factory lads in their struggle against unemployment and starvation turn into outlaws and commit criminal acts. The gang leaders and criminals of the mid nineteenth century are usually of working-class origin.

By the middle of the century, the gentrification of the theatres is accompanied by a greater concentration on the middle- to upper-class male protagonist. Lower-class men tend to be relegated to the position of servants or secondary comic characters. The rise in the social status of the central male character also coincides with a deepening interest in psychology, and a fascination with the secret lives of men. In farce and comedy the revelation of a guilty secret makes the man of high position a subject for ridicule.

Meanwhile, serious drama shows the confrontation with a hidden past as resulting in remorse, near-suicide or even death. Those who have transgressed against the masculine ideal are made a moral example for the audience.

The disintegration, remorse and guilt of transgressors also provide a moral example for those involved with a 'man's world' of philandering and dissipation. Salvation is offered through religion or through the intervention and support of female purity. The true nature of the transgression brings male sexuality into question. Close bonds of friendship between men can seem to border on same-sex love. Sympathy is created for the dissipated profligate who seeks moral purity, but often the true nature of his transgressions cannot be revealed. Censorial restraints mean that in drama the problems created by male sexuality are surrounded by codes and hints. This weakens the position of male supremacy in drama. In a number of plays, emphasis tends to be on the fallen woman, rather than the fallen man.

By the end of the Victorian era, serious drama questions the masculine ideal. Men are shown as flawed, and their dominant position in society is undermined. Middle-class ideals of masculinity survive, however, as a fantasy in the super-human exploits of naval and military heroes in popular melodrama.

Conclusion: Changing power structures in the Victorian theatre

MASCULINE INVOLVEMENT with the Victorian theatre concerns questions of power, subjugation and deviation. Yet within the theatrical sphere we find that the prevailing masculine ideology becomes complicated by the unique conditions relating to stage life. Within its artificiality, the theatre encourages alternatives to the accepted norms of masculinity. It allows men to play roles—both on and off the stage. It places them on public display, enhancing the innate theatricality of masculine self-exhibition. Male performers dress up in costume, they put on make-up, and they take on the personae of other men. In drama, the idealisation and subversion of masculinity is shown through the struggle between good and evil, exemplified by the contest between hero and villain, or even by divisions within an individual psyche.

The unique conditions of the theatre promulgate a masculine-driven hierarchy, dominated by the power of the actor-manager. Yet this dominance is less stable than would first appear. It can easily be undermined by the insecurities of the theatrical profession. There is the fear of unemployment, of rivals, of loss of reputation. Social stigma attached to theatrical performers causes unease over involvement with the stage, and the desire to conform as much as possible to bourgeois respectability.

But the privilege of higher status is only granted to those who have reached the top of the scale. The majority of Victorian actors remain at a subservient level. For some, the vices they portrayed on the stage have become an unfortunate reality. Drink, immorality and debt can easily ruin a career. Yet for those who maintain the leadership of their profession, power may encourage egoism, but paradoxically it can also be beneficial. It gives a position to a man of talent which otherwise may be denied to him. It allows leading men of the theatre to be extremely innovative. It can also generate benevolence toward other theatrical employees in a less fortunate position.

Actor-managers therefore preside over a hierarchy of dominance and subjugation, with nearly every section of the theatre workforce controlled by a male figure of authority. Theatres function through a virtual army of labouring men, working under arduous and hazardous conditions. The necessity for squads of labourers gives the backstage world an industrialised aspect. But, as in outside industry, this backstage army is gradually displaced by contracting out and the replacement of manual labour by machinery. Lack of employment undermines the lower-class masculine need to work and support a family. The lower ranks in the theatrical hierarchy struggle, while those above them enjoy wealth, success and public adulation. Dramatists call for greater control of their output and an equivalent position to that of the actor-manager. Subordinate players who bring attention to appalling backstage conditions are rendered powerless by a managerial lack of concern. Progressives who campaign to abolish censorship are defeated by the stubborn upholding of bourgeois moral values and support for the Lord Chamberlain.

Masculine predominance also places limitations on women in the theatre. Male dramatists are considered superior to female. There are fewer roles and opportunities for actresses. Women are subservient to men in the management of theatres. Even the most successful women managers cannot fully participate in business matters where men hold sway. Yet despite the limitations placed upon them, women may be perceived as a driving force behind the power of men. They come to the fore as partners in management or as co-performers on the stage.

Men are also subservient to women in the demand for physical appeal. Theatre managers usually choose women for their looks, while men are chosen for their ability and supposed intellect. Only with greater female emancipation later in the century does a male actor's erotic appeal rival that of the actress. By the end of the century, an increasing emphasis on the 'manliness' of actors helps to shed their feminised image. By promoting 'manly' interests such as sport and adventure, actors determinedly confirm their heterosexuality. Publicity depicts their private lives as mirroring middle-class domesticity, with careful emphasis on their adherence to bourgeois codes of morality.

It is paradoxical that, while belonging to a world which in many ways is the antithesis of bourgeois conformity, men in the theatre should seek to achieve gentlemanly status. Questions and speculation may arise over masculine moral conduct, particularly in matters such as the exploitation of female performers by male entrepreneurs. However, so far as celebrities of the theatre are concerned, a discreet veil is drawn over any deviation from a carefully promoted image of affluent respectability. Even so, this does not prevent public speculation over issues such as keeping mistresses or homosexual behaviour.

For men in the audience, attending the theatre can give an opportunity for self-display. The auditorium admits those who cast aside the strictures placed upon masculinity by society. Throughout the century, an array of swells, bohemians, cross-dressers, aesthetes and young men wearing green carnations become a highly visible presence. They create disturbances, indulge in immature behaviour or disconcertingly display alternative sexualities.

The escapism of the theatre also allows it to become an outlet for sexual activity. Here, men can meet with prostitutes, both male and female, or indulge in the voyeuristic admiration of actresses and ballet-girls. Meanwhile for the working man, theatre allows the release of aggression. From his space in the gallery he can exert as much power as the swell in the dress circle. All this masculine delinquency is encouraged by the alternatives to reality contained within the theatrical sphere. The Victorian theatre could therefore be viewed as a space for the release of pent-up masculine feelings. It is an alternative world that can either promote make-believe or reflect reality.

The theatre also reflects changes in social attitudes. In the early years of the century the working man sees himself elevated to heroic status in nautical and factory melodramas. With the rise of middle-class values he becomes a more subservient presence on the stage, usually a comic rather than a heroic character. The middle-class man, whose values give credence to the moral outcome of the 'New Drama', gradually usurps his position. This bourgeois predomination gradually drives many lower-class spectators (male and female) from the theatre to the music hall.

The nineteenth-century British theatre thus promulgates many different aspects of masculine behaviour within a class and social framework. It allows men to exhibit egoism, aggression, vanity, self-interest and the need for power. For the actor, it can undermine male authority with questions of deviancy and issues such as unemployment or fall from grace.

At the same time it promotes aspects of a perceived ideal of masculine character. Men of the theatre exhibit loyalty; they are benevolent toward their less fortunate colleagues. They attain positions of authority through struggle and self-promotion. Many, despite the pressures of a theatrical career, appear to have stable family lives. Above all, they make every effort to achieve respectability and the status of a gentleman. This is particularly relevant to the so-called gentrification of the theatre starting from around the middle of the century. Through a masculine-driven quest to accord with middle-class values, the earlier vigour of the nineteenth-century theatre is replaced by a bourgeois dominance and the demand for its reflection on the stage. This engenders contradictions in theatrical masculine behaviour—a veneer of respectability co-exists with elements of bohemianism as well as a transgressive defiance of the ideological restrictions placed by society upon men.

Appendix:
The hard life of the Victorian actor

CONSIDERING ITS DISCOMFORTS AND DIFFICULTIES, why were so many young men in the nineteenth century drawn to the stage? Some possessed genuine talent and had a 'calling'. Many were willing to put up with the difficulties in order to act. Like a life at sea, the stage offered freedom. It appeared to be an adventurous, glamorous alternative to the drudgery of the industrial or commercial work-place. The theatre seemed to offer the opportunity to rise above arduous conditions, to achieve celebrity status and to win the adulation of an adoring public while acquiring a great deal of money. However, to get work in the theatre could prove hazardous. There was a rigidly hierarchical system to be encountered.

Getting on the stage

To get on the stage it helped to be a member of a theatrical family, or have the right connections. While a number of actors had theatrical parentage, quite a few came from non-theatrical backgrounds and had started in jobs far removed from acting. Henry Irving, for instance, was the son of a tailor's salesman and started work as a lawyer's clerk. Others had to fight family prejudice before embarking on a stage career. In 1867, *Chambers's Journal* noted that despite the strenuous opposition of parents and guardians to 'the inclinations of their children and wards towards the theatrical profession, its ranks are constantly recruited from the youth of both sexes in the middle and lower classes of society'.[1] However, talent did not necessarily depend on class or educational background. The achievement of positions of power by actors from humble backgrounds is parallel to the rise to power of the working class factory owner and industrialist.

Evidently, the upper classes 'gave vent to their histrionic ardour by appearing in amateur performances'.[2] This situation altered by the end of the century, when a number of young men and women from upper-class backgrounds began to appear professionally on the stage. The rise in upper-class actors was offset by a decline in the numbers of actors from established theatrical families.[3]

From around the 1870s the majority of actors entering the theatre were better educated than most of their predecessors. Early to mid-nineteenth-century actors were often criticised for their lack of education, even if they had received some kind of rudimentary schooling.[4] Before 1860, it was rare for an actor to have attended public school. Exceptions included Charles Kean, who was sent to Eton, and William Macready, who was educated at Rugby. Henry Irving, born into a lower middle class background, attended the City of London Commercial School, which he left at the age of thirteen to become a clerk.[5] By the 1890s nearly 17 per cent of actors had been educated at public schools, and an increasing number had attended universities.[6] The late nineteenth century also saw a predominance of actor-managers from middle-class backgrounds—notably George Alexander and Charles Wyndham.

Having the necessary connections to embark on a theatrical career could pose a problem for the aspiring actor. How to begin learning his craft was another problem. While there were academies for artists and musicians, there was no specialised Government-funded school for training actors. This meant the actor could not fall back on an accepted body of theory to improve his practice.[7] It was considered difficult to set up training centres for actors because of their unsettled life.[8] Instead, an actor learned on stage, by imitating fellow members of the company. There was a danger in this method—old faults could be perpetuated, and the public often saw barely trained, inexperienced performers trying to imitate star actors. An aspiring actor could also learn through being an understudy, or for a 'small premium and salary' he could tour as a support to a star player. Nor was it unusual for actors to take dramatic pupils.[9]

From the mid to the late nineteenth century various attempts had been made to set up facilities for academic training, but the high fees tended to encourage pupils from affluent backgrounds. The highly regarded school instigated in 1885 by Sarah Thorne at the Theatre Royal, Margate, was partly responsible for an influx of well-to-do young actors onto the West

End stage. According to the actor George Arliss, who trained at the school, his fellow students included 'the sons of prosperous businessmen, of well-to-do actors, of lawyers, authors and clergymen'.[10] Tuition fees were fairly high—£20 for three months or £30 for six months. This meant that the school only admitted pupils from well-to-do backgrounds. By charging high fees, Sarah Thorne kept her school exclusive, excluding student actors from poorer families from receiving a first-class training.

Managers and agents

Whether or not a young actor had been trained, getting on the stage could prove to be time-consuming, difficult and hazardous. His desire to find work placed him in an extremely vulnerable position where he was at the mercy of those who could help or hinder him. He could easily be a victim of other unscrupulous men. While there were many highly respected and respectable teachers, managers and agents, young actors had also to beware of those who were corrupt or fraudulent. A 'guileless aspirant' could easily be defrauded by a 'bogus' professor who took his money with the promise of an engagement after a few lessons.[11]

Aspirants had to be particularly wary of bogus managers who collected fees, assembled a company, and did not show up when rehearsals were supposed to begin.[12] These men were extremely plausible and were 'usually able to impart a feeling of confidence under the most unpromising auspices'.[13] Pretending to have a theatrical company about to go on tour, the bogus manager would 'engage' people willing to pay him a premium for a first appearance. 'If they are foolish enough to part with their money, they find, when too late, that the projected tour is a myth and the "manager" suddenly has changed his address.'[14]

A typical case of the duping of a stage-struck young man was reported in *The Era* on 24 November 1888. William Henry O'Reilly, a former indigo planter returning to England, saw an advertisement for an amateur actor to join a 'first-class touring company at a good salary'. Calling at the address given he met the 'manager', Thomas Everson (or Edward) Terry, who said he would be pleased to engage O'Reilly if he paid a premium of £15 for 'tuition' by Terry's partner, Charles Henry Ward. O'Reilly, led to believe that a tour would start in November at Cardiff, 'shelled-out' a further £10 to study roles as well as to purchase tights and a theatrical wardrobe. When O'Reilly 'suddenly remembered' hearing about a Mr Ward who had been prosecuted for fraud, he was reassured by Terry that this was not 'his Mr Ward'. O'Reilly was met with all sorts of excuses when he asked to meet other members of the tour—although he was allowed a glimpse of a photograph of a Miss Seymour, who Terry claimed had sung before the Prince of Wales. The tour, of course, never started. The extent of Terry and Ward's activities was revealed by the discovery by the police of 'no less than 200 letters and telegrams from people desirous of getting on the stage'. A number of these contained references to premiums that had been demanded preliminary to engagements.[15] Ward and Terry were found guilty in January 1889 and were sentenced to twelve months' imprisonment each.[16]

Evidently, the O'Reilly case was 'only one of hundreds'. O'Reilly was typical of a number of middle-class young men who saw in the theatre an opportunity to continue an adventurous, easy-going life. The ignorance of stage-struck 'simpletons' (usually from the middle to upper classes) was an increasing problem. Vanity, combined with the publicity surrounding wealthy and successful star actors, led some aspirants to believe that entry to a stage career was easy and that large salaries could be earned with the minimum of training or practice.[17] That so many would-be actors were easily duped by unscrupulous men shows just how vulnerable they were. They were victims of their own ambition, desperation, egoism, or sheer ignorance of the workings of the theatre.

Some would-be actors and actresses paid a premium to managers to gain experience by appearing unpaid for several months, with a modest wage guaranteed at the end of the period. While the system of premium apprenticeship was common to other trades and crafts, in the theatre it became the subject of abuse on both sides. There were a number of court cases in the 1890s in which bogus managers had decamped with the premium money paid by stage-struck applicants expecting to be put into a show.[18] Experienced actors and actresses knew the 'chief exponents' of fraudulent management. If they happened to accept engagements with them it was 'in most cases, with open eyes'.[19] However, with so many actors and actresses desperately seeking work it was very easy to fall prey to dishonest men. Anybody with the necessary capital could set up a theatre company and hire a troupe of players. If the venture failed it was invariably the performer who paid for the losses; if it succeeded, a corrupt manager was capable of pocketing the profits. The cost of bringing a suit against an employer would have been prohibitive for the average actor, and managers could easily blacklist anyone trying to do so.[20] In an overcrowded profession, actors were in no position to bargain with employers; exploitation was accepted as a fact of theatrical life. Bogus managers and agents were plausible and cunning men. They mercilessly exploited the situation of the growing number of hopeful young men and women—all anxious to find work and success on the stage.

Even using the services of a *bona fide* agent, the aspiring actor was vulnerable. The theatrical agent was just as able to exploit those constantly hoping for employment as was his bogus counterpart. Theatrical agencies started from around the 1820s and by the late nineteenth century there were scores of them around the West End and as far afield as Lambeth. Some West End agencies had elegantly-fitted offices, luxuriously-appointed waiting rooms, the walls of which were hung with portraits of actors and actresses and files of playbills.[21] But not all agents were so well appointed, and time spent waiting in their offices was not always a pleasant experience. An aspirant also had to be careful, as many agents were unreliable, taking fees but not finding engagements.

The largest and best-known London theatrical agent was Blackmore's, established in 1869 and situated at 11 Garrick Street. According to the actor A. E. Matthews this agency was remembered with 'uniform loathing'. Power was exerted by the unseen and unheard presence of the agent. He summoned the applicants by means of a speaking tube directed at a 'spotty-faced youth sitting at a high desk'. Anxious actors and actresses were forced to wait 'packed together like sheep in a shearing pen'. They might sit and wait from early morning and possibly most of the afternoon, with only a bun and a cup of tea for lunch.[22] Waiting for the summons by speaking tube was a humiliating experience which had to be endured in the hope of obtaining an engagement. Blackmore's agent had crowds of aspiring and unemployed actors at his mercy. He exerted an overriding, unseen power that fuelled tension among the crowd of hopeful aspirants.

Although agencies were not usually pleasant, they did perform a useful service, especially for tours starting from London and for pantomime recruitment. Once a job had been found, a good agent would draw up a standard contract, bearing a letterhead. In return for his services he would take 10 per cent from a client's earnings.[23] The fee paid to the agencies was variable. Sometimes it was a matter of special arrangement between the agent and his client; otherwise it was usual for a sum of '5s. to a guinea' to be paid down, and a commission of 5 per cent on the first fortnight's salaries. The payment of the commission was conditional on the client receiving employment.[24] In 1893 the Actors' Association tried to break the monopoly of privately run, dubious agencies. They resolved to set up a theatrical agency of their own which 'instead of resolving itself a lounge or a school for scandal like some in London' would be a thoroughly business-like institution. They hoped that managers would benefit more from its services than from privately-run agencies.[25]

Another way for an actor to obtain work was through contacts. A head start could be gained from having a member of the family in the theatre, or through being related to an actor or actress. The actor had to keep himself constantly on display for the attention of lessees and managers. He placed advertisements in the theatrical newspapers, *The Stage* and *The Era*, letting his name be known and the address where he could be found. These were an important means of communication between the employer and the employee.

Actors on tour in the provinces took the precaution of advertising their successive addresses and the dates when they were available for fresh engagements. They also sometimes included reviews praising their performances. Actors also had multiple copies of photographs of themselves to be sent to managements and agents. These portraits gave a deliberately respectable appearance, often making the aspiring actor look more like a bank clerk than a bohemian player. Self-advertising was a means by which an actor could keep control of his own career. It allowed him to exert a certain amount of persuasion over managers and agents. However, for most actors this did not alleviate the ever-present anxiety of obtaining employment.

The harshness of conditions for actors

For the majority of actors, a theatrical career was far from being the easy-going life of popular imagination. A novice actor could find work in the theatre as long and arduous as that on the factory floor. It was a paradox of nineteenth-century theatre that the actor, essential to the production, should be among the worst treated of all theatrical staff. Managers had highly arbitrary powers over those performing for their companies. A young man could be given an engagement because he knew, or was related to, the manager; or because he was handsome and had good bearing. Often he was hired simply because he was the cheapest labour available. By providing his basic necessities himself, the actor helped to subsidise financially insecure managements. Most actors had to make do with a basic minimum of items for wardrobe, 'props' and make-up. To own a decent set of 'props' was half-way to securing an engagement.

An actor also had to provide his own make-up. The act of applying, re-touching and taking off make-up had female connotations. It also had associations with degeneracy—with men who passed as women, or dandified young men fond of painting and powdering their faces.[26] Applying make-up to create a different type or character was a transformational art, with the removal of greasepaint after the performance revealing the 'real man' underneath. The nineteenth-century actor had at his disposal specific make-up recipes for creating masculine physiognomies—crepe hair for beards and moustaches, grease paints and powders to create physical effects. In 1899, Leopold Wagner advised on make-up for certain male character types: 'cotton wool roughed over for pimples, Bardolph noses or bloated cheeks'; 'powdered blue' to give an 'unshaven appearance'; nose paste for character roles or to create 'the protuberant cheeks of the stage yokel or genial squire'.[27]

An elaborate character make-up could transform a star role into a mesmeric creation. For instance, Beerbohm Tree as Svengali in *Trilby* (Theatre Royal, Haymarket, 1895) captured the imagination partly because of the elaborate 'Jewish' make-up that he applied to create the character. With 'a few deft touches of grease-paint' Tree was able to change his whole appearance 'and it seemed his whole character'.[28] Make-up was another means by which a star actor could divert attention to himself on the stage.

However effective an actor's performance, backstage conditions were usually far from ideal. Insanitary theatres affected all performers from the star actor-manager down to the 'supers'. Actors needed devotion and stamina to forsake the comfort of a home to perform night after night in conditions that were comparable to those in unhealthy factories or in the slum areas of the major cities. Even the first grade theatres had inefficient backstage facilities. 'Corin' did not exaggerate when he wrote that 'the dressing rooms in many theatres are seldom fit for the reception of any higher animal than a pig'.[29]

Catching a disease that could end a career or prove fatal was a very real fear among performers. Many died comparatively young from consumption and other pulmonary diseases brought on by unhealthy backstage conditions, not the least of which was bad ventilation on stage. As soon as a performer made his appearance on the stage, he was 'enveloped in various odours of oil, turpentine and other delights of stage preparation'. When the curtain rose, players were greeted with 'the whole air of the auditorium and its "orange-peppermint" accompaniments'. This was due to draughts 'created by the intense heat of the footlights and masses of light burning at the wings and borders'.[30]

Gas footlights were also 'a terrible ordeal'. Eyes could be worried by the flickering glare; throats often 'parched up' through the oppressive heat and combustion products. Rising vapours made it necessary for voices to be raised and gas footlights were said to interfere with the proper transmission of sound.[31]

What power did a subordinate actor have when forced to work amid such squalor? He could draw attention to his plight by writing letters to journals such as *The Era* or he could join organisations concerned for his welfare.

In 1885, Edward Rochelle, an actor with the *Silver King* touring company, wrote to *The Era* regarding backstage facilities in a provincial 'Theatre Royal'. Thirteen male actors 'were thrust like rats into a room at the top of a sort of loft ladder leading from the stage'. Crammed in with the baskets 'required for clothes' they were 'without a square foot for each man'. Noxious gases escaping from the stage together with 'combustion and other miasma with which the building reeks' ascended to their dressing room. There was no way foul air could escape or fresh air could be let in. 'We are not only shut in to inhale the exhalations from our own bodies, but those from the mass of spectators in the auditorium, which all ascend to our portion of the stage, over which are the dressing rooms.'

There was also a problem with rats and the lack of fresh water to wash in. According to Rochelle, 'not one of the company' escaped from illness—they all exhibited symptoms of septicaemia and 'well-marked catarrhal and pulmonary attacks'. Others suffered from bad throats or were scarcely able to speak for acute laryngitis. Understudies had to be called in, but even they were affected. It was not necessary, wrote the indignant actor, 'that from six to eleven p.m. we should be stuffed in a fever-den and rat-trap to perspire and be half stifled by foul gas, sewage and other noxious evaporations'. It was in the interests of managements that actors and actresses should remain healthy. They could not display their 'natural abilities' while suffering from headaches 'and the thousand and one ailments produced by sewage contamination'.[32] This letter sparked off an influential debate on dressing-room conditions.

Managers were usually unconcerned about the plight of actors, so long as they made money for their theatres. An actor on the Isle of Man complained that 'The dressing room may generally be a disgrace, but the manager's office is 'always comfortable'; there is warmth, light and … a strip of carpet on the floor.'[33] *The Era* recommended that managers renovating and altering provincial theatres should attend to dressing rooms. It gave the example of the Princess's Theatre, Bristol as having dressing rooms which were 'more than satisfactory'. But this was a building designed under the direction of a lessee who was a former actor.[34] Managements were not always to blame for the low standards of backstage conditions. Progressive or conscientious lessees were often hampered by the reluctance of theatre owners to spend money on improvements. They were more concerned with profit than with high standards and were not prepared to invest in areas where there was no incentive to do so.[35]

As well as having to put up with insanitary conditions, an aspiring actor found he had an extremely heavy workload. The so-called 'bohemian' life of the actor was subject to discipline, hard work and restrictions. There were many rules and regulations for the performer, including fines for bad language, 'violent conduct' and intoxication.[36]

An actor was expected to come to the first rehearsal knowing most of his lines. If ambitious, he would have already learned the roles he hoped to play. If the play was new, 'Each member of the company had to copy out his or her lines, passing the manuscript along until all had been written out. ... To be one of the last to receive the manuscript meant sitting up all night to copy out and study.' This might seem to be an incursion on the actor's precious time, but continual practice in copying out 'made memorizing so easy that writing out a part was almost equivalent to studying it'.[37]

The actor copied out only his own lines and 'business' with the preceding cue line from the prompter's script. Until the rehearsal he would have little idea of the plot or how his character related to others in the play. Even when, later in the century, companies provided type-written parts, they still only gave the character's lines with the cues, so there was still little understanding of the play as a whole.[38] Jerome K. Jerome gives a humorous* example of his part '*in extenso*' as he received it from the management: [39]

Joe Junks
Act I., Scene 1.

——————— comes home.

It's a rough night.

——————— if he does.

Ay. Ay.

——————— stand back.

(*Together*) 'Tis he !

Fall down as scene closes in.

Act IV., Scene 2.

On with rioters.

Rehearsals were mainly for running through lines and arranging exits, entrances and stage business. There was no time for, or notion of, textual interpretation or psychological characterisation. Directing a play was known as 'stage management'. In the early- to mid-nineteenth century stock company the actor was totally controlled and constrained by this system. Any departure from the norm was suppressed by an inflexible

---

* And no doubt fictionalised. —*Ed.*

dependence upon traditional stage business. R. K. Hervey, observing a rehearsal in 1887, noted that the stage manager was 'ready to teach his or her business to every member of the company', supplying the 'brain and thought' which the actors should have brought to the study of their parts. They played 'another man's conception instead of their own'. If it was a play from the repertoire, the manager imparted to them the moves and even speech patterns of their predecessors in the roles.

Hervey noted that there was 'in the rendering of each a certain amount of sameness which would not have been there had the actors thought the parts out for themselves'. However, it would take 'far too much time to rehearse a piece if actors, particularly young actors, were left alone to discover what is right to say and to do'.[40] An actor was admired if he conformed to tradition. The notion of ensemble playing was inhibited by the star system and casts received little or no direction beyond what was necessary to heighten the impact of leading players.[41] A star actor was free to develop his own part in his own way because there was no person in over-all control of the production.

The novice actor was expected to take on a bewildering variety of parts. Because of the frequent changes of the bill, in which there might be two, three or even four pieces, he had to have several roles in readiness. There would often be doubling and trebling of roles in one play. This meant that an actor with a stock company could play an enormous number of roles (Henry Irving at the outset of his career played 451 different roles over three years). If a star player visited a stock company he brought his repertory with him, which could consist of eight 'legitimate', five dramas, four comedies and a farce, to be played over a week. This would create extra roles for the novice actor. Familiarity with an enormous number of roles meant that an actor could gradually reduce the effort of learning and draw on the store of memory. As he climbed higher in the hierarchy, he would play fewer roles and have less to remember.[42]

The system operating in nineteenth-century British theatre tended to 'fragment' the actor. Unless he was favoured by circumstance, he spent his career within a specific income bracket. He was usually confined to a particular type of role with its specific articulation, gestures, make-up and costume. Rehearsals were usually divided so that various sections of the work were practiced simultaneously. Each actor wore his own individual costume usually without any notion of a harmonious stage picture. On the stage he was placed in a designated area according to whether he was playing a leading, supporting, 'utility' or supernumerary role. In a system lacking any conception of an ensemble, each actor was inclined to give an individualised performance—usually with little regard for integration with his fellow performers. The actor had the added strains of battling against noisy audiences, as well as performing in draughty, unhygienic theatres. A theatrical career needed an enormous resilience, which was easier for a man to acquire than for a woman.

The actor on tour

Strength and resilience were needed for a peripatetic life of touring. In the early part of the century leading actors toured by coach, while subordinates travelled by cart, or even walked from town to town. The gradual increase in the efficiency of rail travel not only meant a faster, more efficient means of travel. It gave the actor-manager an opportunity to extend his power and personality through touring with his company. Actor-managers headed their companies like royalty. Beerbohm Tree had a private train including a 'royal coach'. George Alexander had not only his name, but also the names of the occupants of each carriage, printed in large type and pasted on the windows. Improvements in travel meant an increase of profits. Prominent actor-managers were also able to lead their companies by ship to America and the colonies—India, South Africa, Canada, Australia and New Zealand.

In the late nineteenth century, tours usually departed from London on Sunday mornings. There was always a large crowd of admirers at the station to see the company off. Actor-managers were insistent that their actors presented as respectable and smart an appearance as possible when leaving for a tour.[43] A smartly dressed company would reflect on the status of the actor-manager, as well as giving a respectable appearance for provincial towns, where prejudice persisted.

However, on arrival at their destination the social divisions within the company were soon apparent. Stars and wealthy players went to top-grade hotels that could provide room service and cater for the irregular meal times demanded by the theatre.[44] For subordinate actors and actresses, the agent arranged lodgings week by week. If the organiser of the tour did not book accommodation, the actors on arrival had to find digs. So-called 'professional lodgings' were regularly advertised in theatrical journals and notices were also posted at stage-door entrances. Some actors wrote ahead to their favourite digs.[45] However, away from 'the beaten track of the touring companies', there were religious and moral prejudices against actors and actresses. Lodgings could be hard to find. Doors could be slammed in faces and, in some provincial towns, landladies did not take theatricals.[46]

In most towns, however, landladies found that touring actors provided a lucrative market. Theatrical landladies were often recalled with affection. For the actors touring around provincial England, away from home, a landlady could even become a surrogate mother. She cooked for him, washed for him and generally looked after his needs. Motherliness was one of the attributes applied to the best, remembered as warm, hardworking, honest and kind women. They usually charged reasonable rates. Typical prices in the 1890s were 25 shillings for a small room and two guineas for a large one including meals.[47] Landladies and supporting actors were both groups without a high social position. They were mutually dependent on each other—the actor wanted cheap lodgings and the landlady needed money.[48] But however kind the landlady, her regulations—relating to late hours, noise, visitors, meal-times—exerted a matriarchal control over the life of the actor. On tour, he was in a position similar to that of a child in a large family. The manager exhibited a patriarchal interest in his moral welfare, while the landlady showed a motherly concern for his everyday needs.

The economics of acting

Whether he was on tour or doing a season at a particular theatre, life for the average actor could be a long grind on low wages. He had to find the money to pay for his digs, his cleaning, his costumes, props and make-up. While the star performer could earn a great deal, the subordinate actor often had to struggle. The theatre was as much an area of 'sweated labour' as the factory, but it attracted none of the concern felt for miners or mill workers.[49] The stock actor worked an average fifteen- to sixteen-hour day that included study, rehearsal and performance. Sometimes he rehearsed until the small hours of the morning. With his extremely tight schedule—rehearsing, performing and learning lines—he did not even have as much time for rest as the labourer returning home from a sixteen- to eighteen-hour day. As well as working long hours with very little leisure time, the majority of actors were forced to struggle on totally inadequate wages.

Salaries varied considerably between London and the provinces and were subject to the economic and financial fluctuations besetting nineteenth-century Britain. In 1836, Leman Rede noted that wages paid in provincial theatres varied between £7 (presumably for a leading actor) to 15 shillings (for a supernumerary).[50] By the end of the century touring actors were paid even less. Leopold Wagner, in 1899, stated that in small stock companies, 'such as still exist in out-of-the-way places', 30 shillings per week was adequate for a leading man or lady, a guinea for 'other lines of business' and fifteen shillings for a 'small utility actor'. In all touring companies salaries were 'cut down to the lowest possible limit'. They tended to be regulated by the status of the company. The average was 25 to 30 shillings for a small part, £2 to £3 for a 'line of business', with a maximum of £5 for a 'heavy juvenile lead'. Many 'smaller members' of a touring company shared the cost of 'board and bed'.[51]

An actor may have had a lengthy career but it was often beset with financial difficulties. The pay of the average actor varied, not only according to his capabilities, but according to 'the character he assumes' and the theatres or company with which he appeared.[52] Even in West End theatres with their higher salaries, the actor still had the cost of acquiring 'modern costumes and wigs' as well as paying for their cleaning. There was always the danger of a play failing and the manager being unable to pay the wages—after the actor had paid out for his wardrobe. In the late nineteenth and early twentieth centuries, when the theatre strove for respectability, an actor was a 'collar man' and had to appear well dressed when not on stage. Maintaining a smart appearance was another expense—'a serious responsibility on less than £2 per week'.[53]

Income for actors only improved for the middle to upper strata of West End actors. For those lower down the scale, life remained difficult. Money had to be paid out for basic costumes, shoes, make-up and wigs. There were also fines for the infringement of backstage regulations, and amounts had to be found to pay for travel and lodgings. Most performers were not paid for rehearsals. On the other hand, star actors were able to negotiate rehearsal terms. Towards the end of the century, half pay was given for matinée performances and sometimes it was the same rate as for evening performances. But often no extra pay was given.[54] Nor was an actor paid when he was sick or otherwise unable to perform. There was no assistance or compensation for being left stranded by an absconding manager.[55]

A national old age pension did not appear in England until 1908. Sickness benefits and unemployment insurance were not introduced until 1911.[56] Without organised Government assistance, the situation for sick, elderly or failed actors was particularly difficult throughout the nineteenth century. Ending his days in the workhouse was as great a threat for the needy actor as it was for the poverty-stricken factory worker. In 1838, James Grant described the sad sight of the elderly actor rejected partly from the infirmities of his advanced years, and partly from 'the fickleness of public taste' forced to appear in cheap penny theatres (or 'gaffs') as a last resource against the workhouse.[57] Late in the century, the actor-manager Robert Courtneidge encountered—one bitterly cold night in Stockport—an 80 year old ex-actor who had become a night-watchman in order to avoid being sent to the workhouse: 'There was no Benevolent Fund in those days to which he might turn for help.'[58]

Not only supporting players, but those who had been very well known, could be found in a distressed condition. George R. Sims was surprised to discover former star actors and actor-managers among Augustus Harris's 'small-part people' at Drury Lane.[59] Sometimes elderly unemployed actors presented begging letters at stage-doors. Sums were collected for them backstage. Dutton Cook's 'Corin' recalled seeing 'as many as three white-haired decrepit old actors waiting at the stage-door of a theatre at one time. It was pitiful to watch their anxious faces as the stage-manager or prompter returned with their begging letters and sums collected. These were men who never possessed any real talent and their average earnings all their lives had not exceeded 30 shillings a week.'[60]

Robert Courtneidge thought the salaries of actors were 'woefully inadequate' considering the time spent in waiting for engagements and the uncertainties of the profession; long years of service did not qualify 'for pension or reward'. He also noticed how many of the older male actors turning up at auditions showed plainly 'the struggle they have had to live and keep up a decent appearance'.[61] The destitute subordinate actor seemed powerless in his struggle to survive. He was forced to rely on the charity of those who had achieved wealth and status.

Although actor-managers may have been criticised for their egoism and snobbery, nearly all were active in trying to relieve poverty and distress among the less fortunate members of their profession. While this may have been good publicity, there was also genuine concern. Possibly remembering their own early struggles, they did as much as they could to relieve the stress of the subordinate actor: 'A very considerable sum is given away privately, for members of the dramatic profession have the reputation of being very open-handed to professional brethren in distress.'[62]

Henry Irving, John Toole and Squire Bancroft founded the Actors' Benevolent Fund in 1882. The Fund provided a number of services for actors and actresses. It would come to the aid of a company left stranded by a bogus manager. It had its own doctors who would give services free. It would not allow any performer to be buried at the expense of the parish. Grants or loans were made to players down on their luck, sick or temporarily unemployed. Funds were provided for sick actors or actresses to go into hospitals and convalescent homes. Since most of the work was concerned with performers regarding themselves as still in the profession, the Fund increasingly came to serve as a non-contributory pension scheme.[63]

The Actors' Association, founded in 1891, was part of the move toward unionisation. It campaigned against defective sanitation in theatres. It ran arbitration and agency services, and established its own agencies for actors in defiance of exploitative private concerns such as Blackmore's.[64] The Association, like the Benevolent Fund, fought a long campaign against bogus managers, and 153 cases were taken up to extract money from these fraudulent men.*

---

* The campaign against bogus managers continued well into the twentieth century. In 1920, *The Times* reported on the efforts of the Actors' Association to 'successfully eliminate irresponsible and bogus managers'. Even the introduction of a licence

Actors accepted the support of benevolent organisations, but tended to be wary of trade unions with their left-wing connotations. Efforts to organise actors into unions also failed because of the spasmodic, peripatetic nature of theatrical life. A body of workers could not be brought together as could be done in the factory or shop.[65] Also, actors did not join trade unions because of their concerns with the possibility of achieving the status of the actor-manager. In 1908, Daisy Halling and Charles Lister claimed that the 'intimate' relationship between actor and manager was an obstacle to militant unionism for actors—'an artist may be an actor one day and a manager the next'. In trades such as coal mining, there was a social gulf between the boss and the worker; in the theatrical profession this gulf was very often bridged.[66] The actor, according to Halling and Lister, considered himself 'too respectable' to go to pubs for meetings or to buy the sixpenny stamp for the Union contribution.

> His high and mighty views and his abhorrence of anything that savours of the horny-handed make him a very difficult subject for the organiser. Figures fail to raise him from his apathy, and he does not realise that he is being worse paid than the engineer or the cotton operative.[67]

It is ironic that the subordinate actor, who until recently had been a social outcast, should now consider himself to be above an organisation whose object was to champion his rights and agitate for better pay and conditions. Most actors never achieved success and remained fixed in their subordinate position on the hierarchical scale. They survived largely through the munificence of those great and successful men whom they supported as 'juvenile leads', 'comedians', 'utility men' or 'supers' in the lower ranks of the theatre.

---

requiring a name and address failed and attempts to boycott known fraudulent managers could not completely destroy the menace. See *The Times*, 7 August 1920, 8; 8 February 1922: 7.

Notes and references

The notes on the following pages give source information for the numbered references in the body of the text. Notes in the form 'Baker 1978' are further expanded in the 'Books and articles' section of the Select Bibliography; references in the form '*Corsican Brothers* (Boucicault)' are expanded in the 'Plays cited' section.

Notes for Introduction

[1] Adcock 1901: II, 13.
[2] Adcock 1901: II, 9–12.
[3] Baker, M. 1978: 18.
[4] Richards, 1994: 8–9.
[5] Baker, M. 1978: 19.
[6] Woodfield 1984: 1–2.
[7] Palmer 1892: 31.
[8] *Pall Mall Gazette*, 1859, repr. Smiles, 1879: fn. 102–103.
[9] Walkowitz 1992: 44.

Notes for Chapter One

[1] Grant 1836: 83.
[2] *Illustrated London News* 6 November 1858: 429–30, 'New Royal Pavilion Theatre'.
[3] Dickens 1860: 418.
[4] Dickens 1850: 57.
[5] 'S. L. B.' 1896: 376.
[6] Davis and Emeljanow 2001: 48.
[7] Dickens 1860: 418.
[8] Dickens 1877: 277.
[9] Saintsbury and Palmer, 1939: 359.
[10] Roth 1888: 21.
[11] Roth 1888: 25.
[12] Davis and Emeljanow 2001: 50–51.
[13] Davis, J. 1992: 18.
[14] 'S. L. B.' 1896: 376.
[15] Roth 1888: 28.
[16] Booth 1991: 67.
[17] Wright 1867: 162.
[18] Wright 1867: 158–9.
[19] Davis and Emeljanow 2001: 84.
[20] Sanderson 1984: 65–67.
[21] 'Our Local Flaneur' 1870: 3.
[22] Dyer 1833: 138–159.
[23] Dickens 1850: 14.
[24] Morley 1891: 138.
[25] *Here and There* 1 June 1872: 236, 'The Fairy Queen's Rebuke'
[26] *Tower Hamlets Independent*, 16 January 1869: 6, 'Police Intelligence: Worship Street: Disorderly Conduct at the Pavilion Theatre'.
[27] Dickens 1877: 274–5.
[28] Collins 1859: 362.
[29] Wright, 1867: 162.
[30] Bailey 1986: 65–7.
[31] Davis, T. 1991: 83.
[32] 'F. L. G.' 1840.
[33] 'F. L. G.' 1840.
[34] Tristan 1840: 178–179.
[35] Baker, M. 1978: 49.
[36] Acton 1870: 22.
[37] Mander and Mitchenson 1974: 79.
[38] Bristow 1977: 213, 214.
[39] Chant 1894: 27–28.
[40] Bristow 1977: 214.
[41] Anon. 1865: 101.
[42] Grenville-Murray 1881: II, 132.
[43] 'F. L. G.' 1840.
[44] Davis, T. 1991: 92.
[45] Davis, T. 1991: 92.
[46] 'F. L. G.' 1840.
[47] Sala 1859: 238.
[48] Sala 1859: 246–247.
[49] *The Era* 25 January 1852: 12. 'A Word for Ballet Girls'.
[50] Anon. 1888: 210.
[51] Corin 1885: 119.
[52] Corin 1885: 119–120.
[53] Anon. 1888: 208.
[54] Leppington 1891: 245.
[55] Davis, T. 1991: 150–151.
[56] Ryan 1839: 5.
[57] Davis, T. 1991: 109.
[58] Anon. 1888: 203–204.
[59] Anon. 1888: 204.
[60] Anon. 1888: 204.
[61] Davis, T. 1991: 156.
[62] Symons 1896: 78.
[63] Symons 1896: 81.
[64] Askew 1913: 201.
[65] Askew. 202–203.
[66] Symons 1896: 77
[67] Carter 2005: 64.

[68] Carter 2005: 65.
[69] Cook, M. 2003: 29.
[70] Anon. 1850: 6.
[71] Cook, M. 2003: 89.
[72] Croft-Cooke 1967: 265.
[73] Hill 1902: 2, 288; see also Cook, M. 2003: 26.
[74] Letter in the Greater London Record Office, dated 15 October 1894, LCC/MIN/10, 803; quoted Davis, T. 1991: 148–149.
[75] Davis, T. 1991: 149.
[76] Weeks 1990: 197.
[77] 'Stall Swells', *The Era*, 5 August 1877: 10.
[78] Cocks 2003: 110–11.
[79] Adams 1995: 210.
[80] Adams 1995: 10.
[81] Cocks 2003: 100.
[82] Fitzgerald 1888: 319–320.
[83] Cook, M. 2003: 15.
[84] Roughead 1930: 160.
[85] Roughead 1930: 160.
[86] Anon. 1870: 3.
[87] 'Charge Against Gentlemen Personating Women', *Illustrated Police News*, 14 May 1870: 2.
[88] 'The Men in Petticoats—Horrible and Revolting Disclosures', *Reynold's Newspaper*, 29 May 1870: 5.
[89] 'The Boulton and Park Case', *Illustrated Police News,* 20 May 1871: 2.
[90] Cocks 2003: 113.
[91] Sinfield 1999: 28.
[92] Gagnier 1987: 140–141.
[93] cited Gagnier 1987: 108.
[94] Ellmann 1984: 347.
[95] Gagnier 1987: 108.
[96] Ellmann 1984: 346–347.
[97] Ellmann 1984: 344–345.
[98] Kaplan, M. 2005: 226.
[99] Kaplan, M. 2005: 226.
[100] Raffalovich 1896: 247.
[101] 'Meerboom' 1895: 58.
[102] Ellmann 1984, 290–291.
[103] Croft-Cooke 1967: 211–212.
[104] McCormack 2000: 80.
[105] Ellmann 1984: 401.
[106] Kaplan J. and Stowell 1994: 12.
[107] Wilton 1910: 22.
[108] Adcock 1901: II, 9.
[109] Borsa 1908: 4–5.
[110] *The Era*, 11 December 1935; cited Gale 1996: 14.

Notes for Chapter Two

[1] Rohr 2001: 114.
[2] Ehrlich 1985: 237.
[3] 'G. L. S.' 1896: 145.
[4] *British Bandsman,* October 1887: 30.
[5] Rohr 2001: 127.
[6] Rohr 2001: 121.
[7] Ehrlich 1985: 142.
[8] Ehrlich 1985: 143.
[9] *Orchestral Association Gazette*, February 1895: 231.
[10] Reade 1896: 17.
[11] Ehrlich, 1985: 142.
[12] Glover 1911: 62.
[13] Ehrlich 1985: 101.
[14] Rohr 2001: 120–121.
[15] Rohr 2001: 125.
[16] Ehrlich 1985: 142–143.
[17] *Orchestral Association Gazette*, August 1897: 92.
[18] 'Behind the Scenes', *Chambers's Journal*, 21 September 1867: 595.
[19] Reade 1896: 17–20.
[20] 'G. L. S.' 1896: 137.
[21] Ehrlich 1985: 143–144.
[22] Reade 1896: 17.
[23] Maitland 1895: 203.
[24] 'G. L. S.' 1896: 138.
[25] Runciman 1895: 171.
[26] Ehrlich 1985: 144–145.

[27] *Musical Times*, 1 February 1893: 78.
[28] *Orchestral Association Gazette*, December 1897: 134.
[29] Cook 1876: 1, 172–173.
[30] 'G. L. S.' 1896: 138
[31] *Orchestral Association Gazette*, May 1897: 57.
[32] Ehrlich 1985: 144.
[33] *Orchestral Association Gazette*, February 1895: 231.
[34] Ehrlich 1985: 144.
[35] Bancroft 1888: 1, 284.
[36] *Theatre*, 1 December 1880: 378.
[37] Fitzgerald 1881: 70.
[38] Runciman 1895: 170.
[39] Booth 1981: 97.
[40] *Orchestral Association Gazette* August 1897: 46
[41] cited Richards 2005: 245.
[42] Ehrlich 1985: 146.
[43] Davis, T. 2000: 313.
[44] Davis, T. 2000: 327–328.
[45] Leppington 1891: 246–247.
[46] 'Old Lessee' 1885: 6.
[47] Davis, T. 2000: 310.
[48] Davis, T. 2000: 326.
[49] 'Scene Shifting by Electricity' in *Stage Year Book*, 1909: 56–58.
[50] Sala 1851: 291.
[51] Booth 1991: 67: 72–73.
[52] Sala 1859: 238.
[53] Leppington 1891: 261.
[54] Leppington 1891: 248.
[55] Sala 1859: 238.
[56] 'Deaths and Disasters on the Stage', *Chambers's Journal*, 18 January 1876: 13.
[57] 'Alarming Occurrence at the Alhambra', *Illustrated Police News*, 16 June 1870: 2.
[58] Fitzgerald 1881: 49.
[59] Fitzgerald 1881: 43–44.
[60] Harris 1889: 110.
[61] Stoker 1911: 905.
[62] Booth 1991: 85–86.
[63] 'The Destruction of Covent-Garden Theatre', *The Times,* 17 March 1856: 9.
[64] Rees 1978: 122–123.
[65] Booth 1991: 86.
[66] Booth 1991: 86.
[67] 'Old Stager' 1888: 167.
[68] Buckle 1888: 38.
[69] Booth 1991: 86.
[70] Stoker 1906: 906.
[71] Stoker 1906: 911.
[72] Stoker 1906: 906.
[73] Stoker 1906: 910.
[74] Stoker 1906: 911.
[75] Stoker 1906: 911.
[76] Booth 1991: 91.
[77] Telbin 1889: 195–196.
[78] Telbin 1889: 198.
[79] Telbin 1889: 199.
[80] Leppington 1891: 261.
[81] Telbin 1889: 197–198.
[82] Castle 1984: 27.
[83] Harker 1924: 62–63.
[84] Sala 1851: 295.
[85] Harker 1924: 63.
[86] Telbin 1889: 196.
[87] Burgin 1893: 134.
[88] Sala 1851: 292–293.
[89] Leppington 1891: 247.
[90] Leppington 1891: 247–248.
[91] Leppington 1891: 247.
[92] 'Feraldt' 1880: 15.
[93] Sala 1851: 291.
[94] Sala 1851: 291.
[95] Baker, M. 1978: 64.
[96] Varty 2008: 28.
[97] Sala 1851: 294–295.
[98] 'Old Stager' 1888: 67–68.
[99] 'Old Stager' 1888: 67.
[100] Wilhelm 1895: II, 49
[101] Wilhelm 1895: II, 49.
[102] Wilhelm 1895: 53.
[103] Wilde 1890: 18.

[104] Jackson 1989: 34.
[105] Wilhelm 1895: II, 50.
[106] Wilhelm 1895: I, 14.
[107] Wilhelm 1895: I, 16.
[108] 'Obituary "C. Wilhelm": Mr Pitcher's Art', *The Times*, 3 March 1925: 18.
[109] Wilhelm 1895: I, 16.
[110] Leppington 1891: 249.

Notes for Chapter Three

[1] Baker, M. 1978: 62.
[2] Irving, H. B. 1900: 746.
[3] Sala 1851: 290.
[4] Sala 1851: 290.
[5] Booth 1991: 31.
[6] Thomas 1984: 6.
[7] Tomlins 1840: 111.
[8] Tomlins 1840: 111–112.
[9] Hervey 1887: 252.
[10] Hervey 1887: 252–253.
[11] Pearson 1956: 117–118.
[12] see Scott 1900: 323–339.
[13] Scott 1900: 335.
[14] Crawfurd 1890: 934.
[15] Jones 1890: 183–184.
[16] Elliott 1896: 181.
[17] Tree 1890: 926.
[18] Elliott 1896: 181.
[19] Fitzgerald 1878: 358–359.
[20] Sims 1900: 48.
[21] Benson, C. 1926: 62.
[22] Goddard 1891: 219.
[23] Goddard 1891: 247.
[24] Goddard 1891: 179.
[25] quoted *Mascot*, 14 December 1895: 11. 'Masks and Faces (I cannot refrain from quoting …)',
[26] Smythe 1898: ix, 3.
[27] Terriss, 1955: 49.
[28] 'Theatrical Gossip', *The Era* 16 Feb 1895.
[29] from an unsourced cutting in the William Terriss Collection scrapbook.
[30] Sims 1897.
[31] Smythe 1898: 18.
[32] Archer, W. 1898: 347.
[33] 'Theocritus' 1894: 10.
[34] *The Sketch*, 22 December 1897: 322.
[35] Terry 1908: 143.
[36] Sims 1897.
[37] Smythe 1898: 151–152.
[38] Rowell 1987: 32, 34.
[39] Sims 1897.
[40] Smythe 1898: 154.
[41] Millward 1923: 217.
[42] Rowell 1987: 50.
[43] William Terriss Archive cuttings.
[44] Millward 1923: 231.
[45] William Terriss Archive.
[46] Jalland 1996: 221.
[47] Millward 1923: 233–234.
[48] Smythe 1898: 17.
[49] Pearson 1950: 35.
[50] Benson, F. 1930: 312.
[51] Benson, C. 1926: 139.
[52] Trewin 1960: 88.
[53] Benson, F 1930: 312–315.
[54] Benson, C. 1926: 138.
[55] Benson, C. 1926: 135.
[56] Benson, C. 1926: 138.
[57] Benson, C. 1926: 139.
[58] Pearson 1950: 23.
[59] Bettany 1892: 112.
[60] Mason 1935: 199–200.
[61] Pearson 1950: 23.
[62] Pearson 1950: 27.
[63] Senelick 1999: 411.
[64] McKenna 2003: 378–379.
[65] Booth 1991: 136, Plate 17.
[66] De Cordova 1909: fol. 20.
[67] Grein 1899: 108–109.
[68] Pearson 1950: 41.
[69] Pearson 1950: 46.
[70] Pearson 1950: 44.

[71] Pearson 1950: 42.
[72] Courtneidge 1930: 114–115.
[73] Coleman 1888: 2, 287.
[74] Winter 1913: 1, 186.
[75] Coleman 1888: 2, 251.
[76] Coleman 1888: 2, 253.
[77] Coleman 1888: 252.
[78] Coleman 1888: 2, 282.
[79] Coleman 1888: 2, 264.
[80] Coleman 1888: 2, 273.
[81] Coleman 1888: 2, 290.
[82] Coleman 1888: 2, 290.
[83] Cocks 2003: 177–178.
[84] Scott 1899: 2, 39; 369–370.
[85] Stoker, 1906: 2, 178.
[86] Stoker, 1906: 2, 182.
[87] Irving, L. 1951: 671.
[88] Scott, 1899: 2, 369.
[89] Stoker 1906: 1, 33.
[90] Ludlam 1962: ill. opp. 64.
[91] Hopkins 2007: 17.
[92] Stoker 1906: 1, 31.
[93] Showalter 1990: 105–106.
[94] Hopkins 2007: 18.
[95] Belford 1996: 144, 147–148.
[96] Belford 1996: 144.
[97] Belford 1996: [page not identified]
[98] Stoker 1906: 1, 60.
[99] Belford 1996: 132.
[100] Richards 2005: 158.
[101] Ellis and Symonds 2008: 196. fn. 22.
[102] Anon. 1850: 7.
[103] Ellis and Symonds 2008: 196. fn. 22.
[104] Mayne 1908: 399–400.
[105] Cocks 2003: Table 1, 101.
[106] Cocks 2003: 103–104.
[107] Mayne 1908: 399.
[108] Anon. 1888: 212.
[109] Sala 1869: 200.
[110] Carter 2005: 64.
[111] Ellis and Symonds 2008: 164.
[112] Mayne 1908: 399.
[113] Senelick 1993: 87.
[114] cited Busby 1976: 44.
[115] Senelick 1993: 84.
[116] Cook 2003: 108.
[117] Hollingshead 1895: I, 228.
[118] Busby 1976, 53; Senelick 1993, 34.
[119] Hollingshead 1895: I, 228.
[120] Baker, M. 1978: 95.
[121] Coleman 1885: 27.
[122] Roth 1888: 28.
[123] Halling and Lister 1908: 441.
[124] Donaldson, W. 1865: 122.
[125] Halling and Lister 1908: 441.
[126] Halling and Lister 1908: 441.
[127] Faucit 1891: 51.
[128] Faucit 1891: 390.
[129] Carlisle 2000: 57.
[130] Faucit 1891: 51.
[131] Faucit 1891: 52.
[132] Macready 1875: 2, 34.
[133] Terry 1908: 163.
[134] Richards 2005: 47–48.
[135] Terry 1908: 163.
[136] Shaw 1932: 17–18.
[137] Findlater 1976: 151.
[138] Terry 1908: 150.
[139] Richards 2005: 40–42.
[140] Jerome 1885: 123.
[141] Jerome 1885: 124.
[142] Cole 1859: 2, 180.
[143] Terry 1908: 11.
[144] Scott 1899: 2, 362.
[145] Scott 1899: 1, 245.
[146] Ripley 2007: 103.
[147] Matthews and Hutton 1886: 1, 98.
[148] Scott 1899: 1, 245.
[149] Cole 1859: 2, 215.
[150] Terry 1908: 11.
[151] Cole 1859: 2, 376.
[152] 'Drama and Music: Princess's Theatre', *Literary Gazette*, 2 April 1859: 440–441.
[153] Schoch 2004b: 142–143.
[154] Cole 1859: 2, 376.

[155] Coleman 1888: 1, 269.
[156] Coleman 1888: 1, 272.
[157] Pascoe 1879: 384.
[158] Bancroft 1888: 1, 183.
[159] Archer, W 1886: 31.
[160] Bancroft 1888: 1, 340.
[161] Bancroft 1888: 1, 340.
[162] Bancroft 1888: 2, 197.
[163] Bancroft 1888: 2, 199.
[164] Kendal 1933: 70.
[165] Kendal 1933: 69.
[166] Hicks 1939: 54–55.
[167] Coleman 1888: 11, 272.
[168] Downer 1966: 200–201, 348.
[169] Bancroft 1888: 1, 292.
[170] [Source not identified]
[171] Kendal 1933: 80.
[172] Kendal 1933: 71.
[173] Cook, D. 1881: 237.
[174] Marston 1888: 1, 204.
[175] Lewes 1875. 12, 16.
[176] Donaldson, F. 1970: 91, 101.
[177] Robertson, W. 1931: 266.
[178] Pearson 1950: 57.
[179] Robertson, W. 1931: 266.
[180] Robertson, W. 1931: 266.
[181] 'Haymarket Theatre: *The Pretenders*', *The Times*, 14 February 1913: 8.
[182] Pearson 1950: 60, 61.
[183] Richards 2005: 51, 152.
[184] Yates 1863: 186–187.
[185] Macready 1875: I, 280.
[186] Marston 1888: 1, 61.
[187] Ripley 2007: 99–100.
[188] Ripley 2007: 100.
[189] cited Richards, 1944, 93.
[190] Hicks 1939: 55.
[191] Duncan 1964: 185.
[192] Fitzgerald 1881: 150.
[193] Schoch 2004*a*: 180.
[194] Irving, H. 1895: 256.
[195] 'Flashes from the Footlights: A Man who can Play a Cad', *English Illustrated Magazine*, 21 (April–September 1899): 476.
[196] Fitzgerald 1881: 213.
[197] Escott 1885*a*: 300.
[198] Escott 1885*a*: 303–305.
[199] Stoker 1906: I, 310–311.
[200] Escott 1885*b*: 544.
[201] Tosh 1999: 17–19; 126–127.
[202] Leach 1902: 162.
[203] 'Freemasonry', *Chambers's Journal*, 15 September 1866: 583.
[204] Ibid.: 582.
[205] Richards [check date]: 288.
[206] Wintle 1901: 223–227.

Notes for Chapter Four

[1] Archer, F. 1892: 18, 20.
[2] 'Hawk-Eye' 1871: 15.
[3] Archer, W. [check date]: 355-356.
[4] Emeljanow 1996: 156–158.
[5] see Archer, W. 1923: Chapters XI and XII.
[6] Archer, W. 1895: 96–97.
[7] Powell 1997: Chapter 6.
[8] 'Guy Domville', *The Era*, 12 January 1895: 11.
[9] Archer, F. 1892: 71.
[10] Fawkes 1979: 42.
[11] Sims 1917: 41.
[12] Sims 1917: 41.
[13] Stephens 1992: 10–12.
[14] Banham 1990: 833
[15] Banham 1990: 948–949
[16] Lewes 1863: 499.
[17] Lewes 1863: 501.
[18] Smith 1984: 8.
[19] Bunn 1840: 3, 163.
[20] Bunn 1840: 1, 78.
[21] Lewes 1842: 76.
[22] Lewes 1842: 81–82; 87.
[23] Boucicault 1877: 243.
[24] à Beckett 1895: 211–212.

[25] 'Dramatist' 1888: 64.
[26] 'Dramatist' 1888: 64.
[27] 'Dramatist' 1888: 64–65.
[28] Lewes 1863: 507.
[29] Lewes 1863: 502.
[30] Lewes 1863: 505.
[31] 'Dramatist' 1888: 65.
[32] Lewes 1842: 85.
[33] Jackson 2004: 53.
[34] Mayhew 1840: 68.
[35] Mayhew 1840: 64.
[36] Mayhew 1840: 67.
[37] Archer, F. 1892: 97.
[38] Shepherd and Womack 1996: 253.
[39] Barker 1971: 5.
[40] Beerbohm 1930: 258–262; cited Powell 1997: 90.
[41] Bunn 1840: 3, 248.
[42] from a discussion with Dr Laurie Garriston, British Library/Royal Holloway, University of London, *Buried Treasures* Project (Lord Chamberlain's Plays).
[43] Stephens 1992: 185–186.
[44] Boucicault 1877: 243.
[45] Fawkes 1979: 52–53.
[46] Hollingshead 1876: 92–93.
[47] Booth 2004: 134.
[48] Jones 1895: 125.
[49] Booth 1975: 50.
[50] Fawkes 1979: 49.
[51] Booth 1991: 142–143.
[52] Booth 1991: 50–51.
[53] Best 1971: 89.
[54] Stephens 1992: 51.
[55] 'Novelist' 1892: 3.
[56] Stokes 1972: 140–141.
[57] Hardy 1892: 1–2.
[58] Harris [reference not identified] 1892: 3.
[59] Schlicke 1999: 389–391.
[60] Stirling 1881: 1, 191.
[61] Planché 1872: 138 –142.
[62] Planché 1872: 138.
[63] Moody 1999: 100.
[64] Rede 1836: 71.
[65] Moody 1999: 100.
[66] Booth 1975: 57.
[67] Stephens 1992: 52–53.
[68] Fawkes 1979: 68–69; see also Boucicault 1889b: 229.
[69] Fawkes 1979: 126–127.
[70] Stephens 1992: 54–56.
[71] Stephens 1992: 52.
[72] Burnand 1888 [reference not identified]: 169.
[73] Stephens 1992: 114.
[74] Booth 1991: 144–145.
[75] Stephens 1992: 190–191.
[76] *Daily News*, 16 February 1885; cited Archer, W. 1886: 51.
[77] Stephens 1992: 164–165.
[78] Fawkes1979: 87.
[79] Fawkes1979: 87–88; 105.
[80] Walsh 1915: preface, xvii.
[81] Walsh 1915: 179–180.
[82] Watson 1926: 245, 247.
[83] cited Fawkes1979: 208–209.
[84] Booth 1980: xv.
[85] Banham 1990: 833.
[86] Bancroft 1888: I, 201.
[87] Booth 1980: xii.
[88] Watson 1926: 409.
[89] Watson 1926: 410.
[90] Bancroft 1888: I, 202.
[91] Watson 1926: 412.
[92] repr. Jones 1895 164–165.
[93] Archer, W. 1886: 52.
[94] Stedman 1996: 217.
[95] Stephens 1992: 164–165.
[96] Stephens 1992: 165.
[97] Joseph 1994: 45.
[98] cited Stedman 1996: 218.
[99] Smalley 1912: 294.
[100] Crowther 2000: 93.
[101] Stedman 1996: 218.
[102] Campbell 1922: 69.
[103] Maude 1927: 86.

[104] Raby 2004. 191.
[105] 'M' 1889: 260.
[106] British Library Playbill 343.
[107] Booth 1991, 145–146.
[108] Lewes 1853: 241–242.
[109] Shaw 1899: 257.
[110] Archer, W. 1892a: 575.
[111] Goodrich 1892: 236.
[112] Schoch 2004a: 162.
[113] Stephens 1980: 154–155.
[114] Archer, W. 1886: 134.
[115] Gilbert, W. S. 1872: 12.
[116] Crowther 2000: 72–73.
[117] Stephens 1980: 119–124.
[118] Archer, W. 1886: 137.
[119] Archer, W. 1886: 137.
[120] Stephens 1980: 122.
[121] Archer, W. 1892a: 575–576.
[122] Stephens 1980: 155.
[123] Stephens 1980: 113.
[124] Hart-Davis 1962: fn. 317.
[125] Archer, W. 1886: 138.
[126] Stephens 1980: 33–34.
[127] 'The Examinership of Plays', *The Era*, 2 March 1895: 15.
[128] 'The Late Censor', *Saturday Review*, 2 March 1895; Shaw 1932: I, 48–49.
[129] Orme 1936 [page not identified].
[130] Schoonderwoerd 1963: 100; Orme 1936: 107.
[131] Schoonderwoerd 1963: 120.
[132] Kennedy 1996: 134.
[133] Orme 1936: 146–147.
[134] Schoonderwoerd 1963: 128.
[135] Orme 1936: 120.
[136] Orme 1936 [page not identified].
[137] Orme 1936: 8.
[138] cited Richards 2005: 296; see also Orme 1936: 102.
[139] Schoonderwoerd 1963: 99–100.
[140] Grein 1891 [reference not identified]: 167.
[141] Shaw [reference not identified].
[142] *Saturday Review*, 4 January 1895; repr. Shaw 1932: 20.
[143] Shaw 1932: 51.
[144] Shaw 1921: 137.
[145] Schoonderwoerd 1963: 100–101.
[146] 'Mr Archer on Modern Drama', *The Times*, 5 February 1909: 7.
[147] Boucicault 1889b: 229.
[148] Archer, W. 1895: xvi.
[149] Stephens 1992: 168.

Notes for Chapter Five

[1] Mayer 1980: 145–146.
[2] Shepherd and Womack 1996: 198–199.
[3] Mayer 1980: 150–151.
[4] Booth 2004: 131.
[5] Booth 2004: 132.
[6] *Black-Ey'd Susan* (Jerrold): II.1, 19.
[7] Bratton 1991: 47.
[8] Dickens 1844: 183.
[9] 'B. B.' 1853: 319.
[10] Slater 2002: 67.
[11] Slater 2002: 67.
[12] Gilbert, A. N. 1976: 78.
[13] *Harbour Lights* (Sims and Pettitt): II.1, fol. 41.
[14] *My Poll and My Partner Joe* (Haines): I.3, 107–108.
[15] *The Sea!* (Somerset): II.5, 33–34.
[16] *False Colours!* (Fitzball): I.2, 7-8.
[17] *Loss of the Royal George* (Barnett): II.4, 39–40.
[18] *Minute Gun at Sea!* (Barnett): II.5, 29.
[19] Ibid.: I.4, 15.
[20] Ibid.: III.4, 40.
[21] Ibid.: III.4, 44.
[22] Mayne 1908: 186.
[23] *Ashore and Afloat* (Hazlewood): II.1, 21.
[24] Ibid.: I.1, 6.
[25] Bratton 1991: 51.

[26] *Chelsea Pensioner* (Soane): I.2, 9–11.
[27] Ibid.: II.2, 18.
[28] Ibid.: III.3, 37–38.
[29] Crowther 2000: 101.
[30] *H.M.S. Pinafore* (Gilbert and Sullivan): I, 3.
[31] Ibid.: I, 3.
[32] Ibid.: I, 14.
[33] Bradley 1996: 122.
[34] *H.M.S. Pinafore* (Gilbert and Sullivan): I, 14–15.
[35] Ibid.: II, 28–29.
[36] Crowther 2000: 104.
[37] *H.M.S. Pinafore* (Gilbert and Sullivan): I, 13.
[38] Ibid.: I, 12.
[39] Ibid.: I, 10–11.
[40] *Ocean of Life* (Haines): II, 93–95.
[41] Crowther 2000: 104.
[42] Bradley 1996: 180.
[43] Bratton 1981: 120.
[44] Bratton 1981: 122.
[45] 'Astley's Amphitheatre: *The Battle of the Alma*', The Times, 24 October 1854: 10.
[46] Ibid.: 10.
[47] *Battle of the Alma* (Anon.): f. 36.
[48] Ibid.: f. 36.
[49] 'Astley's Amphitheatre: *The Battle of the Alma*', The Times, 24 October 1854: 10.
[50] Bratton 1981: 133.
[51] *Fall of Sebastopol* (Anon.): I.3, f.7.
[52] Ibid.: I.3, f.12.
[53] Ibid.: I.3, 2, f.20.
[54] Ibid.: I.3, f. 37–38. [check reference]
[55] Bratton 1981: 135.
[56] *Ours* (Robertson): III, 63.
[57] Tydeman 1982: Introduction, 18-19
[58] *Ours* (Robertson): III, 43
[59] *Union Jack* (Grundy and Pettitt): I.1, fols. 8–12.
[60] 'Adelphi Theatre' [*The Union Jack*], The Times, 21 July 1888: 15.
[61] Mayne 1908: 214.
[62] Mayne 1908: 220.
[63] *Jessie Brown* (Boucicault): I.3, 19–20.
[64] *Harbour Lights* (Sims and Pettitt): I, fol. 15.
[65] Ibid.: I, fol. 24.
[66] Ibid.: I, fol. 19.
[67] Ibid.: III.1, fol. 59.
[68] Ibid.: V.1, fol. 79.
[69] *Boys Together* (Carr and Chambers): I, fol. 34.
[70] Ibid.: II.1, fol. 13.
[71] *One of the Best* (Hicks and Edwardes): III.2, fols. 24–25.
[72] Ibid.: IV.3, fol. 19.
[73] Ibid.: IV.3, fol. 19.
[74] *Union Jack* (Grundy and Pettitt): IV.4, fol. 18.
[75] Newey 2000: 28–29.
[76] *Foreman of the Works* (Fenn): III.1, fol. 18.
[77] *Factory Lad* (Walker): I.5, 211.
[78] Newey 2000: 36–37.
[79] Newey 2000: 37.
[80] Vernon 1977: 128.
[81] *Factory Strike* (Taylor): I.1, 4.
[82] Ibid.: I.1, 4.
[83] Ibid.: III.5, 16.
[84] Ibid.: II.1, 8.
[85] *Lost in London* (Phillips): I.1, 208.
[86] Ibid.: I.1, 213.
[87] Ibid.: I.1, 210.
[88] Ibid.: I.1, 209.
[89] Ibid.: III.1, 269.
[90] Mayer 1987: 35.
[91] Mayer 1987: 37.
[92] Banham 1985: 13.
[93] *Ticket-of-Leave Man* (Taylor): IV. 3. 222.
[94] 'The Ticket-of-Leave Man', Athenaeum, 6 June 1863.

[95] *Ticket-of-Leave Man* (Taylor): I, 169.
[96] Ibid.: I, 168.
[97] Mayer 1987: 34.
[98] Mayer 1987: 36.
[99] *Ticket-of-Leave Man* (Taylor): IV.3. 221.
[100] Ibid.: III, 202.
[101] Ibid.: IV.1, 215.
[102] Ibid.: IV.1, 214.
[103] Ibid.: IV.1, 211.
[104] '*The Ticket-of-Leave Man*', *Illustrated London News*, 27 June 1863: 697.
[105] *Ticket-of-Leave Man's Wife* (Cheltnam): III.4, 72.
[106] *Corsican Brothers* (Boucicault): I.1, 94.
[107] Ibid.: I.1, 152–156, 95.
[108] Shepherd and Womack 1996: 216.
[109] Taylor 1996: xviii.
[110] *Corsican Brothers* (Boucicault): I.1, 191–197, 96.
[111] Taylor 1989: 25.
[112] *Leader* 28 February 1852; repr. Taylor 1989: 26.
[113] Saintsbury and Palmer 1939: 188.
[114] *The Bells* (Lewis): I. 476.
[115] Mayer 1980: 86.
[116] *The Bells* (Lewis): III. 499–450.
[117] Mayer 1980: 23.
[118] *Observer*, 26 November 1871; repr. Mayer 1980: 102.
[119] Terry 1908: 338.
[120] Mayer 1980: 19.
[121] *The Bells* (Lewis): II. 482–483.
[122] Ibid.: III. 493–494.
[123] Ibid.: III. 494.
[124] 'Lyceum Theatre' [*The Bells*], *The Times*, 30 September 1872: 8.
[125] 'Lyceum Theatre' [*The Bells*], *The Times*, 28 November 1871: 4.
[126] Mayer 1980: 112
[127] Mayer 1980: 94–95
[128] Baker, H. 1904: 503.
[129] Baker, H. 1904: 504
[130] *New York Times*, 28 March 1885: 5; quoted Dawick 1993: 129.
[131] Bratton 1995: xv.
[132] Pinero to Daly, 7 April 1885, repr .in Wearing 1974.
[133] *The Magistrate* (Pinero): I.1.7. l, 138–140.
[134] Ibid.: I.1.13. l, 384–388.
[135] Ibid.: I.1.18 ll, 544–546.
[136] Ibid.: I.1.22. ll, 692–694.
[137] Bratton 1995: 298.
[138] 'The Theatres: Court' [*The Magistrate*], *The Times*, 23 March 1885: 8.
[139] *The Magistrate* (Pinero): III. 1. 49–50.
[140] Ibid.: III. 2. 67.
[141] Ibid.: III. 2. 69. l. 300.
[142] 'The Theatres: Court' [*The Magistrate*] *The Times*, 23 March 1885: 8.
[143] Knight 1885: 418.
[144] Sinfield 1999: 32.
[145] Sinfield 1999: 39.
[146] *Bunch of Violets* (Grundy): IV, 57.
[147] *The Profligate* (Pinero): I, 30.
[148] *Second Mrs Tanqueray* (Pinero): IV.1, 211.
[149] Bland 1995: 9.
[150] Pinero 1889 [reference not identified]: 324. [*The Profligate*].
[151] *The Profligate* (Pinero): IV, fol. 89.
[152] Ibid.: IV, fol. 91.
[153] 'Opening of the Garrick Theatre' [*The Profligate*], *The Times,* 25 April 1889: 9.
[154] Ibid.: 9.
[155] *The Profligate* (Pinero): I. fol.10.
[156] Ibid.: IV. fol. 85.
[157] Bulkeley 1880: 7.
[158] Bulkeley 1880: 9–10.
[159] 'Opening of the Garrick Theatre' [*The Profligate*], *The Times,* 25 April 1889: 9.

[160] *The Theatre*, 1 June 1889: 331 [*The Profligate*].
[161] Bland 1995: 52.
[162] *The World* 22 May 1889, 9: quoted Dawick 1993: 161.
[163] Dawick 1993: 160.
[164] Archer 1892b: 149.
[165] Archer 1892b: 149–150.
[166] Dawick 1993: 175.
[167] Sinfield 1999: 34.
[168] *The Idler*: III. 43.
[169] Senelick 1999: 18.
[170] '*The Blackmailers*', *The Era*, 9 June 1894: 11.
[171] Ibid.
[172] Burgess 1894: 242.
[173] repr. Senelick 1999: 57.
[174] *The Blackmailers* (Gray and Raffalaovich): I. fol.11.
[175] Senelick 1999: 20.
[176] *The Blackmailers* (Gray and Raffalaovich): II. fol. 31.
[177] Ibid.: II. fol. 33–34.
[178] Ibid.: IV. fol. 52.
[179] '*The Blackmailers*', *The Times*, 8 June 1894; repr. Senelick: 56.
[180] Scott 1894; repr. Senelick 1999: 57.
[181] Senelick 1999: 20.
[182] Senelick 1999: 19.
[183] Ellmann 1984: fn.357.
[184] quoted Pearson 1956: 65.
[185] '*A Woman of No Importance*', *The Times*, 20 April 1893: 5.
[186] *Woman of No Importance* (Wilde): I. 475.
[187] Behrendt 1991: 157.
[188] Eltis 1996: 116.
[189] *Woman of No Importance* (Wilde): IV. 514.
[190] 'Mr Oscar Wilde on Mr Oscar Wilde: an Interview', *St James's Gazette*, 18 January 1895: 5.
[191] *Importance of Being Earnest* (Wilde): I, 361–362.
[192] Robb 2003: 150; Behrendt 1991: 35.
[193] 'St James's Theatre' [*Importance of Being Earnest*], *The Times*, 15 February 1895: 5.
[194] Nicholson 1892: 61–62.
[195] *Importance of Being Earnest* (Wilde): I, 363.
[196] Ibid.: IV, 408.
[197] McKenna 2003: 309–310.
[198] *Importance of Being Earnest* (Wilde): IV, 418.
[199] Ibid.: IV, 408.
[200] McKenna 2003: 312.
[201] *Importance of Being Earnest* (Wilde): II, 386.
[202] Ibid.: II, 386.
[203] Ibid.: II, 386.
[204] Ibid.: I. 359.
[205] Ibid.: III, 397.
[206] Ibid.: III, 393.
[207] Ibid.: III, 393.
[208] Ibid.: IV, 418.
[209] Behrendt 1991: 177.
[210] '*The Importance of Being Earnest*', *Theatre* 1 March 1895: 169–170.
[211] *Ideal Husband* (Wilde): III, 556.

Notes for Appendix

[1] 'Behind the Scenes', *Chambers's Journal*, 21 September 1867: 593.
[2] Ibid.
[3] Sanderson 1984: 13.
[4] Baker, M. 1978: 39–40.
[5] Baker, M. 1978: 211.
[6] Sanderson 1984:13.
[7] Baker, M. 1978: 26.
[8] Leppington 1891: 254.
[9] Leppington 1891: 255.
[10] Arliss 1928: 155.
[11] 'Behind the Scenes', *Chambers's Journal*, 21 September 1867: 593.
[12] Booth, 1991: 101–102
[13] Graham 1930: 103.
[14] Wagner 1899: 17–18.

[15] *The Era,* 24 November 1888, 13.
[16] *The Era,* 19 January 1889, 9.
[17] *The Era,* 24 November 1888, 13.
[18] Sanderson 1984: 58–59.
[19] Graham 1930: 103.
[20] Baker, M. 1978: 112–13.
[21] Corin 1885: 85.
[22] Matthews 1952: 31–32.
[23] Sanderson 1984: 55–56.
[24] Leppington 1891: 255.
[25] 'Actors' Association', *The Era*, 4 March 1893: 8.
[26] Cook, M. 2003: 35.
[27] Wagner 1899: 156.
[28] Harker 1924: 146–4.7
[29] Corin 1885: 99.
[30] Roth 1888: 28.
[31] Roth 1888: 32.
[32] *The Era,* 12 September 1885: 14.
[33] Ibid.: 7.
[34] Ibid.: 13.
[35] Baker, H. 1904: 114–15.
[36] 'Behind the Scenes', *Chambers's Journal*, 21 September 1867: 593–4.
[37] Courtneidge 1930: 242.
[38] Booth 1991: 104–105.
[39] Jerome 1885: 38.
[40] Hervey 1887: 249–50.
[41] Baker, M. 1978: 37.
[42] Booth, 1991: 103–104.
[43] Ashwell 1936: 60.
[44] Sanderson 1984: 62–63.
[45] Sanderson 1984: 62.
[46] Benson, C. 1926: 39.
[47] Fairbrother 1939: 106.
[48] Sanderson 1984: 65.
[49] Baker, M. 1978: 136.
[50] Rede 1836: 5–9.
[51] Wagner 1899: 152–53.
[52] Wagner 1899: 257.
[53] Halling and Lister 1908: 442.
[54] Leppington 1891: 256.
[55] Booth 1991: 117.
[56] Sanderson 1984: 86.
[57] Grant 1836: 190–191.
[58] Courtneidge 1930: 115–16.
[59] Sims 1900: 145.
[60] Corin 1885: 178.
[61] Courtneidge 1930: 257–258.
[62] Leppington 1891: 257.
[63] Sanderson 1984: 88–89.
[64] Sanderson 1984: 98–99.
[65] Baker, H. 1904: 133.
[66] Halling and Lister 1908: 445.
[67] Halling and Lister 1908: 446.

Select Bibliography

Books and articles

À BECKETT, Arthur, 1895. 'The Earnings of Playwrights and Players', *Theatre* (1 October).

ACTON, William, 1870. *Prostitution: considered in its moral, social and sanitary aspects* (John Churchill).

ADAMS, James Eli, 1995. *Dandies and Desert Saints* (Cornell University Press).

ADCOCK, A. St John, 1901. 'Leaving the London Theatres' in Sims 1901.

ANON., 1850. *Yokel's Preceptor, or, More Sprees in London! Being a regular and Curious Show-Up of all the Rigs and Doings of the Flash Cribs in this Great Metropolis [etc.]* c. 1850 (Dugdale).

ANON., 1865, *How to Behave: a pocket manual of Etiquette and Guide to correct personal habits etc* (John S. Marr).

ANON., 1870. *The Lives of Boulton and Park: Extraordinary Revelations (Men in Petticoats)* (George Clarke).

ANON., 1888. *Tempted London: Young Men* (Hodder and Stoughton).

ARCHER, Frank (pseud. Frank Bishop Arnold), 1892. *How to Write a Good Play* (Sampson, Low).

ARCHER, William, 1886. *About the Theatre* (Unwin).

—— 1892a. 'A Note on Censorship', *New Review*, 6.

—— 1892b. 'Drama in the Doldrums', *Fortnightly Review*, New Series 52.

—— 1895. *The Theatrical World of 1894* (Scott).

—— 1898. *The Theatrical 'World' of 1897* (Scott).

—— 1923. *The Old Drama and the New: An Essay in Re-Valuation* (Smith, Maynard).

ARLISS, George, 1928. *On the Stage* (John Murray).

ASHWELL, Lena, 1936. *Myself a Player* (Michael Joseph).

ASKEW, Alice and Claude, 1913. *The Actor Manager* (George Newnes).

'B. B.', 1853. 'Sketches of Stage Favourites: Mr T. P. Cooke', *Illustrated London News* (15 October).

BAILEY, Peter, 1986. 'Champagne Charlie: Performance and Ideology of the Music Hall Song' in *Music Hall: Performance and Style*, ed. J. S. Bratton (Open University Press).

BAKER, Henry Barton, 1904. *The History of the London Stage and its Famous Players (1576–1903)* (George Routledge / E. P. Dutton).

BAKER, Michael, 1978. *The Rise of the Victorian Actor* (Croom Helm).

BANCROFT, Sir Squire and Lady [Marie Ellie], 1888. *Mr And Mrs Bancroft on and off the Stage written by themselves. With portraits.* 2 vols. (Bentley).

BANHAM, Martin (ed.), 1985. *Plays by Tom Taylor* (Cambridge University Press).

—— (ed.), 1990. *The Cambridge Guide to World Theatre* (Cambridge University Press).

BARKER, Clive, 1971: 'The Chartists, Theatre, Reform and Resarch', *Theatre Quarterly*, I (Oct–Dec).

BEERBOHM, Max, 1930. 'The Advantage of Writing Plays' in *Around Theatres*. (Knopf).

BEHRENDT, Patricia Flanagan, 1991. *Oscar Wilde: Eros and Aesthetics* (Macmillan).

BELFORD, Barbara, 1996. *Bram Stoker* (Weidenfeld and Nicholson).

BENSON, Constance (Lady Benson), 1926. *Mainly Players* (Thornton Butterworth).

BENSON, Frank, 1930. *My Memoirs* (Ernest Benn).

BEST, Geoffrey, 1971. *Mid Victorian Britain* (Fontana).

BETTANY, W. A. Lewis. 1892. 'Four "Leading Men" A Comparative Estimate', *Theatre* (1 September).

BINGHAM, Madeleine. 1978. *Henry Irving and the Victorian Theatre* (George Allen and Unwin).

BLAND, Lucy, 1995. *Banishing the Beast: Feminism, Sex and Morality* (Tauris Parke; repr. Penguin, 2001).

BOOTH, Michael R., (ed.), 1964. *Hiss the Villain: Six English and American Melodramas* (B. Blom).

—— 1975.'Public Taste, the playwright and the law', in *Revels History of Drama in English*, Vol. VI (1750–1880), ed. Clifford Leech and T. W. Craik (Methuen).

—— (ed.), 1980. *T. W. Robertson: Six Plays* (Amber Lane Press).

—— 1981. *Victorian Spectacular Theatre* 1850–1910 (Routledge).

—— 1991. *Theatre in the Victorian Age* (Cambridge University Press).

—— 2004. 'Comedy and farce', in *The Cambridge Companion to Victorian and Edwardian Theatre*, ed. Kerry Powell (Cambridge University Press).

BOOTH, Michael R. and KAPLAN, Joel H. (eds.) 1996. *The Edwardian Theatre: Essays on Performance and the Stage* (Cambridge University Press).

BORSA, Mario.1908. *The English Stage of Today*, trans. Selwyn Brinton. (John Lane).

BOUCICAULT, Dion, 1877. 'The Decline of Drama', *North American Review*, 125.

—— 1889a. 'The Debut of a Dramatist', *North American Review*, 148.

—— 1889b. 'Leaves from a Dramatist's Diary', *North American Review*, 149.

BRADLEY, Ian (ed.), 1996. *The Complete Annotated Gilbert and Sullivan* (Oxford University Press).

BRAKE, Laurel, 2001. *Print in Transition 1850–1910: studies in Media and Book History* (Palgrave).

BRATTON, J. S., 1981. 'Theatre at War: Crimea on the London Stage 1854–5', in *Performance and Politics in popular drama: Aspects of popular entertainment in theatre, film and television 1800–1976*, ed. David Bradby, Louis James and Bernard Sharratt (Cambridge University Press).

—— 1991. 'British Heroism and the Structure of Melodrama', in *Acts of Supremacy: the British Empire and the Stage 1790–1930*, ed. J. S. Bratton (Manchester University Press).

—— (ed.), 1995. *Arthur Wing Pinero: Trelawny of the 'Wells' and other plays* (The World's Classics, OUP).

BRERETON, Austin, 1908. *The Life of Henry Irving*, 2 vols. (Longmans Green).

BRISTOW, Edward J., 1977. *Vice and Vigilance* (Gill and Macmillan).

BUCKLE, James George, 1888. *Theatre Construction and Maintenance* (The Stage).

BULKLEY, Rev. R. G. [Richard George], 1880. *Social Purity Alliance: 'Purity' an Address to Men delivered in Lincoln Cathedral on 19th September 1879* (Croydon: Jesse W. Ward).

BUNN, Alfred, 1840. *The Stage: Both Before and Behind the Curtain*, 3 vols. (Richard Bentley).

BURGESS, Gilbert, 1894. 'Musical and Dramatic Causerie' [Review of *The Blackmailers*] in *The Artist and Journal of Home Culture* Vol. XV, No. 175 (July 1894): 242.

BURGIN, G. B., 1893. 'The Lyceum Rehearsals', *The Idler*, 3 (February–July).

BUSBY, Roy, 1976. *British Music Hall* (Elek).

CAMPBELL, Mrs Patrick [Beatrice Stella Cornwallis-West], 1922. *My Life and Some Letters* (Hutchinson).

CARLISLE, Carol Jones, 2000. *Helen Faucit: Fire and Ice on the Victorian Stage* (Society for Theatre Research).

CARTER, Alexandra, 2005. *Dance and Dancers in the Victorian and Edwardian Music Hall Ballet* (Ashgate).

CASTLE, Dennis. 1984. *'Sensation' Smith of Drury Lane* (Charles Skilton).

CHANT, Laura Ormiston, 1894. *Why We Attacked the Empire* (Marshall).

COCKS, H. G., 2003. *Nameless Offences: Homosexual Desire in Nineteenth-Century London* (I. B. Tauris).

COLE, John William, 1859. *The Life and Theatrical Times of Charles Kean, FSA*, 2 vols. (Richard Bentley).

COLEMAN, John, 1885. 'The Social Status of an Actor', *National Review*, 5 (March).

—— 1888. *Players and Playwrights I Have Known* 2 vols. (Chatto and Windus).

COLLINS, William Wilkie ['John Bull'], 1859. 'A Breach of British Privilege', *Household Words* (19 March).

COOK, Dutton, 1876. *A Book of the Play*, 2 vols. (Sampson Low).

—— 1881. *Hours with the Player* (Chatto and Windus).

COOK, Matt, 2003. *London and the Culture of Homosexuality 1885–1914* (Cambridge University Press).

CORIN [pseud. E. Lind], 1885. *The Truth about the Stage by Corin* (Wyman).

COURTNEIDGE, Robert, 1930. *I was an Actor once* (Hutchinson).

CRAWFURD, Oswald, 1890. 'The London Stage: a Rejoinder', *Fortnightly Review*, New Series 47.

CROFT-COOKE, Rupert, 1967. *Feasting with Panthers: a new consideration of some late Victorian writers* (W. H. Allen).

CROWTHER, Andrew, 2000. *Contradiction Contradicted: the Plays of W. S. Gilbert* (Fairleigh Dickinson University Press).

DAVIS, Jim, 1992. *The Britannia Diaries 1863–1875: Selections from the Diaries of Frederick C. Wilton* (Society for Theatre Research).

DAVIS, Jim and EMELJANOW, Victor, 2001. *Reflecting the Audience: London Theatregoing, 1840–1880* (University of Hertfordshire Press).

DAVIS, Tracy C., 1986. 'The Employment of Children in Theatres' *New Theatre Quarterly* 2.6.

—— 1991. *Actresses as Working Women* (Routledge).

—— 2000. *The Economics of the British Stage 1800–1914* (Cambridge University Press).

DAVIS, Tracy C. and DONKIN, Ellen (eds.) 1999. *Women and Playwriting in Nineteenth Century Britain* (Cambridge University Press).

DAWICK, John, 1993. *Pinero, a Theatrical Life* (University Press of Colorado).

DE CORDOVA, Rudolph, 1909. *Parts I Have Played* (Abbey Press).

DICKENS, Charles, 1844. 'Letter to Clarkson Stansfield, 24 August 1844', repr. in *The Letters of Charles Dickens*, vol. 4, 1844–1846, ed. Kathleen Tillotson. (The Pilgrim Edition. Clarendon, 1977).

—— 1850. 'Amusements of the People', *Household Words* (30 March).

—— 1860. 'The Uncommercial Traveller', *All the Year Round* (25 February).

—— 1877. 'Some Theatrical Audiences', *All the Year Round* (19 May).

DONALDSON, Frances Annesley, 1970. *The Actor Managers* (Weidenfeld and Nicholson).

DONALDSON, Walter, 1865. *Recollections of an Actor* (publisher not named).

DOWNER, Alan S., 1966. *The Eminent Tragedian: William Charles Macready* (Harvard University Press).

'DRAMATIST, a', 1888. *Playwriting: A Handbook for Would-be Dramatic Authors* (Stage Office).

DUNCAN, Barry, 1964. *The St James's Theatre: Its Strange and Complete History 1835–1957* (Barrie and Rockliff).

DYER, Robert, 1833. *Nine Years of an Actor's Life* (London and Portsmouth: publisher not named).

EHRLICH, Cyril, 1985. *The Music Profession in Britain since the Eighteenth Century: A Social History.* (Clarendon).

ELLIOTT, Henry, 1896. 'The Actor-Manager', *Theatre* (1 October).

ELLIS, Havelock and SYMONDS, John Addington, 2008. *Sexual Inversion: A Critical Edition*, ed. Ivan Crozier (Palgrave Macmillan).

ELLMAN, Richard, 1984. *Oscar Wilde* (Hamish Hamilton; repr. Penguin 1987).

ELTIS, Sos, 1996. *Revising Wilde: Society and Subversion in the Plays of Oscar Wilde* (Clarendon).

EMELJANOW, Victor, 1996. 'Towards an ideal spectator: theatergoing and the Edwardian critic', in *The Edwardian Theatre: essays on performance and the stage*, ed. Michael R. Booth and Joel H. Kaplan (Cambridge University Press).

ERLE, Thomas William. 1880. *Letters from a Theatrical Scene-painter: Being sketches of the minor theatres of London as they were twenty years ago* (London: 'printed for private circulation').

ESCOTT, Thomas Hay Sweet ('A Foreign Resident'), 1885a. *Society in London* (Chatto and Windus).

—— 1885b. *England: Its People, Polity and Pursuits* (Chapman and Hall).

'F. L. G., Hon', 1840 [or 1841]. *The Swell's Night Guide throughout the Metropolis* (London: 'Roger Funnyman for the author' unpaginated).

FAIRBROTHER, Sydney, 1939. *Through an Old Stage Door* (Frederick Muller).

FAUCIT, Helen (Lady Martin), 1891. *On Some of Shakespeare's Female Characters* (Blackwood).

FAWKES, Richard, 1979. *Dion Boucicault a Biography* (Quartet).

'FERALDT', 1880. 'The Hive of Pantomime', *Theatre* (1 January).

FINDLATER, Richard, 1976. *The Player Queens* (Weidenfeld & Nicolson).

FINKEL, Alicia 1996. *The Romantic Stages: Set and Costume Design in Victorian England* (McFarland).

FITZGERALD, Percy, 1878. 'Actors' Faces', *Theatre* (1 December).

—— 1881. *The World Behind the Scenes* (Chatto and Windus).

—— 1888. *Chronicles of Bow Street Police-Office; with an account of the magistrates, "runners" and police: and a selection of the most interesting cases*, 2 vols (Chapman and Hall).

FONTANE, Theodore, 1999. *Shakespeare in the London Theatre 1855–58*, trans. Russell Jackson (Society for Theatre Research).

FOULKES, Richard, 2005. *Lewis Carroll and the Victorian Stage. Theatricals in a Quiet Life* (Ashgate).

FULLER-MAITLAND, J. 1895. 'Incidental Music in Plays', *Theatre* (1 April).

'G. L. S.',1896. 'Gentlemen of the Orchestra', *The Orchestral Association Gazette* (October).

GAGNIER, Regenia, 1987. *Idylls of the Marketplace: Oscar Wilde and the Victorian Public* (Scolar).

Gale, Maggie B., 1996. *West End Women* (Routledge).

GARCIA, Gustave, 1882. *The Actor's Art*, illustrated by A. Forestier (Pettitt).

GILBERT, Arthur N., 1976. 'Buggery and the British Navy 1700–1861', *Journal of Social History*, 10, 1.

GILBERT, William Schwenck, 1872. 'Dramatic Censorship', *The Era* (14 January).

GLOVER, James M. ['Master of Music at Drury Lane Theatre'], 1911. *Jimmy Glover his Book* (Methuen).

GODDARD, Arthur, 1891. *Players of the Period.* Two Series in one volume. (Dean).

GOODRICH, Arthur, 1892. 'The Dramatic Censorship', *Theatre* (1 May).

GRAHAM, Joe, 1930. *An Old Stock Actor's Memories* (John Murray).

GRANT, James, 1836. *The Great Metropolis* (Saunders and Otley).

GREIN, J. T., 1899. *Dramatic Criticism* (John Long).

GRENVILLE-MURRAY, E. C., 1881. *Side-lights on English Society*, 2 vols. (Vizetelly).

HALLING, Daisy and LISTER, Charles, 1908. 'A Minimum Wage for Actors', *Socialist Review* (August).

HARDY, Thomas, 1892. 'Why I Don't Write Plays: I—by Mr Thomas Hardy', *Pall Mall Gazette* (31 August).

HARKER, Joseph, 1924. *Studio and Stage* (Nisbet).

HARRIS, Augustus, 1889. 'Art in the Theatre: Spectacle', *Magazine of Art* Vol. 12 (October).

HART-DAVIS, Rupert (ed.), 1962. *The Letters of Oscar Wilde* (Rupert Hart-Davis).

'HAWK-EYE' [R. H. Carlisle], 1871. *The Stage of 1871: A Review of Plays and Players* (Bickers).

HERVEY, R. K., 1887. 'On Stage Management', *Theatre* (1 November).

HICKS, Sir Edward Seymour, 1939. *Me and My Missus* (Cassell).

HILL, Graham, 1902. 'Bar and Saloon London' in Sims 1901–03: II.

HOLLINGSHEAD, John, 1876. 'Authors and Managers' in *The Era Almanack 1876, dramatic and musical*, conducted by E. Ledger.

—— 1895. *My Lifetime*, 2 vols. (Sampson Low, Marston).

HOPKINS, Lisa, 2007. *Bram Stoker a literary life* (Palgrave Macmillan).

IRVING, H. B., 1900. 'The Art and Status of the Actor', *Fortnightly Review* (January–June).

IRVING, Henry, 1895. 'The Profession of Acting', *Theatre* (1 May).

IRVING, Laurence, 1951. *Henry Irving: The Actor and his World. By His Grandson* (Faber and Faber).

JACKSON, Russell (ed.), 1989. *Victorian Theatre* (Adam and Charles Black).

—— 2004. 'Victorian and Edwardian stagecraft: Techniques and issues', in *The Cambridge Companion to Victorian and Edwardian Theatre*, ed. Kerry Powell (Cambridge University Press).

JALLAND, Pat, 1996. *Death in the Victorian Family* (Oxford University Press).

JEROME, Jerome Klapka, 1885. *On the Stage—and Off: The Brief Career of a Would-be Actor*. (Field and Tuer).

JOHNSON, A. J. (illustrator), 1893. 'Transformation Scenes: How they are made and worked', *Strand Magazine* (December).

JONES, Henry Arthur, 1890. 'The Actor Manager', *Fortnightly Review*, New Series 48 (July–December).

—— 1895. *The Renascence of the English Drama* (Macmillan).

JOSEPH, Tony, 1994. *The D'Oyly Carte Opera Company 1875–1982: An Unofficial History* (Bunthorne).

KAPLAN, Joel H. and Stowell, Sheila, 1994. *Theatre and Fashion: Oscar Wilde to the Suffragettes* (Cambridge University Press).

KAPLAN, Morris B., 2005. *Sodom on the Thames: Sex, Love and Scandal in Wilde Times* (Cornell University Press).

KENDAL, Madge, 1933. *Dame Madge Kendal by Herself* (John Murray).

KENNEDY, Dennis, 1996. 'The New Drama and the new audience', in Booth and Kaplan 1996.

KNIGHT, Joseph, 1885. '*The Magistrate*' review, *Athenaeum* (28 March).

LAWRENCE, David Haldane, 2007. 'Charles Brookfield: a Paradoxical Life' *The Wildean* 34 (January).

LEACH, Henry, 1902. 'In London's Lesser Club Land' in Sims 1901.

LEPPINGTON, C. H. d'E., 1891. 'The Gibeonites of the Stage', *National Review*.

LEWES, George Henry, 1842. 'Authors and Managers: Regeneration of the Drama', *Westminster Review*, 37.

—— 1853. 'La Dame aux Camélias', *The Leader*, 2 April; repr. in *Dramatic Essays by John Forster and George Henry Lewes*, ed. William Archer and Robert W. Lowe, 1896 (Walter Scott).

—— 1863. 'The Miseries of a Dramatic Author', *Cornhill Magazine*, 8 (July–December).

—— 1875. *On Actors and the Art of Acting*. (Smith, Elder).

LUDLAM, Harry, 1962. *A Biography of Dracula: The life story of Bram Stoker* (Fireside Press, Foulsham).

'M', 1889. 'A Few Words from the Unseen', *Theatre* (1 May).

MACREADY, William Charles, 1875. *Reminiscences and selections from his diaries and letters* (ed. Sir Frederick Pollock). 2 vols. (Macmillan).

MANDER, Raymond and MITCHENSON, Joe, 1974. *The British Music Hall* (Gentry Books).

MARSTON, John Westland, 1888. *Our Recent Actors*, 2 vols. (Sampson, Low).

MASON, A. E. W., 1935. *Sir George Alexander and the St James's Theatre* (Macmillan).

MATTHEWS, A. E. [Alfred Edward], 1952. *Matty* (Hutchinson).

MATTHEWS, Brander and HUTTON, Laurence (eds.), 1886. *Actors and Actresses of Great Britain and the United States: From the Days of David Garrick to the Present Time*, 5 vols. (Cassell).

MAUDE, Cyril. 1927. *Behind the Scenes with Cyril Maude* (John Murray).

MAYER, David, 1980. *Henry Irving and The Bells* (Manchester University Press).

—— 1987. '*The Ticket-of-Leave Man* in Context', *Essays in Theatre*, 6.1 (November).

MAYHEW, Edward, 1840. *Stage Effect, or, the Principles Which Command Dramatic Success in the Theatre* (London: publisher not stated).

MAYNE, Xavier [pseud. Edward Irenaeus Prime Stevenson], 1908. *The Intersexes: A History of Similisexualism as a problem in social life* (Naples: privately printed).

MCCORMACK, Jerusha Hall, 2000. *The Man Who Was Dorian Gray* (St Martin's Press).

MCKENNA, Neil, 2003. *The Secret Life of Oscar Wilde* (Century).

—— 2013. *Fanny and Stella: The Young Men who Shocked Victorian England* (Faber and Faber).

'MEERBOOM, Max', 1895. 'From the Queer and Yellow Book—Book I 1894'. *Punch* (2 February).

MILLWARD, Jessie, 1923 (in collaboration with J. B. Booth). *Myself and Others* (Hutchinson).

MOODY, Jane, 1999. 'Illusions of Authorship' in *Women and Playwriting in Nineteenth Century Britain*, ed. Tracy C. Davis and Ellen Donkin (Cambridge University Press).

MORLEY, Henry, 1891. *The Journal of a London Playgoer from 1851 to 1866* (Routledge).

NEWEY, Katherine, 2000. 'Climbing Boys and Factory Girls: Popular Melodramas of Working-Class Life', *Journal of Victorian Culture* (Spring 2000).

—— 2005. *Women's Theatre Writing in Victorian Britain* (Palgrave Macmillan).

NICHOLSON, John Gambril F., 1892. 'Of Boys' Names' in *Love in Earnest: Sonnets, Ballades and Lyrics* (Elliot Stock).

'NOVELIST, a, 1892. 'Why I Don't Write Plays: XI—By a Novelist', *Pall Mall Gazette* (5 September).

'OLD LESSEE, an', 1885. 'The Theatrical Business—I'. *St James's Gazette* (10 January).

'OLD STAGER, an', 1888. 'Some Stage Trades', *Chambers's Journal of Popular Literature and Science* (31 January).

'OUR LOCAL FLANEUR', 1870. 'The City of London Theatre', *Hackney and Kingsland Gazette and Shoreditch Telegraph* (15 January).

ORME, Michael [pseud. Alice Augusta Grein, née Greeven], 1936. *J. T. Grein: the story of a pioneer 1862–1935: by his wife* (Murray).

PALMER, Rev. A. Smythe, 1892. *The Perfect Gentleman* (Cassell).

PASCOE, Charles Eyre. 1879. *The Dramatic List: A Record of the Principal Performances of Living Actors and Actresses on the British Stage, with criticisms from contemporary journals* (Hardwicke and Bogue).

PEARSON, Hesketh, 1950. *The Last Actor-Managers* (Methuen).

—— 1956. *Beerbohm Tree: his Life and Laughter* (Methuen).

PLANCHÉ, James Robinson, 1872. *Recollections and Reflections* (Sampson Low).

POWELL, Kerry, 1990. *Oscar Wilde and the Theatre of the 1890s* (Cambridge University Press).

—— 1997. *Women and the Victorian Theatre* (Cambridge University Press).

RABY, Peter. 2004. 'Theatre of the 1890s: breaking down the barriers', in *The Cambridge Companion to Victorian and Edwardian Theatre*, ed. Kerry Powell (Cambridge University Press).

RAFFALOVICH, Marc-André, 1896. *Uranisme et Unisexualité: Études sur différentes manifestations sur l'instinct sexuel* (Lyons: Storck; Paris: Masson).

READ, Michael, 2008. 'The Chief and his Champion: Irving and J. L. Toole', in Richard Foulkes (ed.), *Henry Irving: A Re-Evaluation of the Pre-Eminent Victorian Actor-Manager* (Ashgate).

READE, Charles, 1896. *Readiana: Comments on Current Events* (Chatto and Windus).

REDE, Leman Thomas, 1836. *The Road to the Stage* (J. Onwhyn).

REES, Terence, 1978. *Theatre Lighting in the Age of Gas* (Society for Theatre Research).

RICHARDS, Jeffrey, 1994. *Sir Henry Irving: Theatre, Culture and Society* (Rybum).

—— 2005. *Sir Henry Irving: a Victorian Actor and his World* (Hambledon).

RIPLEY, John, 2007. 'We are not in little England now: Charles and Ellen Kean in Civil War America', *Theatre Notebook*, 61, 2.

ROBB, Graham, 2003. *Strangers: Homosexual Love in the Nineteenth Century* (Picador).

ROBERTSON, Michael, 2008. *Worshipping Walt: The Whitman Disciples* (Princeton University Press).

ROBERTSON, Walford Graham, 1931. *Time was: Reminiscences* (Hamish Hamilton).

ROHR, Deborah, 2001. *The Careers of British Musicians 1750–1850: A Profession of Artisans* (Cambridge University Press).

ROTH, Walter Edmund, 1888. *Theatre Hygiene: A Scheme for the Study of a Somewhat Neglected Area of Public Health* (Baillière).

ROUGHEAD, William, 1930. *Bad Companions* (W. Green).

ROWELL, George, 1987. *William Terriss and William Prince: Two Players in an Adelphi Melodrama* (Society for Theatre Research).

RUNCIMAN, J. F., 1895. 'Music in Theatres', *Monthly Musical Record* (1 August).

RYAN, Dr Michael, 1839. *Prostitution in London: With a Comparative View of That of Paris and New York* (Baillière).

'S. L. B., 1896. 'Saturday Night at the Britannia', *The Sketch* (24 June).

SAINTSBURY, H. A and PALMER, Cecil, 1939. *We Saw Him Act: a Symposium on the art of Sir Henry Irving* (Hurst and Blackett).

SALA, George Augustus, 1851. 'Getting up a Pantomime', *Household Words*, 20 (December).

—— 1859. *Twice Round the Clock, or the Hours of the Day and Night in London* (J. & R. Maxwell).

—— 1869. 'Behind the Scenes', *Belgravia*, 8 (February).

SANDERSON, Michael, 1984. *From Irving to Olivier: A Social History of the Acting Profession in England* (Athlone).

SCHLICKE, Paul (ed.), 1999. *The Oxford Reader's Companion to Dickens* (Oxford University Press).

SCHOCH, Richard W., 2004a. *Queen Victoria and the Theatre of her Age* (Palgrave Macmillan).

—— 2004b. *Shakespeare's Victorian Stage: Performing history in the theatre of Charles Kean* (Cambridge University Press).

SCHOONDERWOERD, N, 1963. *J. T. Grein Ambassador to the Theatre 1862–1935: A Study in Anglo-Continental Theatrical Relations* (van Gorcum).

SCOTT, Clement, 1894. '*The Blackmailers*', *Illustrated London News* (16 June).

—— 1899. *The Drama of Yesterday and Today*, 2 vols. (Macmillan).

—— 1900. 'Sir Henry Irving, Actor: Manager: and Diplomatist', *International Monthly*, 1 (March).

SCULLION, Adrienne (ed.) 1996. *Female Dramatists of the Nineteenth Century* (J. M. Dent, Everyman).

SENELICK, Laurence. 1993. 'Boys and Girls Together: Subcultural Origins of Glamour Drag and Male Impersonation on the Nineteenth-century Stage', in *Crossing the Stage*, ed. Lesley Ferris (Routledge).

—— 1999. *Lovesick: Modernist Plays of Same-Sex Love, 1894–1925* (Routledge).

SHAW, George Bernard, 1899. 'The Censorship of the Stage in England', *North American Review*, 169 (August) repr. in E. J. West, *Shaw on Theatre* (MacGibbon & Kee) 1958.

—— 1921. 'Letter to J. T. Grein', used as 'Introductory' to *The World of the Theatre: Impressions and Memoirs*, repr.in E. J. West, *Shaw on Theatre* (MacGibbon & Kee) 1958.

—— 1932. *Our Theatres in the Nineties*, 3 vols. (Constable).

SHEPHERD, Simon and WOMACK, Peter, 1996. *English Drama: A Cultural History* (Blackwell).

SHOWALTER, Elaine, 1990. *Sexual Anarchy: Gender and Culture in the Fin-de-siècle* (Bloomsbury).

SIMS, George R., 1897. 'Terriss As He Was', *Evening News* (17 December).

—— 1900. *Without the Limelight—theatrical life as it is* (Chatto and Windus).

—— (ed.) 1901. *Living London*, 3 vols. (Cassell; 1901–03).

—— 1917. *My Life: Sixty Years' Recollections of Bohemian London* (Eveleigh Nash).

SINFIELD, Alan, 1999. *Out on Stage: Lesbian and Gay Theatre in the Twentieth Century* (Yale University Press).

SLATER, Michael, 2002. *Douglas Jerrold 1803–1857* (Duckworth).

SMALLEY, George W., 1912. *Anglo-American Memories, Second Series* (Duckworth).

SMILES, Samuel, 1879. *Self-Help: with Illustrations of Character and Conduct* (John Murray: New Edition) [first edition 1859].

SMITH, James L. (ed.), 1984. *London Assurance by Dion Boucicault* (New Mermaids, Adam and Charles Black / W. W. Norton).

SMITH-ROSENBERG, Carroll, 1986. 'The Female World of Love and Ritual,' in *Disorderly Conduct* (Oxford University Press).

SMYTHE, Arthur J, 1898. *The Life of William Terriss Actor* (Constable).

STEDMAN, Jane W., 1996. *W. S. Gilbert: A Classic Victorian and His Theatre* (Oxford University Press).

STEPHENS, John Russell, 1980. *The Censorship of English Drama 1824–1901* (Cambridge University Press).

—— 1992. *The Profession of the Playwright: British Theatre 1800–1900* (Cambridge University Press).

STIRLING, Edward, 1881. *Old Drury Lane: Fifty Years' Recollections*, 2 vols. (Chatto and Windus).

STOKER, Bram, 1906. *Personal Reminiscences of Henry Irving*, 2 vols. (William Heinemann).

—— 1911. 'Irving and Stage Lighting', *Nineteenth Century and After*, 69 (January–June).

STOKES, John, 1972. *Resistible Theatres: Enterprise and Experiment in the Late Nineteenth Century* (Elek).

SYMONS, Arthur, 1896. 'At the Alhambra: Impressions and Sensations', *Savoy*, 5 (September).

TAYLOR, George. 1989. *Players and Performance in the Victorian Theatre* (Manchester University Press).

—— (ed.). 1996. *Trilby and Other Plays: Four Plays for Victorian Star Actors* (The World's Classics, Oxford University Press).

TELBIN, William, 1889. 'The Painting of Scenery', *Magazine of Art* (October).

TERRISS, Ellaline, 1955. *Just a Little Bit of String* (Hutchinson).

TERRY, Ellen, 1908. *The Story of my Life* (Hutchinson).

'THEOCRITUS', 1894. 'Mr William Terriss', *The Sketch* (31 October).

THOMAS, James, 1984. 'The Art of the Actor-Manager, Wilson Barrett and the Victorian Theatre', *Theater and Dramatic Studies* No. 15. (U. M. I. Research / Bowker).

TOMLINS, F. G., 1840. *A Brief View of the English Drama: From the Earliest Period to the Present Time, with Suggestions for Elevating the Present Condition of the Art* (Mitchell).

TREE, Sir Herbert Beerbohm, 1890. 'The London Stage: 1 A Reply' *Fortnightly Review*, New Series 47 (January–June): 922–931.

TOSH, John, 1999. *A Man's Place* (Yale University Press).

TREWIN, J. C., 1960. *Benson and the Bensonians* (Barrie and Rockliff).

TRISTAN, Flora, 1840. *Flora Tristan's London Journal: A Survey of London Life in the 1830s*, trans. Dennis Palmer and Giselle Pinsett. (Prior).

TYDEMAN, William (ed.), 1982. *Plays by Tom Robertson* (Cambridge University Press).

VARTY, Ann, 2008. *Children and Theatre in Victorian Britain: All Work, No Play* (Palgrave Macmillan).

VERNON, Sally, 1977. 'Trouble up at T'Mill: the Rise and Decline of the Factory Play in the 1830s and 1840s', *Victorian Studies*, Vol. XX, 2 (Winter).

WAGNER, Leopold, 1899. *How to Get on Stage and how to succeed there* (Chatto & Windus).

WALKOWITZ, Judith R. 1992. *City of Dreadful Delight* (Virago).

WALSH, Townsend, 1915. *The Career of Dion Boucicault* (Dunlap Society).

WATSON, Ernest Bradlee. 1926. *Sheridan to Robertson* (Harvard University Press).

WEARING, J. P. (ed.), 1974. *The Collected Letters of Arthur Pinero.* (University of Minnesota Press).

WEEKS, Jeffrey, 1990. 'Images, Perverts and Mary-Annes: Male Prostitution and the Regulation of Homosexuality in the Nineteenth and early Twentieth Centuries' in *Hidden from History: Reclaiming the Gay and Lesbian Past*, ed. Martin Bauml Duberman, Martha Vicinus and George Chauncey. (Meridian).

WILDE, Oscar, 1890. *The Picture of Dorian Gray*, in Wilde 2003.

—— 2003. *The Complete Works of Oscar Wilde*, introduced by Merlin Holland, fifth edition (Collins).

WILHELM, C. (pseud. William Pitcher), 1895. 'Art in the Ballet (In Two Parts)', *Magazine of Art*, 18.

WILTON, C. D., 1910. 'Judging a Man by his Buttonhole', *Modern Man* (15 January).

WINTER, William, 1913. *The Wallet of Time*. 2 vols. (Moffat, Yard).

WINTLE, W. J., 1901. 'Mr Lewis Waller on and off the stage—a popular actor at work and play', *Harmsworth Magazine*, 7 (August).

WOODFIELD, James, 1984. *English Theatre in Transition, 1881–1914*. (Croom Helm).

WRIGHT, Thomas, 1867. *Some Habits and Customs of the Working Class: By a Journeyman Engineer*. (Tinsley).

YATES, Edmund, 1863. 'The Social Position of Actors', *Temple Bar*, 8 (July).

Plays Cited

ANON., *The Battle of the Alma* (Astley's Theatre 1854). BL Lord Chamberlain's Collection, Add Mss. 52950H.; 'An Additional Act', Add. Mss. 52952W.

—— *The Fall of Sebastopol* (Astley's Theatre 1855). BL Lord Chamberlain's Collection, Add. Mss 52955T.

—— *The Siege of Sebastopol, or, The Horrors of War* (Britannia Theatre 1855). BL Lord Chamberlain's Collection, Add. Mss. 52952M.

BARNETT, C. Z. [Charles Zachary], *The Loss of the Royal George, or, The Fatal Land Breeze* (Sadlers Wells Theatre 1840). Duncombe's *British Theatre*, vol. 42.

—— *The Minute Gun at Sea!* (Surrey Theatre 1845), Duncombe's *British Theatre*, vol. 55.

BARRETT, Wilson. *The Sign of the Cross* (1895).

BOUCICAULT, Dion. *The Corsican Brothers* (Princess's Theatre 1852) in *Trilby and other plays*, ed. George Taylor. (The World's Classics, Oxford University Press) 1996, 85–125.

—— *Jessie Brown, or, The Relief of Lucknow* (Theatre Royal, Plymouth, 1858). Lacy's Acting Edition, vol. 38, [1859?].

—— *London Assurance* (Theatre Royal Covent Garden, 1841).

—— *The Colleen Bawn* (Adelphi Theatre 1860).

—— *The Long Strike* (Lyceum Theatre 1866), (Samuel French, 1870?).

CARR, J. W, Comyns and CHAMBERS, C. Haddon. *Boys Together* (Adelphi Theatre, 1896) BL Lord Chamberlain's Collection, Add. Mss. 53609K.

CHAMBERS, Charles Haddon *The Idler* (St James's Theatre 1891). (Samuel French c.1902).

CHELTNAM, Charles Smith. *The Ticket-of-Leave Man's Wife, or, Six Years After* (New Theatre, Greenwich, 1866), T. H. Lacy [1875], French's Acting Edition, vol. 69, no. 1032.

FENN, George Manville. *The Foreman of the Works* (Standard Theatre 1886). BL Lord Chamberlain's Collection, Add. Mss. 53354A.

'FIELD, Michael' [pseud. BRADLEY, Katherine Harris and COOPER, Edith Emma]. *A Question of Memory* (Opera Comique 1893).

FITZBALL, Edward *False Colours! or, The Free Trader!* (Theatre Royal, Covent Garden, 1837), Duncombe's *British Theatre*, vol. 25, [1837?].

'FLEMING, George' (pseud. FLETCHER, Constance), *Mrs Lessingham* (Garrick Theatre 1894).

GILBERT, W. S., *The Happy Land* (Court Theatre 1873).

—— *The Realm of Joy* (1873).

GILBERT, W. S. and SULLIVAN, Arthur, *H.M.S. Pinafore; or the Lass that Loved a Sailor* (Opera Comique, 1878). (Chappell, undated).

GRAY, John, *The Kiss* (translation of Théodore de Banville's one-act play *Le Baiser*) (Royalty Theatre 1892).

GRAY, John and RAFFALOVICH, Marc-André, *The Blackmailers* (Prince of Wales's Theatre 1894). BL Lord Chamberlain's Collection, Add. Mss. 53552H.

GRUNDY, Sydney and PETTITT, Henry, *The Union Jack* (Adelphi Theatre 1888). BL Lord Chamberlain's Collection, Add. Mss. 53398C.

GRUNDY, Sydney, *A Bunch of Violets* (Theatre Royal Haymarket 1894). (London/New York: 1901).

HAINES, J. T. [John Thomas], *My Poll and My Partner Joe* (Surrey Theatre 1835), in Booth 1964.

—— *The Ocean of Life, or, Every Inch a Sailor* (Surrey Theatre 1836), in Lacy (T. H.), Lacy's Acting Edition of Plays, vol. 69 [1850 etc.].

HAZLEWOOD, Colin H. *Ashore and Afloat* (Surrey Theatre 1864), in Lacy (T. H.), *Lacy's Acting Edition of Plays*, vol. 106, [1850 etc.].

—— *Lady Audley's Secret*.

HICKS, Edward Seymour and EDWARDES, George. *One of the Best* (Adelphi Theatre 1895). BL Lord Chamberlain's Collection, Add. Mss. 53589C.

IBSEN, Henrik, *The Pretenders* (Theatre Royal Haymarket 1913).

—— *Ghosts* (Royalty Theatre 1891).

JAMES, Henry, *Guy Domville* (1895).

JERROLD, Douglas, *Black-Ey'd Susan, or, All in the Downs* (Surrey Theatre 1829) in *Nineteenth Century Plays*, ed. George Rowell (Oxford University Press, 1953; repr. 1972), 1–43.

JONES, Henry Arthur, *The Dancing Girl* (Theatre Royal Haymarket 1891). (Samuel French, 1907).

JONES, Henry Arthur and HERMAN, Henry. *The Silver King* (Princess's Theatre 1882).

LEIGHTON, Dorothy, *Thyrza Fleming* (Terry's Theatre 1895).

BULWER-LYTTON, Edward, *The Lady of Lyons* (1838).

—— *Money* (Theatre Royal Haymarket 1840).

LEWIS, Leopold *The Bells* (Lyceum Theatre 1871) in *Nineteenth Century Plays*, ed. George Rowell. Oxford University Press, 1953; repr. 1972).

MOORE, George *The Strike at Arlingford* (Opera Comique, 1893).

PHILLIPS, Watts *Lost in London* (Adelphi Theatre 1867) in Booth 1964, 201–269.

PINERO, Arthur Wing *The Magistrate* (Court Theatre 1885) in Bratton 1995.

—— *The Profligate* (Garrick Theatre 1889), 'printed as a manuscript' (London: J. Miles, June 1887); BL Lord Chamberlain's Collection, Add. Mss. 53425G.

—— *The Second Mrs Tanqueray* (St James's Theatre 1893) Oxford University Pressin Bratton 1995.

PITT, George Dibdin, *The Battle of Inkerman* 'a Petite Military Drama in Two Acts' (Pavilion Theatre 1854), BL Lord Chamberlain's Collection Add. Mss. 52950AA.

POTTER, *Trilby* (Theatre Royal Haymarket 1885).

ROBERTSON, T. W. [Thomas William], *Ours* (Prince of Wales's Theatre 1866), prompt copy [1870].
—— *Caste* (1867).
—— *Society* (Prince of Wales's Theatre 1865).
SARDOU, Victorien, *Madame Sans-Gêne* (Lyceum Theatre 1897).
SHAW, George Bernard, *Mrs Warren's Profession* (New Lyric Club 1902).
—— *The Philanderer* (1893).
—— *Widowers' Houses* (Royalty Theatre 1892).
SIMS, George R. and PETTITT, Henry, *The Harbour Lights* (Adelphi Theatre 1885). BL Lord Chamberlain's Collection, Add. Mss. 53347H.
SOANE, George, *The Chelsea Pensioner* (Queen's Theatre 1835). *Duncombe's Edition*, vol. 19, [1825 etc.]
SOMERSET, Charles A., *The Sea!* (Queen's Theatre 1834). *Cumberland's Minor Theatre*, vol. 7 [1825 etc.]
TAYLOR, G. F. *The Factory Strike, or, Want, Crime and Retribution* (Royal Victoria Theatre 1838). Dick's Standard Plays, No. 790 [1886].
TAYLOR, Tom *The Ticket-of-Leave Man* (Olympic Theatre 1863) in *Plays by Tom Taylor*, ed. Martin Banham (Cambridge University Press, 1985).
—— *Our American Cousin* (Theatre Royal Haymarket, 1861).
TENNYSON, Alfred Lord, *The Cup* (Lyceum Theatre 1881).
WALKER, John, *The Factory Lad* (Surrey Theatre 1832) in Hudston, Sara *Victorian Theatricals: From Menageries to Melodrama* (Methuen, 2000), 199–223.
WILDE, Oscar, *A Woman of No Importance* (Theatre Royal Haymarket 1893) in Wilde 2003: 464–514.
—— *An Ideal Husband* (Theatre Royal Haymarket 1895) in Wilde 2003: 515–582.
—— *The Importance of Being Earnest* (St James's Theatre 1895; Four-act version) in Wilde 2003: 356–419.
—— *Salomé*, translated from the French of Oscar Wilde by Lord Alfred Douglas, in Wilde 2003: 583–605.
—— *Lady Windermere's Fan* (St James's Theatre 1892) in Wilde 2003: 420–464.

Sources for illustrations

Figure 18 is reproduced under the Creative Commons Attribution-Share Alike 2.5 Generic license.* Figure 30 is reproduced under licence from the University of Bristol Theatre Collection / ArenaPAL. All other images are believed to be out of copyright or in the public domain.

Figure 1: Adcock 1901: II.
Figure 2: Adcock 1901: II.
Figure 3: *Wikimedia Commons*: 'File:Gaiety-interior-1868.jpg'.
Figure 4: *Here and There*, 1 June 1872, 240.
Figure 5: Sala 1859: 257.
Figure 6: Grenville-Murray 1881: II, 132.
Figure 7: *Wikimedia Commons*: 'File:George Augustus Sala British journalist.jpg'.
Figure 8: Sala 1859: 249.
Figure 9: Grenville-Murray 1881: II, 132.
Figure 10: Wikimedia Commons:
    'File:Italian Opera House Covent Garten interior c1847.jpg'.
Figure 11: *The Entr'acte Almanack*, 1873: 13.
Figure 12: *Wikimedia Commons*: 'File:Park and Boulton (Fanny and Stella) restored.jpg'.
Figure 13: *Wikimedia Commons*: 'File:Oscar Wilde frock coat.jpg'.
Figure 14: *Wikimedia Commons*: 'File:John2gray.JPG'.
Figure 15: Burgin 1893: 139.
Figure 16: Johnson 1893: 708.
Figure 17: Johnson 1893: 710.
Figure 18: *Wikimedia Commons*: 'File:Limelight diagram.svg'. Author Theresa Knott.
Figure 19: *The Graphic*, 3 January 1874 (repr. in Rees 1978).
Figure 20: Johnson 1893: 706.
Figure 21: Johnson 1893, 707.
Figure 22: Wilhelm 1895: II, 52.
Figure 23: *Wikimedia Commons*: 'File:Sir Squire Bancroft.jpg'.
Figure 24: *Wikimedia Commons*: 'File:Henry Irving portrait.jpg'.
Figure 25: *Wikimedia Commons*: 'File:Sir Herbert Beerbohm Tree.png'.
Figure 26: Garcia 1882: Fig 42, 74.
Figure 27: *Wikipedia*: 'File:Williamterriss7.jpg'.
Figure 28: *Wikimedia Commons*: 'File:F. R. Benson I.png'.

---

* See https://creativecommons.org/licenses/by-sa/2.5/deed.en

Figure 29: De Cordova 1909. Part IV: 'Mr George Alexander, a Photographic Biography' fol. 79.
Figure 30: University of Bristol Theatre Collection / ArenaPAL (repr. in Booth 1991: 136, Plate 17).
Figure 31: London Printing and Publishing Company, c. 1856.
Figure 32: *Wikimedia Commons*: 'File:John L.Toole.jpg'.
Figure 33: *Wikimedia Commons*: 'File:Bram Stoker 1906.jpg'.
Figure 34: *Wikimedia Commons*: 'File:Lulu aka El Niño Farini.jpg'.
Figure 35: *Wikimedia Commons*:
'File:William Charles Macready by John Jackson crop b&w.jpg'.
Figure 36: *Wikimedia Commons*: 'File:Ellen Terry 1886 Hollyer.jpg'.
Figure 37: *Wikimedia Commons*: 'File:Charles Kean as Macbeth 1858.jpg'.
Figure 38: *Wikimedia Commons*: 'File:Effie Bancroft.jpg'.
Figure 39: *Wikipedia*: 'File:Pygmalion and Galatea.jpg'.
Figure 40: *Wikimedia Commons*: 'File:Edward bulwer-lytton.jpg'.
Figure 41: *Wikimedia Commons*: 'File:DionBoucicault.jpg'.
Figure 42: *Wikimedia Commons*: 'File:Thomas William Robertson.jpg'.
Figure 43: *Wikimedia Commons*: 'File:Ironmaster of the Savoy.png'.
Figure 44: *Wikimedia Commons*: 'File:Jones HenryArthur-001.jpg'.
Figure 45: *Wikipedia*: 'File:JTGrein.jpg'.
Figure 46: *Wikimedia Commons*: 'File:George Bernard Shaw 1936.jpg'.
Figure 47: 'From a photograph by Mayall', *Illustrated London News*, 15 October 1853, 320.
Figure 48: *Wikimedia Commons*:
'File:HMS Pinafore, The Captain and sweet little Buttercup.jpg'.
Figure 49: *Illustrated London News*, 1843.
Figure 50: Smythe 1898: 131.
Figure 51: *Wikimedia Commons*: 'File:Tom Taylor06.jpg'.
Figure 52: National Library of Scotland, *Digital NLS*:
http://digital.nls.uk/theatre-posters-1870-1900.
Figure 53: *Wikimedia Commons*:
'File:Houghton MS Thr 709 - Courbold, Corsican Brothers - crop.jpg'.
Figure 54: *Wikipedia*: 'File:Irving-the-bells.jpg'.
Figure 55: *Wikimedia Commons*:
'File:Arthur Wing Pinero Vanity Fair 7 March 1891.jpg'.
Figure 56: National Library of Scotland, *Digital NLS*:
http://digital.nls.uk/theatre-posters-1870-1900.
Figure 57: *Theatre* 1 June 1889, 333.
Figure 58: *Wikimedia Commons*: 'File:Raffalovich, Marc André (1864-1934).jpg'.
Figure 59: *Wikimedia Commons*:
'File:The Importance of Being Earnest - Cigarettecase.jpg'

Index

Page numbers in italics indicate illustrations. Page numbers in bold indicate the main passage about the item in question.

à Beckett, Arthur, 164
Achurch, Janet (Mrs Charrington), 281
Acton, William, 23
actor-managers, 45, 61, 73, 95, 96, 97, **91–97**, 105, 108, 137, 140, 141, 155, 157, 165, 177, 181, 188, 195, 204, 237, 301, 302, 311, 316, 320, 321, *See also* matinée idols and their leading ladies, **132–36**
Actors' Association, 94, 152, 310, 320
Actors' Benevolent Fund, 94, 320
Adams, James Eli, 38
Adcock, Arthur St John, 1, 2
Adelphi Theatre, The Strand, 36, 55, 100, 101, 103, 175, 178, 213, 215, 232, 233, 234, 237, 239, 245, 274, 284, 298
After Dark (Boucicault), 180
Ahern, Robert William, 36
Ainley, Henry, 106
Albion Tavern, Drury Lane, 176
Alexander, Florence, 44
Alexander, Sir George, *108*, **107–10**, 274, *291*, 306, 316
and Oscar Wilde's arrest, 109
Alhambra Music Hall. *See* Alhambra Theatre, Leicester Square
Alhambra Theatre, Leicester Square, 24, 29, 32, 33, 34, 36, 40, 41, 66, 99, 126, 127, 215
Amalgamated Musicians' Union, 61
Antoine, André, 196, 198, 203
Archer, Frank, 158, 167
Archer, William, 101, 102, 158, 159, 188, 190, 191, 192, 194, 195, 196, 281
Arliss, George, 307

Arms and the Man (Shaw), 58
Artist and Home Journal, The (magazine), 46, 282, 285
As You Like It (Shakespeare), 134
Ashore and Afloat (Hazlewood), 220
Askew, Alice and Claude, 33
Astley's Royal Amphitheatre, Westminster Bridge Road, 227, *228*, 229
Aynesworth, Allan, *291*
Baker, Michael, 131
Bakst, Leon, 85
Balcombe, Florence. *See* Stoker, Florence
ballet dancers, 55, 84, 126
male, 126, 127
ballet girls, 25, 27, 28, 29, *30*, 31, 32, 34, 49, 80
Bancroft, George Pleydell, 146
Bancroft, Marie Effie (née Wilton), 5, 59, *142*, 143, 164, 181, 182, 183, 184
Bancroft, Sir Squire, 5, 59, 60, 86, *90*, 94, 142, 143, 146, 153, 182, 320
appearance, 91
Barnett, C. Z.
The Loss of the Royal George, 218
The Minute Gun at Sea, 218–20
Barrett, Wilson, 100, 153, 181
Barrie, J. M., 180
Bateman, Ellen, 131
Battle of Inkerman, The (Pitt), 229
Battle of the Alma, The (Anon.), 227–29, 231
Becket (Tennyson), 74
Bedford Park, 100, 103
Beerbohm Tree. *See* Tree, Sir Herbert Beerbohm

Beere, Mrs Bernard, 279
behind the scenes, *28*
Bells, The (Lewis), 149, 255, *262*, **260–65**, 265
Bennett, Arnold, 203
Benson, Lady, 107
Benson, Sir Francis (Frank), 99, *105–7*
Berne Convention, 180
Bernhardt, Sarah, 194, 279
Bettany, W. A. Lewis, 107
Black-Ey'd Susan (Jerrold), 180, *214*, **213–15**, 233
blackmail, 37, 44, 123, 269, 274, 275, 282, 284–88
Blackmailers, The (Gray and Raffalovitch), **284–88**
Blackmore, R. D., 173
Blackmore's (theatrical agency), 309, 320
Blanchette (Brieux), 198
Borsa, Mario, 50
Bosie. *See* Douglas, Lord Alfred
Bouchier, Arthur, 152
Boucicault, Dion, 170, *178*, **177–81**, 205
  After Dark, 180
  as director of his plays, **181–82**
  attitude to censorship, 191
  centre of all-male writers circle, 160
  Jessie Brown; or The Relief of Lucknow, 233
  London Assurance, 160, 163, 165, 170
  opposition to the power of managers, 164
  The Colleen Bawn, 178, 179
  The Corsican Brothers, 67, 255, *259*, **256–60**, 265, 292
  The Long Strike, 245
  willingness to accept alterations to his plays, 163
Boulton and Park, 3, 38, *39*, 40, 41, 42, 48, 127, 128, 130, 293
Bow Street Magistrates's Court, 42
Bower Saloon, Lambeth, 175
Boys Together (Carr and Chambers), 237
Braddon, Mary Elizabeth, 173
Bradley, Katherine. *See* Field, Michael
Brandes, Edward

A Visit, 199
Brissebarre, Edouard
  Léonard, 247
Britannia Theatre, Hoxton, 14, 15, 16, 141, 162, 168, 174, 181, 229
Browning, Robert, 5
Buckle, James, 71
Buckstone, John, 172
Bulwer-Lytton Act. *See* Dramatic Copyright Act 1833
Bulwer-Lytton, Edward, Lord Lytton, 172, *175*, 205
  Money, 173
  The Lady of Lyons, 173
Bunch of Violets, A (Grundy), 275
Bunn, Alfred, 161, 163, 168
burlesque, 29, 54, 98, 127, 128, 142, 167, 192, 215, 221
Burnand, F. C., 177, 180
Byron, H. J., 143
Café Royal, 44
Campbell, Mrs Patrick, 187
Carpenter, Edward, 119, 293
carpenters, 62, *79*, 78–80
carpenters' scenes, 167
Carr, J. W. Comyns, 195
  Boys Together, 237
Caste (Robertson), 183, 184
Castle Spectre, The (Lewis), 257
censorship, 5, 157, **188–96**, 197, 204, 282, 302
Chambers, Charles Haddon
  Boys Together, 237
  The Idler, 283
Champagne Charlie, 22, 34
Chapman, Patty, 140
Charrington, Charles, 281
Charrington, Janet. *See* Achurch, Janet
Chekhov, Anton, 203, 205
Chelsea Pensioner, The (Soane), 221
Cheltnam, Charles Smith
  The Ticket-of-Leave Man's Wife, **253–55**
children on stage, 80, 145
chirruping, 41
chivalry, 6, 99, 234
Christianity, 100, 116
Church, Roman Catholic, 155
Churchill, Sir Winston, 24

Cinderella (Lyceum Theatre), 83
City of London Theatre, Bishopsgate, 14, 17, 18
Cleveland Street affair, 124
clubs, gentlemen's. *See* gentlemen's clubs
Cocks, H. G., 42, 124
Cole, John William, 138, 140
Coleman, John, 113, 115, 141
Colleen Bawn, The (Boucicault), 178, 179
Collins, Wilkie, 21
Comédie Française, 96
Comedy Theatre, Panton Street, 110, 293
Comedy, The (magazine), 196
competition, 7, 155
Contagious Diseases Acts, 277
contracting out, 63, 72, 74, 302
Cook, Dutton, 58
Cooke, Thomas Potter, 213, *214*
Cooper, Edith. *See* Field, Michael
copyright, 170, 172, 175, 176, 180, *See also* Dramatic Copyright Act 1833
Corsican Brothers, The (Boucicault), 67, 255, 259, **256–60**, 265, 292
Corsican trap, 257
costume, 27, 30, 31, 32, 34, 55, 63, **80–85**, *98*, 99, 100, 110, *111*, 126, 132, 210, 219, 234, 316, 318
Court Theatre, Sloane Square (later the Royal Court), 192, 266
Courtneidge, Robert, 319
Covent Garden. *See* Theatre Royal, Covent Garden
Coventry Street, 2
Craven, Hawes, 77
Crimean War, **226–31**
Criterion Bar, 36
Criterion Theatre, Piccadilly Circus, 24, 54, 270
cross-dressing, 40, 46
  among audiences, **39–42**
  on the stage, **125–30**
Cup, The (Tennyson), 68
D'Oyly Carte Company, 185, 187
Daly, Augustin, 180, 268
Dancing Girl, The (Jones), 275
Davis, Tracy, 26, 37, 145

de Lange, Herman, 198
demi-monde, 9, 38, 189, 269
Dickens, Charles, 10, 12, 14, 18, 174, 213
Dillon, Charles, *114*, **113–16**
Disraeli, Benjamin, 174
divorce, 137, 146
Dog of Montargis, The (Pixérécourt), 114
Doll's House, A (Ibsen), 281
Donne, William Bodham, 192
Douglas, Lord Alfred, 109, 282, 286, 295
Dracula (Stoker novel), 118, 122
Dramatic Authors' Society, 176–77
Dramatic Copyright Act 1833, 172, 175, 176
Dream of Eugene Aram, The (Hood poem), 120, 122, 261
dressing rooms, 26, 91, 95, 113, 126, 131, 312, 313
Drury Lane. *See* Theatre Royal, Drury Lane
Dublin, 118, 120, 122
duels, 258, 260
Dumas, Alexandre, *fils*
  La Dame aux Camélias, 189
Dumas, Alexandre, *père*
  Les Frères corses (novel), 256
  The Three Musketeers (novel), 111
Dutch metal, 78
Dutton Cook, 319
Dyer, Robert, 18
East End, 5, 12, 14, 17, 20, 124, 174, 179, 210
Edwardes, George
  One of the Best, 237, *238*
effeminacy, 22, 38, 40, 43, 46, 84, 125, 126, 130, 238, 268, 274, 294, 296
El Niño Farini, *129*, **128–30**
electric lighting, 63, 69, 73, 84
Eliot, George, 174
Ellis, Edwin, 55
Ellis, Havelock, 36, 122, 123, 126
emigration, 9, 254, 273
Empire Music Hall, Leicester Square, 9, 24, 32, 34, 36, 99
Erckmann-Chatrian (Emile Erckmann and Pierre Alexandre Chatrian)

Le Juif polonais, 261
Ernest (codeword for homosexuality), 293
Ervine, St John, 146, 151
Escott, T. H. S. (Thomas Hay Sweet), 153
Examiner of Plays, 189, 190, 191, 192, 194, 195, 197, 249
Factory Lad, The (Walker), **241–43**, 254
factory plays, 212, 227, **239–47**, 299
Factory Strike, The (Taylor), 243–44
Fairy Queen, 19, *20*
Fall of Sebastopol, The (Anon.), 229
fallen man, 210, 253, 274, 275, 277, 279, 287, 294, 300
fallen woman, 24, 189, 247, 274, 276, 280, 300
False Colours! Or, The Free Trader! (Fitzball), 217
families, theatrical, 3, 74, 80, 103, 104, 136, 137, **145–50**, 151, 161, 304, 305, 310
family life, 3, 7, 8, 89, 136, 137
Farini, El Niño. *See* El Niño Farini
Farren, William, 166
Father, The (Strindberg), 203
Faucit, Helen, 132, 133, 134, 135, 136
Fenn, George
  The Foreman of the Works, 241
Field, Michael (Katherine Bradley and Edith Cooper)
  A Question of Memory, 201
Fisher, Mary Elizabeth, 84
Fitzball, Edward, 161
  False Colours! Or, The Free Trader!, 217
Fitzgerald, Percy, 40, 60, 68, 87, 97, 151
Fleming, George. *See* Fletcher, Constance
Fletcher, Constance ('George Fleming')
  Mrs Lessingham, 159
flogging, 215, 216, 217, 219
Fontane, Theodore, 53
food and drink, 14, 230, 295
Forbes-Robertson, Johnston, 95
Foreman of the Works, The (Fenn), 241
Frankau, Julia, 198

Fraser, Claud Lovat, 85
Freemasonry, **154–55**
French plays, 110, 114, 159, **169–71**, 180, 190, 199, 203, 205, 247, 260, 270, 274
Gaiety Theatre, Aldwych, *13*, 191, 237
Gaiety Theatre, New Orleans, 181
gallery, **12–19**, 22, 36, 44, 49, 50, 111, 225, 303
Garrick Club, 154
Garrick Theatre, Charing Cross Road, 159, 171, 274, 277, 278
Garrick, David, 12
gas lighting, 69, 70, 73, 86, 312, *See also* limelight
Gaskell, Elisabeth
  Mary Barton (novel), 245
gentleman, 3, 4, 6, 7, 107, 110, 147, **150–56**, 235, 259, 268, 304
gentlemen's clubs, 9, 120, 131, 141, **153–54**, 268
gentrification, 4, 49, 50, 93, 299, 304
Ghosts (Ibsen), 197, 198, 199, 280
Gilbert, W. S. (William Schwenk), 173, 181, *186*, 205
  atitude to censorship, 192
  control of production, 185–87
  H.M.S. Pinafore (with Sir Arthur Sullivan), *223*, **221–25**
  Pygmalion and Galatea, 144
  The Happy Land, 192, 193
  The Realm of Joy, 193
Gissing, George, 173
Gladstone, William Ewart, 192
Goddard, Arthur, 100
Godwin, E. W., 134
Grant, Duncan, 289
Grant, James, 319
Granville Barker, Harley, 180, 203
Gray, John, *46*, 47, 201, 284, 285, 287
  The Blackmailers (with Marc-André Raffalovich), **284–88**
  The Kiss, 47
Grecian Theatre, Shoreditch, 175
green carnation, 44, *45–48*, 48, 298
Green Carnation, The (Hichens novel), 294
green room, 25, 26, 27, 29
Green Room Club, **154**

Grein, Alice Augusta (Alix), née
   Greeven ('Michael Orme'), 196,
   198, 199
Grein, J. T. (Jacob Thomas), 47, 111,
   197, **196–204**
Gribsby scene (*The Importance of
   Being Earnest*), 295
Grieve family, 74
Grimston. *See* Kendal
Grundy, Sydney, 281
   A Bunch of Violets, 275
   A Pair of Spectacles, 171, 180
   The New Woman, 180
   The Union Jack, 232, 239
Guy Domville (James), 159, 160
H.M.S. Pinafore (Gilbert and Sullivan),
   223, **221–25**
Haines, J. T.
   My Poll and My Partner Joe, 216,
      236
   The Ocean of Life, 215, 225
half-price admission time, 21, 23
Halling, Daisy, 132, 321
Hamilton, Henry
   The Three Musketeers, 111
Hamlet (Shakespeare), 120, 131, 149
Hankin, St John, 203
Happy Land, The (Gilbert), 192, 193
Harbour Lights, The (Sims and Pettitt),
   102, 103, 215, 234, 235
Hardy, Thomas, 173, 174
Hare, John, 145, 278
Harker, Joseph, 76, 77
Harris, Frank, 173, 198
Harris, Sir Augustus, 68, 81, 154
Hawick, 115
Haymarket. *See* Theatre Royal,
   Haymarket
Hazlewood, Charles H., 167, 168
   Ashore and Afloat, 220
   Lady Audley's Secret, 167
Hemans, Felicia, 177
Henry IV (Shakespeare), *133*
Henry V (Shakespeare), 110, *111*, 139
Her Majesty's Theatre, Haymarket, *26*,
   35, 54, 56, 74, 96, 189
Hervey, R. K., 96, 315
Hichens, Robert
   The Green Carnation, 294

Hicks, Sir Edward Seymour, 104, 145
   One of the Best, 237, *238*
Hollingshead, John, 128, 171, 191
Holywell Street, 31
   Unity Club, 161
homosexuality, 9, 35, 37, 43, 44, 48,
   100, 109, 119, 123, 275, 282, 285,
   287, 288, 293
   among actors, **122–25**
   at sea, 215, 216, 222
Hood, Thomas
   The Dream of Eugene Aram (poem),
      120, 122, 261
Hoxton, 15, *See* Britannia Theatre,
   Hoxton
hypnotism, 120, 264
Ibsen, Henrik, 193, 195, 203, 204, 276,
   281, 285, 288
   A Doll's House, 281
   Ghosts, 197, 198, 199, 280
   The Pretenders, 149
Ideal Husband, An (Wilde), 109, 110,
   275, 282, 298
Idler, The (Chambers), 283
Importance of Being Earnest, The
   (Wilde), 43, 109, 110, 205, 225,
   291, **290–98**
Incorporated Stage Society, 203
Independent Theatre Society, 47, 160,
   196–204
Ireland, 122, 227
Irving, Florence, 149
Irving, H. B. (Henry Brodribb), 90, 147,
   148
Irving, Laurence, 147, 149
Irving, Sir Henry, 3, 4, 67, *92*, 94, 95,
   96, 104, 152, 259, 315, 320, 339,
   348
   and Dame Ellen Terry, **134–36**
   appearance, 91
   attitude to censorship, 195
   attitude to music, 60, *61*
   background, 305, 306
   freemasonry, 154
   his sons, 147, **148–49**
   hospitality, 153
   in *The Bells*, 149, 255, *262*, **260–65**
   knighthood, 6, 93, 152
   lighting, 73
   Lyceum Theatre, 15

marriage, 149
opposition to the Independent Theatre Society, 199
relationship with Stoker, **118–22**
relationship with Toole, **116–18**
Italian Opera, *35*, 36, 54, 56
James, Henry, 45, 153
Guy Domville, 159, 160
Jarvis, Charles W., 198
Jerome, Jerome K., 136, 314
Jerrold, Douglas, 173
Black-Ey'd Susan, 180, *214*, **213–15**, 233
Jessie Brown; or The Relief of Lucknow (Boucicault), 233
Jones, Henry Arthur, 96, 157, 169, 171, 184, *193*, 195, 204, 205, 289
attitude to censorship, 194
The Dancing Girl, 275
The Silver King, 179, 312
Jones-Evans, Eric, 263, 264
Kaplan, Morris B., 46
Kean, Charles, 4, 5, 95, *138*–**40**, 147, 148, 150, 255, 306
Kean, Edmund, 147
Kean, Ellen, *138*–**40**, 150
Kean, Mary, 140
Kemble family, 151
Kendal, Dorothy, 146
Kendal, Madge, *144*, **143–45**, 146, 151, 161
Kendal, Margaret, 146
Kendal, William, *144*, **143–45**, 146, 151
King Lear (Shakespeare), 261
Kingsley, Charles, 207
Kiss, The (Gray, after de Banville), 47
Knowles, James Sheridan
Virginius, 146
La Dame aux Camélias (Dumas), 189
Labouchère Amendment, 43
Lady Audley's Secret (Hazlewood), 167
Lady of Lyons, The (Bulwer-Lytton), 173
Lady Windermere's Fan (Wilde), 44, 45, 47, 110
Lane, Sarah, 141, 162

Le Juif polonais (Erckmann-Chatrian), 261
Leighton, Dorothy, 198, 201
Thyrza Fleming, 160
Lemon, Mark, 160
Léonard (Brissebarre and Nus), 247
Leppington, C. H. d'E., 86
Les Frères corses (Dumas novel), 256
Lewes, George Henry, 148, 162, 163, 165, 166, 189, 259
Lewis, Leopold
The Bells, 149, 255, *262*, **260–65**
Lewis, M. G.
The Castle Spectre, 257
Leybourne, George, 22
lighting
electric. *See* electric lighting
gas. *See* gas lighting
limelight, *71*, **70–73**, 86
Limelight, *72*
Lister, Charles, 132, 321
Litton, Marie, 192
London Assurance (Boucicault), 160, 163, 165, 170
Long Strike, The (Boucicault), 245
Lord Chamberlain, 5, 157, 168, **188–96**, 197, 249, 286
Loss of the Royal George, The; or the Fatal Land Breeze (Barnett), 218
Lost in London (Phillips), 245–47
Lyceum Theatre, The Strand, 15, 60, 61, 68, 74, 77, 83, 85, 100, 110, 115, 120, 121, 122, 134, 135, 151, 153, 180, 200, 245, 255, 260
Lytton, Lord. *See* Bulwer-Lytton, Edward
M'lle Lulu. *See* El Niño Farini
Macbeth (Shakespeare), *98*, 99, *138*, 261
Macready, William Charles, 3, 4, 5, 132, *133*, 134, 146, 147, 148, 150, 306
Madame Sans-Gêne (Sardou), 60
Maeterlinck, Maurice, 198, 203, 261
Magistrate, The (Pinero), *272*
Magistrate, The (Pinero), **266–74**
Maiden Tribute of Modern Babylon, The (Stead), 278

make-up, 132, 192, 210, 213, 311, 315, 318
manliness, 38, 43, 89, 100, 101, 106, 111, 112, 120, 125, 126, 155, 238, 297
Married Women's Property Acts, 8
Marston, John Westland, 147
Mary Barton (Gaskell novel), 245
Marylebone, 15
Mason, A. E. W., 107
Mathews, Charles, 163, 170
Mathews, Lucia. *See* Vestris, Lucia
matinée idols, **97–112**, 123, 125, 233
matinée performances, 6, 50, 99, 200, 202, 319
Maugham, W. Somerset, 203
Mayhew, Edward, 167
Mayne, Xavier (Edward Stevenson), 123, 232
mechanisation, 65, 241
Melvin, Henri de, 128
Merrill, George, 293
Mesmerism. *See* hypnotism
Metropole Theatre, Camberwell, 110
Millward, Jessie, 103–4
minor theatres, 5, 114, 171, 174, 212, 240, 246
Minute Gun at Sea, The (Barnett), 218–20
Mitford, Mary Russell, 177
Modjeska, Helena, 182
Money (Bulwer-Lytton), 173
Monsieur Beaucaire (Sutherland, after Tarkington), 110
Moore, George, 47, 173, 196, 198
   The Strike at Arlingford, 201
Morley, Henry, 18, 19
motor-cars, 155
Mrs Lessingham (Fletcher), 159
Mrs Warren's Profession (Shaw), 199, 201
Much Ado About Nothing (Shakespeare), 134
Mudie's Circulating Library, 191
music halls, 5, 11, 22, 24, 29, 32, 33, 34, 36, 37, 40, 49, 58, 99, 127, 128, 232, 303, *See also* Alhambra Theatre, Leicester Square; Empire Music Hall, Leicester Square

My Poll and My Partner Joe (Haines), 216, 236
National Theatre, 204
Neville, Henry G., 100, 249
New Drama, 50, 158, 207, 234, **274–82**, 288, 303
New Theatre, Greenwich, 254
New Woman, The (Grundy), 180
Nightingale, Florence, 227
Novelty Theatre, Great Queen Street, 281
Nus, Eugène
   Léonard, 247
O'Reilly, William Henry, 307, 308
Ocean of Life, The; or Every Inch a Sailor (Haines), 215, 225
Olivier, Sir Laurence, 106
Olympic Theatre, Drury Lane, 36, 141, 159, 160, 172, 175, 247, 249, 254
One of the Best (Hicks and Edwardes), 237, *238*
opéra bouffe, 54
Opera Comique, The Strand, 201, 221
orchestra pit, 53, 59, 60, 62, 86
Orchestral Association, 61
orchestras, *61*, **53–62**, 86
Orme, Michael. *See* Grein, Alice Augusta
Ormiston Chant, Laura, 24, 32, 37
Othello (Shakespeare), *114*
Our American Cousin (Taylor), 172
Ours (Robertson), 183, 230, 231
painting, **74–78**, 166
Pair of Spectacles, A (Grundy), 171, 180
patent theatres, 5, 22, 188
Pavilion Theatre, Whitechapel, *1*, 12, 14, 20, 24, 36, 229
Pearson, Hesketh, 105, 107, 108, 112, 149
Penal Servitude Act 1853, 248, 250
Pettitt, Henry
   Harbour Lights, 102, 103, 215, 234, 235
   The Union Jack, 232, 239
Phelps, Samuel, 5
Philanderer, The (Shaw), 201
Phillips, Watts
   Lost in London, 245–47

Piccadilly, 23, 36, 40
Picture of Dorian Gray, The (Wilde novel), 47, 83, 280, 289
Piggot, Edward F. S., 194–96
Pinero, Arthur Wing, 107, 157, 169, 193, 195, 204, 205, 266, *267*, 289, 298
  control of production, 187
  The Magistrate, *272*, **266–74**
  The Profligate, *279*, **277–82**
  The Second Mrs Tanqueray, *108*, 187, 276, 277
  Trelawny of the 'Wells', 185
pit, 12, 13, 16, 18, 44, 49, 60, 111, *See also* orchestra pit
  removal of, 143
Pitt, George Dibdin
  The Battle of Inkerman, 229
Pixérécourt, René Charles Guilbert de
  The Dog of Montargis, 114
plagiarism, 180
Planché, Eliza, 159, 177
Planché, James Robinson, 162, 176, 180
platonic friendship, 6, 37, 38, 103, 116, 118, 119, 122, 208, 210, 219, 220, 269, 283
poison, 275, 278, 288
portable theatres, 175, 176
Portman Market, 114
Potter, Paul M.
  Trilby, 188, 311
press gang, 212, 216, 219
Pretenders, The (Ibsen), 149
Prince of Wales. *See* Wales, Prince of
Prince of Wales Theatre, Liverpool, 110
Prince of Wales's Theatre (Queen's Theatre), Charlotte Street, 5, 59, 142, 143, 165, **182**, 184, 217, 221, 230, 284
Prince, Richard, 100
Princess's Theatre, Bristol, 313
Princess's Theatre, Oxford Street, 5, 138, 139, 140, 255, 256, 259
printed editions of plays, 175, 176, 180
private boxes, 18, 20, 23, 284
private theatre clubs, 196, 197, 203
Profligate, The (Pinero), *279*, **277–82**

prostitution, 4, 9, 22, 23, 26, 27, 44, 199, 253, 274
  homosexual. *See* renters
Punch, 46, 160, 162, 192
Pygmalion and Galatea (Gilbert), *144*
Queen's Theatre, Charlotte Street. *See* Prince of Wales's Theatre
Queen's Theatre, Liverpool, 55
Queensberry, Marquess of, 109
Question of Memory, A (Field), 201
queuing, 49
Quiller-Couch, A. T., 173
Raffalovich, Marc-André, 46, 47, 201, 284, 285, 287, 293
  The Blackmailers (with John Gray), **284–88**
Reade, Charles, 55, 191
Realm of Joy, The (Gilbert), 193
Rede, Leman, 318
Reeves, John, 40
Regent Street, 35
renascence of English drama, 193, 194, 201
renters (homosexual prostitutes), 36, 37, 40, 127, 232, 286, 295
respectability, 3–4, 7–9, 10, 17, 18, 40, 89, 99, 104, 107, 137, 138, 145, 146, 147, 149, 150, 151, 152, 154, 155, 190, 250, 253, 255, 263, 267, 287, 297, 301, 303, 304, 318
Richards, Jeffrey, 134
Richmond, 28
Ricketts, Charles, 266
Robertson, T. W. (Thomas William), 157, 161, 165, 171, 173, 181, *183*, 182–85
  Caste, 183, 184
  Ours, 183, 230, 231
  School, 183
  Society, 183
Robertson, W. Graham, 149
Rochelle, Edward, 312
Roth, Walter, 15, 16
Royal Effingham Theatre, Whitechapel, 14
Royal Holborn Empire, 128
Royal Princess Theatre, Edinburgh, *251*
Royal Standard Theatre. *See* Standard Theatre, Shoreditch

royalty system, 178, 179
Royalty Theatre, Dean Street, 47, 53, 198, 200, 201
Runciman, J. F., 58, 60
Ruskin, John, 207
Ryan, Dr Michael, 30
Sadler's Wells Theatre, 5, 18, 218
sailors, 14, 101, 209, **211–21**, 221–25, 225, 229, 230, 232, 233, 235, 236, 237, 240, 299
Sala, George Augustus, *27*, 28, 32, 65, 66, 77, 79, 80, 87, 90, 126
Salomé (Wilde), 190, 194, 195
Sardou, Victorien
  Madame Sans-Gêne, 60
Savoy Hotel, 44, 295
Savoy operas. *See* Savoy Theatre
Savoy Theatre, The Strand, 185, 186, 205
scene-painter's studio, *75*
scenery, 65–68, 74, 77, *79*, 95, 200
School (Robertson), 183
Scotland, 227
Scott, Clement, 45, 96, 118, 139, 195, 285, 288
Scottish soldiers, 230, 232, 233, 237
Sea!, The (Somerset), 217
seamstresses, 63, 65, 80
Second Mrs Tanqueray, The (Pinero), *108*, 187, 276, 277
Sentence, The (Webster), 160
Shakespeare, William, 5, 18, 84, 99, 103, 105, 106, 110, 112, 115, 131, 139, 140, 148, 170
  As You Like It, 134
  Hamlet, 120, 131, 149
  Henry IV, *133*
  Henry V, 110, *111*, 139
  King Lear, 261
  Macbeth, *98*, 99, *138*, 261
  Much Ado About Nothing, 134
  Othello, 114
Shannon, Charles, 266
Shaw, George Bernard, 135, 180, 193, 201, *202*, 237
  Arms and the Man, 58
  attitude to censorship, 188, 189, 191, 194, 195
  Mrs Warren's Profession, 199, 201

The Philanderer, 201
Widowers' Houses, 201, 202
Siege of Sebastopol, The; or the Horrors of War (Anon.), 229
Silver King, The (Jones), 179, 312
Sims, George R., 98, 161, 319
  Harbour Lights, 102, 103, 215, 234, 235
Sinfield, Alan, 43, 282
Singla, Etienne, 265
slavery, 220, 236
Smiles, Samuel, 6–7, 93, 150, 207
Smythe, Arthur, 100
Soane, George
  The Chelsea Pensioner, 221
Society (Robertson), 183, 184
sodomy. *See* homosexuality
Soho, 15
Soho Theatre. *See* Royalty Theatre, Dean Street
soldiers, 212, 221, **225–39**, 258, 299
  as male prostitutes, 232
Somerset, Charles A., 175
  The Sea!, 217
Spitalfields, 14
sport, 104, 105, 106, 107, 155, 302
St James's (district), 274
St James's Theatre, King Street, 36, 44, 107, 108, 109, 131, 145, 274, 276, 283, 290
St John's Wood, 28, 95, 100, 155
stage boxes, 19, 20
Standard Theatre, Shoreditch, 14
Stead, W. T.
  The Maiden Tribute of Modern Babylon, 278
Stevenson, Edward. *See* Mayne, Xavier
stock system, **64**, 109, 115, 132, 137, 145, 169, 185, 314, 317
Stoker, Bram, 69, 73, 116, 117, *119*, 258, 338
  Dracula (novel), 118, 122
  relationship with Irving, **118–22**
Stoker, Florence, née Balcombe, 121
Stoker, Irving Noel Thornley, 121
Strachey, Lytton, 289
Strike at Arlingford, The (Moore), 201
Strindberg, August, 203, 261
  The Father, 203

sub-contracting, 64
suicide, 209, 275, 276, 279, 288, 295
supernatural appearances, 257
supernumeraries, 55, 62, 85, 104, 229, 316, 318
Surrey Theatre, Blackfriars, 40, 175, 212, 213, 215, 218, 220, 240, 241
Sutherland, Evelyn
    Monsieur Beaucaire, 110
swells, 12, **19–22**, 26, 27, 28, 29, 32, 37, 38, 42, 48, 50, 51, 91, 211, 250, 269, 303
Symonds, John Addington, 119
Symons, Arthur, 32, 33, 34, 201
Taylor, G. F.
    The Factory Strike, 243–44
Taylor, Tom, 162, 179, 191, *248*, 255
    Our American Cousin, 172
    The Ticket-of-Leave Man, 132, 162, 172, 179, *251*, **247–53**, 254
Telbin family, 74
Telbin, William Lewis, 74, 75, 76
telepathy, 256
Tennyson, Alfred, Lord, 174
    Becket, 74
    The Cup, 68
Terriss, Ellaline, 101, 104
Terriss, Tom, 102
Terriss, William, *102*, **100–104**, 154, 233, 234, *238*, 260
    and Jessie Millward, 103
    murder, 100
Terry, Dame Ellen, 102, 120, *135*, 136, 138, 149, 263
    and Sir Henry Irving, **134–36**
Terry, Edward O'Connor, 154
Terry, Thomas Everson, 307
Terry's Theatre (The Strand), 160
Texeira de Mattos, Alexander, 198
Théatre Libre (Paris), 196, 203
Theatre Regulation Act 1843, 5, 188
Theatre Royal, Covent Garden, 5, 12, 22, 23, *35*, 54, 56, 69, 74, 80, 132, 161, 163, 165, 166, 217, 237
Theatre Royal, Drury Lane, 5, 22, 23, 54, 56, *64*, 68, *75*, 77, *79*, 80, 81, 82, 85, 95, 154, 161, 162, 163, 168, 176, 257, 319
Theatre Royal, Haymarket, 5, 44, 59, 60, 86, 109, 149, 170, 172, 188, 274, 275
Theatre Royal, Margate, 306
Theatre Royal, Plymouth, 233
Theatre Royal, Wigan, 62
Thorne, Sarah, 306
Three Musketeers, The (Hamilton, after Dumas), 111
Thyrza Fleming (Leighton*)*, 160
Ticket-of-Leave Man, The (Taylor), 132, 162, 172, 179, *251*, **247–53**, 254
Ticket-of-Leave Man's Wife, The (Cheltnam), **253–55**
toilets, 15
Tomlins, F. G., 95
Toole, John Laurence, 94, *117*, 122, 320
    relationship with Irving, **116–18**
trade unions, 61, 65, 321, *See also* Actors' Association; Amalgamated Musicians' Union; Orchestral Association
Trafalgar Square, 35
transpontine theatres, 5, 12, 161, 175, 226
transvestism. *See* cross-dressing
trapdoors, 65, 66, *67*, 257, 265, *See also* Corsican trap
Tree, Sir Herbert Beerbohm, 4, *94*, 95, 96, 97, 188, 289, 311, 316
Trelawny of the 'Wells' (Pinero), 185
Trewin, J. C., 106
Trilby (Potter, after du Maurier), 188, 311
Tristan, Flora, 23
tuberculosis, 59
typewriters, introduction of, 168
unhygienic conditions in theatres, 15–16, 313
Union Jack, The (Grundy and Pettitt), 232, 239
Unity Club, Holywell Street, 161
Uranian, 285
Uranianism, 37, 43, 46, 47, 123, 268, 282, 285, 286, 288, 289, 292, 293, **297–98**
Vaudeville Theatre, The Strand, 12

venereal disease, 31, 231, 275, 278
Vestris, Lucia Elizabeth, née
 Bartolozzi, 163, 164, 170
Victoria Theatre, Waterloo, 12, 18
Victoria, Queen, 217, 232, 260
Virginius (Knowles), 146
Visit, A (Brandes), 199
voyeurism, 24, **29–33**, 49, 303
Vyner, James D., 201
wages, 54, 55, 56, 57, 74, 76, 78, 132,
 167, 232, 240, 244, 308, 317, 318
Wagner, Leopold, 311, 318
Wagner, Richard, 60
Wales, 115, 227
Wales, Prince of (later King Edward
 VII, 308
Wales, Prince of (later King Edward
 VII), 153, 154
Walker, John
 The Factory Lad, **241–43**, 254
Waller, Florence (neé West), 155
Waller, Lewis, 95, 109, *111*, **110–12**,
 155
Walsh, Townsend, 182
Ward, Charles Henry, 307
Wareing, Alfred, 15
Webb, Eliza, 115
Webster, Augusta
 The Sentence, 160
Webster, Ben, 45
Webster, Benjamin, 170, 178
West End, 2, 5, 21, 35, 99
West, Florence. *See* Waller, Florence
Whelen, Frank, 203
Whistler, James McNeill, 266
Whitechapel. *See* Pavilion Theatre;
 Royal Effingham Theatre
Whitman, Walt, 119
Widowers' Houses (Shaw), 201, 202
Wigan, Alfred, 141, 145, 259
Wigan, Leonora, 141
Wild, Sam, 175

Wilde, Oscar, 3, *45*, 107, 157, 193, 201,
 204, 205, 259, 266, 282, 284, 285,
 287, 295, 298
 A Woman of No Importance, 279,
  288–90
 An Ideal Husband, 109, 110, 275,
  282, 298
 engagement to Florence Stoker, née
  Balcombe, 121
 green carnation, **45–48**
 Lady Windermere's Fan, 44, 45, 47,
  110
 leader of a queer circle, 43–44
 opening nights, 44–46
 Salomé, 190, 194, 195
 The Importance of Being Earnest,
  43, 109, 110, 205, 225, *291*,
  290–98
 The Picture of Dorian Gray (novel),
  47, 83, 280, 289
 trial, 36, 109, 124, 152, 238
 visit to Walt Whitman, 119
Wilhelm, C. (William J. C. Pitcher), *82*,
 81–85
Wills's (restaurant), 44
Wilton, Marie. *See* Bancroft, Marie
Winter, William, 113
Woman of No Importance, A (Wilde),
 279, **288–90**
women, 3
 backstage jobs, 63
 in boys' roles, 34
 in orchestras, 54
 in the audience, 99, 111
 legal position of, 8
 on the stage, 30, 33
 worship of matinée idols, 111
Woods, Margaret L., 173
workhouse, 241, 243, 244, 319
Wright, Thomas, 16, 21
Wyndham, Charles, 270, 306
Wyndham's Theatre, Charing Cross
 Road, 274
Yates, Edmund, 150
Zola, Émile, 198, 199, 203

Some recent books from Paradise Press

Biography
Gay Life, Straight Work, by Donald West
A Life's Tales, by Joseph Hucknall

Poetry
Coming Clean, edited by John Dixon & Jeff Doorn
Ivor Treby, Poems 2007–2012, edited by John Dixon
Seeking, Finding, Losing, by John Dixon
Oysters and Pearls, edited by Jeffrey Doorn and Adrian Risdon

Fiction
The Bexhill Missile Crisis, by David Gee
Twenty-Two Eighty-Four, by Christopher Preston
The Carrier Bag and other stories, by John Dixon
The Dropout, by David Gee
Eros at Large, edited by Michael Harth
Ghosts and Gargoyles, by Elsa Wallace
Guru on Hire, by Michael Harth
Queer Haunts, edited by G. Abel-Watters
The Best of Gazebo, edited by Michael Harth
Bokassa's Last Apostle, by Rod Shelton
My Life Outside, *Nothing Stays the Same* and *Prisoner 537*, by Elizabeth Lister
A Short History of Lord Hyaena, by Elsa Wallace
Behind the Mask, by Winston Green
The Monkey Mirror, by Elsa Wallace
People Your Mother Warned You About, edited by G. Abel-Watters
The Queer Businessman, by Paul Mann
First and Fiftieth and other stories, by Martin Foreman